FRANCESCO MARIA GUAZZO

COMPENDIUM MALEFICARUM

THE MONTAGUE SUMMERS EDITION

TRANSLATED BY E. A. ASHWIN

DOVER PUBLICATIONS, INC., NEW YORK

This Dover edition, first published in 1988, is an unabridged, slightly altered republication of the work originally published in 1929 by John Rodker, London, in an edition of 1275 copies. The 1929 title page reads: "Compendium Maleficarum / Collected in 3 Books from many Sources by Brother Francesco Maria Guazzo of the Order of S. Ambrose *ad Nemus* / showing the iniquitous and execrable operations of witches against the human race, and the divine remedies by which they may be frustrated / Edited with notes by the Rev. Montague Summers . . . Translated by E. A. Ashwin." The dedication and the Preface to the Reader originally occupied two pages each. The page numbers in the prefatory matter have accordingly been altered.

Manufactured in the United States of America
Dover Publications, Inc., 31 E. 2nd St., Mineola, N.Y. 11501

Library of Congress Cataloging-in-Publication Data

Guazzo, Francesco Maria.
    [Compendium maleficarum. English]
    Compendium maleficarum : the Montague Summers edition / Francesco Maria Guazzo : translated by E. A. Ashwin.—Dover ed.
        p.   cm.
    Translated from the Latin.
    Slightly altered ed. of the work originally published: London : John Rodker, 1929.
    ISBN 0-486-25738-X (pbk.)
    1. Witchcraft—Early works to 1800. 2. Demonology—Early works to 1800. I. Summers, Montague, 1880–1948. II. Title.
BF1565.G8313   1988
133.4—dc19   88-9575
                                  CIP

THE MOST ILLUSTRIOUS AND RIGHT REVEREND

LORD ORAZIO MAFFEI

CARDINAL OF THE HOLY ROMAN CHURCH AND
EVER VIGILANT PROTECTOR OF THE
ORDER OF S. AMBROSE

FRA FRANCESCO MARIA GUAZZO

A HUMBLE BROTHER OF THE
SAME ORDER

GIVETH GREETING

O *MOST vigilant Prelate, three years ago when I was attending the Court of His Serene Highness the Duke of Cleves and Jülich (who was vexed and bound by many spells of witchcraft), I put together and composed this book which I have called "Compendium Maleficarum" and I have, moreover, filled it with various and most ample examples, with the sole purpose that men, considering the cunning of witches, might study to live piously and devoutly in the Lord. And although it may provoke the idle jests of the censorious (for what is more difficult than to satisfy every palate?), yet I conceive that it will be of some avail to those who would escape the mortal venom of sorcerers. When I had, then, determined to print it, I began to look for a Patron under whose auspices it might be more securely brought to the light. Then, O most illustrious and Most Reverend Protector, whom no one has excelled in genius, gifts of mind and body and countless graces, did you stand out in my mind as one who has given public proof that your most eminent courage is joined to a like degree of learning, a Patron who, far from despising a humble writer, would rather extend to him your greatest favour and more than ordinary kindness. Having these considerations in my mind, therefore, I was assured that you were pre-eminently suited to act the part of a Maecenas towards such as devoted themselves to the furtherance of sound doctrine, among whom I count myself the humblest: and I determined to light this new-born work upon its way with the torch of your most Famous Name; and although you are worthy of a far nobler work, I venture to dedicate to you this little book which has not been compiled without some labour. And if (as is my hope) you will accept it wholly and generously with that fair candour which is yours, it may assuredly be expected that those carping critics, who will tolerate nothing that does not savour of perfect genius and unremitting industry, will turn a blind eye to its faults. Farewell: and may Guazzo be written among those who are whole-heartedly attached to you.*

Milan, May, 1608.

PREFACE TO THE READER

AMONG the countless blessings which the Divine mercy daily confers upon the whole human race, and especially upon His faithful, I esteem this to be the most particular: the power to discover the malice and wickedness of our enemies, both visible and invisible. So that, recognising their cunning, we may counteract their stumbling-blocks and temptations. And since (Ps. lxxiii) the pride of them that hate God is daily increased and ever grows, and the venomous Enemy of the human race, whose fierceness waxes ever greater, does not fear to sow in our path the sharpest thorns of sorrow and tribulation and all sorts of maladies, although he himself is fearful of being tormented; therefore he essays his utmost to increase his own eternal punishment by leading as many men as he can to hell, and to deride, despise, and insult the most excellent and divine likeness of God which has been washed in the Precious Blood of Christ, and to turn man's freedom to slavery. Therefore each one of us ought to search his heart to keep it free from the malice of the devil; for he goeth about as a roaring lion, seeking whom he may devour; and even though his heart may be pierced and torn by his enemy's weapons, yet the devil leaves nothing unattempted and dares everything. When he sees men of weak and timid mind, he takes them by storm: when he finds them dauntless and firm, he becomes as it were a cunning fox to deceive them: for he has a thousand means of hurting us, and he uses countless methods, superstitions and curious arts, to seduce men's minds from God and lead them to his own follies; and all these he wondrously performs by means of illusions and witchcraft. Therefore it is agreed that this sort of evils has been disseminated to the destruction of men's bodies and souls by the devil and his fiends through the agency of warlocks, witches, sorcerers and diviners; and in proof of this the present book will give a sure indication of the truth. And that each man may be able to guard himself, let him seriously read and carefully digest this book, which I have called *Compendium Maleficarum*; for just as there are shown to be various means and methods of inflicting injury, so there are various remedies by which these harms may be met and dispersed when they are recognised. If therefore, reader, there be anything in this book which holds your attention and points you to the way to a remedy, I lift up my hands in thanks to God, who to His own greater glory, and the confusion of devils, has permitted the temptation of our souls that the just may be made perfect and the wicked cast into hell. Therefore the demons do but work in accordance with the design and permission of Almighty God.

EDITOR'S INTRODUCTION

THE ancient origins of the local Milanese Order Ambrosiani or Ambrosini, of which Francesco-Maria Guazzo was so eminent and honoured a member, are buried in obscurity, although the Brethren themselves, perhaps with more devotion than exactness, were ever wont to refer their foundation to no less a figure than the great S. Ambrose himself. It is very possible, and even probable, that some old traditions had actually been handed down from the illustrious Father who had taken so deep an interest in monasticism and so closely watched the beginnings of the cloister throughout his diocese. However that may be, in the earlier decades of the fourteenth century certain solitaries and hermit priests dwelling near Milan gradually adopted the cenobitic life, making it their pious custom to assemble at stated intervals during the day for solemn office and united prayer. About this very time three young nobles, Alessandro Crivelli, Alberto Besozzo, and Antonio della Pietra-Santa, disgusted with the licentiousness of the aristocratic society and court of Giovanni II, had sought refuge in retreat from the world, and taking as their anchorhold a wood not many leagues from the city, here they built a humble chapel which soon became the common oratory of a regular community, and this forest sanctuary may not untruly be said to have been the cradle of the Ambrosian Order. In 1375 Pope Gregory XI, who some twelve months before had approved the Congregation of the Spanish Hermits of S. Jerome, gave the Milanese frati the Rule of S. Augustine, adding thereto a number of particular constitutions, and assigning as their name "Fratres Sancti Ambrosii ad Nemus." They were, moreover, empowered to elect their own superiors, subject to the confirmation of the Archbishop of Milan. A habit was prescribed with broad scapular, a stuff girdle pendent as is the Augustinian cincture, a voluminous cowl and capuce, a mighty mantle in which to walk abroad, in colour all of chestnut brown.* The Ambrosian Liturgy, both for

---

* It does not seem certain whether the Ambrosians (ad Nemus) were by rule discalced or shod. Hélyot, "Histoire des Ordres Monastiques," 1715, vol. IV, p. 52, gives an engraving, "Religieux de l'Ordre de S. Ambroise ad Nemus," who is wearing sandals. But there appear to have been modifications, and this detail differed from time to time. Originally no doubt the brethren were discalced, but a mitigation tolerated some form of foot-gear.

Mass and choir, must be followed. The Order henceforth was canonically established.

Of the history of the Ambrosiani comparatively few details are known, and it is hardly necessary here to rehearse them at any length. It will suffice to say that various houses were founded, and that for more than half a century each monastery remained entirely independent, their only connexion being the fact that each adopted the same rule. In 1441 Eugenius IV united all the existing foundations in one Congregation under a Master-general who was to reside at the original convent where in future a full Chapter met every three years. It was found that the old discipline had become somewhat relaxed in the time of S. Carlo Borromeo, but at the request of the brethren this great Saint presided in person over their Chapter of 1579, and with his encouragement the earlier strictness was soon restored. Subjects, none the less, were few, and on 15 August 1589 Sixtus V issued a bull joining the Ambrosiani with the Apostolini or Barnabites,* who claimed the Apostle S. Barnabas as their founder, but whose constitution, as then followed at any rate, had been approved by Rome early in the fifteenth century. The Congregation thus formed was now generally known as the Brethren of S. Ambrose ad Nemus and S. Barnabas, and upon the engraved title-page of the second edition (1626) of Guazzo's "Compendium Maleficarum," the two Saints are duly depicted as patrons in full pontificalia.

Outside the archdiocese of Milan the Ambrosiani held for a while only two houses, both of which were at Rome: San Clemente,† and San Pancrazio. In Milan itself their most important monastery was that attached to the Church of San Primo, a parish which in more recent years was divided among three other churches, S. Bartolomeo, S. Babila, and San Andrea. The Church of San Primo and the adjoining cloister stood hard by the Porta Orientale where was the Collegio Elvetico at the opening of the Strada Marina. The religious also served the church of S. Ambrogio della Vittoria, which was built (1348) at Parabiago ‡ in thanksgiving for the famous battle won there by the Milanese in 1339.

---

* *The Brothers of S. Barnabas, not to be confused with the Barnabites, Clerks Regular, "Clerici Regulares Sancti Pauli," founded by S. Antonio Maria Zaccaria in 1530.*

† *Now served by the Irish Dominicans. S. Pancrazio fuori le Mura was seriously damaged in 1849, but has been restored.*

‡ *For an account of the connexion of the Ambrosini with this church and the jealousy of the civic authorities who wished to appoint their own chaplains, see the article "Ambrosiani" by Monsignor Giovanni Galbiati in the "Grande Enciclopedia Italiana."*

However popular at Milan, where they were held in high honour, even in the day of their greatest prosperity the Ambrosiani had never been more than a purely local Congregation, and when their numbers sensibly diminished and several of their houses fell vacant it is not surprising to find that the question of suppressing the Order was more than once debated. Eventually, on 1 April, 1645, by the bull "Quoniam," Innocent X dissolved the surviving monasteries, including that of Parabiago, which remained, directing that they should be assigned to secular priests. The details of these arrangements were entrusted to two Cardinals, Odescalchi and Monti, who acted on behalf of the Holy See. It must not be supposed that the dissolution was in any way intended as a censure or reflection upon the Ambrosiani. At that time certain reforms were being essayed in various directions, and of these one was the diminution of the very many provincial Congregations and obscurer local Orders, whose continuance involved a vast complexity of business and affairs, whose members were few and dwindling, whose purpose had been served, in most cases admirably and devotedly served throughout the years, but whose day was gone. Even as one of our own poets has said:

> God fulfils Himself in many ways,
> Lest one good custom should corrupt the world.

The Ambrosiani were not without their holy names. There were Beati in the calendar of the Order; Blessed Alberto Besozzo; Blessed Antonio Gonzaga of Mantua, Blessed Filippo of Fermo, Blessed Gerardo of Monza, Blessed Guardate, Blessed Giovanni, Blessed Placido, and many more, a noble roll of sanctity. They boasted too eminent scholars and writers of renown; the pious and strictly orthodox Paolo Fabulotti whose authoritative "De potestate Papae super Concilium," first published at Venice in 1613, ran into several editions; Ascanio Tasca, who left the Society of Jesus to follow the more cloistered Ambrosian life, and who rose to be Master-general; Michele Mulazzani, a Piedmontese, who in his day had also governed the Order; Zaccaria Visconti; and Francesco-Maria Guazzo.

Even the recent and particular researches of Monsignor Professore Giovanni Galbiati, the distinguished Prefect of the Ambrosian Library, have failed to discover any details of the life of Guazzo. Perhaps this is because there is really little to know of the contemplative and monastic life, little to know of Guazzo save what we may gather from his own printed works. The archives and cartularies of the Ambrosiani whence *we might at least have learned the dates of Guazzo's birth, of his profession in the Order, and his death, have been lost for many a century. There remain then his writings, three in number, the first and most important being the "Compendium Maleficarum," which was originally published at Milan, "Apud Haeredes Augustini Tradati," in 1608. This golden treatise is dedicated to the Protector of the Ambrosiani, Cardinal Orazio Maffei, and the preface is signed in the month of May. Guazzo was indeed no mere prodigy of the lecture-room and the schools, for he brought his genius to bear upon the pressing problems of a much-distracted time, and perhaps there was no business which more immediately required examination and remedy than the evil of witchcraft. The north of Italy and the remoter Alpine villages had for some reason long been infected to an almost unexampled degree. It was at Asti in Piedmont that well-nigh six hundred years before a society of devil-worshippers had been almost accidentally discovered, largely owing to their zeal for proselytism, and in spite of all efforts, both ecclesiastical and civil, it would seem that these had never wholly been stamped out, but that the dark tradition lingered and was perpetuated in obscure and evil ambuscades. It may be that throughout the thirty years' incumbency of the Cardinal Archbishop Ippolito d'Este (1520–1550), always absent from his see, this cult waxed strong in common with many another dereliction and abuse. Certain it is that during the tenure of S. Carlo Borromeo, that great prelate was well-nigh overwhelmed by the corruptions of Milan, and indeed of his whole diocese. On one occasion he received the submission and confessions of no less than one hundred and thirty sorcerers. Another time as he was passing through a certain village it was noticed he refused to give his blessing to any house or to any individual save the parish priest alone, whom he informed that the folk were, one and all, secret Satanists.*

In Milan itself the votaries of this hidden worship were to be met on every side. They vended charms and love-brews, poisons and philtres; almost openly they boasted of their skill in necromantic lore, their traffic with demons, their sabbats and sorceries, enormously corrupting the whole city.

It was at the instant request of a prelate of rare learning and keenest intelligence, Cardinal Federico Borromeo, the cousin and successor of San Carlo, and Archbishop of Milan from 1595 to 1631 that Fra Francesco-Maria Guazzo composed his encyclopaedic "Compendium Maleficarum," "in the which is fully set forth the vile craft and enmity of witches against the whole race of mankind. Whereunto is further added a most salutary and potent Exorcism to dissolve and dispel all iniquities and delusions of the devil." Guazzo tells us that he has been engaged upon these chapters for some three years, and in addition to his earnest desire to satisfy the Cardinal-Archbishop he was yet further induced to employ his pen on the theme of witchcraft owing to what he had personally witnessed and heard at the court of the Serene Duke John William of Jülich-Cleves. Owing to the great reputation Guazzo had acquired throughout the Milanese Archdiocese as being one of the most learned, most patient and most acute Judges and Assessors in the prosecutions for witchcraft, he was summoned in the year 1605 to Cleves to advise and direct in the case of the Duke himself, who as it was feared and proved had been overlooked and ensorcelled by an aged Satanist, a warlock ninety years old, named John, who dwelt at Lauch, in the archdiocese of Cologne. This wretch confessed that by his charms and certain evil runes he had indeed afflicted the Duke with a wasting sickness and a frenzy, whereupon, being guilty in the highest degree, he was, as the law directed, condemned to the stake. However, in the madness of desperation, as he lay in prison on Sunday morning, 25 September, with a sharp knife he inflicted a fearful wound in his throat, and it was said the very fiend stood by him in his death throes.

It is not to be wondered at that the whole cohort of witches aimed their utmost malice at the Duke, for he was very active in the suppression of that sect throughout his dominions.* Thus on 24 July, 1581, he sent to the upper bailiff at Vlotho, Bertram von Landsberg, a woman accused of sorcery and deeply implicated, bidding the officers examine her straitly "both by gentle means and under torture," and adding an express injunction that "in case of her still refusing to confess, she was to be subjected to trial by water." It was to Duke John William, his territorial prince, that in 1596 Franz Agricola, pastor of Sittard, a strong opponent of Weyer, Hermann Neuwaldt, Wilckin, Anton Praetorius, and the rationalising school, dedicated his "Von Zauberern, Zauberinnen und Hexen," in the preface to which pamphlet he very plainly says: "I know not whether any Catholic writers have hitherto treated this subject in German, but at any rate the rulers are not yet sufficiently informed as to the horror and monstrosity of this sin; . . . . so that most scandalous, dangerous and abominable sin of sorcery and witchcraft has spread in all

---

* *For the witch prosecutions in the Lower Rhine district see Kuhl's "Geschichte der Stadt Jülich," 3 Teile, Jülich, 1891–94.*

directions; no country, town, village, or district, no class of society is free from it."

Lambert Daneau writing in 1574 tells us that in some districts "the witches are so defiant and audacious that they say openly, if only they had an eminent and renowned man for their captain they should become so strong and numerous that they could march against a powerful king in open battle and easily vanquish him with the help of their arts." Well might James I whilst yet he only held his Scottish throne fear the dark Earl of Bothwell. In later years too the boast of the witches has been fearfully fulfilled.

Timely indeed was the writing of the "Compendium Maleficarum," and necessary. A second edition "Ex Collegii Ambrosini Typographia," appeared in 1626. The text here is very considerably amplified by further examples and the extended discussion of nice theological points. An exorcism is added together with various Benedictions, especially for the sick, such as the "Modus Curandi Febricitantes."

The second work of Guazzo was a Life of Blessed Alberto Besozzo, one of the earliest of the Ambrosiani, and especially venerated as the Propagator of the Order, "Vita del Beato Alberto Besozzo," Milan, Nava, 4to, 1625. This notable piece was widely esteemed for the elegance of its style, and brought Guazzo no small increase of reputation as a skilled hagiographer. The monograph was reprinted by the Milanese house of Corrada, 4to, 1684. In 1643 was issued at Venice Guazzo's last book, "Il principe perfetto," 12mo.

It has been conjectured that "Il principe perfetto" may be a posthumous volume, in which case we should date Guazzo's death "circa" 1640, and it has further been suggested that the dissolution of the monasteries of the Ambrosiani—a suppression determined some years before —was purposely delayed until after the demise of so honoured and famous a member of that community.

Francesco Maria-Guazzo comes before us as a writer and scholar of no mean order. In the course of the "Compendium Maleficarum" I have counted quotations from and references to more than two hundred and fifty authors, and these illustrations are never those of some mere commonplace book or random excerpts, but pertinent, illuminative, well chosen and aptly employed. His reading and erudition were prodigious. Steeped in the lore of Councils and in the Fathers, both Greek and Latin, the writings of S. Basil, S. Gregory Nazianzen, S. Athanasius, S. John Chrysostom, S. Cyril, Tertullian, Lactantius, S. Augustine, S. Ambrose,

S. Jerome, S. Bernard, S. Peter Damian, Dionysius the Carthusian, and many other a mighty name are easily familiar to him. With equal facility will he cite Cedrenus and Pontano; Pliny and the Dominican Silvester; Lucian and Luitprand; Hippocrates and Francesco Mattioli; the Catholic champion, Bishop Dubravsky of Olmütz and the Protestant Philip Camerarius, the son of Melancthon's partner in the Augsburg Confession.

Although the "Compendium Maleficarum" was at once accepted as supremely authoritative by all contemporaries, and later demonologists have not been slow to commend, apprize, and make final appeal to this most salutary and excellent treatise—the learned and judicious Sinistrari manifestly and formally not merely follows but actually paraphrases entire more than one chapter when discussing dark problems of witchcraft —it is surprising indeed that Francesco-Maria Guazzo has never generally achieved the wide renown and high reputation of a Bodin, a Remy, a Boguet, or a De Lancre. The reason for this no doubt lies in the fact that these writers were also men of action, each of whom perforce from his very office and estate stood largely in the public eye, and wrought zealously for the public weal. Jean Bodin won fame as a politician, a deputy of the Third Estate to the States-General of Blois, Attorney-General at Laon; Nicolas Remy for fifteen years held the helm as Privy-Councillor and chief Judge in the Duchy of Lorraine; Boguet was "Grand Juge de St. Claude au Comte de Bourgogne"; Pierre De Lancre, the wealthy magistrate of Bordeaux, served as Commissioner Extraordinary in the witch trials of Labourd. Francesco-Maria Guazzo remained but a humble friar, the subject of an obscure and solitary Congregation.

And yet the "Compendium Maleficarum"* is a treatise of no less value and importance than the famous "Démonomanie des sorciers" and the "Tableau de l'inconstance des mauvais anges et démons." Guazzo analyses and describes as perhaps no other demonologist has set out with equal conciseness and clarity the whole practice and profession of witchcraft. Although never sparing of illustration and detail he does not indeed draw examples from the trials of those whom he had examined and judged as do Boguet and De Lancre, a feature which lends their work an especial and personal value, but the "Compendium Maleficarum" may be taken to be in some sort a complementary volume, an essential text-book of the subject, as it were, a tractate which probes and proves every circumstance of Satanism and sorcery.

---

* *Curiously enough there is no mention of the book either in Graese or Brunet.*

To the historian, to the occult student, Guazzo's work is of incalculable worth, and it is not too much to say that he can pretend to little knowledge of that evil Society and their horrid devices who is not intimately conversant with these pages. It will be found moreover that not the least valuable of these chapters are those which treat "De Remediis Diuinis," and in particular the sections "De Eucharistia," "De Signo Sanctae Crucis," and "Auxilium singulare Beatae Mariae Virginis," per Quam, ut ait Bernardus, Deus nos uoluit totum habere.

MONTAGUE SUMMERS.

In Festo B.M.V. Diuini Pastoris Matris, 1929.

FOREWORD

ALTHOUGH the "Compendium Maleficarum," both from the encyclopaedic learning of the author and the scientific precision of his details, must rank as one of the most important of all Witchcraft Manuals, not only—largely owing to his severe concentration of thought and expression and the many technicalities—is the original Latin more than ordinarily difficult, but Guazzo was ill-served both in 1608 and in 1626 by his printers, for these two (which are the only) editions of the book are marred by a superabundance of most riddling typographical errors. Indeed before the work could be well rendered into English I found that it was necessary to prepare something like a definitive recension of the text, a preliminary which, if mechanical enough, has cost me no little time and labour.

To write a full excursus upon the "Compendium Maleficarum," giving further and later examples of the many ill observances and devices of witchcraft, the transvection of the sorcerers to their rendezvous, the abominations of the Sabbat, the worship of the demon, the pledges of diabolical servitude, the "osculum infame," the revelry, the dances, the lewdness of the Incubus and the Succubus, the malice and evil charms of Satanists, all of which and many more black secrets of goety Guazzo has so amply and so authoritatively displayed, would be to pen a second "History of Witchcraft," another volume as copious and as detailed as the "Compendium" itself. However interesting and useful it would have proved to afford modern instances of the continued practices of this horrid Society I have judged it best to reserve so extensive a relation for a separate occasion, and therefore I have furnished this work of Guazzo with a minimum of annotation. Even so I am very well aware that in the glosses will be found information some may perhaps deem superfluous. On the other hand I am constantly being requested to illustrate these manuals of the demonologists by far more extensive commentaries than my wont, so that in fine it is, I fear, not possible entirely to satisfy every student and reader. In the present case I frankly acknowledge that on *account of practical limitations of space, if for no other reason, I have felt obliged entirely to pass over no small number of points concerning which I was minded to write something fully, as also was it necessary for me to treat with economy other details not unworthy of closer investigation.*

To the most learned Prefect of the Ambrosian Library, Monsignor Professore Giovanni Galbiati, I am greatly indebted for the trouble and pains he has so generously bestowed on my behalf in making very particular researches concerning Francesco-Maria Guazzo and in communicating to me important bibliographical and historical details of the Ambrosiani.

My best thanks are due to Dr. H. T. Norman, not only for the loan of many rare pieces on witchcraft from among the treasures of his library, but also for the very real and inspiring interest he has so cordially taken in the present series.

MONTAGUE SUMMERS.

TABLE OF CONTENTS

THE FIRST BOOK

THE SECOND BOOK

DEALING WITH THE VARIOUS KINDS OF WITCHCRAFT, AND CERTAIN OTHER MATTERS WHICH SHOULD BE KNOWN

THE THIRD BOOK

TREATING OF THE DIVINE REMEDIES FOR THOSE WHO ARE BEWITCHED, AND OF CERTAIN OTHER MATTERS

COMPENDIUM MALEFICARUM

BOOK I ☆ CHAPTER I

The Nature and Extent of the Force of Imagination.

ARGUMENT.

MANY authors have written at length concerning the force of imagination: for example Pico della Mirandola,* *De Imaginationibus;* Marsilio Ficino,† *De Theologia Platonica,* Book 13; Alonso Tostado,‡ *On Genesis,* Chapter 30; Miguel de Medina,§ *De Recta in Deum Fide,* II, 7; Leonard Vair,‖ *De Fascino,* II, 3; and countless others. All are agreed that the imagination is a most potent force; and both by argument and by experience they prove that a man's own body may be most extensively affected by his imagination. For they argue that as the imagination examines the images of objects perceived by the senses, it excites in the appetitive faculty either fear or shame or anger or sorrow; and these emotions so affect a man with heat or cold that his body either grows pale or reddens, and he consequently becomes joyful and exultant, or torpid and dejected. Therefore S. Thomas (*Contra Gent.* III, 103) has well said that a man's body can be affected by his imagination in every way which is naturally correspondent with the imaginative faculty, such as local motion in those

---

* *"Mirandola."* Giovanni Pico della Mirandola, *1463–1494. There are many editions of his Complete Works: Bologna, 1496; Venice, 1498; Strasburg, 1504; Basle, 1557; 1573; 1601.*

† *"Marsilio Ficino." 1433–1499. "Theologia Platonica de animarum Immortalitate," perhaps his most important work, was published at Florence 1482.*

‡ *"Alonso Tostado." Circa 1400–1455. A famous exegete often quoted as Abulensis or Alonso Abulensis owing to his having been consecrated Bishop of Avila in 1449. The latest edition of his works is 27 volumes, folio, Venice, 1728.*

§ *"Miguel de Medina." 1489–1578. A Spanish Franciscan, esteemed as one of the most distinguished theologians of his day. "Annales Ordinis Minorum," xix, xxi.*

‖ *"Leonard Vair." Born at Benevento, of Spanish descent, c. 1540; Bishop of Pozzuoli, where he died in 1603. His "De Fascino," Libri III, Paris, 1583; Venetiis apud Aldum, 1589, is a work of singular erudition.*

who are asleep: but that his other bodily dispositions which bear no natural relation with the imagination cannot be so affected; so that imagination cannot, for example, cause any man to add one cubit to his stature.

The argument is proved also by the daily experience of sleep-walkers who do wonderful things in their sleep: for it is agreed that such things are done through the power of imagination while the senses are asleep. Many such matters are discussed by Martin Delrio,* *Disquisitiones Magicae*, Quaest. I, 3.

☆

Examples.

MARTIN DELRIO† tells of what happened at a monastery at Liège a few years ago. There was a certain lay brother whose duty it was during the day to teach the rudiments of the Catechism to a class of boys: and when he slept his thoughts were occupied with the same subject, so that he used to teach in his sleep, encouraging and scolding the boys as loudly and fervently as he did when he was awake; and in this way he disturbed the sleep of those near him. Another lay brother who slept next to him often complained to him about it; and one day he jokingly threatened that, if he made that noise again, he would get up in the night and go to his bed and beat him with a rope whip. And what did Gundislaus, as

his name was, do? In the middle of the night he arose in his sleep and went from his bed to his fellow's cubicle with a pair of scissors in his hand which he pointed straight at the bed of the other who had threatened him. But see the providence of God! The moon was shining, and the night was clear and cloudless; so that the brother, who was awake, saw him coming and at once threw himself from the bed on that side where the partition was farthest removed. The sleeper came up to the bed and stabbed the mattress three or four times with the scissors, and quickly went back where he came from. In the morning he was questioned, and said that he remembered nothing of it, adding that he had never had the least thought of doing such a thing; but that he had only contemplated frightening that brother and driving him off with the scissors if he had approached him with a whip.

Two friends ‡ were travelling together back to their own country and came one day to a town where one of them had an acquaintance with whom he lodged, while the other went to an inn for the night, intending to resume their journey the next day. But while his guest was sleeping the innkeeper, conceiving a greedy desire to take his money, killed him; and having done so began to think how he could smuggle the body out of the town to

---

* *"Martin Delrio." This famous Jesuit scholar was born at Antwerp, 17 May, 1551, and died at Louvain, 19 October, 1608. His encyclopaedic "Disquisitionum Magicarum Libri Sex," 3 vols., 4to, 1599, was frequently reprinted. Of these the folio, 1603, Mainz, is among the most highly esteemed. It is sometimes said that the first edition of Delrio's work was Mainz, 1593, but this folio is a mere myth.*

† *"Delrio." "Disquisitiones Magicae," III, q. 3.*

‡ *"Two friends." This history is very famous in English literature as having been introduced by Chaucer into the Nonne Preestes Tale of the Cok and Hen, Chauntecleer and Pertelote. Guazzo had it from Cicero, "De Diuinatione," I, 27. It is also related by Valerius Maximus, I, 7 ("De Somniis"), where Warton wrongly supposed that Chaucer had found it. But it is plain that Cicero was the author to whom Chaucer refers, since in the "De Diuinatione" are two histories and both these the poet gives, but in a changed order and notes before the second narrative:*

And certes, in the same book I rede,
Right in the nexte chapitre after this . . .

bury it. The same night the murdered man appeared in a dream to his companion who was sleeping in his friend's house, and said: "My friend, my friend, help me; for the innkeeper means to kill me." An hour or two later he appeared again, saying: "Ah, my friend, you did not help me; and behold, the cruel innkeeper has destroyed me." A little later on the same night he came the third time in his dream, and said: "My friend, you did not help me to escape from my murderer's hands, and now I am lying dead. And the murderer is considering how to dispose of and bury my body in the fields outside the town walls; and already he has hidden it in a cart-load of dung. I beg you, as you love me, not to allow this, but at least to see to it that I go to my burial in an honourable and befitting manner." In the morning the man awoke and, terrified by his dream, went to look for his friend. He asked the innkeeper: "Where is my friend?" He answered, in the words of Cain: "Am I his keeper? He arose and went away, taking his belongings with him. I do not know where he went." The friend stood for a while in doubt what he should do: but meanwhile he saw in the yard a cart laden with dung. The unhappy man was then struck with the vision he had seen in his imagination and, since he could not find his friend, quietly thought the matter over with himself. He waited some time to see whether his friend would come back; and when he did not return, he said that perhaps he had started on his journey, and added: "Good-bye then: if my friend comes, say that I have gone on, and tell him to follow me." He then went straight to the mayor and told what had happened to his friend, mentioning the load of dung and adding all other necessary information. The mayor sent his officers, who stood at a distance and watched what the innkeeper would do. The murderer, thinking that all was safe since the dead man's friend had gone away, started off with his cart to go out of the town. Seeing this the officers ran up and said: "Where are you off to, my good fellow, and what is this dung for? We have been ordered to take possession of it." And overturning the cart they found the murdered man lying amidst the dung. The murderer was taken, and met with the terrible punishment which his crime deserved.

☆

CHAPTER II.

Of Artificial Magic.

Argument

MAGIC is of two kinds, natural and artificial. Natural or legitimate magic was, together with all other knowledge, a gift from God to Adam, who by peopling the world handed it down to posterity. This, as Psellus* (*De Daemonibus*) and Proclus † (*De Magia*) have noted, is no more than a more exact knowledge of the secrets of Nature, which by observing the courses and influence of the stars in the heavens, and the sympathies and antipathies subsisting between separate things, compares one thing with another and so effects marvels

---

* "*Psellus.*" *Michael Constantine Psellus, 1020–1110 (Caillet); or c. 1018–c. 1078 (Adrian Fortescue), the celebrated Byzantine philosopher, attained a vast reputation at Constantinople, and even now Krumbacher, "Byzantinische Litteraturgesch." (2nd ed., Munich, 1897), regards him as "the first man of his time." At Paris, 1615, was published the "'De Operatione Dæmonum' Dialogus Gilbertus Gaulminus Molinensis primus Græce edidit et notis illustrauit."*

† "*Proclus.*" *Born at Constantinople, 410; died at Athens, 485. "The scholastic of Neo-Platonism." His writings were collected by Cousin, "Procli Opera," Paris, 1820–25.*

which to the ignorant seem to be miracles or illusions. As when Tobias dispersed his father's blindness with the gall bladder of a fish, a virtue which Galen and many others attribute to the dragonet.* Also the sound of a drum made from a wolf's skin will burst a drum made from the skin of a lamb. Many other notable examples are mentioned by S. Augustine :† such as the peacock's flesh which cannot decompose; chaff which by its coldness preserves snow, and by its heat ripens fruit; a chalk which is set on fire by water, but will not burn if oil be poured upon it; the salt of Girgenti which melts in fire, but becomes hard and groans in water; and many other such things.

The other kind is artificial magic, which effects marvels by means of human skill. This again is two-fold, Mathematic and Prestidigital. Mathematical magic involves the principles of Geometry, Arithmetic or Astronomy: and examples of this are the setting fire to the ships at the siege of Syracuse ‡ by means of mirrors; the flying wooden doves of Archytas § of Taren-

tum; the golden singing birds ‖ of the Emperor Leo; and such matters. Yet we affirm that by this means nothing can be effected which is opposed to the nature of things, but rather that it necessarily requires the help of natural causes and the correct application of certain movements and dimensions. The other sort, which may be called Prestidigital, is ludicrous and illusionary, and its effects are not such as they seem to be. To this sort belongs much that is believed to be done by conjurers and ropewalkers by means of feigned incantations as well as by the agility of their hands and feet. Such feats are at times performed by carefully trained brute animals; sometimes they are effected by the stealthy movements of hidden persons, as in the case of the priests of Bel ¶ who claimed that the food was eaten by the Dragon. Now thaumaturgy and natural magic are in themselves good and lawful, as any art is of itself good. But it may happen to become unlawful: first, when it is done for an evil purpose; second, when it gives rise to scandal, being thought to be done with the help of demons; third, when it involves any spiritual or bodily danger to the conjurer or the spectators. And it must be noted that, for every ten tricks of prestidigital illusion, these men perform one of pure sleight of hand, so as to foster the belief that there is no illusion or sorcery in any-

---

* "*Dragonet.*" *Cf. Pliny,* "*Historia Naturalis,*" *XXXII, 7:* "*Callionymi fel cicatrices sanat, et carnes oculorum superuacuas consumit.*"

† "*S. Augustine.*" "*De Ciuitate Dei,*" *XXI, 4, 5, and 6.* "*A chalk which is set on fire by water,*" "*Eam uiuam calcem loquimur,*" *i.e.* "*quicklime.*" "*The salt of Girgenti.*" *Cf. Pliny,* "*Historia Naturalis,*" *XXXI, 7:* "*Agrigentinus (sal) ignium patiens ex aqua exsilit.*" *This is repeated by Solinus,* "*Polyhistoria,*" *XI; and S. Isidore* "*Etymologiae,*" *XVI, 2, 4.*

‡ "*Siege of Syracuse.*" *Syracuse was captured by Claudius Marcellus in 212 B.C. The story of the burning of the Roman fleet by the reflected rays of the sun, a device said to be due to the genius of Archimedes, is not found in Plutarch, Polybius, or Livy. It is first mentioned by Galen,* "*De Temp.*" *III, 2; and Lucian,* "*Hipp.*" *II, 2. In fuller detail it is recorded by Joannes Tzetzes,* "*Chiliades,*" *II, 103, sqq.*

§ "*Archytas.*" *He probably lived about*

400 B.C. Our chief authority for the little known of his life is Diogenes Laertius, VIII, 79–83.

‖ "*Golden singing birds.*" "*When the Crusaders came from their grey castles to Constantinople, they were dazzled by the magnificence they saw at the Emperor's Court. They told, when they came back, almost fabulous tales of the wonders they had seen, the costly toys, golden lions that roared, trees of jewels where enamelled birds flapped their wings and sang, thrones of ivory and sheets of porphyry.*" *Fortescue,* "*The Orthodox Eastern Church,*" *Part I, chapter 3.*

¶ "*Bel.*" "*Daniel*" *xiv.*

thing that they do, but that all is done by pure skill and dexterity. Ulricus Molitor * states that the devil is able to make one thing seem as if it were another; and Nider † tells us that many other tricks are practised by conjurers. For this prestidigital art was taught by the giant demons before the Flood, and from them Ham ‡ learned it, and from him the Egyptians, then the Chaldaeans and Persians, and so in succession. S. Clement in his *Recognitions* (IV) says: Zoroaster was the first of the Chaldaeans, and he was struck by lightning as a fit reward for his deeds.

☆

Examples.

A certain virgin of Cologne was said to have performed in the presence of the nobles wonders which seemed to be due to magic art: for she was said to have torn up a napkin, and suddenly to have pieced it together again before the eyes of all; she threw a glass vessel against the wall and broke it, and in a moment mended it again; and other like things she did. She escaped from the hands of the Inquisition with a sentence of excommunication.

From the same source we hear of a conjurer in France named Trois Eschelles,§ who in the sight of all and in the presence of Charles IX, called the Praiseworthy King, charmed from a certain nobleman standing at a distance from him the rings of his necklace, so that they flew one by one into his hand, as it seemed; and yet the necklace was soon found to be whole and uninjured. This man was convicted of many actions which could not have been due to human art or skill or any natural cause, and confessed that they were all devil's work, although he had obstinately denied this before.

John Trithemius ‖ tells that much earlier, in the year 876 during the time of the Emperor Louis,¶ a certain Zedechias, a Jew by religion and a physician by profession, worked wonders in the presence of Princes. For he appeared to devour a cart loaded with straw, together with the horses and the driver; he used to cut off men's heads and hands and feet, and exhibit them in a bowl dripping with blood, and then suddenly he would restore the men unharmed each to his own place; and in mid-winter he created in Caesar's palace a most beautiful garden, with trees, grass, flowers, and the singing of suddenly produced birds.

---

* *"Ulricus Molitor."* *A learned lawyer of Constance, who being consulted by Sigismund of Austria on various problems of witchcraft published in January, 1489, his famous treatise "De laniis [sic] et phitonicis mulieribus." Molitor died in 1492.*

† *"Nider." Jean Nider, O.P., prior of the important Dominican house at Basle, papal inquisitor and Rector of the University of Vienna. He died in 1438. His work is very famous and there are constant appeals to his authority. The edition of the "Formicarius" (or "Formicarium") which I have used is that of Douai, 1602.*

‡ *"Ham." Cf. "Malleus Maleficarum," Part I, Question 2: "Vincent of Beauvais in his 'Speculum historiale,' quoting many learned authorities, says that he who first practised the arts of magic and astrology was Zoroaster, who is said to have been Cham (Ham), the son of Noe." This tradition is very frequently found. See my note on above passage in my translation of the "Malleus Maleficarum" (p. 15), John Rodker, 1928.*

§ *"Trois-eschelles." For whom see "The Geography of Witchcraft," by Montague Summers, c. v, pp. 398–9 and 426. Also Bodin, "Demonomanie" (ed. Lyons, 1593), III, 5, pp. 329–30; IV, 4, pp. 421–2; and IV, 5, p. 509.*

‖ *"John Trithemius." The famous Benedictine abbot was born at Trittenheim, 1 February, 1462; and died at Würzburg, 13 December, 1516.*

¶ *"Louis." Louis le Germanique, third son of Louis le Debonnaire, born 806; died 876.*

Thomas Fazelli, O.P.,* relates in his *De rebus Siculis*, Decade II. v. 2 (also Dec. I. iii. 1) wonders of a certain Diodorus, commonly known as Liodorus, who was endowed with magic art and flourished at Catania by means of his marvellous skill in illusions. This man, by the force of his incantations, appeared to change men into brute beasts, to effect a metamorphosis of nearly all things into new shapes, and instantly to bring to himself objects very far distant from him. Moreover by slandering and insulting and reviling the people of Catania he bound them with such vain credulity that he incited them to worship him. When he was delivered up to be punished with death, by means of his pre-eminent skill in incantations he had himself carried out of his gaolers' hands through the air from Catania to Byzantium, to which Sicily was then subject, and back again from Byzantium to Catania in a very short space of time. And the people so wondered at this magic that they thought there was some divine power in him, and in sacrilegious error began to worship him. At length Leo, the Bishop of Catania, received a sudden power from God and in the midst of the city caused him to be cast in the sight of all into

a furnace of fire, in which he was burned. In this way divine justice prevailed; for he who had escaped death at the too lenient hands of the judges, could not escape from the hands of the Holy Man.

In our own times they say that one Cesare, a Maltese, was captured by the Parisians, but cunningly escaped from prison; and this, among other charges, was brought up against him in judgement by Bazius the Inquisitor. But as he was being exhorted to fear damnation, and the Governor of that time had required the Ecclesiastical Judges to preside over the enquiry, he broke away into the midst of the Court and there began to do many fresh marvels. He caused another person to hold magic cards in his hands, and standing at a distance he altered their appearance two or three times: he charmed to himself vessels placed on another part of the table by merely moving a small piece of glass: at times he divined the thoughts of others, as when he scattered on the table a great number of small grains of sugar, and told each man which grain he was thinking of; and even if any one was doubtful of his choice, he would then come to a decision after a little hesitation, boasting that he had long before known which they would choose: and many other such marvels he claimed to perform. Wherefore he was a third time called to trial by the illustrious Archbishop of Malines, the learned Hovius,† in the year 1600; and though he undertook to appear, he escaped to a refuge with a Prince who was the chief champion of Antichrist.

---

* "*Thomas Fazelli, O.P.*" This famous historian, one of the glories of the Dominican Order, was born in 1498 at Sacca, a town of Sicily, not far from Palermo, where whilst yet young he joined the famous Priory of San Domenico. "*In omni scientiarum genere excelluit. Orator enim euasit, poeta, philosophus, theologus Patauii laureatus.*" Thus the old biographer. Amongst the works of Thomas Fazelli the most important are: the posthumous "*Thesaurum Antiquitatum et Historiarum Siciliarium,*" Tomi x, 1579, and the history which is quoted here, "*De rebus Siculis decades duo,*" "*nunc primum in lucem edita,*" Panormi, folio, 1558. This was soon translated into Italian. Fra Fazelli died at the Palermo convent, 8 April, 1570. For fuller details see Quétif-Echard, "*Scriptores Ordinis Praedicatorum,*" vol. II, pp. 212–13.

† "*Hovius.*" Matthias Hovius was consecrated Bishop of Malines, 18 February, 1596; died 30 May, 1620. This great prelate, "*qui coaeuos omnes et discendi celeritate et ingenii facilitate antecelluit,*" is highly praised by his contemporaries for his "*ingentes dotes,*" which were the admiration of all. Cornelius à Lapide in the preface to his Commentary on the Epistles of S. Paul pays a remarkable tribute to the learning of Bishop Hovius.

This Prince who unlawfully kept the conjurer from the Judge's authority hardly lived two years longer, but died in the prime of his life; and after he had undertaken the defence of an evil cause nothing prospered in his government. From this it is clear that God never leaves unpunished those Princes who defend His enemies; for He has expressly commanded: "Thou shalt not suffer a witch to live" (*Exodus* xxii, 18).

☆

CHAPTER III

Whether this Magic can produce True Effects

Argument

ANY man who maintained that all the effects of magic were true, or who believed that they were all illusions, would be rather a radish than a man. Most often the devil, being the father of lies, deceives us and blinds our eyes or mocks our other senses with vain illusory images: and not seldom God prevents him from achieving on behalf of witches what he would and could truly essay; and when he sees that this is so he has recourse to glamours, so that his impotence may not be perceived. But when God permits it, and the devil wishes to produce a true effect, provided that it does not exceed his power, then there is nothing to prevent him from effecting a genuine result; for he then applies active to passive principles, and natural causes engender a true effect. Dionysius of Athens (*De Diuinis Nominibus*, IV.) proves this when he affirms that the Devil did not, in sinning, lose his natural gifts, so that he has the greatest natural strength together with age-long and unlimited experience to enable him to produce a true effect when he desired. But witches' works are illusions, not real but apparent. This is shown by Glycas * where he speaks of the Egyptian Magicians who seemed to do as Moses did, and says: "They indeed changed their rods into serpents, but the rod of Moses swallowed their rods. And they also changed the water into blood, but once it had been changed, they could not restore it to its former state. They brought forth frogs also, but they were unable to protect the houses of the Egyptians from them. They had power to plague the Egyptians, but they had no power to ease their afflictions. Rather did God afflict the magicians with the same boils and blains as the rest of the people suffered; that it might be shown that not only were they unable to avert the divine punishment, but they must themselves partake of it."

☆

Examples.

We read that the sorcerer Pasetes by means of certain enchantments caused a sumptuous feast to appear, and again he made all vanish at his pleasure. He used also to buy things and count out the price, and shortly the money would be found to have passed back secretly from the seller to the buyer. In S. Clement of Rome we also read much concerning Simon Magus: that he made a new man out of air, whom he could render invisible at will; that he could pierce stones as if they were clay; that he brought statues to life; that when cast into the fire he was not burned; that he had two faces like another Janus; that he could change himself into a ram or a goat; that he flew in the air; that he suddenly produced a great quantity of gold; that he could set up kings and cast them down; that he com-

---

* "*Glycas.*" *Michael Glycas, Byzantine historian. His "Annals" commence with the Creation and conclude with the death of Alexis I, Commenus, 1118. Editions; Bekker, Bonn, 1836; Migne, Paris, 1866.*

manded a scythe to go and reap of itself, and that it went and reaped ten times as much as the others; and that when a certain harlot named Selene was in a tower, and a great crowd had run to see her and had entirely surrounded that tower, he caused her to appear simultaneously at all the windows and exhibit herself to all the people.

Anastasius * of Nicaea says: "Simon Magus made statues walk, and when thrown into the fire he did not burn, and he flew in the air, and made bread from stones. He changed himself into the form of a serpent and other beasts; he had two faces: he was changed into gold; he would cause all sorts of spectres to appear at feasts; he caused many shades to go before him, which he said were the souls of the departed; he made the vessels in a house move as though of their own accord with apparently none to carry them."

Bishop Dubravsky † of Olmütz tells that a Bohemian sorcerer Zyto ‡ ex-

hibited his skill now in his own appearance and form, and now under that of another; also that he appeared before the King in purple and silk, which suddenly changed to sordid woollen rags; and that he walked upon the ground as if he were sailing over water. Sometimes he would drive in a four-wheeled coach drawn by cocks. He used also to make sport in many ways with the King's guests; sometimes causing them to be unable to reach their hands to the dishes, by changing their hands into the hooves of oxen or horses; and sometimes he fixed spreading stag's antlers to their foreheads when they looked out at window at some passing spectacle, so that they could not draw their heads in again. He made thirty fat pigs out of bundles of straw and drove them to a certain rich baker named Michael, saying that he might buy them at his own price; only he warned the buyer not to drive his new herd to the river to water. The baker took no notice of the warning, and saw his pigs sink into the water while bundles of straw floated on the top: he then sought out the seller and at last found him in a tavern lying stretched out on a bench; and when he angrily tried to stir him by pulling one of his legs, Zyto caused his foot and leg to come away in the other's hand. Zyto then loudly complained and, seizing him by the throat, had him taken before the Judge. The baker seemed to have been caught in a manifest crime, and suffered punishment in addition to his loss. For this power of sorcerers to throw off their limbs, see Pliny, Books 25, 26 and 28, and Aulus Gellius, Book 10, chapter 12.

---

* "*Anastasius.*" *A theologian and exegete of the sixth century. The reference is to his* "*In Sacra scriptura,*" *q. xxiii.*

† "*Bishop Dubravsky.*" *John Dubravsky, Bishop of Olmütz, was the great Catholic champion of the sixteenth century, who refuted Speratus, Hubmaier, Huter, Socinus and other sectaries. His various writings include five books on piscatology; the work entitled "Ueber das heilige Messopfer"; and the thirty-three volumes of his monumental History of Bohemia. The present reference is to Book XXIII of this work.*

‡ *Zyto was the favourite magician of the Emperor Wenceslas, and upon the occasion of the marriage of this latter in 1389 with Sophia of Bavaria, is said to have far outexcelled in his art all the warlocks and conjurers of the land. His feats are recorded in not a few chronicles: e.g. Concil. Pragens. anno 1355, c. 61 (Hartzheim, IV, 400); Höfler, "Prager Concilien," p. 2 (Statuta breuia Arnesti anno 1353); Raynaldus, anno 1400, No. 14. Most of these tricks—the sprouting of antlers on the heads of persons looking through a window; fardels of straw sold as pigs and sinking in running*

water (fatal to sorcery); the leg coming away when pulled; passed into common folk lore and chap-books, being attributed to every conjurer of popular renown. These three illusions are introduced in Marlowe's "Dr. Faustus," 4to, 1604.

✪

CHAPTER IV

That Witches Effect their Marvels with the Help of the Devil

Argument

THE demon can effect the most rapid local movement of bodies, so that he can withdraw an object from sight and substitute another so quickly that he deludes the understanding and the eyes of the onlookers into a belief that the first object has been changed into the second. We must believe that the metamorphoses of the heathen were of this sort; such as the transformation of Diomedes' companions into birds, and of Iphigeneia into a hind, as S. Augustine* observes. These deceptions were exposed by Astirius also, whose deeds were saved from oblivion by Eusebius.

We must, then, consider marvels as of two kinds. The first is when the effect is not due to any local motion and is beyond the sphere of applied natural causes, as, for example, the raising of the dead or the healing of true blindness; for in such there is always some glamour or deception. The other is when a visible object suddenly vanishes; and this is due to some prestidigital contrivance. An example of the first is when a sorcerer places in a room a bow made of a certain wood, and an arrow of another wood, and a string of a certain material, and shoots the arrow and causes a river to appear in the place as wide as the length of the bow shot: of the second, when a horse appears to be torn in pieces, and then is found to be whole. Of the same sort is that trick mentioned by Nicetas,† to which we shall refer later, in which a

conjurer produces what appears to be a serpent. But for a better understanding of this it must be known that the devil deceives our senses in many different ways. First when he wholly or in part hides from our eyes an object which is present. Secondly, when he so affects the medium of our vision that an object seen through it seems different from what it is: as when salt is mixed with acid and a linen cloth soaked in it, if that cloth be lighted at a candle the faces of those present will assume a ghastly appearance; or if a candle made from an ass's semen and wax be lighted, all those present appear to have asses' heads. Thirdly, when the vapours of the intermediate air are thickened and so it appears that a cock is drawing along a beam, when it is really only a straw. Fourthly, when objects seem to move through the air, as trees appear to sailors to move along together with their ship. Fifthly, when there is shown to the onlookers an aerial or a fantastic body similar to that which they suppose it to be. Sixthly, by a swift agitation or a sudden concealment of visible objects, and by various secret arrangements and divisions of them, as conjurers do with strings and little balls, etc. Seventhly, if the bodily humours be agitated or disturbed things appear to be different from what they are, as happens to drunkards and madmen. Finally, I say that the devil can so compound and arrange fantasms that even when a man may be said to be awake he is as one who sleeps, and thinks he sees what he does not see, according to Gaetani,‡ 2. 2, q. 95, artic. 3.

---

* "*S. Augustine.*" "*De Ciuitate Dei,*" XVIII, *18.*

† "*Nicetas.*" *Acominatus, also called Choniates (from his birthplace Chonae in Phrygia). He ranks among the most important Byzantine historians. Of his "Annales" there are editions by Bekker, Bonn, 1835; by Migne, Paris, 1865. "Annales," IV, 23.*

‡ "*Gaetani.*" *Tomaso de Vio Gaetani, Dominican Cardinal, philosopher, theologian, and exegete, 1469–1534. His Commentaries on the "Summa" of S. Thomas are recognised as a classic of scholastic literature, and were by order of Leo XIII incorporated in the official Leonine edition of the works of S. Thomas, of which the first volume appeared at Rome in 1882.*

Examples.

At Caesarea Philippi, which the Phoenicians call Paneas, it is said that at a certain Festival of the Heathen a woman was solemnly sacrificed and thrown into the spring which there arises from the base of Mount Paneus, from which the Jordan is said to flow: and this woman, through the potent might of the demon, vanished in a wonderful manner from their eyes so that they thought that a memorable miracle had been performed. On one occasion Astirius chanced to be present while this was being done and, seeing so many people dumbfounded with wonder at this thing, he had pity on their ignorance and, raising his eyes to heaven, prayed God the Ruler of all through the mediation of Christ to restrain from his deception that demon who had so blinded the people with error, and to prevent him from those illusions with which he used to mock them. When he had thus prayed to God, the victim suddenly appeared floating on the water; and this matter which had caused so great wonder came to nothing, so that thereafter the like was no more practised in that place.

Michael Sicidites looked from a high place in the Palace of Constantinople and saw a ship laden with pots and dishes; and by a magic spell he caused the captain to rise and start beating those dishes until they were reduced to powder. Soon, when his blindness had passed, the wretched man tore his beard and began to utter loud lamentations: and when he was asked why he had treated his merchandise in that manner, he sorrowfully answered that, while he was intent upon his oars, he saw a horrible serpent stretched upon the dishes and glaring at him as if it were about to devour him, and that it had not ceased from its twistings and contortions until all the dishes were broken.

Hear another example which is so well told and instructive that I cannot refrain from relating it.

In the time of Sigismund I,[*] King of Poland, Jacob Melstinch, the Mayor of the town of Brezinium, was induced by some lightness of the mind to take upon himself the authority and name of Christ. He chose Peter Zacorski of Cracow and eleven other robbers like him, and gave them the names of the Apostles; but himself he called Jesus Christ. They visited the towns doing miracles after the manner of conjurers; they suborned other rogues and robbers to feign death and raised them to life; they planted fish in muddy marshes where they could not naturally be, and then in the name of Christ caught them in their hands; they hid loaves in ovens, and then in the name of their Christ brought them out as if they had not been there before, to the great wonder of the simple vulgar people. At one time he came with his disciples to Czenstochowa,[†] a monastery famous for its picture of the Blessed Virgin Mary; and staying there some days incited one of their number to behave as if he were possessed of the devil, and by means of this man they obtained food: for he went among the guest rooms, and snatched meat from the kitchen and threw it to his comrades, who blessed the meat with the cross and ate it. And when there was a great gathering of people before the Holy Image, these rogues led their possessed companion to the altar wearing a two-fold robe within which he could secrete what was required. They put stones within his garment. As he was being led to the altar, he

---

[*] *"Sigismund I." 1506–1548.*
[†] *"Czenstochowa." Our Lady of Czenstochowa, Królowa Korony Polskiej. Czenstochowa is a small town in the palatinate of Kalisz, near the Silesian frontier. The most Holy and Miraculous Picture of Our Lady, the work of S. Luke, is painted on cypress, and, says an old author, "has a majesty which passes the conception of art."*

broke away from their hands raging, and rushed upon the altar, which was covered with alms money which he seized and thrust between his two-fold garment. The monk who was at the altar broke off the divine office and fled; and the other monks ran up and undid the man's belt. The stones then fell to the ground, but the money remained between the folds of his garment. The monks thought that the money had been changed into stones by the devil, and tried by exorcisms to restore it to its proper shape: but when the stones still remained, the exorcist angrily threw down the holy book, saying: "We have never had such a devil. Depart with him to all the devils!" The rogues escaped with the real money into Silesia where in a certain village they approached a noble matron who, in the absence of her husband, would not receive them. They asked her to give them at least a napkin or a piece of flax as alms; and she offered them a bundle of flax, upon which they said: "This we will take and Christ will bless you, that your linen may increase more abundantly. Show us, if you have it, another bundle." And when they would likewise have taken this, the woman, fearing her husband, refused: whereupon they secretly put a piece of lighted tinder in the flax as they returned it to her. And so by means of the flax the house was set on fire and burned. When the husband returned, the woman said that this was a just punishment for her bad behaviour to Christ and His disciples. But the husband was smitten with anger and said: "There has been no Christ here, but a very vile rogue." So with his neighbours he went in pursuit and found them in a certain town. Then the false Christ said to him he called Peter: "Now my Passion draws near, Peter, and the cup which I am to drink." Peter answered: "And, Lord, I think it threatens me also." He replied: "Peter, I can in no other wise escape from this than by the window." Peter answered: "And as long as I live I will not leave you, but will follow you wherever you go." So they escaped through the window, and the other Apostles by whatever means they could: but the peasants followed them smiting them with staves and ropes, saying: "Prophesy unto us, thou Christ and thy Apostles, in what forest did these sticks grow." So, being chastened with blows, they thereafter chastened their lives, saying: "It is hard for us to bear the Passion of Christ and the persecutions of the Apostles as well." This story is told in the Chronicles of Poland.

☆

CHAPTER V.

The Men of Old Accredited Witches with Marvellous Deeds.

Argument.

JOHN of Salisbury * says that, when God permits, witches can with the help of demons shake the elements together and alter the true appearance of things. They can foretell much of the future. They confuse the minds of men with dreams; and merely by the potency of their charms can cause death, etc. Saxo Grammaticus † writes that giants and sorcerers in the North practised unheard-of wonders with various illusions, and could so skilfully deceive men's eyes that they hid their own features and those of others under various fantasms, and obscured the true shape of things under seductive forms, and did other marvels like those which we have already told of Simon Magus. Pythagoras made his thigh appear to be golden, and by his spells tamed an eagle with which he often conversed. Baianus ‡ the King of Bulgaria was

---

* "John of Salisbury." "Polycraticus," I, 10.
† "Saxo Grammaticus." "Hist. Dan." I.
‡ "Baianus." This is from Marcantonio Cocceius Sabellius, III, "Ennead." 2.

seen to change himself whenever he would into a wolf or any other animal, and sometimes did so in such a manner that no one perceived it. Glycas * tells of Simon Magus, besides what we have already mentioned, that once when Caesar would have apprehended him he was stricken with terror and escaped by leaving another man in his own likeness. He says also that he had a dog chained to the door of his house, which devoured those who tried to come in without his permission: but the dog told S. Peter to enter, and announced in human speech that S. Peter was present. You see how the power of the devil yielded to the divine virtue in S. Peter; for that Cerberus fawned upon S. Peter and was unable to harm him. Numa Pompilius produced a sumptuous feast when he had no food in his house. Ollerus sailed over the open sea on an enchanted bone as if it were a ship, as we are told by John Trithemius in his *Chronica Hersaugiensis*. Eric, King of the Goths, could draw a favourable wind from any quarter by turning his hat towards it. Apuleius † himself, according to many, was skilled in magic, and he relates a wonderful story of two women, the first of whom was a Queen among witches, as follows.

☆

Examples.

This woman, because her lover had seduced another woman, changed him with one word into a beaver; since that animal, when it is in fear of being caught, escapes its pursuers by cutting off its stones: and so also it happened to this man, because he had loved another woman. She changed a neighbouring innkeeper into a frog because he was jealous of her: and now (says Apuleius) in his old age he swims about in a large vessel of his own wine, and squatting in the dregs of it greets his former customers with hoarse servile croakings. Another man who spoke against her in public she changed into a ram. Also when her lover's wife, who was heavy with child, loaded her with insults, she closed up the woman's womb and by checking the growth of the foetus condemned her to a perpetual pregnancy; so that it is agreed that the wretched woman went for eight years swollen like an elephant ‡ about to give birth. The same author writes of one Pamphile who was said to be a witch of the first order and a mistress of every necromantic spell. This woman, by breathing upon pebbles and twigs and such small articles could plunge the heavenly light of the world into hellish and primeval darkness. Again, when she saw any beautiful youth she was at once smitten by his charms and turned her whole eyes and soul upon him; but if they would not comply with her, or proved in any way defective, she would detest them and at once change them into rocks or cattle or some other animal; while some she killed outright.

It is certain that all the wonders we have just instanced were due to some magic illusion. But the Saints, as S. Paul § says (*Hebr.* xi, 34), performed miracles and wonders in the name of God and in perfect faith: "The Saints through faith quenched the violence of fire," as did the Hebrew children, and S. Francis of Paula, and many others. Hear the following example of faith and praiseworthy religious obedience.

Bernardino Scardeone writes as follows. A certain Dominican Prior of the Preaching Friars was invited to dine with the Jesuates, the sons of Blessed John Colombini, and sat down

---

* "Glycas." "Annales," II and III.
† "Apuleius." "Metamorphoseon," I.

‡ "Elephant." Pliny, "Historia Naturalis," VIII, 10, says of the elephant: Decem annis gestare in utero uulgus existimat. Cf. Plautus, "Stichus," I, 3, and Achilles Tatius, Lib. IV.
§ "S. Paul." "Hebrews" XI, 34.

to the meal. When the food had been removed and leave was given to talk, this Prior began to speak of the Passion of Our Lord and His sufferings in good set phrase indeed, but somewhat arrogantly, tacitly criticising his hosts because, although they were monks they did not, as other monks did, make public and private profession of the three vows. To this the Jesuate Prior, a simple man, but prudent and beloved of God, answered: "Since we have fallen into this talk, Father, do you agree that we see whether one of our Brothers, who has humbly devoted himself to God, or that companion of yours who has publicly professed the three vows, will show the more sincere obedience to his Superior?" Without thinking, the other willingly agreed. Then the Jesuate turned to our Brother Mark here as he ministered to those at the table, and said: "Brother Mark our guests are cold: in the name of your holy obedience bring them quickly from the kitchen in your bare hands some burning coals that they may be warmed at once." The Brother promptly and unhesitatingly obeyed, not dreaming that anything could be impossible which he was commanded to do in the name of his obedience, and brought straight from the kitchen to the table as many burning coals as he could hold in his two hands, without taking the slightest hurt, and offered them to the two guests to warm themselves with: and at the Prior's command, to the wonder of all, he then carried them back again to the place where he had fetched them from. The Dominican Prior was beyond measure astonished, and looked at his companion as if he were about to command him to do likewise; but this man, recognising this, thought there was not a moment to lose and broke out into the following words: "I beg you, Father, not to command me to tempt God. If you wish I will bring you fire as I always do in a potsherd, but not in my hands." The

other monks were looking at each other in silent amazement at this great miracle; but when they heard him blurt out those words, they quietly smiled at each other.

☆

CHAPTER VI

Of the Witches' Pact with the Devil.

Argument.

THE pact formed between a witch and the devil may be either expressed or tacit. The expressed pact consists of a solemn vow of fidelity and homage made, in the presence of witnesses, to the devil visibly present in some bodily form. The tacit pact involves the offering of a written petition to the devil, and may be done by proxy through a witch or some third person when the contracting party is afraid to see or have speech with the devil. Grilland* calls this a tacit pact, yet although it is made with another person than the devil, it is expressly made in the devil's name, as is clear from the examples he gives. Perhaps we should class as an expressed pact that rather rare instance of a German woman who, jumping backwards out of her bath, said: "As far as I thus leap away from Christ, so much nearer may I come to the devil." But there are certain matters common to all their pacts with the devil, and these may be arranged under eleven heads.

First, they deny the Christian Faith and withdraw their allegiance from God. They repudiate the protection

---

* " Grilland." Paul Grilland of Castiglione wrote his famous "Tractatus de hereticis et sortilegiis, omnifariam coitu eorumque poenis" about 1525. Grilland was "diocesis Aretinae (Arezzo) criminalium causarum auditor, Andreae de Iacobatiis, sanctissimi domini nostri papae almaeque urbis uicarii generalis." The reference is Q. III, N. I sqq. of the "De hereticis."

of the Blessed Virgin Mary, heaping the vilest insults upon her and calling her Harlot, etc. And the devil arrogates honour to himself, as S. Augustine notes (*contra Faustinum*, cap. 22).

Therefore S. Hippolytus * the Martyr writes that the devil compels them to say: "I. deny the Creator of Heaven and earth. I deny my Baptism. I deny the worship I formerly paid to God. I cleave to thee, and in thee I believe." The devil then places his claw upon their brow, as a sign that he rubs off the Holy Chrism and destroys the mark of their Baptism.

Second, he bathes them in a new mock baptism.

Third, they forswear their old name and are given a new one; as, for example, della Rovere of Cuneo was renamed Barbicapra.

Fourth, he makes them deny their godfathers and godmothers, both of baptism and confirmation, and assigns them fresh ones.

Fifth, they give the devil some piece

of their clothing. For the devil is eager to make them his own in every particular: of their spiritual goods he takes their Faith and Baptism; of their bodily goods he claims their blood, as in the sacrifices to Baal; of their natural goods he claims their children, as will be shown later; and of their acquired goods he claims a piece of their clothing.

Sixth, they swear allegiance to the devil within a circle traced upon the ground. Perhaps this is because a circle is the symbol of divinity, and the earth is God's footstool; and so he wishes to persuade them that he is the God of heaven and earth.

Seventh, they pray the devil to strike them out of the book of life, and to inscribe them in the book of death. So we can read written in a black book the names of the witches of Avignon.

Eighth, they promise to sacrifice to him: and certain fiendish hags, as Bar-

tolomeo Spina † tells, vow to strangle

---

* "*S. Hippolytus.*" *Died c. 236. This Saint was a prolific author, but many of his works have not come down to us, and there is much in his history which is obscure.*

† "*Bartolomeo Spina.*" *c. 1475–c. 1546. A Dominican theologian, Master of the Sacred Palace under Paul III. His "Tractatus de Strigibus et Lamiis," Venice, 1523, has been often reprinted.*

or suffocate for him one child every month or two weeks (*De Strigibus,* II).

Ninth, they must every year make some gift to the demons their masters

been observed by Lambert Daneau * and Bodin and Gödelmann.† And just as God in the Old Testament marked His own with the sign of circumcision, and in the New Testament with the sign of the Holy Cross which took the place of circumcision, according to S. Gregory Nazianzen and S. Jerome; so also the devil, who loves to imitate God, has from the very infancy of the Church marked those heretics who were implicated

---

* "*Lambert Daneau.*" A Calvinist theologian, born at Beaugency. He was minister to Protestant communities at Gion, Orthez and Castres, in which latter town he died in 1595. His dialogue "Les Sorciers" (Geneva ?), 1574, was translated into Latin, English, and other languages. See Paul de Félice "Lambert Daneau," Paris, 1881, and Paulus "Lambert Daneau et la Sorcellerie," in "Études hist. et relig. du diocèse de Bayonne," 1895, pp. 573, sqq.

to avoid being beaten by them, or to purchase exemption from such of their pledged undertakings as are obnoxious to them; but, as Nicolas Remy says, these gifts are only legitimate when they are completely black in colour (*Demonol.* I, 11).

Tenth, he places his mark upon some part or other of their bodies, as fugitive slaves are branded; and this branding is sometimes painless and sometimes painful, as we learn from examples of it. He does not, however, mark them all, but only those whom he thinks will prove inconstant. And the mark is not always of the same description; for at times it is like the footprint of a hare, sometimes like that of a toad

or a spider or a dog or a dormouse. Neither does he always mark them upon the same place: for on men it is generally found on the eye-lids, or the arm-pit or lips or shoulder or posterior; whereas on women it is found on the breasts or private parts, as has

† "*Gödelmann.*" John George Gödelmann, Doctor of Law and Professor at the University of Rostock. He gave public lectures at Rostock on the Carolina, and then published a part of these in Latin, "Tractatus de magis, ueneficis et lamiis." The first edition is probably 1590. They were often reprinted.

in witchcraft with a certain sign, as we learn from Irenaeus, I, 24, and Tertullian, *de praescript. aduers. haeret., post medium.*

Eleventh, when they have been so

marked they make many vows : as never to adore the Eucharist; that they will both in word and deed heap continual insults and revilings upon the Blessed Virgin Mary and the other Saints; that they will trample upon and defile and break all the Relics and images of the Saints; that they will abstain from using the sign of the Cross, Holy Water, blessed salt and bread and other things consecrated by the Church; that they will never make full confession of their sins to a priest; that they will maintain an obstinate silence concerning their bargain with the devil, and that on certain stated days they will, if they can, fly to the witches' Sabbat and zealously take part in its activities ; and finally that they will recruit all they can into the service of the devil. And the devil in his turn promises that he will always stand by them, that he will fulfil their prayers in this world and bring them to happiness after death.

It must be known too that, as Remy notes (I, 13), it is an inviolable rule among witches that, when several of them are met together for the purpose of doing ill to some person, and through the will of God their plans come to nothing since, perhaps, he whom they wish to harm daily commends himself to God in his prayers, defending himself from their devilish works with Holy Water and the Sacrament; then they have to settle among themselves which of their number shall herself incur the evil, so that they may observe their contract, which provides that, if they try to send misfortune upon another and fail, it must return upon themselves. For the devil will not endure that the injunctions he has laid upon them should all come to nothing. And she to whom the fateful lot falls has to suffer the evil for them all. The devil

exacted this condition in the case of Catherine Praevotte in the town of Freising. This woman had a wish to poison the only daughter of her neighbour Michael Cocus, and tried often to do so, but in vain (for the mother guarded her every day with prayers and lustrations against the evil of witchcraft); and finally the devil repeatedly accused her of cheating him of his prey, and in the end the wretched woman was forced to poison

her own son Odilo, a babe in his cradle.

But to return to our argument: the way to the pact between the devil and witches and the vow of service and allegiance seem to be prepared by some sympathy in wickedness between the witches and the devil, which gives rise to a familiarity approaching friendship, and so to a gradual feeling of confidence; and this begets in the weaker party a certain presumptuousness and boldness in making requests from the stronger, and in the stronger some pleasure in fulfilling his federate's requests. And so it comes that the witch confides in the devil, thinking that he can command him, and the devil pretends to acknowledge his power. This has been well and fully proved by Abbot Trithemius: (*Questionum.* VIII, 5). "Such pacts with the devil are usually vain and empty; for the devil never keeps faith, nor thinks himself bound by any promise, who

dared to lie to Christ when he said, 'All these will I give to thee, if thou wilt fall down and worship me'" (*S. Matthew* iv).

He promised the sorcerer Cyprian * that he should enjoy Justina, and yet he did not keep his word: for IT IS THE HEIGHT OF MADNESS TO EXPECT THE TRUTH FROM THE FATHER OF LIES (see Origen, *contra Celsum*, Bk. 8). But these pacts with the devil are not only vain and useless; they are also dangerous and immeasurably pernicious, as I shall show by the two following examples, and by many others in their proper places.

☆

* *"Cyprian." "Martyrologium Romanum,"* 26 September: "At Nicomedia the birthday of the holy martyrs Cyprian and Justina the Virgin, the latter whereof suffered much for Christ

under the Emperor Diocletian and the governor Eutholomius, and converted to Christ the said Cyprian, who was a mage, and who had attempted with his wizard arts to make her mad, and presently she underwent martyrdom with him." The birthday is the heavenly birthday, that day upon which a Saint passes to bliss.

Examples.

Remy (I, 9) relates that a youth named Theodore Maillot desired in marriage a maiden of very wealthy family, but was quite without hope of winning her since he was poor and of humble birth, and his family was engaged in commerce, which was then despised as ignoble; therefore he could see no honourable means of declaring his love. Now when matters are desperate and entirely without hope, men readily turn to any conceivable remedy and engage themselves to follow any plan, whether it be lawful or not. Consequently young Maillot approached a fellow servant from Germany who, as he had heard, had a demon always at his service, and told him of his trouble, asking him not to begrudge him any help that he could give him, for he would not prove ungrateful. The German gladly accepted this chance: for such were the terms of his pact with the demon that he was compelled within a few days either to deliver up another man to take his own debt upon him, or to have his neck twisted and be killed by the demon. He therefore appointed the following day at dawn for their business at a close and secret place; and they had hardly met there before the doors suddenly opened and there entered a maiden of the most beautiful and pleasing aspect (for so the demon chose to appear at first, lest Maillot should be revolted by his terrible appearance), who said that she would easily bring to pass the marriage which he so ardently desired, on condition that he would follow her instructions: and as he waited in anxious suspense, she gave him her advice. First she said that he must abstain from theft, obscenity, lust, blasphemy and other vices which soil the soul, and must practise piety and relieve the poor according to his ability, and fast twice a week, and not cease from solemn prayer every day, and be diligent in doing all that befits and becomes a Christian man; and that if he would bind himself by an oath to do all this, he would without difficulty obtain the marriage he desired. Saying this, and having appointed a day for his answer, she went out at the door. Maillot, seeing that so great a benefit was offered him on such holy and honourable conditions, thought that he need have no hesitation in gratefully and willingly accepting them. But on thinking more and more deeply of the matter, and being tossed between hope and fear, there was that in his face which caused a certain priest of his house to guess that there was some cause for his distraction. This priest approached him kindly and searched out what was troubling his mind and succeeded in persuading him not to sink to any further communing with the devil. The German, thus cheated of his hope, soon after paid the debt of his pact; for not many days later he fell on to his head from his horse on a level and open road, and was instantly killed.

Johann Nider (*Formicarius*, V) relates that, a little before the present General Council, there dwelt in Lesser Basle a man of evil life and strongly suspected of witchcraft, whose daughter was married and living in her father's house. At length the old father began to sicken and, showing his daughter and son-in-law a certain casket, said: "Do not move this chest, but let it rest in its place even after my death, or you will be sorry for it." And soon afterwards he died. After some time had passed neither the daughter nor her husband paid much attention to her father's words: but as they were moving the rest of their furniture to a new house, the man began to carry the chest, which was only a small one, to their new dwelling. On the way it began to grow so heavy that it was too much for his strength, and he called on his wife to help him. I do not know whether the woman opened the casket afterwards in the house, or whether she rashly interfered with it in some other way; but it is certain that when they entered their new house with the child that had been born to them the woman suddenly became stark lunatic and rushed upon the cradle to kill the child. Seeing this, the husband forcibly restrained her, recognising that she was possessed by a demon. She was exorcised, whereupon the demon threatened that he would not come out without killing her; and so it happened, under the very hands of the exorcist. The next day, as the husband was walking in public, a stone suddenly fell from the top of a conduit and, by the agency of the devil, as it seemed, struck him in the face and so deformed him that he no longer looked human.

See how the demon exacted payment in accordance with the pact which he had no doubt formed with the old father, namely, that he should kill whoever opened or moved the casket. Pierre Crespet* has much to say concerning such imprisoned demons, namely, that in serving their masters some are saturnine, some jovial, some venereal, some mercurial, etc.; that they must be approached with a certain ritual, and that at certain times in the night they arouse their owners and require to be worshipped by them, if they do not demand a worse thing.

It remains to quote another instance of how, when a witch attempts to do evil and fails, the evil rebounds upon herself, as I said in my argument. At Freising on the 4th September, 1589, Catharine Praevotte, whom I have mentioned before, told the following with her own lips. "Several of us witches met together to plot how to bewitch the cattle of a certain shoemaker of Freising; but in some way we were thwarted so that we could not do this. Nevertheless our bargain had to be fulfilled, so that he who was await-

ing a sure prize should not be disappointed. So we decided to cast lots to see who should suffer for it, and it fell upon Agnes Eyswitz, the vilest and wickedest of all us women. She did not hesitate, but with the utmost readiness gave a drugged drink to her twenty-year-old son Peter in the presence of his companions, which soon caused his whole body to become monstrously distorted and deformed." This was doubtless done so that he might suffer pains even worse than death at the hands of the demon, who never forgoes one tittle of his bargain.

☆

CHAPTER VII

By their Terrible Deeds and Imprecations Witches Produce Rain and Hail, etc.

Argument.

IT is most clearly proved by experience that witches can control not only the rain and the hail and the wind, but even the lightning when God permits. Therefore Andrea Césalpino, in his *Daemonum inuestigatio peripatetica*, says that men have been known who could raise, not only hail storms, but lightning also; but they confessed that they could not injure whomsoever they pleased, but only those whom God had forsaken, that is (for so I understand it) those who had fallen from God's grace by mortal sin. They can also evoke darkness; wherefore we read in Marco Polo that the Tartars are so potent in devilish illusions that they can cause darkness when and where they will, and that he once narrowly escaped from robbers through the protection of this art. Bishop Haito† of Basle also tells that when the Tartar army was being beaten in battle, the witch Vexillarius

---

* *"Pierre Crespet." A monk of the Celestine Order. A mystical and ascetical writer, author of "Deux livres de la haine de Satan et des malins esprits contre l'homme," Paris, 1590.*

† *"Bishop Haito." Born in 763 of a noble house of Swabia; died 17 March, 836, in the Abbey of Reichenau on an island in the Lake of Constance. Vautrey, "Histoire des évêques de Bâle," I, (Einsiedeln, 1884).*

encompassed their enemies with a thick darkness by means of his spells, so that they rallied and won the victory. They can moreover cause rivers to stop flowing, and dry up springs, and irrigate the land with fresh springs produced from rocks and stones: they can make the water of a river turn back and flow to its source, a thing which Pliny* says happened in his time (II, 103). Many examples are to be found in Remy, of which I shall quote a few here.

☆

Examples.

In the district of Treves a peasant was planting cabbages in his garden with his eight-year-old daughter, and praised the girl highly for her skill in the work. The young maid, whose sex and age combined to make her talkative, boasted  that she could do more wonderful things than that; and when her father asked what they were, she said: "Go away a little, and I will quickly make it rain on whatever part of the garden you wish." He was astonished, and said: "Come then, I will go a little away." And when he had withdrawn the girl dug a trench and pissed in it, and beat the water with a stick, muttering I know not what, and behold there fell from the clouds a sudden rain upon the said place. The astounded father asked:

"Who taught you to do this?" She answered: "My mother did; and she is very clever at this and other things like it." The peasant nobly faced his right and plain duty, so a few days later, on the pretence that he had been invited to a wedding, he took his wife and daughter dressed in festal wedding robes to the neighbouring town, where he handed them over to the Judge to be punished for the crime of witchcraft.

It is recorded in the *Malleus Maleficarum* that certain Inquisitors determined to prove by means of a witch whom they had in custody the truth of the power claimed by witches of stirring up tempests. They therefore released her; since it is certain that, as long as they remain in prison, all magic powers desert them. She then went to a thickly wooded place and there dug a trench with her hands and filled it with water, which she continued to stir with her finger until there arose from it a vapour which grew into a dense cloud. This cloud at once became alive with thunder and lightning, to the great awe and terror of the onlookers. But she said: "Be of good heart; I will cause all this cloud to be removed to whatever place you wish." And when they named a desert place near by, the cloud was at once borne thither by the force of the wind and tempest, and let loose its hail upon the rocks, so confining all its damage within the prescribed and indicated limits.

The following example is very like the first. A Suabian peasant was bit-

---

* "*Pliny.*" "*Historia Naturalis,*" *II, 103:* "*Amnes retro fluere et nostra uidit aetas, Neronis principis annis supremis, sicut in rebus eius retulimus.*"

terly complaining of the drought from which they were suffering, and as he was doing so his daughter, who was eight or ten years old, came to him and said that if he wished she would at once bring a heavy shower upon the field in which they were together. When the father said that he very greatly wished it, she asked him to give her a little water. So they came to a neighbouring stream where she beat the water in the name of that Master, as she said, to whom her mother was dedicated; and thereupon there fell rain from the skies abundantly enough to water that field, while it left all the other fields as dry as they were before.

Remy relates how a witch named Alexia Granjean told that she was once being carried through the clouds and came to a place where, from her point of vantage, she could see a man named Johann Vehon pasturing his horses. Suddenly there appeared to her a huge black man who, as if eager to serve her, asked her whether she had any grudge against that peasant, for he would quickly avenge her upon him. She answered that she hated the man bitterly because he had once beaten her only son nearly to death while he was pasturing his horse. "Very well," replied he; "I agree to avenge you at once." So saying, he quickly rose up in the air so high that no eye could see him, and thereupon the lightning, with a mighty flash and thunder, fell upon the horses and smote down two of them, while the peasant looked on in terror about thirty paces away, according to his own evidence.

Giovanni Pontano* tells that Ferdinand II, King of Naples, laid close siege to Sessa Aurunca, which is situated near Monte Massico. Now this town was for the House of Anjou, and he hoped to force it to surrender

---

* "Pontano." "De Bello Neapolitano," V. "Pontani Opera Omnia," Basileae, 1538, II, pp. 574-75.

through lack of water. But a number of wicked priests dared to summon rain by means of magic. For some of the besieged townsmen went out in the dark of night evading the camp sentries, and stealthily made their way to the sea shore dragging with them over rugged rocks the image of the Crucifix, which these execrable sinners reviled with foul curses and incantations and then cast into the sea. At the same time certain priests, the vilest sinners of all men, being anxious to assist the soldiers' profane practices, performed a wicked rite in order to produce rain of this sort. They stood an ass before the Church door and sang a funeral dirge as for a living soul: then they placed the Divine Eucharist in its mouth, and continued their funeral chants about the living ass, and finally buried it before the Church doors. Hardly had this rite been performed before the air grew dark and the sea began to be lashed with the wind, and at midday the darkness of night descended, and now the heavens were rent with lightning, and now all was black darkness, and the heavens and the earth shook with thunder, and trees were hurled through the air by the wind, and rocks were split by lightning and filled the air with crashing explosions: and so heavy a downpour of rain fell from the clouds that the cisterns were not adequate to collect the water, but the torrents swept away stones and rocks which had before been parched and dried by the sun. The King therefore, whose whole hope of taking the town had rested upon the townsmen's thirst, was baffled in his intention and returned to his former camp by the river Savone.

I purposely set down this example, reader, that you may be advised of what abuses have crept into certain regions; such as dragging the Crucifix and the images of the Saints over the ground. In Germany and Aquitaine also they boldly resort to such evil means for ensuring seasonable weather; and Martin de Arles* has written against similar foul practices prevailing in Spain in his book on Superstitions.

☆

CHAPTER VIII

The Power of Witches over External Things.

Argument.

IT is one of the obligations that witches owe to the devil that, when they assemble at the Sabbat, they must show that they have wrought some fresh evil since the last meeting; and if they cannot do so they do not escape with impunity. And that they may not be able to plead ignorance as an excuse,

their evil Master instructs them in all those activities which he demands from them: as in infesting the trees and fruits with locusts, caterpillars, slugs, butterflies, canker-worms, and such pestilent vermin which devour everything, seeds, leaves and fruit; or in bewitching cattle; or in casting a spell on the crops so that they are destroyed by leeches or wasted in some other way; or in the use of poisons, and in working as far as in them lies for the destruction of the whole human race. For all this we know from their own confessions; as, for example, those of Helena of Armentières at Douzy on the 30th September, 1586; of Anna Ruffa at the same place and time; of Jean the Fisher at Gerbeviller on the 13th May, 1585; of his wife Colette; and of several others whom we pass over for the sake of brevity. For these, see Remy, Book I, chap. 22, and elsewhere.

They can also destroy the flocks and herds, either by scattering poison or by sending into their bodies a demon which throws them down and strangles them or tears them in pieces. They can remove a man's crops and fruits to another place, as is told by Servius (*In. Eclog. Verg.*) and Apuleius (*In Apologia*), and by S. Augustine (*Ciu. Dei,* VIII). They can cause houses to be consumed by fire, as was done in a certain town of Suabia in the year 1533 by a certain witch, as we shall tell in the proper place.

They can conjure up feasts: and these are either sheerly fantastic like those of Scoto† of Parma, from whose

---

* *"Martin de Arles." Martin de Arles y Andosilla, author of the rare "Tractatus insignis de Superstitionibus, contra Maleficia, seu Sortilegia quae hodie uigent in Orbe terrarum," Paris, 1517. Another edition, Rome, 1559.*

† *"Scoto." There is an allusion to Scoto of Parma, a notorious Italian necromancer and adept in the black art, in the "Defensative against Supposed Prophecies" of Henry Howard, Earl of Northampton, 1583: "I was present my selfe when diuers Gentlemen & noble men, which vndertooke to descry the finest sleights, that Scotto the Italian was able to play by Leger du main before the Queene, were notwithstanding no lesse beguiled then the rest: that presumed lesse vppon theyr owne dexteritie and skyll in those matters." In J. Harvey's "Discoursive Problem concerning Prophecies,"*

banquets the guests departed apparently satisfied, but soon they were tortured by hunger; or else they may be composed of true food, but bad tasting and of an evil odour, since God does

not permit them to conjure savoury food. Generally salt is lacking, and often bread; perhaps because salt is used in Baptism, and in the Eucharist we are fed with the life-giving flesh of our Lord Christ veiled under the form or accident of bread. But with God's permission they can also produce bread and salt and savoury foods, as the witches themselves have confessed to their Judges; but this is rarely the case. Again when God wills they can by mere local motion free captives from their prisons and fetters: but this does but require the breaking of something; and since this can be done by men, why not by a devil? Trithemius narrates a story worth recording, which we shall tell later.

Examples.

There was put to death at Treves some years ago a very famous witch who had inserted a pipe into the wall of her house, through which she charmed all the milk of her neighbours' cows: that is to say, the demon milked the cows and instantly carried the milk to her house.

Remy tells (I, 23) of a certain peasant named Desiré Finance, who dwelt among the Vosges mountains, and who, whenever he sat down to eat in company, had a dog lying at his feet from which he used secretly to take poison which he then administered to whomever he wished: and by him a considerable number of men were killed before any suspicion rested upon him as being the cause of it.

The same author tells that Antoine Welsch was asked to lend the garden of his house for the approaching cele-

bration of the witches' Sabbat. At first he said that he could not do so

---

1588, Scoto is named together with the well-known juggler Feates as a member of the "foisting crue." Also in Nash's "The Unfortunate Traveller," 1594, mention is made of Cornelius Agrippa, who is said to bear "the

fame to be the greatest coniurer in Christendome, 'Scoto,' that dyd the iugling tricks before the Queene, neuer came neere him one quarter in magicke reputation."

because he had to go out that night: but when they still continued to press him and insist upon it as their right, he knew that he was overpersuaded; yet, as he had said, he himself went out. When he came home in the morning and happened to go into his garden, he found it all devoured by caterpillars and slugs, and the whole garden filled with such animals: but he bore all in silence, recognising the usual traces of that ungodly Assembly.

In the year 1323 Frederick Duke of Austria marched against the Emperor Louis of Bavaria, and was defeated in a great battle between Öttingen and Moldova, and was captured by Louis, who placed him under guard in his fortified citadel. Meanwhile a witch promised his brother Leopold in Austria that he would by his art bring back Frederick within an hour if he should have a sufficient reward; and the Prince made liberal promises. The demon then flew to Frederick in Bavaria, and entered his prison in the form of a pilgrim, saying: "If you wish to be freed from captivity, mount this horse, and I will take you safe into Austria to your brother Leopold." The Duke asked: "Who are you?" But he answered: "Do not ask who I am, for that does not concern you; but mount this horse which I bring you." But when even this most valiant Duke was seized with horror and protected himself with the sign of the cross, the evil spirit disappeared together with his black horse, and went back empty to him who had sent him; in reply to whose complaints that he had not brought the captive home, he told all that had happened.

Among the Swedes Ollerus attained to such fame in arms by means of his magic art that, as Saxo Grammaticus (*Hist. Dan.* 3) says, he was thought to be divine. The same author writes as follows (Book 5) of the Danish pirate Oddo: "He sailed the seas without any ship, and by raising up storms often wrecked his enemies' fleets. He was a foe to merchants and a friend to

barbarians. He embarked upon a war with the Normans; and by his spells so deluded his enemies' eyes that they thought they could see the flashing of the Danish swords at a distance, so that when it came to hand to hand fighting they were so dazzled that they could not see to fight, and were thus defeated by magic."

Bishop Martin Kromer * writes as follows of the memorable victory of the Tartars over the Poles: "In the year 1240 the Poles joined battle with the Tartars near Legnitz and pressed them strongly and were putting them to rout. In the extreme rear of the Tartar army there was, among other banners, a notable one bearing a picture of the letter X, while at the top was a hideous bearded black head. As the standard bearer strongly waved this banner, it exhaled a dense and horribly stinking cloud of smoke, which not only hid the barbarians from the Poles, but even killed the Poles with its overpowering stench. The Tartars had done this by their spells; for they were much addicted to consultation with soothsayers and diviners, especially in war but also in peace, in order to foreknow the future. When they saw that the Poles were in a panic, the barbarians roused themselves and charged them, and put them to rout with great slaughter. So great a number of Christians was killed in that battle that nine huge sacks were filled with the ears that were cut off, one from each dead man.

The Chinese, according to Juan Gonzáles de Mendoza,† worship the

---

* "*Kromer.*" *The famous Polish bishop of Ermland and historian. Born, 1512; died 1589. His "De origine et rebus gestis Polonorum," a vast work in thirty books treating of the history of Poland from the earliest times until 1506, was published at Basle in 1555. It has been twice translated into Polish, and also into German, 1562. Walewski, "Martin Kromer," Warsaw, 1874. The reference here is to Book VIII of the "De origine . . . Polonorum."*

† "*Mendoza.*" *This eminent early geographer was of the Order of Augustinian*

Virgin Noema as sacred; and he says that she owed her cult to magic art. For when a certain captain named Compo had, by order of the King, taken the fleet to a certain island, he could by no force weigh anchor to sail away again; but at last he suddenly saw Noema sitting in the stern of his ship. He approached reverently and begged her for help and advice; and she replied that the Chinese would never win the victory except under her leadership. She set out with the fleet therefore; and though the enemy relied upon their magic spells she defeated them with more potent charms. For the enemy threw their god into the sea and made the Chinese fleet appear to be burning and everything to be consumed in the false flames: but Noema put the flames out and, by her more powerful art, sent a similar spell upon the enemy who, finding that all their efforts were unavailing, surrendered themselves to Compo as beaten.

The people of Pergamus also once tried to raise a siege of the town by means of magic, but without success, as Paul the Deacon* tells (*Rerum Romanarum*, XX).

In the time of Leo Isaurus, Masalmas the Saracen chief occupied Pergamus with no difficulty, although the citizens, trusting to a witch, had offered up a terrible sacrifice to the devil by cutting open a pregnant woman and taking out the living foetus, which they boiled in a pot, and all the soldiers defiled their right sleeves with this abominable sacrifice. Theophanes is our authority for this.

Duke Wratislaw, the founder of Breslau (says Aeneas Silvius), went to war with his grandson Gremozislav, Duke of Bohemia. There was a woman

---

Hermits. It was he who made the first really intelligible map of China, 1585.

* "*Paul the Deacon.*" *c. 720–799. The Benedictine historian also known as Casinensis, Levita, Warnefridi. His "Historia Romana," an amplified and extended version of Eutropius, was formerly much esteemed.*

who foretold that her own son-in-law, together with Wratislaw and the greater part of the people, would fall in that war; but that the young man could escape if he would obey her. When the youth answered that he would obey her commands, she told him to kill the first man he met, then to make the sign of the cross with his sword on the ground between his horse's forefeet, then to cut off both the dead man's ears and put them in a bag and make haste to flee. The battle was fought in a plain near Tuscus; and when Wratislaw had been killed, the young man, having done as the old woman bade him, returned safe to his home; but he found his dearly loved wife killed and with her ears cut off and her breast pierced, and was amazed and grieved to find that the ears he had cut off from his enemy were those of his wife. This was indeed a fit reward for consulting with a witch: and it may be that the wife also was a witch and had joined in the battle after the manner of Bohemian women; or else the demon set some deadly image in the battle and transferred the wounds which it received to the wretched woman in the house.

☆

CHAPTER IX

Whether the Devil can Truly Enrich His Subjects.

Argument.

WE read that Stuphius paid his army with magic money. Psellus writes that the devil cannot veritably fulfil any of his promises, but only offers empty mockeries to his worshippers: but this view, while it may be true of some of the things that the devil is said to do, is false if it be made applicable to everything that he is able to do. For I say that the devil, if God permits and he himself wishes, can enrich his subjects: and if God commanded him to do so, he would be compelled to obey, however unwilling he were: but only rarely does the devil wish this, and never does God command it, and very seldom does God permit it. The devil's reluctance in this matter is clear, since we see that he most often cheats his subjects; and although he enriches a few with a little money at times, as he did Doctor Vlaet at Treves, he usually deceives them with empty hope and vain appearances. Remy proves this by many examples taken from eye-witnesses as follows.

At Douzy on the 30th September, 1586 it transpired that Seneel of Armentières, having received from the devil what appeared to be a gift of money, hurried home rejoicing to count it; but when she shook out her purse she found nothing but charred bits of clay and coal. Catherine of Metz, on the 31st October, 1586, found nothing but pigs' excrement. Claude Morelle, at Barr in December 1586; Benedict Driget, at Héricourt in January; Dominique Petronine, at Pargny in October 1586; all were proved to have been similarly deceived. Jeanne de Bans, at Châlons-sur-Marne in July 1585, stated that she found on the road a sum of money wrapped in paper as the demon had foretold, and gleefully showed it to her husband; but to her shame she found that instead of gold she had a rusty-looking pebble which crumbled at the first touch. Others have been given the leaves of a tree for money. But Catherine Ruffa, at Val-de-Villé near the Moselle, in 1587, admitted that she had once been given three genuine coins.

I have freely quoted these examples because they are publicly vouched for in the Courts of Justice. I could add many more, but think it unnecessary since the above are sufficient.

Lorenzo Anania* (de Natura Dae-

monum, II) adduces another reason why the devil is loath to enrich his votaries. He says that evil spirits are given to avarice, and that they amass treasures and money to meet the needs of Antichrist, the son of perdition, and that a certain soothsayer was told this by a demon. And although the demon is a liar and little faith can be placed in him, yet this is not far from the truth. But we are nearer to the true reason when we say that God never bids the devil to enrich his votaries (since He has no part in evil), and only very rarely permits it: for indeed these to whom the devil promises riches, dignity, honours and the favour of Princes are the most vile, abject, needy and despicable: and if they were rich before, they become poor: and if they were poor, they never become rich. And those who seek to acquire riches at the instance of the devil by their magic and against human laws, as may be seen from the first Canon Law de thesauris, the devil frightens to death or cruelly strangles. André Thevet† (Cosmog. VIII, 1) tells that he heard from an eye-witness that a certain Greek named Macrianus was looking for treasure in the island of Paros, and was swallowed up by the earth. Anastasius quotes Cedrenus as telling the like, and many others have such stories, one of which I shall set down as being a wonder not unworthy of record.

☆

Examples.

About the year 1520 at Basle a certain simple-minded tailor afflicted with a stammer somehow or other

---

* "Anania." Giovanni Lorenzo Anania, born at Taverna in Calabria, died c. 1582. His chief patron was the Archbishop of Naples,

Caraffa. In 1581 was published at Venice his "De Natura dœmonum, libri quatuor." A second edition followed in 1589. The reference here is to Book II.

† "Thevet." This great French explorer is best known for his voyage to America when with others in 1556 he landed on the banks of the Penobscot. He has left a very complete account of his visit.

entered the cave which has its entrance at Augst and going further into it than any had ever gone before, said that he saw marvellous sights. He said that, after burning consecrated corn, he went into the cave and first went through an iron gate, and then from one room to another, and so into a most beautiful flower garden. In the midst was a magnificently decorated hall where he saw a very beautiful Virgin with a golden diadem upon her head and her hair flowing loose; but the lower part of her body ended in a horrible serpent. This Virgin led him by the hand to an iron chest which was guarded by two black Molossian hounds, which by their baying prevented any from approaching: but the Virgin in some wonderful manner calmed them, and taking a bunch of keys from her neck, opened the chest and displayed every sort of gold, silver and copper money. And he said that the Virgin gave him no small sum of this money, which he brought back out of the cave. He added that the Virgin said that she was a King's daughter who had always led a devout life, but that she had been changed by an evil spell into that monstrous shape and that there was no other hope of her recovery than for her to be kissed three times by a youth of unimpaired chastity; for then she would be restored to her former shape, and would give as dowry to her liberator the whole treasure hidden in that place. He asserted also that he twice kissed the Virgin, and twice saw upon her face such a horrible gloating at the thought of her liberation that he was afraid that he would not escape from her with his life. Afterwards he was taken by some loose boys into a brothel, and could never thereafter find the approach to the cave, to say nothing of entering it again.

Who does not understand the illusion? The young man was not quite in his right senses: or a devil of the class of the Lamiae tempted him to kiss her, so that she might devour him after the third kiss; but God did not permit it. The two dogs were other demons, or may have been the true or pretended guardians of the treasure. The money was perhaps real, and given with the permission of God.

Some years later another citizen of Basle entered that cave purposing to relieve his family's poverty. He found nothing but the bones of human corpses, and seized with a sudden panic rushed out, and behaved so extravagantly that he perished miserably in three days. See Stamphius as above, and Beatus Rhenanus,* Book III, *Historia Germanorum.*

A few years before a certain Prior of Margulina, being in search of treasure, went with two companions into a pit in the cave of King Salaus near Pozzuoli, and met with a wretched death, never being seen again. This I have from Jacques de Villamont (*Les Voyages,* livre I, 23).

Andreas of Ratisbon ‡ writes: " We know that many treasures have been collected by magic art, but it is not known who obtained possession of them."

In our own time certain men began to dig for treasure at Pisa, but at last were beaten by the difficulty of the work and ceased from it.

Finally last year men started to dig where Nero's § palace is said to have

---

* *"Beatus Rhenanus." 1485–1547. Humanist and classical scholar, the friend of Erasmus and Gelenius.*

† *"Les Voyages." "Les Voyages du Seigneur Jacques de Villamont." I have used the Arras edition, 1598, of this very popular book. There were reprints Paris, 1600; Lyons, 1606 and 1607; Paris, 1609; Rouen, 1618; and Paris, 1698, which purports to be the Third Edition. This is, of course, incorrect.*

‡ *"Andreas of Ratisbon." All that is known of this historian is gathered from his works. Ordained priest at Eichstätt in 1405, he joined the Canons Regular of S. Augustine at Ratisbon in 1410. His writings have won him the title of the "Bavarian Livy."*

§ *"Nero." Nero's "Golden House" extended from the Palatine across the valley of* stood, in a place which is to-day a cloister for Holy Virgins, where there is a huge pine tree: but they were so tormented by devils that fear compelled them to desist from the work which they had begun; and meanwhile many of the nuns dwelling in that place were possessed by devils. And what wonder, when they permitted this unlawful treasure search in their own grounds? Therefore God punished them in this life that He might pardon them in the future. Paul Grilland (*De sortileg.* q. 3, n. 12) writes more exactly on this subject than do any others.

☆

CHAPTER X

Whether Witches Can by their Art Create any Living Thing.

Argument.

IT is the opinion of S. Augustine (*De Trinitate*, III, 7), supported by all other Theologians, particularly S. Thomas and S. Bonaventura, that witches can in a moment produce imperfect animals, such as flies, worms, frogs and such insects and other animals which are generated by putrefaction; not by creating them, but by applying active to passive principles. It is usually the demon who, in accordance with his pact with the witch, produces such animals by the application of active to passive forces: for the witches themselves for the most part do not know how they are produced, and are ignorant of the causes: as when the devil gives a witch a little dust which she throws into the air, and there are born various kinds of locusts and grasshoppers and mice and caterpillars and suchlike animals. The devil could also, having produced such things,

tend them and nourish them and give them breath in remote places where they appear to be generated; as among rocks, where imperfect animals are often born, such as flies and mice and similar things. And I believe that this is what happened in the case of those dogs mentioned by William of Newburgh (*Hist. Anglorum*, I, 28) as follows. A huge stone was being split open in a certain quarry, when there appeared two dogs equal in size to that stone; and from no perceptible hole there sprang these same dogs, which were of the kind called harriers, but fierce-looking, strongly smelling and very shaggy; and one of them, it is said, quickly disappeared. But the other, which is said to have been extraordinarily voracious, was kept in luxury for several days by Henry, Bishop of Winchester. These dogs could not, I think, have been generated except from prolific semen; but the devil was able to take them from their mother's womb and hide them in that place. Demons can also bring forth strange monsters, like that in Brazil which is seventeen palms high, has a lizard's skin, very swollen paps, the forelegs of a lion, deadly eyes and a flaming tongue: or like those monsters in the forests of Saxony, of half human appearance, which were captured in 1240 (Anania, *De Natura Daemonum*, IV). Unless perhaps such were the issue of an abominable coition of men and beasts, which is undoubtedly the cause of most monsters. For in this way in the Marsic war Alcippe gave birth to an elephant. And Alexander ab Alexandro,* II, tells us that in the year 1278 in Switzerland a woman gave birth to a lion. So in 1471 at Pavia one produced a cat, and another at Brixen a dog. So in 1531 a woman of Augsburg brought forth at one

---

the Colosseum and far up the Esquiline. It would be difficult—and it is perhaps not necessary—to identify the Convent of which Guazzo speaks.

---

* "*Alexander ab Alexandro.*" *Alessandro Alessandri, a famous Neapolitan jurisconsult and archaeologist, born 1461; died c. 1523. The reference is to his "Genialium Dierum," an encyclopaedic work, often reprinted.*

birth first a human head covered in a caul, then a two-legged serpent, and thirdly a complete pig. We read of many such births in more recent times; but the most astounding of all is that recorded in the Chronicles of Portugal.

☆

Examples.

A woman was deported for some crime to a desert island and there left, and was at once surrounded by a chattering crowd of apes, of which there were many in that place. Then one larger than the rest, for whom they all made way, came and took her gently by the hand and led her into a big cave, where he and some other apes brought her a plentiful variety of fruit and nuts and roots, and signed to her to eat. Finally she was forced into foul sin with the ape, and so continued for many days until she gave birth to two children by the animal. The wretched woman lived in this way for some years, until God took pity upon her and sent a ship there from Portugal, from which some sailors came ashore to fetch water from a spring which was near her cave. It happened that the ape was not at hand; so the woman ran up to the men, whose like she had not seen for so long, and throwing herself at their feet implored them to set her free from her criminal and disastrous servitude. They consented, having pity on her misfortune, and she embarked upon the ship with them. But behold, the ape then appeared calling with extravagant gestures and groans to his wife, who was not his wife; and when he saw the sails set for departure, he quickly ran and held out one of her children to the mother, threatening to drown it in the sea if she did not come back. And he was not slow to carry out his threat. Then he ran back to the cave and as quickly came again to the shore with the other child, which he likewise threatened and drowned. After

this, in his fury, he swam after the ship until he was overcome by the waves. This story became the talk of all Portugal; and the woman was condemned by the King of Lisbon to be burned: but certain men petitioned for her, and her sentence was commuted to imprisonment for life. Does this surprise you, reader? Hear what Saxo Grammaticus and two great Bishops of Upsala say. They say that the Gothic Kings sprang from a bear and a nobly born virgin; and João de Barros * says that the Pegusian and Sianite Indians originated from the physical union of a dog and a woman.

Yet I am sceptical in this matter, for man must be generated by man. And if there is any truth in what we have just told, I shall say that an Incubus devil injected the warm semen of those animals into the women: and as for the report concerning the Gothic Kings, I think this is to be said; that the devil in the form of those beasts tumbled the women. And that he can do this is shown by the next example, and the following chapter.

There was a lewd fellow in Belgium who had to do with a cow, and the cow soon became pregnant and after some months gave birth to a male foetus, which was not a calf but human. There were many present who saw it come from its mother's womb, and they picked it up from the ground and gave it to a nurse. The boy grew up and was baptised and instructed in the Christian life, and applied himself seriously to piety and works of penance for his father; and so came to manhood. But he felt in himself certain bovine propensities, as that of eating grass and chewing the cud. What must be thought of this? Was he not a man? Certainly I believe he

---

* "João de Barros." 1496–1570. His classical work "Asia," giving an account of explorations and conquest, is highly esteemed as a masterpiece of Portuguese literature. See De Feria, "Vida de João de Barros," Lisbon, 1778.

was; but I deny that his mother was a cow. What then? The devil was aware of his father's sin, and at his pleasure made the cow appear to be pregnant: he then secretly brought an infant from elsewhere, and so placed it by the labouring cow (which was big only with wind) that it seemed to be born from the cow.

☆

CHAPTER XI

Whether there Truly are Incubus and Succubus Devils; and whether Children can be Generated by Copulation with them.

Argument.

ALMOST all the Theologians and learned Philosophers are agreed, and it has been the experience of all times and all nations, that witches practise coition with demons, the men with Succubus devils and the women with Incubus devils. Plato in the *Cratylus*, Philo, Josephus, and the Old Synagogue; S. Cyprian, S. Justin Martyr, Clement of Alexandria, Tertullian, and others have clearly proved that devils can at will fornicate with women. But a more substantial proof is to be found in S. Jerome on *Ephesians* vi, and S. Augustine (*Civ. Dei.* XV, 23), who is followed by the consensus of all Theologians, and especially by S. Isidore, chapter 8. The same belief is championed in the Bull of Pope Innocent VIII * against witches.

This truth can be proved by argument. For demons can assume the bodies of dead men, or make for themselves out of air a palpable body like that of flesh, and to these they can impart motion and heat at their will.

They can therefore create the appearance of sex which is not naturally present, and show themselves to men in a feminine form, and to women in a masculine form, and lie with each accordingly: and they can also produce semen which they have brought from elsewhere, and imitate the natural ejaculation of it.

I add that a child can be born of such copulation with an Incubus devil. To make this clear, it must be known that the devil can collect semen from another place, as from a man's vain dreams, and by his speed and experience of physical laws can preserve that semen in its fertilising warmth, however subtle and airy and volatile it be, and inject it into a woman's womb at the moment when she is most disposed to conceive, making it appear to be done in the natural way, and so mingling it with the woman's ova. Yet it is true that the devils cannot, as animals do, procreate children by virtue of their own strength and substance: for neither between themselves have they any propagation of their own kind, nor are they endowed with any semen which can in the least degree prove fertile. And how should they have semen of their own, since semen is a vital part of the corporeal substance, and (according to Symposianus in his *Problems*) a secretion from well-digested food; whereas devils are substances without corporeal bodies? We say, then, that a child can be born from the copulation of an Incubus with a woman, but that the father of such a child is not the demon but that man whose semen the demon has misused. There are countless examples told by many authors (Jornandus, *de rebus Gothicis*, and Luitprand) that the Huns were descended from the union of Fauns with Gothic witches. Chieza (*Hist. Peru*, II, 27) writes that in Spanish America a demon named Corocoton lies with women and that there are born children with two horns. The Japanese claim that their Shaka is of the same

---

* "*Innocent VIII.*" *The Bull "Summis desiderantes affectibus," 9 December, 1484, a translation of which will be found in my "Geography of Witchcraft," pp. 533–6, as also prefixed to the "Malleus Maleficarum," John Rodker, 1928.*

sort. Nor are there wanting those who place Luther * in this class. And not ten years ago a woman was punished in the chief city of Brabant because she had been brought to bed by a demon. It remains for us to reply to the arguments which are brought forward to contradict this belief.

The first argument is that of Remy as follows. Devils and human beings are of a different species, and therefore no issue can come of a copulation between them. I answer that this argument bears no weight; for from a horse and an ass, and from other differing animals, are born mules, wolves, leopards, panthers, etc. Also, the procreation is not ascribed to the demon, but to the man whose semen is used, as S. Thomas says (*Quodlib.* VI, art. 6 and 8).

The second argument is that the devil has no part in life, but is the source of death; therefore he cannot be the author and origin of the vital act. I answer that this vital force is not in the devil, but in the semen itself; just as the warming virtue of wine is not in the vat or the goblet, but in the wine itself. See S. Thomas as above, and the *Malleus Maleficarum*, I, 4.

The third argument is that witches confess that the semen injected by the devil is cold, and that the act brings them no pleasure but rather horror; and therefore no issue can come of such a union. This is the argument of Mark of Ephesus, who is followed by Remy, and it is based on the confessions of witches who say that such copulations are entirely devoid of pleasure, and that they rather feel the most acute pain in them. I answer that when the devil wishes to disguise himself in the form of a certain man, and would not have it known that he

is a devil, then he must as far as possible imitate every detail of true copulation between a man and a woman: and then, if he wishes any issue to result (which is very rare; for he never desires propagation for his own sake, since nothing of like nature to himself can be generated: although sometimes at least he humours the woman's wish and seeks to make her pregnant by means of another's semen), he must necessarily take care to provide everything needful for procreation. Therefore he seeks for fertile semen and, having found it, conserves it and so quickly transports it that its vital essence is not wasted; and when need is, he injects it. But when he does not mean to beget issue he injects some substance in the likeness of semen, which is warm so that the deception may not be detected. As for the cold semen, that is only found in the case of witches who are fully aware that he is a devil. Moreover, as Sprenger says (*Malleus M.* I, 1, c. 4), he usually asks the woman if she wishes to become pregnant; and if she does, he provides true semen from another source, as I have described.

The fourth argument was that it is incredible that God should allow such a thing to be done, or would endow with a living soul anything born of such a union, for this would be adding the final touch to the devil's work. The answer to this is that, as far as natural operation is concerned, the devil is only the instrument which applies the principal agent, namely, true human semen; and therefore God concurs in the final disposition of an organic body born from human semen, although it is abnormal; and the sin lies entirely at the door of the witch and the devil's malice. God, the author of nature, delights in all things natural: but if this argument held good, since He is not the author or abettor of sin, no issue could be born of fornication or adultery or uncleanness or incest. It is further objected

---

* "*Luther.*" *Malvenda,* "*De Antichristo*" (*1604*), *II, vi, certainly says of Luther:* "*Ex incubo dæmonio genitum haud leuibus futilibrisque coniecturis deprehensum est a plerisque, ut Coclaeus refert.*" *Coclaeus is Johann Dobeneck, 1479–1552.*

that the root of all procreation is the heart, and that when the necessary cordial heat and virtue are wanting there can be no procreation. The answer is that, whether its source is the heart or the brain, the vital fertilising germ is contained in the semen in the actual ejaculation of that semen from the human body; and that the devil can preserve that germ in its necessary warmth.

We shall set down certain instances of the activities of Succubus devils, as well as some more of Incubus devils.

☆

Examples.

Fifteen years ago, at Bamberg, a certain Peter Stumpf was sentenced to death because he had sinned with a Succubus devil for more than twenty-eight years. This devil had given him a girdle which he had only to put on, and it appeared both to himself and others that he was changed into a wolf. He tried to devour two of his daughters-in-law. He lived with his own daughter and her godmother as his wives. This is all vouched for in the Court records, and is memorised in pictures carved in brass which are for sale.

Remy tells an example which he heard from a trustworthy man named Melchiore Errico, taken from the most closely guarded secrets of the Most Serene Duke of Lorraine. " There was at Hemingen," says this man, "while I was watching my Lord's interests in that place, a certain warlock who, when he was asked by the Judge how he had first been led into such wickedness and, especially, by what wiles the devil had seduced him, freely and openly declared as follows: 'I was a common herdsman, and at dawn of day was gathering my herds from their several houses, when of all the girls who let the cattle out of the stables one especially fired my soul with love, and I began to think more

and more of her by night and by day. At last as I was burning with desire for her at my solitary pasturage, there appeared to me one like her coyly hiding behind a bush. I ran to my longed-for prize, wooed her and at last embraced her although against her will; but after some repulses, she consented to make me free of her on condition that I acknowledged her as my Mistress and behaved to her as if she were God Himself. I accepted the condition, and possessed her; but she also so possessed me that from that time I have been unhappily subject to no will but hers.' "

Hector Boece (*De rebus Scoticis*, liber 8) tells that in the coasts around Moray Firth a highly born girl of great beauty refused several noblemen in marriage and fell into an abominable familiarity with an Incubus devil. When her parents commanded her to tell whether this were true, and to discover her paramour, she said that a marvellously beautiful youth had frequent intercourse with her by night, and sometimes by day, but that she did not know whence he came or whither he went. Her parents did not entirely believe the girl, and formed a plan by which they should learn more exactly who it was who had stormed the fortress of their daughter's virginity; and when, three days later, they were informed by a serving maid that the paramour was present, they bolted the house doors and, lighting many torches, went into the bedroom, where they saw in their daughter's arms a horrible monster whose appearance was terrible beyond human imagination. Others quickly ran up to see the foul sight, among them a priest of most holy life not unlearned in rituals and exorcism, who, while the rest were running away in terror or stood rooted to the ground with horror, began to recite the Gospel of S. John; and when he had come to " The Word was made flesh," the evil demon gave a terrible cry, set fire to all the furniture, and departed, carrying with him the roof of the bed chamber. The girl, having escaped from this danger, gave birth to a monster of utterly loathsome appearance, such as had never before been seen, as it was said; and lest it should be seen and bring disgrace upon her family, the midwives lit a huge fire and quickly burned it.

A little earlier the same author tells of a Succubus devil as follows. In the district of Gareotha in a village not fourteen miles from Aberdeen, a young man of great beauty openly complained before the Bishop of Aberdeen that for many months he had been tormented by a Succubus devil, as they say, more beautiful than any woman that he had ever seen. He said that she came to him by night through locked doors, coaxed and forced him into her embraces, and went away as the dawn

began to break, with scarcely any sound; and that he could by no means, though he had tried many, be delivered from so great and foul a madness. The excellent Bishop at once ordered the young man to remove himself to another place, and to apply his mind more than usual to the Christian Religion, with more devout fasting and prayer; and so, following the advice of the venerable Bishop, the young man was after a few days delivered from the Succubus devil. Elsewhere I shall describe other examples.

☆

CHAPTER XII

Whether Witches are Really Transported from Place to Place to their Nightly Assemblies.

Argument.

MANY of the followers of Luther and Melancthon maintained that witches went to their Sabbats in imagination only, and that there was some diabolical illusion in the matter, alleging that their bodies had often been found lying at home in their beds and had never moved from them; and they support their contention with that passage in the Life of S. Germanus concerning the women who met together, as it seemed, in a feast, and yet were all the time sleeping at home. It is certain that such women are very often the victims of illusion, but it is not proved that this is always so. But as Michal the wife of David deceived the soldiers of her father Saul by putting an image in David's room, so we say that the devil can and does place a false body in the bed to deceive the husband while a witch has gone to the Sabbat; and in order that the husband may not suspect she is absent, he either causes him to fall into a heavy sleep, or substitutes a likeness of his wife so that the husband on awaking may think that it is indeed his wife. Nicolas Remy proves this from judicial records. A barber's wife confessed at Forbach on 1st September, 1587, that she had often done this to her husband Bertrand, and had put him to so deep a sleep by anointing him with a certain ointment that she could tweak him by the ear without rousing him; and she used the same ointment upon herself when she wished to go to the Sabbat. On the same day at the same place Eller, the wife of a beadle of Öttingen, was said to have substituted for her own body a child's cradle, or as some said a bundle of twigs marked with the name of her Familiar, and so often duped her husband. At Homberg on the 5th June, 1590, Maria, the wife of a tailor in Metzer Esch, anointed a bundle of straw and so created an illusion which vanished as soon as she herself returned to the house. Catharine Ruffa declared that the devil himself had at times taken her place in bed and acted in her stead. These instances are taken from Remy, *Demonolatreia*, I, 12.

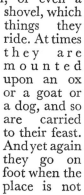

Further I hold it to be very true that sometimes witches are really transported from place to place by the devil who, in the shape of a goat or some other fantastic animal, both carries them bodily to the Sabbat and himself is present at its obscenities. This is the general opinion of the Theologians and Juriconsults of Italy, Spain, and Catholic Germany; while a great many others are of a like opinion. Turrecremata (Torquemada) on Grilland, *De sortileg.* libre 2, q. 7, num. 8: Remy, *Demonolatreia*, I, 14, 24, 29: S. Peter Damian, *Epist.* IV, 17: Francesco Silvester,* *In uerbo*

haeresis, num. 3: Gaietani on *S. Mark* iv, quest. 47: Alfonso à Castro†: Sisto of Siena‡: Crespet: Spina, *Contra Ponzinibium* §: Anania: and very many others whom for the sake of brevity I omit.

But it must be known that before they go to the Sabbat they anoint themselves upon some part of their bodies with an unguent made from various foul and filthy ingredients, but chiefly from murdered children; and so anointed they are carried away on a cowl-staff, or a broom, or a reed, a cleft stick or a distaff, or even a shovel, which things they ride. At times they are mounted upon an ox or a goat or a dog, and so are carried to their feast. And yet again they go on foot when the place is not

* *"Silvester of Avila."* Francesco Silvester, c. *1474–1526. Dominican theologian, and*

sometime Master-General of the Order. A prolific and esteemed writer.

† *"Alfonso à Castro. 1495–1558. A Franciscan theologian of great eminence. Confessor to Charles V and Philip II. Among his chief works are "Aduersus omnes hæreses," first edition, Cologne, 1539; and "De Iusta Hæreticorum punitione," Salamanca, 1547.*

‡ *"Sisto of Siena." Dominican theologian and demonologist. His chief work is "Bibliotheca Sancta," Libri V., Francofurti, folio, 1575 (secunda editio).*

§ *"Contra Ponzinibium." The jurist Gianfrancesco Ponzinibio wrote a rationalistic monograph on witchcraft in which he strove to regard the Sabbat, the flight of witches and much beside as a sick illusion. He was completely answered and routed by Bartolomeo Spina, who devoted no less than three tractates to these points and very properly arraigned Ponzinibio as himself vehemently suspect of heresy and an advocate of heretics.*

far distant. Examples of all these were to be found in Remy, I, 14.

When these members of the devil have met together, they generally light a foul and horrid fire. The devil is president of the Assembly and sits on a throne in some terrible shape, as of a goat or a dog; and they approach him to adore him, but not always in the same manner. For sometimes they bend their knees as suppliants, and sometimes stand with their backs turned, and sometimes kick their legs high up so that their heads are bent back and their chins point to the sky. Then they offer him pitch black candles, or infants' navel cords; and kiss him upon the buttocks in sign of homage. Having committed these and similar crimes and execrable abominations, they proceed to other infamies

as we shall tell later: but first let us discuss the hour of their Sabbat.

Remy says that he learned from the witches' own answers at their trials that the fixed time for the nocturnal assembly of witches is one or two hours before midnight, this being most suitable and opportune not only for such assemblies but also for certain other devils' terrors, sports, runnings about and hubbub which follow, and are not at such an hour so obnoxious. Witches do not explain the cause of this, neither do I inquire into it. But it has been sworn to by Johannes à Villa and Agatina the wife of Francis the tailor. This one thing will I add: that no hours of the night are more suspect nor more favourable to the apparition of fearful and terrifying shades. In-

deed it is known from experience that such hours are chiefly notorious for spectres and hideous ghosts, as the classical authors have testified in their writings. For example, Aristomenes,* in Apuleius, *Golden Ass*, Bk. I: Pliny,† VII, 6: Pliny the Younger,‡ *Epist.* 7: and among more modern writers Alexander ab Alexandro (*Genial. Dierum*, V, 24) tells that he heard in the silence of midnight a terrible noise of ghosts from certain houses in Rome. And authors of weight say that this silent time is the dead of night which comes (according to Censorinus,§ *De Die Natali*, cap. XXIV) just before the stroke of midnight. Eusebius of Caesarea argues that the untimely hour of the night is just before cock crow, and that this is the most suited to the demon's wicked purposes. Servius (in

---

* *"Aristomenes."* The traveller who relates the story of witchcraft, *"Metamorphoseon, I.*" The hags appear "circa tertiam ferme uigiliam," and long after their departure "nox ibat in diem."

† *"Pliny, H.N."* VII, 6: Plenilunium, "quod tempus editos quoque infantes praecipue infestat."

‡ *"Pliny the Younger."* The allusion is to the well-known history of the haunted house at Athens, *"Epist."* VII, 27. The spectre appeared with a noise of chains "per silentium noctis," and when the philosopher Athenodorus was watching "Initio, quale ubique, silentium noctis, deinde concuti ferrum, uincula moueri."

§ *"Censorinus."* "Concubium," cum itum est cubitum. Exinde "intempesta," id est, multa nox, qua nihil agi tempestiuum est: tunc "ad mediam noctem," dicitur: et sic "media nox."

the Fifth Book of the *Aeneid*) says that it is the middle of the night: Macrobius* that it is just after midnight; since such time is aptest to the Prince of Darkness for his dealings

with men, being an uncouth and vacant time. And, to return to the subject of the cock crow, Remy in the same place says that he had it in judicial examination from a witch named Latoma that nothing more baleful and hostile to them could happen than that the cock should crow while they were still about their business. Johann Pulmer and his wife Desideria, both of them witches, likewise deposed in Court that their Masters often used to cry out, when it was nearly time to break up the Sabbat: "Now go quickly away all, for the cocks begin to crow." And this can only mean that they are unable to prolong their business any further. But I know not the reason of their fear of the cock crow. From Pliny and Aelian I know that the cock crow is feared by lions and *Scolopendrae*. Also that it portends much when they crow out of time during the night, as Zacchia da Volterra † (*Philologiae*, libre 25) records it to have happened on the birth night of the eldest son of Matteo Visconti the Great, Lord of Milan: for on that night the cocks did not cease from crowing to the point of tediousness, and therefore the child was named Galeazzo, and grew up to great eloquence and military glory, as Paolo Giovio tells.

Remy (I, 16) tells that the witches themselves assert that a great number of both sexes meet at their nocturnal Sabbats, but that there are far more women than men. This was affirmed by Barbellina Raiel of Blainville-la-Grande on the 13th January, 1587. In 1585 Jeanne de Bans and Nicole Ganette from the town of Mainz in Lorraine said that they were sometimes present among so great a num-

ber of witches that they felt no small pity for the human race when they saw it assailed by so many enemies and betrayers, and that it was indeed

---

* "*Macrobius.*" "*Saturnalia,*" I, 3: "*magistratus . . . post mediam noctem auspicantur.*"

† "*Volterra.*" *A famous professor of the University of Pisa.*

wonderful that mortals did not suffer more harm from them. Catharine Ruffa of Val-de-Villé near the Moselle said in July 1587 that she saw no less than five hundred on that night when she was first lured into their number.

There are tables placed and drawn up, and they sit and start to eat of the food which the demon has provided, or which they have themselves brought. But all who have sat down to such tables confess that the feasts are all foul either in appearance or in smell, so that they would easily nauseate the most ravenously hungry stomach. The above-mentioned Barbellina and Sybil Morelle said at Bar-le-Duc in September 1586 that all sorts of food were there, but so vile and mean and badly cooked that they were scarcely worth eating. At Bar-le-Duc in Feb-

ruary 1587 Nicolas Morelle said that their taste was so evil and dry and bitter that he had to spue them out as soon as he had eaten them; and that the demon was so angry when he saw this that he hardly kept his hands from him. Their wine also is black like stale blood, and is given to the feasters in some filthy sort of drinking horn. They say that there is plenty of everything except bread and salt. In 1583 at Ribeauville, near the Château de Girsberg, Dominique Isabelle added that human flesh was also set out, and that this was a frequent practice among the Scythian witches we learn from Belleforest (*Cosmographiae*, II, 6). Most of the partakers of such feasts say that the food and drink satisfy neither their hunger nor their thirst, but they are just as hungry and thirsty afterwards as they were before. Joanna Michaelis, of Château-Salins, in 1590 added that the eyes of those who attend such assemblies are not sure and clear of sight, but that all is confused and disturbed and appears vague to them, like those who are blinded by drunkenness or some sin or some magic. Thus witches sometimes are actually present at the Sabbat; and often again they are fast asleep at home, and yet think that they are at the Sabbat; for the devil deceives their senses, and through his illusions many imaginings may enter the minds of sleepers, leaving them with a conviction of their reality when they awake, as if it were not a dream but an actual experience and an undoubted physical action. For so for the most part does the crafty devil manage his affairs.

Then follow dances, which are performed in a circle but always round to the left; and just as our dances are for pleasure, so their dances and measures bring them labour and fatigue and the greatest toil. And they return home from them so weary, according to the confession of Barbellina and nearly all witches who have attended them, that they have often had to lie abed for a full two days. And the most sorry and most iniquitous thing about it is that no one is allowed to excuse herself from the dance; and if any of them, by reason of ill health or old age, shirks that labour, she is soon beaten and bruised by fists and feet, just as salted fish is beaten with hammers.

When they approach the demons to venerate them, they turn their backs

and, going backwards like crabs, put out their hands behind them to touch him in supplication. When they speak they turn their faces to the ground; and they do all things in a manner altogether foreign to the use of other men. Indeed it is sufficiently clear from our own experience that the desire of men for wanton dancing and treading light measures nearly always lead by evil example to more lust and sin; in his day this was complained of by Scipio Aemilianus, in his oration *contra legem iudiciariam Tiberii Gracchi*, and by Macrobius, *Saturnalia*, III, 4.

Sometimes they dance before eating, and sometimes after the repast. Some three or four tables are set apart for the richest and most honoured among them. Sometimes each sits next to his own Familiar Spirit; sometimes the witches on one side, and the demons opposite them. There is not lacking a grace said at this table, worthy of such

an assembly, composed of blasphemous words in which Beelzebub himself is acclaimed the Creator and Giver and Preserver of all. The same spirit inspires their actions after the tables have been removed. For when the banquet is done each demon takes by the hand the disciple under his guardianship, and all the rites are performed with the utmost absurdity in a frenzied ring with hands joined and back to back; and so they dance, throwing their heads like frantic folk, sometimes holding in their hands the candles which they have before used in worshipping the devil.

They sing in honour of the devil the most obscene songs to the sound of a bawdy pipe and tabor played by one seated in the fork of a tree; and then in the foulest manner they copulate with their demon lovers. They come to these Sabbats, as we have said, in the silence of midnight when the

powers of darkness are strong; but sometimes they even meet at noontide; and this is referred to in the passage of the *Psalms* (xci, 6) where it speaks of the noon-day demon. They have also fixed days which differ in various localities. In Italy they meet about midnight on Thursday, according to Sébastien Michaelis.* The witches of Lorraine meet on Wednesday night, and on Saturday night with the Sunday following, according to Remy: and I have read that others meet on Tuesday night.

From what we have already described, therefore, and from the confessions of witches themselves before their Judges, it is clearer than light, and will be confirmed by particular instances, that witches are carried bodily through the air to the Sabbat by demons; and not only are they themselves so carried, but with the help of the devil they can carry others on their own shoulders, as the examples will show. Sometimes indeed, when the Sabbat has been suddenly dispersed, tables and silver furnishings have been found and recognised by their owners, which the women have confessed that they have carried with them to the Sabbat.

Only I will add this: that they who assert that all this is not true, but only a dream or an illusion, certainly sin in lack of true reverence to our Mother the Church. For the Catholic Church punishes no crime that is not evident and manifest, and counts no one a heretic unless he has been caught in patent heresy. Now for many years the Church has counted witches as heretics and has ordered that they be punished by the Inquisitors and handed over to the Secular Courts, as is clear from the works of Sprenger, Nider, Nicolas Jacquier,† and Michaelis, as well as from our own knowledge. Therefore either the Church is in error, or they who maintain this belief. But he who says that the Church is in error over a matter concerning the faith is Anathema Maranatha. I conclude therefore that witches are most often actually transported by the devil, and that sometimes they go afoot: and when they wish to be transported bodily they anoint themselves, as I have said already, with an ointment made from the fat of infants' bodies; but when they wish to attend the Sabbat only in dream, they lie down on their left side: but when they prefer to keep awake, and yet see what is done at the Sabbat as if they were present at it, then by some devils' work they send a thick vapour from their mouths, in which they can see all that is done as if in a mirror.

---

* "*Sébastien Michaelis.*" *A Dominican of great sanctity, born at Saint Zacharie in Provence, 1543; died at Paris, 1618. He was widely known for his deep study of the demonologists, and as a most powerful exorcist he was summoned to deal with the possession of Madeleine de la Palud, who had been bewitched by Gaufridi. For an account of this see my "Geography of Witchcraft," pp. 408–12. The cause of Sébastien Michaelis has been introduced at Rome, and he has been declared Venerable.*

---

† "*Nicolas Jacquier.*" *Dominican and Inquisitor. Author of "Flagellum Haereticorum fascinariorum," a piece of great value, which with some other tractates was first printed at Frankfort by Basse in 1581.*

It is stated by some authors * as a fact that there have been women who have manifestly spent the night in bed with their husbands, and yet on the next morning have confidently remembered and spoken about many things pertaining to the Sabbat, at which they have maintained that they were present on the preceding night. Others have been observed by their family and relations, who have formed some suspicion of them, to start violently in their sleep as if they were in great pain; or even to bestride a chair or some other object as if it were a horse, and spur it on with their heels: yet they have not gone out of the house, but on awaking have been as tired as if they had returned from a long journey, and have told of marvellous things which they thought they had done. And what is more, they are angry and incensed against those who do not believe them. This has led many to believe that this is no more than a matter of dreams sent by the devil into the minds of those whom he has caught in his net.

☆

Examples.

In the County of York in England a wonderful thing happened which is recorded by Martin Delrio of the Society of Jesus, who quotes from William of Newburgh,† to whom it was known from boyhood (for it was not far from the birthplace of this historian). There is a village some miles from the North Sea, near which are those famous waters which the common people call "the Gipsies"‡ or the "Gipsey-race." A certain peasant went on a visit from this village to a neighbouring village to see a friend and as he was returning late at night not very sober, behold from a mound some two or three furlongs from the village came the sound of voices singing and of people feasting. He wondered who could be breaking the silence of the night in that place with these formal celebrations, and was curious enough to wish to enquire into it; and seeing an open door in the side of the mound he went and looked in, and saw a wide and well-lit hall filled with men and women sitting down to a grand feast. But one of the servers saw him standing at the door and brought him a cup,§ which he took but purposely refused to drink from it; for he spilled its contents and at once went away with the cup. An outcry arose among the feasters at the theft of the cup, and the guests went in pursuit of him; but he escaped thanks to the speed of his horse, and came back to the village with his rare prize. Afterwards this cup, which was of unknown material and unusual colour and uncommon shape, was offered as a gift to Henry I, King of England, and then to the brother of the Queen of David, King of Scotland, and was for many years kept in the Treasury of Scotland, as may be read in the First Book *Rerum Anglicarum*, cap. 28.

Sébastien Michaelis tells that among

---

* "*Some authors.*" e.g. Bodin, "*Démono-manie,*" II, 5.

† "*William of Newburgh.*" "*Historia Anglicana,*" I, 28.

‡ "*Gipsies.*" "*Gipse*" is the reading of Lambeth MS.; Cotton MS.; and Hearne's edition of William of Newburgh. MS. Reg. 13 B ix gives "*Vipse.*" The village of Wold Newton, eight miles from Bridlington, has a large mere principally supplied by the "*Gip-seys,*" streams of water which appear after intervals of two or three years and disappear after two or three months. Allen, "*History of County of York,*" vol. II, p. 330.

§ "*A cup.*" Hamilton in his edition of William of Newburgh has the following note on this passage: "*This Scandinavian legend is common, with variations, to the ballad and romantic literature of most countries of Europe. It may be sufficient to direct attention to a version very similar to the above, named the 'Altar-cup in Aegerup,' a story of the Trolls, quoted in Keightley's 'Fairy Mythology,' from Thiele's 'Danske Folkesagen.'*"

the witches of Avignon a boy was taken who told the Judge that he had been led by his father to the Synagogue (for so they called their Assembly), and had there seen many wicked and horrible things done; so that in his terror he had signed himself with the cross and said "Jesus, what is this!" And as soon as he had said this the whole rout disappeared, leaving him there alone; and the next day he returned home, which was three German miles distant from the place of the Synagogue, and brought his father before the Judges. And therefore in that district the boy was given the name Masquillon, that is, Little Magician: and this boy was still in captivity at Avignon when Michaelis wrote this in 1582.

Bartolomeo de Spina (*De Strig.* Tom. II, p. 11, cap. 17) relates the following: Master Socino Benci, a famous physician of Ferrara who was Public Intendant of the sick in that city, lately told me as the faithful truth that when he was in the country about three years ago to see after his properties, he fell into conversation with his bailiff about witches. The physician said that all the talk about witches was madness, especially that they could be bodily transported wherever they wished. But the bailiff (who is still living, one Tommasino Polastros from the district of Mirandola, but now living in the place called Clavica Malaguzi) replied that there was another peasant living close by, who said that he had seen great numbers of men and women dancing in the night and abandoning themselves to pleasures. The physician was astounded and asked the bailiff to bring that peasant to him; and when he was brought and asked about those things, he answered as follows: "One night I rose about three hours before dawn and came with my own oxen and wagon to this bailiff of yours to help him in a job of work; and I had got as far as that plain I am pointing to" (for it was near by) "when I saw

afar off a big fire in different places, like great lights, among which I saw a great crowd of men and women wrestling or dancing together. Going nearer, I saw more than six thousand people in the clear light of the fires, and tables spread, and some of them eating and drinking; but more were dancing and playing different sorts of games, while most of them were acting bawdy in a way that it is not right to speak of. I saw some men and women among them whom I knew, and spoke to some of them: but after an hour a signal was given and they all seemed to run away very quickly indeed, and they were nowhere to be seen, as if they had been carried away in a cloud." On hearing this evidence the physician changed his opinion, and not only believed that what he had formerly thought to be madness was possible, but that it did actually happen.

The following, which is a witch's own statement, is taken from Grilland. After she had paid her homage, the chief of the devils at once appointed as her guardian a demon who must never leave her but serve her in all that she wished; and whenever their rendezvous and games were to be held he was to inform her of it and take her there fully instructed: and this demon used her carnally as a husband serves his wife. She said that witches often go to these Assemblies, where a great number of women meet; and that it is no matter of a mere mental or intellectual or apparent vision, for in their true and natural shape they go to such places in the following manner. A day or two before the Sabbat the witch is told by her guardian demon to prepare to go to the games on such a night at such an hour; and if she has any just cause to hinder her she adduces it and is heard, provided that it is a true and legitimate excuse: but if she invents a false reason to excuse her attendance, she is not carried there against her will, but remains in her house; yet as a punishment for her lies the demon so mightily torments her both in mind and body with continuous torture of the sharpest degree, and aches and pains both within and without, that she can have no rest by day or by night, but is always plagued; and everything that she does comes to nothing and is abortive. So that, to put an end to such great pain, she must confess her fault and promise on oath that she will no more refuse to go to the Sabbat. When she has so promised, as soon as the night and the hour have arrived she is summoned in a sort of human voice by the demon himself, whom she does not call demon but Little Master, or Martinet Master, or Martinellus. And on this summons she goes out of her house and always finds her Little Master waiting by the door in the form of a goat, upon which this woman said that she rode holding tightly to its hair, and the goat rose into the air and in the shortest time carried her to the wizard walnut tree of Benevento * and gently put her down there.

Paul Grilland (*De sortileg.* II, 7) tells that in 1524 there was brought to him as Inquisitor a certain Lucretia who, while she was being carried home from the Sabbat, came at dawn within sound of the bells calling the people to morning prayer, and was suddenly left by the devil who was carrying her near a river in a field covered with thorns. It happened that a young man well known to her was walking across it, and the unhappy woman called to him by his name. The young man, seeing her quite naked except for a covering over her

private parts, and with her hair all loose, was afraid to go near her: but she coaxed him with flattering words, and at last he went up to her and asked her how she came to be there in that state. At first she invented many lies, but the young man did not believe her and said he would not help her unless she told the truth. Then, binding him to secrecy, she told the truth of what had happened to her, and the reason for it. The young man took her secretly to her home, and she gave him many gifts; but in the end he forgot his promise and spoke of the matter first to one and then to another, and so by degrees the disgraceful story was spread abroad, and the woman was taken, and the young man was compelled to give evidence of the truth and he told all this to Grilland.

A woman in the Diocese of Sabina practised this diabolic art, and her husband becoming suspicious repeatedly questioned her, but she always denied the charge. But the husband retained his suspicions and anxiously sought to know the truth, and contrived so cunningly that one night he saw her anointing herself with some ointment, after which she flew away as quickly as a bird. He followed to see where she was going, but lost sight of her; and going to the door of the house he found it shut, which caused him great surprise. On the following day he again asked his wife what he so eagerly wished to know, and she firmly denied all knowledge; until, so that she could no longer plead ignorance, he openly told her all that he had seen her do the night before, and then soundly thrashed her, since it is wisely said that an obstinate heart is broken by the rod; and he threatened to beat her even more severely unless she told the truth, promising her a full pardon if she would freely confess. The woman, seeing that she could no longer hide it, told the truth and asked pardon of her husband, which he

---

* "*Benevento.*" *The magic walnut tree of Benevento was reputed to be the general rendezvous of all the witches in Italy. Peter of Piperno has a pamphlet, "De Nuce Maga Beneuentana," which gives many of the legends connected with this ill-omened spot. See Montague Summers, "Geography of Witchcraft," pp. 546–48; and A. de Blasio, "Inciarmatori, Maghi, e Streghe di Benevento," Naples, 1900.*

granted on condition that she would take him to the Sabbat. To obtain forgiveness she readily promised this, and, with the permission of Satan, fulfilled her word. The husband was taken to the place of the Sabbat and saw the games and dances and everything else, and finally sat down with the rest at the tables to eat; but finding the food insipid, he asked for salt and, although there was none on the table, kept asking again and again for it, but was not given any until after much importunacy and long waiting. Then he said: "Praise be to God, for at last the salt has come!" As soon as he had uttered these words the demons immediately departed, and all the rest vanished, and the lights were put out and he remained there alone and naked. In the morning he saw some shepherds whom he asked in what country he was; and they answered that it was Benevento in the Kingdom of Naples, which was a hundred miles from the man's own country. So, although he was a rich man, he had to beg his way home; and on his arrival he at once accused his wife of the crime of witchcraft, and told the Judges the whole story and how she had departed. And when they had well and duly examined the matter, they found all that we have related to be true, and it was all confirmed by the woman's own confession.

Bartolomeo Spina,* Master of the Sacred Palace, records some equally certain examples, one of which is as follows. A girl who lived with her mother at Bergamo was found one night at Venice in her brother-in-law's bed. In the morning she was found naked and was recognised as a kinswoman, and was asked why she had come there. When they had clothed her she told with tears the following story: "Last night I was lying in bed awake and saw my mother, who

thought I was asleep, rise from her bed and take off her vest and anoint her body with an unguent from a pot which she took from a secret place; and then she mounted a staff which was at hand as if it were a horse, and rose up and was carried through the window, so that I could no longer see her. Then I also rose from bed and anointed my body as my mother had done, and was at once borne through the window and brought to this place, where I saw my mother threatening with horrid gestures the boy lying in this bed. I was frightened at this, and saw that my mother also was disturbed by my appearance and began to menace me: so I called upon the Name of the Lord Jesus and of His Mother, and then I no longer saw my mother, and was left here alone and naked." When they heard these words of the girl, her brother-in-law wrote all down and brought it before the Inquisitor-General of Bergamo, who took the woman into custody. She was exposed to torture and confirmed everything in confession, adding that the demon had carried her more than fifty times to kill the son of that brother-in-law, but that she had never succeeded in doing so because she had always found him too well protected by his parents with the sign of the cross and holy prayers.

Spina also relates that a certain Antonio Leone, a charcoal burner of Ferrara, who was then living in the Valtellina, that very same year, attested that he knew intimately the man to whom the following occurred in his native district. This man, on account of many hints which had been given him, suspected his wife of going to the witches' Sabbat while he himself was asleep. One night, therefore, he pretended to be in a deep sleep, and saw his wife rise from her bed and anoint herself from a hidden vase, and immediately vanish. In astonishment not unmixed with curiosity the man also rose from his bed and did as his wife had done; and at once, as

* "Spina." This is from "De Strigibus," c. xviii. It was told Spina by Andrea Magnani of Bergamo, who personally knew of these events.

it seemed to him, he was carried up the chimney just as his wife appeared to have been, into the wine cellar of a certain noble Count, where he found his wife together with many others. When she saw him, his wife and all the rest of the company made a certain occult sign and disappeared, the husband being left all alone in that place. There he was found in the morning by the servants of the house, who raised an outcry, and seizing him as a thief haled him before the Count. When he had been granted leave to speak, he shamefacedly told what had happened; and so his wife was accused before the Inquisitor, and at last confessed, and suffered the punishment well merited by her crimes.

Nicolas Remy (I, 14) tells the following examples. At Luthz at the foot of the Vosges Mountains in May 1589 the villagers were celebrating a pagan festival. Claude Cothèze was returning in the evening from that village to the next, which is called Wisembach, and had already climbed a good part of the hill which separates the two villages, when he was suddenly caught in a whirlwind and stood looking about him in amazement to see if he could find any cause for such an unusual occurrence, for the air was most calm and still everywhere else. Then he saw in a sheltered place six witch women dancing round a table sumptuously decked with gold and silver, tossing their heads about like people afflicted with madness; and near them was a man like a black bull watching them as if he were a casual passer by. He therefore stood still for a while collecting himself and making sure that he saw quite clearly; and when he had done so, they all suddenly vanished from his sight. Recovering from his fright he then started on his road again and had already passed the top of the hill when behold, those women were following him from behind, throwing their heads about as before and keeping a deep silence, while before them went a man

with a black face and hands curved like talons, with which he would have clawed his forehead if he had not turned and opposed him with his drawn sword; but then the man ceased to threaten him and vanished as if in fear of his life. The women showed themselves yet again, and with them the man like a bull, who, as I have said, was looking on at their dances. Cothèze now felt more confident towards this man, and went up to him, saying: "Are not you my friend Desirée Gazète?" (for so he was named). "I beg you to protect me if you can; for I promise you that I will tell no one anything of what I have seen." Hardly had he said this when he was encompassed by a fresh whirlwind or cloud, and when he had come out of it as soon as he could, he went home. Three days after he had given evidence as above, he was recalled for examination by the Judge, and added the following: that he remembered that when he had gone near the table to see what food there was upon it, the demon had instantly flown at his face with his talons, and that while he was defending himself with his sword he had been lifted up by a violent wind and carried to the cataracts of Comber Hill, which was no less than two hundred paces away. And lest anyone should think that this was the imagining of a drunken man frightened by the darkness and solitude, the story was confirmed at St.-Dié in June 1589 by Barbelline Gazète, one of the women in question, who told it in almost the same words to the Inquisitor, adding that her husband Desirée Gazète had given to Cothèze as a gift three measures of wheat and as many cow's cheeses which he kept hidden, and that she had seen them. All this was admitted and agreed to, except that Barbelline said that the demon had not raised his hands against Cothèze because he came near the table, as he had falsely stated in his evidence, but because he was about to steal a golden cup from it.

When Johann of Hembach was scarcely more than a child, his witch mother took him to the nocturnal assembly of demons and, because he was so clever a crowder, ordered him to play his kit and to climb up a tree from which he could be heard better. He did so and, having leisure to watch their lewd reels and rigadoons, found it very unusual (for everything at their Sabbat was uncouth and ridiculous), and cried out: "Good God, whence came that extraordinary mob of madmen?" No sooner had he said this than he fell to the ground and hurt his shoulder; and when he called for help, he found himself alone. He told this story openly and various opinions were formed about it; some saying that it was only a vision, whilst others contended that it had really happened. But not long afterwards the opportunity arose to remove all doubt. For Catharine Prevotte, one of those who had taken part in those dances, was soon afterwards taken on suspicion of witchcraft, and confessed the whole matter as we have told it, although she was unaware of the story told by Johann and was not pressed by any questions.

As Nicole Langbernard was returning home from Marainviller to Igney-Avricourt in July 1590, and was walking at full noonday along a wooded path, she saw in a neighbouring field a company of men and women dancing in a ring, not in the usual manner of men but in the opposite direction and with their backs turned. She looked more closely and saw further some who were deformed with hooves like goats or oxen among the dancers; and being struck with terror she began to call upon the Most Holy Name of Jesus, and earnestly to pray that she might come back safe and unharmed to her own people. Thereupon all the dancers vanished except one named Peter, and he quickly rose into the air and was seen to let fall to the earth a little brush of the sort used by bakers to clean their ovens before they bake bread. Meanwhile she was caught in a violent wind so that she could hardly draw her breath; and then returned home, where she lay sick for three whole days. This thing became known through the talk of herself and her neighbours, and had soon spread all over the village. This Peter, lest by ignoring the story he should seem to admit and confess to so heavy a charge, went first to the Judge and angrily laid a complaint before him; but in the end he was afraid he would lose his suit and lay himself open to a greater danger, and so desisted from it. This brought him into far greater suspicion of the crime, since many were of opinion that his guilty conscience had caused him to withdraw the complaint which he had started so bitterly against her. Accordingly the Judge made diligent enquiry into his life and character, and found some indications that this was no empty suspicion, and arrested him (at Dieuze, Feb. 1591). And he was with little trouble induced to confess his guilt, and finally to name and indicate those others who had been partners in that crime, among whom were Barbelia the wife of Johann Latomer, and Mayette the wife of Laurentius, the Chief Magistrate, all of whom told the same story of their dancing back to back with the cloven-hoofed creatures, maintaining that it was all true. Their confession was yet further substantiated by Johann Michel, a herdsman, who stated that during those proceedings he had been playing upon his pipes, beating time with his foot and moving his fingers quickly over the pipes. But when Nicole in panic called upon Jesus, and moreover signed herself with the Cross, he fell from the high branch of an oak on which he was sitting, and was then caught in a whirlwind and carried to a field called Veiler in which he had shortly before left his flock grazing. But the gravest and weightiest proof was that the place where the dance had been performed had been found, on the day following that mentioned by Nicole, marked with a ring such as is seen in circuses where horses run round in a circle, and there were recent tracks of goats or oxen, all of which could be seen until that field was again ploughed up in the following winter.

In Holland there was in the village of Oostbruck not far from Maestricht a widow woman whose circumstances required her to keep a man-servant to manage the affairs of the house. This man was, like most servants, inquisitive, and often used to look through a window and see his mistress go at the dead of every night, as soon as the servants had gone to sleep, to a certain fixed spot in the stables, where she stretched up and laid fast hold of the nearest rack of hay. At last, wondering what she could be about, he made up his mind to do the same just once, unbeknown to his mistress, and to try the same venture. So when his mistress went as usual to that place and seemed to be out of sight, he followed and looked about the place and, as his mistress had done, grasped the hay. Then he was at once carried to the town of Wijk into a secret underground cave, where he found himself in the midst of a company of witches brewing their evil plots. The mistress was surprised at her servant's unexpected appearance, and asked how he had managed to come there in a moment of time. He told her how it was; and she waxed very angry and highly incensed, being afraid lest by this means their nocturnal and clandestine meetings should become known. She therefore asked her associates what they advised in this doubtful pass, and they at length agreed that he should be received in friendly fashion and be sworn to keep silence, and that he would never communicate or tell to any one those mysteries which chance had allowed him to witness, beyond his desert or expectation. He gave his promise and spoke fairly to them; and, that they might treat him more leniently, pretended that his one chief wish was that they should thereafter admit him into the fellowship and company of witches. Meanwhile the hours passed until it was time for their return; and then a new question was posed by the mistress, whether he should be sent back home to be a danger to the whole assembly, or whether he should be killed for the general good. They arrived at the more merciful decision of binding him by an oath and sending him home. This duty was undertaken by his mistress, who promised that when he had given his oath she would carry him home on her shoulders; and to this business they set themselves, and were carried by an east wind through the air. But when they had covered the greater part of their journey a lake overgrown with reeds came in sight; and the old witch, fearing lest the young man should be led by penitence to disclose what he had seen at those frantic orgies, saw her chance of getting rid of him, and to cast him from her as she flew, hoping, as it is thought, that he would die either from the violence of his fall or in the deep waters of the lake. But God, who is merciful and desireth not the death of a sinner but rather that he should turn from his wickedness and live, frustrated the evil design of that witch, and did not allow the innocent young man to be drowned, but most justly granted that he should live to this very day. As he fell among the reeds he received no mortal hurt indeed, for the violence of his fall was a little broken by the reeds: but the unhappy man was unable to do anything but use his tongue, and lay there till daylight in the most dreadful agony, sighing and groaning, until some passers by were surprised to hear this unusual lamentation, and searched and found a young man with both his hips dislocated. They asked how he had fallen into such misfortune; and when he had told all they took him in a cart to Maestricht. There a nobleman, Jehan

Chulenburgh, the Mayor of the city, being struck by the strangeness of the affair, wonderingly enquired into it all; and having examined the matter he ordered the youth's mistress to be seized and put in chains. As soon as she fell into the hands of the Mayor, she denied nothing, but confessed to every particular.

Bernard of Como * in his *De Strigiis*, 3, tells that about sixty years ago in the Diocese of Como proceedings were being taken against such witches by an Inquisitor named Master Bartolomeo de Homate, with Master Lorenzo da Concorezzo the Podesta and Giovanni da Fossato as Notary. One day the Podesta, out of curiosity, wished to prove by experience whether witches go to the Sabbat really and in their bodies. Accordingly he agreed to go one Thursday evening with his Notary and another companion to a place outside the town † which had been indicated by the witches. While they were standing there they saw many people assembled before one who was the devil in the form of a goat enthroned like some great Lord: and behold, at the command of the devil all those persons there assembled fell upon that magistrate and his companions and, with God's permission, so beat them with sticks that they all three died from their blows within fifteen days.

Florimond de Raymond,‡ Senator

of the King at the Parlement of Bordeaux, a pious catholic and learned man, in his *L'Antéchrist*, VII, tells of some unspeakable and sacrilegious rites in the following words.

At this Court in the year 1594 was tried a young girl of Aquitane, a wench of intelligent appearance who, without being tortured, freely confessed that she had been corrupted at a tender age by a certain Italian. In the middle of the night before the day of S. John Baptist the Italian had led her to a certain field, where he had traced a circle on the ground with a beech twig, muttering some words out of a black book. Suddenly there appeared a large and perfectly black goat, well horned, and accompanied by two women, and soon there came up a man clothed and vested like a priest. The goat asked the Italian what girl that was; and he answered that she had been brought by him to be enrolled among the goat's subjects. Hearing this, the goat ordered her to make the sign of the cross with her left hand, and all who were present to approach and perform their act of veneration. Thereupon they all kissed him with their lips under his tail. Between the goat's horns a black candle gave a horrid light, and from this they all lit the candles they were holding; and as they worshipped the goat, they dropped money in a bowl. This is what happened the first time. Afterwards the Italian again took the girl to the same place; and then the goat asked her for a tress or lock of her hair, which the Italian cut off and gave to him. By this sign the goat led her apart as his bride into a neighbouring wood and, pressing her against the ground, penetrated her: but the girl said that she found this operation quite lacking in any sensation of plea-

---

* *"Bernard of Como." Dominican Inquisitor. The "De Strigiis" is a short but very important tractate which is usually found appended to his famous "Lucerna Inquisitorum Haereticae Prauitatis." My own copy is Venice, 1596, and this edition also contains the valuable Commentaries of Francesco Pegna.*

† *"Place outside the town." Mendrisio. For other accounts of this celebrated episode see —"Mémoires de Jacques du Clercq," IV, 4; "Chron. Cornel. Zanfliet," ann. 1460 (Martene, "Ampl. Coll." V, 502); and Prierias, "De Strigimagarum mirandis," I, 2, 14; II, 1, 4.*

‡ *"Raymond." Or Raemond; sometimes Rémond. Born at Agen c. 1540; died at Bor-*

---

deaux, c. 1602. His famous work, "L'Anté-christ," first appeared at Lyons in 1597, and was frequently reprinted. There are editions of Paris, 1599 and 1607; Arras, 1613; Cambrai, 1613.

sure, for she rather experienced a very keen pain and sense of horror of the goat's semen, which was as cold as ice. On a Wednesday and a Friday in each month these rites were performed by the well of Dôme, and she attended them countless times with more than sixty others, all of whom brought candles with them which the goat lit by blowing upon them from his behind, after which they danced round with joined hands and their backs turned. They also performed a travesty of the Mass, celebrated by one clothed in a black cope with no cross woven upon it. At the time of the Holy Sacrifice and the Elevation of the Host, he lifted up a segment or round of turnip stained black, upon which they all with one voice cried out: "Master, help us!" The Chalice contained water instead of wine; and they made their Holy Water as follows:—The goat pissed into a hole dug in the ground, and with this undiluted water the celebrant sprinkled them all with a black aspergillum. In this assembly each witch has his or her particular duty assigned, and each gives a report of what he has done. So writes Raymond; and he discusses the question of poisons, spells, charms and magic remedies, as also the destruction of the fruits of the earth, and many such crimes.

Let us now consider how witches are borne through the clouds by demons at other times than that of the nocturnal assembly. In Belgium a nobleman of proved faith named Vanderburch, Dean of the Cathedral Chapter and an honoured citizen of Mechlin, was walking outside the town with an arquebus, when suddenly he heard the screaming of crows and crowds of obscene crows and pies in a tree near his path. He levelled his arquebus and discharged it at them, and thought he had fairly hit one and brought it down from the tree; but all he found was an iron key from a woman's girdle. He took this home and told a friend what had happened,

asking whether he recognised the key. His friend said that he knew it for the key of a neighbouring house. They then went to the house, found the door locked, opened it with their key and, shutting the door behind them, went in, since they were acquainted with the good man of the house; and there they found a woman, the owner's wife, wounded in the side with an arquebus shot.

Martin Delrio (*Disqu. Magic.* V, 3) makes the following observation:—I was at the Nieulay Bridge at Calais when it was stormed under the auspicious leadership of the Serene Archduke Albert and held by the soldiers of His Catholic Majesty. A company from Valogne was stationed as outpost to keep a watch upon the men of Boulogne, who were then on the enemy's side; and towards the evening two of these men saw a black cloud floating out of the clear sky, and from the midst of it there seemed to come a confused sound of many voices, although no one could be seen. At last the bolder of these two men said: "What is this? Are we safe? If you consent, I will discharge my arquebus into that cloud." His comrade agreed, and after the report of the arquebus, there fell to their feet from the cloud a drunken naked woman, very fat and of middle age, wounded right through the thigh. On being seized she pretended to be feeble minded, and would answer nothing to their questions but, "Are you friends or foes?" Now what do they say to this, who deny that these witches are transported? They will say that they do not believe it. Then let them remain sceptical; for they will not believe any number of eye-witnesses whom I could produce. Why? Because they themselves have never seen or heard such a thing, and they have examined certain witnesses who have maintained that they knew nothing of such happenings. So says Delrio.

Now, reader, I will take further instances from Nicolas Remy, the truth of which has been sworn on oath and given in evidence at trials. There is, he says, at Gironcourt in the Vosges Province a strong-built castle which was struck by lightning so that some of its roofing was torn away. Not long afterwards, namely, in October 1580, one Sebastienne Piccarde was accused of witchcraft in that village, and confessed to the Judge that this had been the work of herself and her demon. For, she said, we together rushed from a cloud upon the castle meaning to bring it entirely to ruin; but it was not in our power to do so, and we could only inflict a little damage so that our attempt should not be altogether abortive.

The following instance is similar. A man named Cunin, who was a magistrate in the bailiwick of S. Clement in Ronchamp, was attending to his hay with his servants on the 1st December, 1586, when he noticed the sky grow very stormy. He was getting ready to go home, when suddenly he saw six oak trees near him struck by lightning and torn up by the roots, and a seventh appeared as if it had been all rent and lacerated with claws. He then made the more haste towards home, in his hurry leaving behind his hat and all his tools, and again heard the crash of lightning striking and saw perched in the top of an oak near him a woman who seemed to have come from the clouds. He looked at her more closely and recognised her as an old neighbour of his, and at once began to revile her as follows: "Are not you that vile hag Marguerite Warens, who, as I now find, thoroughly deserve the general suspicion of witchcraft which every one has long harboured against you? Whence come you now in that costume?" To this she answered: "Spare me, I entreat you, and keep silent about what you now see. If you will promise me this, I will manage so that no harm at all shall ever come from me to you and yours." And lest any should doubt the truth of this, let him know that it was proved not only by the evidence of Cunin, but by the confession of that very Warens which was often repeated even without the stimulus of torture, and confirmed by her in the hearing of many at the very last moment of her life.

To the same effect are instances arising out of other capital trials, vouched for as true by those who conducted them. A great thunder-storm arose while some shepherds were watching their flocks in the Vosges, and since they were exposed in the open they took shelter in the neighbouring woods. There all at once they saw two peasants perched, or rather entangled, in the tops of the trees, so terrified that it was easy to see that they were not there of their own will, but quite by accident and through some unexpected impetus. But then the filth and muddiness of their clothing, and the fact that they were all scratched with brambles, gave rise to an increasing suspicion that they had been cast out and hurled into that place by their Master after he had dragged them hither and thither according to his custom. This suspicion was the more confirmed because, after they had sat there long enough for the shepherds' eyes to make sure that they saw clearly, in an instant, without anyone marking how, they seemed to fall to the ground. Finally all doubt was removed when their own words, and the report of the shepherds, were fully borne out by spontaneous confession when they were questioned in prison.

There is also a village lying to the left as you go from Bellemont to Vittel, where the same two peasants fell headlong from a storm cloud on to the top of a roof. One of them, whose name was Rouet, was terribly troubled as to how they could get safely to ground from so difficult a place. But the other, Amant, had been led into the devil's service by his parents as soon as he reached puberty and very soon adapted himself to the conditions, saying: "Cheer up, you fool; for he in whose power we are is Master of far more difficult matters than this, and will very soon manage this affair for us." And no sooner said than done; for they were suddenly caught up together in a whirlwind and set down safe on the ground, while the house itself shook so that it seemed to be torn from its foundations. This was told by each of them separately in the same words: moreover their story agreed in every respect with that of the villagers, as to the day, the storm, and all the panic. Finally, they who in life had been associated together in crime, perished in one fire by the Judge's sentence. So says Remy.

☆

CHAPTER XIII

Whether Witches can Transmute Bodies from One Form to Another.

Argument.

NO one can doubt but that all the arts and metamorphoses by which witches change men into beasts are deceptive illusions and opposed to all nature. I add that any one who holds the contrary opinion is in danger of Anathema; and in this I am supported by the opinion of S. Augustine,* as also by logical reasoning. For a human soul cannot inform the body of a beast, any more than the soul of a lion can inhabit the body of a horse, or the soul of a horse the body of a man: because every substantial form, to be true to its own nature, requires the peculiarly adapted dispositions and physical organism which are natural to its own body, and the soul regulates the motions of the

organic body. Therefore, as I have said, no animal's soul can inform the human body, and no human soul an animal's body. The belief in such monstrous transformations is nothing new, but was firmly held by the Ancients many ages ago. Euanthes,† an author of great note, says that it is recorded in the Annals of Arcadia that there was a certain family of the tribe of Anthus which used every so many years to go to a certain pool across which, having taken off their clothes, they swam, and they were at once changed from men into beasts: and after nine years, if they had not in that time tasted human blood, they returned to their former shape. Herodotus in *Melpomene*, and Solinus in the *Polyhistor*, chapter 8, record that the Neuri, who live by the river Dnieper, are changed into wolves on certain days in every year, and after the appointed time has elapsed they return to their true shape. But this did not happen to them only in times before the light of Christian truth shone upon the world; for in Bulgaria a certain official had in his charge the son of that Symeon who had formerly ruled over the country, and this boy could when he wished change himself into a wolf or any other animal by black magic. And a certain Russian chieftain, hearing that there was in his territory a man who could change himself into whatever form he pleased, summoned him and put him in chains and commanded him to give instant proof of his power. The man said he would willingly do so if he might withdraw into the next room for a while; and when this had been granted, he suddenly came back in the form of a wolf, but still bound with his chains, to the great astonishment of all who were present. But the chieftain had two very fierce dogs at hand, which fell upon the unhappy creature and tore him to pieces.

---

* "*S. Augustine.*" "*De Ciuitate Dei*," XVIII, *18*.

† "*Euanthes.*" *A Greek author as quoted by Pliny*, "*Historia Naturalis*," VIII, *22*.

But, as I have already said, no one must let himself think that a man can really be changed into a beast, or a beast into a real man; for these are magic portents and illusions, having the form but not the reality of those things which they present to our sight. For the devil, as I have said elsewhere, deceives our senses in various ways. Sometimes he substitutes another body, while the witches themselves are absent or hidden apart in some secret place, and himself assumes the body of a wolf formed from the air and wrapped about him,

and does those actions which men think are done by the wretched absent witch who is asleep. William of Paris tells how a certain Holy Man made this stratagem clear to all. Sometimes, in accordance with his pact, he surrounds a witch with an aerial effigy of a beast, each part of which fits on to the correspondent part of the witch's body, head to head, mouth to mouth, belly to belly, foot to foot, and arm to arm; but this only happens when they use certain ointments and words, as in the case of the above example of the man who was torn in pieces by dogs: and then they leave the footprints of a wolf upon the ground. But in this last case it is no matter for wonder if they are afterwards found with an actual wound in those parts of their human body where they were wounded when in the appearance of a beast; for the enveloping air easily yields, and the true body receives the wound. But when the witch is not bodily present at all,

then the devil wounds her in that part of her absent body corresponding to the wound which he knows to have been received by the beast's body. Bartolomeo Spina* tells the following example of this sort.

☆

Examples.

A certain day-labourer named Philip bore witness in this very city of Ferrara to this apparent conversion of witches into cats. For he swore to me on oath that, three months before, a certain witch had told him not to drive them away if he saw any cats come coying playfully up to his son, whom she had strongly bewitched and had undertaken to cure. The same day, about an hour after she had gone away, he and his wife saw a big cat which they had never seen before go deliberately up to the boy. They were frightened and kept driving it off, and were at last goaded to exasperation by its insistence, and the man shut the door and chased it about for a long time, striking it with a stick, until finally he made it jump out of a high window, so that the cat's body seemed to be all bruised and broken. After that, the old witch kept her bed for many days with a bruised and broken body. Consequently, where there had already been a slight suspicion that she was a

---

* *"Spina." "De Strigibus," XIX. "Experientiae apparentis conuersionis strigum in catos."*

witch and had bewitched the boy who lay very sick under the spell of his infirmity, this now grew into a strong and grave suspicion; for the blows and wounds which were given to the cat were found upon the corresponding parts of the witch's body.

Remy (II, 5) writes that nearly all those who came into his hands charged with witchcraft told him that they changed themselves into cats whenever they wished to enter other people's houses in secret, so that they could scatter their poison there by night. Barbelline Rayel, at Blainville-la-Grande on the 1st January, 1587, confessed that she was turned into a cat so that in that shape she might more easily enter the house of Jean Louis and wander about it in greater safety; and when she had done so and found his two-year-old infant unguarded she dusted it with a drugged powder which she held in the pad of her paw, and killed it.

The Shepherd Petronio, who was tried at Dalheim in 1581, whenever he felt moved with hatred or envy against the shepherds of neighbouring flocks (as is the way of such men), used to change himself into a wolf by the use of certain incantations, and so for a long time escaped all suspicion of being the cause of the mutilation and death of his neighbours' sheep.

The following example is told by the famous Count of Salm, chief Gentleman of the Bedchamber at the Palace of Lorraine. In Hesse-Langhau, over which town he was Lord, the inhabitants, in accordance with the ancient custom, came to pay him their yearly tribute of labour. As they came with their cart-loads of timber, and waited in turn for their reward of food, the dogs which were with them began to fight in the castle hall. One of these dogs hid itself in one of the bathroom furnaces, and the rest barked violently at it. One of the townsmen looked at it and, finding it uglier than the rest, began to suspect the truth (for that part is said to be

infested with witches); so he thrust his weapon into its face and grievously wounded it, whereupon it rushed out of the door and was no more seen. Then a rumour crept all over the town that there was an old woman in bed with a wound of which no one knew where she had received it. They all began to suspect the truth, namely, that she was the mad dog who had been wounded in the castle hall. This suspicion, on the top of a long standing rumour that she was a witch, led to her being seized and imprisoned; and at last, after she had been carefully questioned, she freely confessed all that has just been told, together with very many other sorceries.

Hear also what Remy reports to have been told him by the Noble Baroness Lady Diana of Dommart, the wife of the illustrious Prince Charles Philip of Croy, Marquis of Haurech, as follows. Not long since there was in Thiaucourt, a village of that country, a woman addicted to these evil practices and credited with the power of assuming different shapes with the help of the Devil. This woman had conceived a bitter hatred against the village shepherd on account of his having bested her in some money transaction, and fell in the form of a wolf upon his flock as it was feeding. The shepherd ran up and wounded her in the thigh with an axe so grievously that, in her weakness, she was forced to flee into a neighbouring thicket. He followed her there, and found her trying to stop the freely flowing blood by binding her wound with strips torn from her clothes. With this evidence against her she was taken into custody and acknowledged all that we have said, and finally expiated her crimes at the stake.

In Flanders at a town not far from Dixmude a peasant was drinking at an ale-house with his son, a lively youth, and watched the hostess scoring up the beer which she brought him. He noticed that she marked up double the quantity that he drank, but kept quiet until he had finished drinking. Then he called the hostess and asked what he owed; and she demanded the amount that she had scored. He refused to pay it and, thrusting many persons aside, threw on to the table what he knew to be a sufficient sum of money, and was going out. The enraged hostess said: "You will not go home to-day, or my name is not So-and-so!" But he went away despising the woman's threats. He came to a stream where he had left his boat, but he could not, however much he tried, even with the help of his son, who was a lusty lad, move it from the bank; so that you would have said that it was nailed to the very ground. Two or three soldiers happened to come that way, and he called to them, saying: "Good friends, come and help me launch this boat from the bank, and I will give you a good drink." They came and exerted themselves to the utmost for a long time in vain, till one of them, panting and sweating, said: "Let us unload the boat. Perhaps when it is empty we shall manage better." And behold, when the goods were exposed to view, a lurid great toad stood in the road looking at them with gleaming eyes. One of the soldiers at once spitted it through the throat with his sword and threw it into the water, where it floated belly upwards as if dead. The rest gave it more wounds as it floated, and suddenly the boat was launched. The overjoyed peasant took his helpers back to the same inn and ordered beer. This was brought by a serving maid; and he asked where the hostess was. He was told that she was very ill in bed. "What!" said he. "Do you think I am drunk, you fool? It is hardly half an hour since I left her as well as you are. I am going to see what the matter is." He went into the bedroom and found that the woman had died from wounds in the neck and stomach. "How did she get these wounds?" he exclaimed.

The serving maid said she did not know and that, to her knowledge, she had not set foot outside the house. They went to the Magistrate, and the cuts and stabs were found to be in the same places as those in which the soldiers had wounded to death the toad, which was never found.

☆

CHAPTER XIV

Whether Witches have Power to Make Beasts Talk.

Argument.

AT times it happens that God grants the power of speech to that which naturally has no such power, as in the case of Balaam's ass in Holy Scripture. How this may be, none knows but He who is the author of all speech: but I think that for the most part it is the voice of an Angel speaking in such inanimate objects or brutes. As for brute animals speech is created in their own bodies and is a physical action of the beast itself; yet such action is intellectual only on the part of the Angel. This is true of such animals as have organs adapted to speech, as magpies, parrots, ravens and their like: but when the animal's organs are not so adapted, as in asses, oxen, etc., I think that the Angel creates a voice from the air about the animal. The same would be true in the case of inanimate objects, such as fire, water, earth, air, or corpses, which likewise could easily be made to appear to speak.

Porphyry, considering the question whether magicians can truly understand the speech of animals, writes that in his own time it used to be said of Apollonius of Tyana that, having heard a sparrow twittering to a flock of its fellows, he explained to his friends who were with him that the sparrow was telling the others that an ass laden with corn had fallen by the city gate, and the corn had been spilled on the ground. In this way Apollonius wished to pretend that he could understand the chattering of birds; but such a thing is incredible. Yet we have daily evidence of the fact that beasts, at any rate those of the same kind, understand each other; and Porphyry tried to prove this. For when a fish has broken from the net it warns the others of the danger, so that no more fish of that sort will be caught that day. Petrus Gregorius* in his *De Republica*, XV, 5, mentions this matter, prudently adding that animals are incapable of true intelligence and conversation.

☆

Examples.

Antonius Bonfinius † in his *Histories*, III, writes that about three years after the defeat of the Emperor Sigismund by the Turks at Ternowar, a number of people went to the battlefield and heard a voice from among the bones calling upon the Names of Jesus Christ the Saviour and the Virgin Mary: and a talking head among the corpses, seeing that there were men standing by, said: "Why do you stand so amazed, O men? I am a Christian who died in this battle unconfessed; but Mary our Mother would not have me condemned to eternal punishment, and has granted me to keep my power of speech till now so that I may confess my sins and purge my soul with holy absolution. I beg you, then, to bring me a priest to hear my confession and give me absolution." When he was asked how he had earned so great a benefit from the Virgin, he answered that he had been peculiarly devout to

Her during his life, and had with great reverence observed Her seven yearly Feasts, fasting religiously on bread and water. Therefore a priest was brought from the next village, who duly heard the confession; and when the head had obtained remission and absolution for all its sins, it at once and for ever fell silent.

The devil, who is the Ape of God, at times performs many false miracles of a similar nature, which God permits in His own avenging justice. Phlegon of Tralles says that Polycritus married a Locrian woman and, after having slept with her for three nights, died on the third day, leaving her pregnant. The woman gave birth to an hermaphrodite monster, which was brought before a council of the people to decide what it portended and what should be done about it: and then the ghost of Polycritus appeared in the midst of the people and foretold a massacre of the Locrians and Aetolians; and with the people powerless to interfere he took off the head of his monstrous son and devoured him and vanished; and afterwards the head also spoke of the same massacre.

The same author quotes the following from Antisthenes the Peripatetic Philosopher. When the Consul Acilius Glabro conquered Antiochus, King of Asia, the Romans were frightened by oracles from invading Asia any further. And the Roman General, Publius, moved as it is thought with a divine madness, foretold that he would be devoured by a wolf, which would leave his head: and this head made a long speech foreshowing the coming defeat of the Romans.

With the help of a demon a witch can easily vitiate a man's organs so that, while trying to speak, he barks or howls or clucks or neighs; for we have known many such cases. We read that in 1546 Margarita of Essling had pains in her belly, and that it swelled to such a size as completely to hide her face, being more than ten palms in circumference.

---

* *"Petrus Gregorius."* A famous jurist who in 1570 was appointed to the Chair of Civil Law at the University of Cahors.

† *"Antonius Bonfinius."* *"Rerum Ungaricarum Decades Quattuor cum Dimidia."* Folio, Basle, 1568.

Those who stood about her bed heard the crowing of cocks, the clucking of hens, the braying of asses, the barking of dogs, the bleating of sheep, the grunting of pigs, the lowing of oxen and the neighing of horses. Then she voided from her side about a hundred and fifty worms and serpents. This was believed to be a miracle; but it was in truth only a devil's illusion created by the girl's mother for the sake of gain.

☆

CHAPTER XV

Whether the Devil can Make Men Insensible to Torture.*

Argument.

DEALING with the question whether the devil can render insentient that which is naturally sensitive, so that, for example, a man should feel no pain when put to torture, Iamblichus (*De myster. Aegypt.*) writes that many heathen seers have been thrown into the fire and have either not been burned or have not felt their burning or any other tortures; and he says that this is due to some god who drives back the flames, or nullifies the other tortures. And what is this god of the sorcerer Iamblichus but the Cacodemon Eurycles? What are those seers but witches? In our own day there are impious soldiers who think that they are invulnerable if their armour is charmed with a certain spell, or if they have the hardihood to commit the sacrilege of piercing, threatening or breaking the image of the Crucifix. So Baptista Codronchi† (*De morbis ueneficis*, III, 12) tells that they wear a shirt inscribed with a terrible and most horrid character, which they call the Shirt of Hell; or else they wear trinkets engraved with various magic signs; or they make use of prayers, which

---

* "*Insensible to torture.*" It was well known that witches had charms which enabled them to bear the severest tortures without flinching. Damhouder, whilst member of the council at Bruges, relates a case which came under his own eyes. A witch during three examinations not only endured the fiercest engines, but actually laughed at and mocked the officers. At length a piece of parchment covered with cabalistic characters was found on her person, and after its removal she soon confessed her pact with Satan. ("Rerum Crimin. Praxis," Cap. XXXVII, Nos. 21, 22. Cf. Brunnemann, "Le Inquisit. Process," Cap. VIII, Memb. v, No. 70.) Grilland tells us that he had met instances of insensibility to torture only to be explained by magic. "De Quaestione et Tortura," Art. III, 12–16. He gives several conjurations which were used completely to deaden all pain: "Quemadmodum lac Beatae Gloriose Mariae Uirginis fuit dulce et suaue Domino Nostro Iesu Christo, ita haec tortura sit dulcis et suauis brachiis et membris meis." Another ran:

Imparibus meritis tria pendent corpora ramis.
Dismas et Gestas, in medio est Diuina Potestas.
Dismas damnatur, Gestas ad astra leuatur.

At Innsbruck a witch boasted that if she had but a thread of a prisoner's tunic she could enable him to endure torture to the death without confessing. W. B. Seabrook in his study of sorcery in Haiti, "The Magic Island," relates that during a military engagement there was slain a notorious warlock, a member of the "culte des morts." Upon the body was found a small book of secret formulas written in creole by himself. Of these one is: "When confronted with Torture." When one finds himself tied up, it is very necessary to make this prayer: 'For the sake of the great pain which Jesus Christ suffered from Judas, the traitor, in walking along Golgotha's hilly road, may I be relieved from the rope which is piercing through my [mention the part] to the heart, just as the left side of Christ's Body did abundantly spill Blood by Herod, the infamous executioner. Amen.' Order a mass in the name of all the Saints "

† "Codronchi." This famous Italian physician was born at Imola c. 1560. The work to which reference is made is: "Batistae Codronchii de Morbis Ueneficis ac Ueneficiis, libri quattuor, in quibus non solum certis rationibus ueneficia claro demonstratur sed eorum species . . . aperiuntur." Venice, 1595.

the sorcerers blasphemously and falsely ascribe to S. Leo or Charlemagne, invoking the mighty Names of God. So does the devil delude his own, as may be seen from the examples.

☆

Examples.

Martin Delrio (*D.M.* I, 21) tells that he knew a certain law student named Quirino, a Bachelor of Law, who, relying upon such a charm, boldly mingled in brawls and fights and, though often struck, was never wounded. At last, in 1572 or 1573, he was killed at a drinking-bout in Rome through some trifling wound. The following example is similar.

Nider writes in his *Formicarius* that in the district of Berne there was a notorious witch named Scavius,* who dared to boast publicly that whenever he wished he could change himself into a mouse in the sight of all his rivals; and so he is said to have often escaped from the hands of his mortal enemies. But, when it was the will of Divine Justice to make an end of his wickedness, his enemies stole upon him as he was sitting in a warm bath by the window suspecting no attack, and suddenly struck him through the window with swords and spears, so that he perished miserably for his crimes.

---

* *"Scavius." This wretch was not only a warlock of most ancient impiety, but also an instructor of younger witches. Peter of Berne judged that he spread sorcery like a plague, and Nider tells us that this holy Inquisitor when bewailing the iniquities and necromancy practised in Berne added "quorum primus auctor fuit quidam Scauius dictus . . . Hic tamen suae fraudis commenta discipulo, qui Hoppo uocabatur, reliquit. Et idem supra dictum Staedelin in maleficiis magistrum fecit." Staedelin or Stadlin dwelt at Boltigen in Simmenthal. He was brought to trial before Peter of Berne and confessed many secrets of the horrid craft. See "Malleus Maleficarum," Part II, Qn. 1, Ch. 6.*

It is a common matter for witches to escape the torture of the rack; for they overcome all the pain by laughter or sleep or silence. Loys Charondas le Caron† in his *Antichrist Unmasked*, I, tells a wonderful story of this sort as follows. He knew a woman of fifty who endured boiling fat poured over her whole body and severe racking of all her limbs without feeling anything. For she was taken from the rack free from any sense of pain, whole and uninjured, except that her great toe, which had been torn off during her questioning, was not restored, but this did not hinder or hurt her at all. After she had undergone every torture and had obstinately denied all her crimes, she cut her throat in prison. So the devil, having accused her of witchcraft through the mouth of a possessed woman, killed her.

Near Amiens in 1599 a girl witch was imprisoned, who felt nothing when her feet were cruelly burned or when she was heavily scourged, until at the suggestion of a priest they hung about her neck a waxen image of the Blessed Lamb. Then, by virtue of the sacred amulet, the wiles and guile of the devil were defeated, and she began to feel the force of pain. Therefore it is clear that this indifference to torture, which even Tostado (*In Genesim.* XIII) recognises, springs from no physical cause, but is due to the devil's work.

Remy (I, 5) tells the following. When Isabella Pardea was seized for witchcraft at Epinal on the 6th May, 1588, and had shown the magistrate a part of her body branded by the devil, it occurred to the magistrate to test the truth of this alleged insensitiveness to pain. So he ordered a pin to be thrust and pressed deeply into her, and this was done in the presence of sufficient witnesses, and no blood flowed from the wound,

---

† *"Loys." "Charondas de Caron." Born at Paris, 1530; died 1617.*

and the witch gave not the least sign of pain.

At Brindisi in November 1590, when Claudia Bogarta was about to be tortured, she was closely shaved, as the custom is, and so a scar was exposed on the top of her bare brow. The Inquisitor then suspecting the truth, namely, that it was a mark made by the devil's claw, which had before been hidden by her hair, ordered a pin to be thrust deep into it; and when this was done she neither felt any pain, nor did so much as a drop of blood come from the wound. Yet she persisted in denying the truth, saying that her insensitiveness was caused by an old blow from a stone. But when she was brought to the torture, she not only acknowledged that the scar had been given her by the devil, but confessed to many other abominable crimes which she had committed.

In June 1591 at Iesi, a village a mile distant from Brindisi, the Judge ordered a gaoler to search Mugeta, who was charged with witchcraft. The gaoler therefore stripped her to see if he could find any devil's mark, and at last found on her left thigh a mark like a shell. Into this he thrust his weapon with all his force, but Mugeta uttered no cry, nor could he get one drop of blood from the wound; but when he lightly pricked the place next to the mark, she roared aloud in pain, and much blood flowed from it.

☆

CHAPTER XVI

Whether by Witchcraft and Devil's Work the Sexes can be Interchanged.

Argument.

CORNELIUS GEMMA inquires into the mutation of the feminine into the masculine sex, and the masculine into the feminine, which is admitted by modern physicians to be natural. We read of many women who have become men. Hippocrates writes that at Abdera Phaetula, the wife of Pitheus, had borne him children; but when her husband was sent into exile, after a few months her menstrual courses ceased, and she was smitten with terrible pains all over her body, and acquired the physical features of a man. He says that the same thing happened to Anamisia, the wife of Gorgippus, at Thasos. Livy tells the same story in Book 24 (*de Spoletana muliere*). Pliny says that it is no fable that women are changed into men. Martin Delrio uses the following words (quoting from Pliny, *Historia Naturalis*, VII, 4): "I myself saw in Africa L. Cossicius, a Tisdritanian citizen, changed into a man on his wedding day." S. Augustine* mentions heathen records of women becoming men, and of hens being changed into the masculine sex, not, however, by witchcraft but naturally: for witches cannot actually do this thing, but only in appearance to deceive us by casting a glamour over our senses with the help of the devil, as we have shown elsewhere.

☆

Examples.

Giovanni Pontano† (*Hist. Neapolit.*) tells that at Gaeta a woman changed into a man after having been married for fourteen years to a fisherman: and another, named Emilia, after having been for twelve years the wife of Antonio Spensa, a citizen of Eboli, dissolved her marriage, married a wife and begot children. He speaks also of another woman who had borne one son to her husband, and suddenly assumed virility, left her husband,

---

* "S. Augustine." "De Ciuitate Dei," III, 31.

† "Pontano." "De Bello Neapolitano," V, "Pontani Opera Omnia," Basileae, 1538, II, pp. 574-75.

and married a woman who bore children to her.

Cocceius Sabellicus* has some similar stories which I shall omit, and will set down two instances which occurred in Spain in our own time, and were faithfully described by Antonio de Turrecremata† in his *Jardin de las Flores curiosas*.

In the town of Ezgueira in Portugal, about nine leagues from Coimbra, there lived a nobleman who had a daughter named Maria Pacheco. When this girl was at the age when a woman's monthly courses usually begin, instead of a fluid excretion there broke or otherwise grew from those parts a virile member; and so, from being a girl, she suddenly became a pubic young man endowed with virility, and assumed the name of Manoel Pacheco. He then took ship for India and endured much hardship and performed great deeds as a soldier. Returning to his country he married a noble wife: yet Amatus the Portuguese, writing in his *Centuries*, makes no mention of any children, but says that he remained unbearded and with a feminine cast of countenance, these being indications of imperfect virility. Finally Torquemada adds that he heard this from a most trustworthy friend of great authority.

Not far from Benaventana in Spain the wife of a farmer of moderate fortune was ill-treated by her husband because she was barren. Weary of such bad treatment she ran away one night dressed as a man-servant, and in this guise went from place to place earning her living by menial work. After some time, either because of the efficacy of her natural heat or through imagination induced and strengthened by her continuous masculine clothing and work, she found that she had actually turned into a man. Therefore she, who had long been a wife, determined to act the husband, and consummated her marriage with a woman. The secret was kept for a long time, since she did not dare to tell it to any one, until a certain man who had been very well known to her noticed that she was in face very like that farmer's wife who had run away. He asked if he were her brother; whereupon she told him the whole story as it happened, and so it came to light.

Baptista Fregoso‡ (*Exemplorum*, I, 6) writes as follows. At Naples, in the reign of Ferdinand I, Ludovico Guarna, a citizen of Salerno, had five daughters, the two youngest of whom were named Francesca and Carola. When these two girls reached the age of fifteen the genital parts of both of them sprouted into masculinity, so that they changed their clothes and were taken for men, being called Francesco and Carolo.

At Eboli in the same region, a girl had been betrothed for four years. On the first night of her marriage she went to bed with her husband: but either owing to the friction or to some other unknown cause, when the hymen which gave her the appearance of a woman was broken, a male organ stood out. She then went home

---

* *"Cocceius Sabellicus."* Marcus Antonius Cocceius Sabellicus, a Venetian writer of eminence. He is the author of *"Epistolarum libri XII"*; *"Orationum libri XII"*; *"De situ Uenetae libri tres"*; and many poems, of which some are devotional, such as *"De laudibus Deiparae Uirginis Eligiae XII."* I have used the collected edition of his *"Opera,"* Venice (23 December), 1502.

† *"Antonio de Turrecremata."* In Latin Torquemada. The first edition of the *"Jardin de las Flores curiosas, en que se tradan algunas materias . . . etc.",* is Salamanca, 1570. *"Olivante de Laura,"* a romance by Turrecremata was discovered in Don Quixote's library and condemned to the flames by the curate. Turrecremata was a very popular author in his day, and the *"Jardin de las Flores"* was translated into French by Gabriel Chappuys as the *"Hexameron"* as early as 1579. It was reprinted Lyons, 1582; Paris, 1583; Rouen, 1610.

‡ *"Baptista Fregoso."* An Italian writer of the fifteenth century.

and sued in the Courts for a return of her dowry, and was thereafter reckoned as a man.

Phlegon writes: "A virgin born at Smyrna named Philotis was, on reaching maturity, given by her parents in marriage to a man: but a masculine organ appeared and she changed into a man. Also in Laodicea in Syria a woman named Aeteta was changed into a man while in the very act with her husband, Aetetus. This was when Macrinus was Governor of Athens, and Lucius Lamia and Aelianus were Consuls at Rome."

Michel de Montaigne says that in his time there was at Viering a girl named Maria who, as she was dancing rather vigorously, was suddenly made a man by the sprouting of male organs, and was given in the Sacrament of Confirmation by the Bishop of Soissons the name of Germain, by which she began to be known. A beard grew upon her chin, and she lived long, even to a decrepit old age, but never married a wife.

If this can come about naturally, as so many authors maintain, I should think that with God's permission it is possible to the devil, relying upon natural causes.

☆

CHAPTER XVII

Whether the Spirits of the Dead can Appear to Men.

Argument.

ALL the faithful of Christ are agreed that, through the power and might of God, the souls of the departed can and do at times appear to the living. For we read that Christ appeared to S. Peter when the Apostle was fleeing from persecution, and said that He was going to Rome to be crucified again.

Our Holy Father Ambrose bears witness to the appearance of spirits in his *Contra Auxentium de basilicis tradendis.* Dionysius the Areopagite writes that Jesus appeared with a great company of Angels and blamed him for his harshness in seeking to punish the sins of his brother and seducer.

S. Justin Martyr testifies that the souls of the dead return and at times appear, maintaining that the spirit of Samuel was actually called up. Tertullian supports this view in the following words: "But if the Divine Power has recalled the souls of some to their bodies to witness to His truth, we must not on that account give credence to the claims of witches, to illusive dreams, or to poetic fables." Origen speaks as follows in refutation of Celsus: "The wicked spirit, which is bound to the earth by horrid crimes so that it may not aspire to Heaven, goes wandering about the earth haunting graveyards; and in such places shadowy ghosts are most often seen dwelling upon this earth. And it is to be thought that of such sort are the spirits of those in every age who have been snared and bound in witchcraft." And in the time of Origen, the Blessed Potamiaena appeared to the murderer Basilides and converted him to the faith, as we are told by Eusebius, and by Origen himself, *contra Celsum*, Bk. 1.

S. Gregory of Nyssa, in his most authoritative *Life of S. Gregory the Thaumaturge*, writes that the Blessed Virgin Mary and S. John the Evangelist appeared to him. See also S. Cyprian, *De Uisionibus Nocturnis, Epist.* 12 and 69, where he argues against those who despise such visions. S. Ambrose, in *Sermon 90*, says that while her family were watching by the tomb of S. Agnes one night, she appeared to them and said: "Do not mourn for me as dead, my kinsmen," etc.

In the year of Our Lord 300 Christ appeared to S. Peter of Alexandria in the form of a boy asking for his robe which had been torn by Arius (Surius, tom. 6, 15th Nov.). See also Pope Adrian I, *Epist. tom.* 2: *Decret. et Synod.* 7: *Concil. Nicene* 2, *act.* 2: S. Gregory of Tours, *apud Laurentium, tom.* 6, *12th December:* S. Gregory of Neocaesarea, *In oratione de Nicena Synodo:* Nicephorus, VIII, 23: S. Basil, *de uera Uirginitate, paulo post medium,* and S. Gregory of Nazianzus, *In oratione in Laudem Caesarii.*

In the year 400 the death of S. Martin was made known to S. Severinus and S. Ambrose when they were absent from him. This is told also by S. Gregory of Tours in his *Book on the Miracles of S. Martin,* and in his *Book on the Glory of the Confessors.* We have the authority of S. Augustine* that SS. Gervasius and Protasius appeared to S. Ambrose and told him where their bodies were lying.

About the year 429 the Blessed Virgin Mary with S. John the Baptist and S. John the Evangelist appeared to Abbot Ciriacus and said that she would not enter his cell because, unknown to him, there were in it two books by the heretic Nestorius written against the Blessed Virgin Mary.

There is the signal authority of S. Jerome which at one blow silences all the heretics who say that the spirits are all held imprisoned until the Day of Judgement. These are S. Jerome's own words: "Thou sayest that the souls of the Apostles and Martyrs abide in Abraham's bosom, or in the outer cold, or under the Altar of God, and that they cannot appear at their tombs or wherever they wish: for they are forsooth of senatorial dignity, and are shut, not in a foul prison together with murderers, but in free and honourable keeping in the Islands of the Blessed and the Elysian Fields. Wilt thou make laws for God? Wilt thou put chains upon the Apostles? So that they should be held in bondage up to the Day of Judgement, and not be with their Lord, of whom it is written that

they follow the Lamb wherever He goes. They therefore who are with the Lamb must be believed to go everywhere, if the Lamb goes everywhere: and can the Devil and his demons wander all over the earth and with great speed appear in every place, while the Martyrs, after their blood has been shed, are shut down in a box and cannot come out from it?" So says S. Jerome (*Aduersus Uigilantium.*)

But we must understand that such apparitions are not the ordinary rule, but occur in accordance with the special and singular permission of God. S. Augustine (*De cura pro mortuis agenda,* c. 13), wrote about his mother in words which our opponents have scandalously twisted against us, as follows: "If the souls of the dead were concerned with the affairs of the living, I am sure that my mother (to say nothing of any others) would not fail to visit me every night." Elsewhere he speaks openly about that exceptional permission, saying in Chapter 15 that it is no common or ordinary thing for the souls of the dead to appear to the living; but that the appearance of Samuel and Moses in the Scriptures proves that they can do so.

To conclude shortly, there is unlimited authority on this matter. Therefore, that I may not be tedious, I will only quote the authority of certain Theologians; such as Richard de Middleton†; Peter of Palude,‡ 4,

---

† "*Richard de Middleton.*" "*Doctor solidus et fundatissimus*"; *the date of his birth is unknown; most authorities name 1300 as the year of his death; but some say 1304, and others 1307 or 1308. This great schoolman paid due attention to the important problems of demoniality,* "*Quaestiones disputatae*" (*1284*), *q. xxxi; and he also treats of the Incubus and Succubus,* "*In secundo Sententiarum,*" *d. viii, a. 1, q. 6. For a full study see Edgar Hocedez, S.J.,* "*Richard de Middleton, Sa Vie, Ses Œuvres, Sa Doctrine,*" *Louvain, 1925.*

---

* "*S. Augustine.*" "*De Ciuitate Dei,*" *XXII, 8; and* "*Confessiones,*" *IX, 7.*

‡ "*Peter of Palude.*" *A Dominican theologian of the fourteenth century; died 1342.*

distinct. 45, *q.* 3; Scotus, *quest.* 1, *art.* 4; Denys the Carthusian, *Compendium Theologicum*, 4, *distinct.* 45, *q.* 1., and in his work on the Four Last Things, and in his book inscribed to the Novices of his Order; Dominic Soto* and Peltanus† in their several treatises, *de Purgatorio, cap.* 5; S. Peter Canisius, S.J.‡ and Gregory of Valencia, S.J.§ in the Third Part, of his *Commentarii theologici, distinctions* 6, 9, *and* 11, *point* 1. *disposit.* 11, *quest* 1, *part* 1; and very many others. Let us now turn to some examples.

☆

Examples.

Socrates and Rufinus record that S. Spiridion had a daughter named Irene who, having well ministered to him, died a virgin. After her death there came a man who said that he had given her something to keep for him.

---

* "*Dominic Soto.*" *A renowned Spanish theologian of the Order of S. Dominic. Born at Segovia, 1494; died at Salamanca, 1560. See Echard-Quétif, "Scriptores Ordinis Praedicatorum," II, p. 171, sqq.*

† "*Peltanus.*" *Theodore Peltanus, a Biblical scholar of note, who translated several commentaries from Greek into Latin. His own glosses are very highly esteemed. One of his most important works is his version of the "Commentary on the Apocalypse," by Bishop Andrew of Caesarea (sixth century), which was published, 4to, 1584.*

‡ "*S. Peter Canisius, S.J.*" *1521–1597. Doctor of the Church.*

§ "*Gregory of Valencia, S.J.*" *Professor of the University of Ingolstadt. Born at Medina, March 1550 (some say 1551; others 1540); died at Naples, 23 April, 1603. He wrote many theological works of great value. The lectures given at Ingolstadt (1575–92) appeared as "Commentariorum theologicorum tomi quatuor," 1591–1597. There have been many subsequent editions. Gregory of Valencia has been much criticised for holding ("Commentarii," Liv. III, col. 2008, sqq.) that where the guilt of witchcraft is legally established the judge must inflict the penalty, even though he himself were personally convinced of the nullity of the charge.*

The father knew nothing about it, but searched the whole house without finding what the man wanted. But he insisted and said with tears that he would lose his life unless he recovered the thing. The old man was touched by his tears, and went to his daughter's tomb and called her by name. Then she said from the tomb: "What do you wish, father?" He answered: "Where did you put that thing which this man gave you to keep?" She indicated the place, saying: "If you dig there, you will find it." He went home and found it just as his daughter had said, and gave the thing to the man. If she could speak, could she not also appear? Certainly she could. Hear also how the dead subscribed to the Council of Nicaea.

Gregory of Neocaesarea records the following marvel, writing of the Council of Nicaea. Two Holy Bishops, Chrisantus and Musonius, happened by God's will to die before they had appended their signatures to the Council's decisions. So the Holy Fathers met together at the last resting-place of the two who had gone before, and when they were where they could be heard, they said: "Brethren and Fathers, you have fought a noble fight with us, and have run your course and kept your faith. If therefore, in the light of your clearer knowledge, you judge that our decisions are pleasing to God, let there be nothing to prevent you also from adding your signatures." Saying this, and leaving there the signed decisions of the Holy Fathers, they passed all that night in prayer: and on the next day when they came there, they found added to their own signatures those of the two Holy Fathers in the following words: "We, Chrisantus and Musonius, who sat with all the Fathers in the First Holy Oecumenical Council, although we are translated in body, with our hands we agree to and sign this document." From this it is clear that with God's permission the souls of the dead can return to us.

Blessed Paul the Deacon (not S. Paul of Nola) says in his *Life of S. Ambrose*: "On the day of his death a letter was received from the East by his venerable successor Simplicianus, written by S. Ambrose as if he were still living, and this letter is still preserved in a monastery at Milan. He appeared to certain saintly men, praying with them and laying his hands upon them; and we found that the letter bore the same date as that of his death. And in Tuscany at Florence, where the good Zenobius is now Bishop, because he had promised that he would often visit them, he was seen praying at the altar in the Ambrosian Basilica which had been built there by him, as we learn from Zenobius himself. When Radagais the Ostrogott was besieging Florence and the citizens were in despair, he appeared to some one in the house where Eugenius lay sick, and promised that they would be relieved in two days; and at this the citizens took heart, and on the second day Count Stilicho came with an army and defeated the enemy. The following we learned from Pansofia, a religious woman who was mother of the boy Pansofius. When Mazcezel was in despair for his own safety and that of his army which he was leading against Gildo, S. Ambrose appeared to him in a vision at night holding a stick; and when Mazcezel cast himself at the Saint's feet, the old man struck the ground with his stick and said: 'Here, here, here,' pointing out the place, and giving the man who had been deemed worthy of the visitation to understand that in the same place where he had seen the Saint he would in three days gain the victory. And so he brought his war to a prosperous conclusion.

"But we who are dwellers in Milan know these things on the authority of Mazcezel himself; for in this our Province he related this matter to many priests, and therefore we have set it down in our book with the greater confidence.

"Further, we received at Milan with the greatest reverence the Relics of the Martyrs Sisinnius and Alexandrinus* who in our time, after the death of S. Ambrose, gained the Martyrs' crown in the parts of Anaunia through the persecution of the heathen. And we know that on that day there came a blind man who touched the coffin in which the Relics of the Saints were being carried, and received his sight. For in a dream he had seen a ship coming to the shore with a number of men clothed in white; and as they came to the shore he prayed one of them to tell him who they were, and was told that they were S. Ambrose and his companions. Hearing this name he prayed that he might receive his sight, and was told by the man: 'Go to Milan to my brethren who will come there on such a day, and you shall receive your sight.' For the blind man was, as he said himself, from the coast of Dalmatia and had never been to the city before he came straight to the Holy Relics, although he was yet blind; and when he had touched them, began to see."

Constantius Presbyter† in his *Life of S. Germain of Auxerre*, chapter 17, writes as follows: The Saint was fearlessly abiding in a ghost-haunted house, when suddenly there appeared before the master of the house a terrible Shade which slowly raised itself before his eyes, and the stone walls were hidden by a cloud. In terror the man begged for the priest's protection; and the Saint ran forward and saw a fearful apparition. He first invoked the Name of Christ, and then asked who he was and what he did

---

* *"Sisinnius and Alexandrinus." "Roman Martyrology," 29 May. "In the district of Trent, the birthday of the holy Martyrs Sisinnius, Martyrius, and Alexandrinus, who in the time of the Emperor Honorius, as Paulinus writeth in his "Life of S. Ambrose," obtained the crown of martyrdom, being persecuted by the heathen in the parts of Anaunia."*

† *"Constantius Presbyter." See Constantius, "Vie de St. Germain d'Auxerre, tr. franç. avec une étude," 1874.*

there. The spectre at once put off its empty frightfulness and answered humbly as a suppliant that he and his companion had been guilty of many crimes, and lay unburied; and therefore they haunted men because they themselves could not rest quiet: and he asked him to pray God for them that they might be granted rest. The Saint was grieved at this, and asked to be shown the place where they lay: and the ghost went before them and by the light of a wax taper, at dead of night among ruins most difficult of access, showed them the place where they had been thrown. When it was light he called upon the neighbours and urged them both by word and his own example; and they threw aside all the rubbish and searched the place with rakes, and at last found the bodies lying quite disordered, with the bones still bound in chains. He directed a grave to be dug, freed the bodies from their chains and clothed them in shrouds, and buried them decently in the ground, uttering a prayer of intercession over them; and so the dead found rest. After that day the house was happily inhabited without any sign of haunting.

Every faith may be placed in the following history of Sinesius, Bishop of Cyrene, and the Philosopher Evagrius, which is preserved by Sophronius* from Leontius. Sinesius tried diligently to convert Evagrius to Christianity; but he objected that he could only regard as fables the Christian doctrine of the Resurrection of the body, and the teaching that almsgiving would be rewarded a hundred fold after this life. At last, however, by sparing no effort, the Bishop persuaded him to become a Christian and to be baptised together with his children. Not long after his baptism he gave the Bishop three hundred pieces of gold for the use of the poor, saying: "Take this gold and distribute it to the poor; and give me a written undertaking that Christ will restore it to me in the next life." He took the gold and at once gave him the undertaking required. The Philosopher lived for some years after his baptism, and at last fell sick to death. When he was near his end, he said to his sons: "When you arrange for my funeral, put that paper in my hand and bury it with me." When he was dead they did as he had asked, and buried the paper with him. On the third day after his burial he appeared to the Bishop as he was sleeping at night, and said: "Come to the tomb where I lie, and take your paper: for I have received my debt and am satisfied. And to convince you of this, I have signed it with my own hand." Now the Bishop did not know that they had buried that paper. In the morning he went to the sons and asked: "Did you place anything in the grave with your father?" They, thinking that he was asking about money, said: "Nothing, Lord, except the customary garments." "What, did you not bury a certain paper with him?" Then the sons remembered and said: "Certainly, Lord; for when he was dying he gave us a paper and said, 'When you bury me, place this paper in my hand'; but we did not know what it contained." Then the Bishop told them his dream which he had seen in the night; and taking them with the Clergy and Elders of the city to the Philosopher's grave, they opened it and found the Philosopher lying, holding in his hand a paper written in the Bishop's writing. They took it from his hand and opened it, and found newly written in the Philosopher's handwriting the following words: "I, Evagrius the Philosopher, to thee, Sinesius the Most Reverend Lord Bishop, greeting. I have received the debt stated by you in this letter and am satisfied; and I have no legal claim against you for the gold

* "Sophronius." c. 560–638; Patriarch of Jerusalem and Greek ecclesiastical writer, much of whose work is preserved in "Symeon Metaphrastes."

which I gave to you and, through you, to Christ Our Lord and Saviour." Hugh Etherianus relates the same story.

In his *De regressu animarum ab inferis*, XVI, Hugh Etherianus relates how the Abbot Menas told that he heard S. Eulogius* of Alexandria say as follows: "When I had set out for Constantinople, I was lodging with Master Gregory, Archdeacon of Rome and a famous man, who told me the following concerning the most Holy and Blessed Pope Leo. He said that Pope Leo had written in the Church at Rome a letter to S. Flavian, Bishop of Constantinople, against the heretics Eutyches and Nestorius; and that he placed the letter upon the tomb of S. Peter, the First of the Apostles, and devoted himself to prayers and vigils and fasts, beseeching the mighty Apostle as follows: 'If I, being but a man, have put anything in this letter ill-advisedly, do thou, to whom this Church and See were committed by our Lord and Saviour Jesus Christ, amend it.' After four days the Apostle appeared to him and said: 'I have read and amended it.' Then he took the Letter from S. Peter's sepulchre and, on opening it, found it amended by the Apostle's hand."

Theodore, the Holy Bishop of Dorna in Lybia, told us as follows: When I was lodging with the Holy Father Eulogius I saw in a dream a man in the habit of a monk and of huge stature, who said to me: "Announce my arrival to Eulogius." I said: "Who are you who tell me to announce you?" He answered: "I am Leo, the Pope of Rome." So I went in and told him, saying: "The Most Holy and Blessed Pope Leo, Bishop of Rome, desires you to come to him." Hearing this, Father Eulogius quickly arose and ran to him; and they saluted each other and, having prayed, sat down together. Then the Exalted Lord Leo said to S. Eulogius: "Do you know why I have come to you?" And when he said "No," he told him: "To thank you for your just and eloquent defence of my Letter which I wrote to my Brother Flavian, Patriarch of Constantinople, expounding its sense and meaning, and closing the mouths of heretics. For know, my Brother, that your holy zeal and labour were not for me only, but also for S. Peter, the Chief of the Apostles, and for Him whose truth we all preach, namely, Christ Our Lord." I saw this vision not once only, but twice and three times; and so, being assured of its truth, I told it to S. Eulogius.

About the year 587 a vision of this sort appeared to King Guntram about Chilperic, that terrible tyrant of the Franks; and the King related it as follows to S. Gregory of Tours: "And I saw another vision which foretold the death of this man. For he was led before me in chains by three Bishops, the first of whom was Tetricus, the second Agricola, and the third Nicetus of Lyons. Two of these Bishops were saying: 'Loose him, I beg, and scourge him and let him go.' But the third Bishop answered them bitterly: 'Not so; but he shall be burned in the fire for his crimes!' While they were disputing together at great length, I saw at a distance a bronze vessel set on a fire and glowing fiercely. Then, as I wept, they seized Chilperic and broke his limbs and threw him into the pot, where he was soon dissolved by the flames so that no trace remained of him."

In the year 600 the Most Blessed Gregory I, Pope of Rome and Doctor of the Church, tells (*Dialogorum*, IV, 17) the following of S. Musa. One

---

* "*S. Eulogius.*" *Patriarch of Alexandria from 580 to 607. He was a warm friend of S. Gregory the Great, who bestowed upon him many signal marks of esteem. S. Eulogius stoutly refuted the many heresies which were vexing the Church, but unfortunately with the exception of one sermon and a few fragments his writings have perished. Those that remain are in Migne, "Patrologia Graeca," LXXXVI (2), 2913–64.*

night there appeared to her in a vision the Blessed Mother of God the Virgin Mary, together with some maidens of her own age clothed in white. She wished to mingle with these, but dared not; but she heard the voice of the Blessed Virgin Mary ask if she wished to be of their company and live in Her service. The girl said that she did, and was at once ordered to behave in no foolish or girlish manner, and to abstain from laughter and joking; for she must know that on the thirtieth day from then she would enter Her service with those other virgins. The girl followed these precepts and became changed in all her habits and with great gravity put away all her girlish levity; and when her parents expressed surprise at the change in her, she told them what the Blessed Mother of God had commanded her and on what day she was going to enter Her service. On the twenty-fifth day she was taken with a fever; and on the thirtieth day, as the hour of her death drew near, she saw the Blessed Mother of God come to her with the same virgins whom she had seen in her vision, and spoke to Her aloud with eyes reverently lowered, saying: "Behold, Lady, I come." And with these words she gave up the ghost.

Hugh Etherianus* again writes of the spirit of the owner of a bath who for his sins was, after his death, deputed to the heat of the hot rooms where he was compelled to attend carefully upon the bathers. He had performed this duty to a priest of Civita Vecchia more than once when, in charity, the priest gave him two pieces of Blessed Bread. But he, weeping and lamenting, said: "Why do you give me this, Father? This bread is holy, and I cannot eat it. For I whom you see was once the Master of this place; but for my sins I was deputed after my death to serve here. If, however, you wish to help me, offer this bread for me to Almighty God and intercede for my sins: and you will know that you have been heard when you come here and do not find me." Saying this, he disappeared and so showed that, although he seemed to be a man, he was a spirit.

In the year 1139 Alfonso, King of Portugal, when about to join battle with five Saracen Kings, was told by Christ in a dream to be of good heart, and to use in the battle a Standard on which the Five Wounds were depicted. He won a notable victory which was the foundation of the glory of the Kingdom of Portugal. Fourteen years later Alfonso, King of Castille, was besieging Baeza, when S. Isidore appeared to him and advised him to make an assault, which resulted in one of the most remarkable victories ever won.

A very wonderful thing is told as an eye-witness by Bishop Constantine concerning the translation of the Relics of S. Euphemia† the Martyr. In order to put a stop to her marvellous miracles, Leo III‡ the Isaurian secretly removed the Martyr's Relics, putting dry bones in their place and throwing into the sea the true Relics in their coffin. Some sailors chanced upon this coffin, knowing nothing about it; and thinking some treasure was hidden in it, they took it and opened it. But by the miraculous scent which came from it they knew that they were Holy Relics. While they were still

---

* "Hugh Etherianus." A Tuscan employed at the Court of Constantinople under the Emperor Manuel I (Comnenus 1143–1180). He was a very learned theologian and on account of his treatise commonly known as "Aduersus Graecos" he is esteemed as one of the most eminent Catholic controversialists against the Eastern Church. His "De regressu animarum ab inferis" was composed at the request of the clergy of Pisa. His works are in Migne, "Patrologia Latina," CCII.

† "S. Euphemia." Virgin and Martyr. She suffered under Diocletian. Feast Day, 16 September. Her Relics were venerated at Chalcedon.

‡ "Leo III." The Iconoclast; Emperor of Byzantium, 717–741.

ignorant of whose they were, on the same night they saw lights and candles and men wondrously chanting and praising God. And when they had reached Levinum and had gone to sleep, in the quiet of the night they saw Glycerias the Martyr come to Euphemia the Virgin and embrace and kiss her, congratulating her on her arrival; and so they knew whose Relics they were. Three times they sailed from that place, and three times the winds drove them back again. At last S. Euphemia came to them in a dream and told them what would happen, saying that she wished to remain in that place, from which she had been cast into the sea by the impious Leo.

In the year 800 Ramiso I, King of Spain, fought fiercely all day with a mighty host of Saracens. Towards night he retired to a hill with a small band of his followers. As he was watching and praying to God, S. James appeared to him and commanded that they should all purge themselves by confession and take the Eucharist, and then give battle. In the morning, when they had all obeyed the divine warning, they advanced their standards and slew sixty thousand of the enemy. In that battle the Apostle was seen riding on a white horse bearing a snow-white banner with a red transverse cross upon it. This is told by Bishop Roderick in his *Chronicum generale Alphonsi Regis*,* and by Mariana,† Bk. VII, 13.

---

* "*Alphonsi Regis.*" *Alfonso X "el Sabio," 1220–84. It was under his patronage that the "Crónica de España," more commonly known as "Crónica general," was compiled from many historical sources.*

† ."*Mariana.*" *Juan Mariana, S.J., 1536–1623. His most important work is the great history of Spain which during the lifetime of the author himself went through several editions, to which he added, continuing his chronicle of events. The work first appeared as "Historiae de rebus Hispaniae, libri XX," 1592, but the Spanish version made by Mariana, which was published at Toledo in 1601, has Thirty Books.*

In the year 1117, among other prodigies which were appalling Italy, an infant was lying in its cradle at Cremona wrapped in clouts and, contrary to all nature, opened its mouth and began to speak, calling from her bodily cares its mother as she was preparing food for its elder brother who was crying for something to eat. The babe said that it had seen Mary the Mother of God standing before the Judgement Seat of Christ, interceding with Him with the most earnest prayers for the doom which was coming upon the world because of its sins. After this it ceased to speak until the natural time for a child to begin talking. This is told by Dodechinus in his History.

Fregoso (*Exemplorum*, IX, 12) tells the following: Since Udo, Bishop of Magdeburg, would not for any sign and warnings from God keep himself from impudicity, certain religious men prayed God either to correct or to remove the Bishop. One night, as one of these, Canon Frederick, was so praying in the Cathedral of S. Maurice, all the lights of the Church were suddenly put out by a violent gust of wind, and soon afterwards two young men came bearing lighted wax candles, and following them came Christ with His Mother and the Apostles, calling upon the Holy Men whose bones were resting in the Church. Among these came S. Maurice, who spoke gravely and at length in denunciation of Bishop Udo. Soon afterwards Christ passed sentence that Udo should be brought there naked by two of them. The Bishop struggled and one of those who were fetching him struck him in the belly; and he vomited into the Chalice upon the Altar the Host which he had taken the day before in Communion. Udo was struck down with an axe, and then all that vision vanished. Frederick was greatly frightened and went up to the Altar, where he saw the Chalice with the Host in it, and the dead body of the Bishop lying on the ground. He then roused the other religious men, who took the Bishop's body away and buried it in a field.

Two rich merchants of no mean birth were entering France by the Mont Cenis Pass, when they met a man of more than human stature who ordered them as follows: "Speak to my brother Lodovico Sforza and give him this letter in my name." As they stood wondering who he was, he told them that he was Galeazzo Sforza, and soon vanished from them. They at once returned to Milan and thence to Vigevano where the Moor lived. They delivered the Duke's letter, which was written in these terms:

" Oh, Oh, Oh, Lodovico, beware! For the Venetians and French are about to come against you and destroy your Dukedom. But if you will give me three thousand pieces of gold I will help you to conciliate the Spirits and avert your evil fate; and this I hope to do if you do not oppose me. Farewell! " The signature was: "The Spirit of your brother Galeazzo."

And though some may laugh at this thing, yet it is true that not long afterwards the Duke was thrust from his Dukedom by Louis XII,* King of France, and was led away captive. Bernard of Arles testifies that he was an eye-witness of this.

The father of Lodovico Alidosi, the Lord of Imola, not long after he died appeared like one on horseback with a hawk, to a man secretly sent by his son Lodovico to Ferrara as he went on his way, and told him to tell his son to meet him in that place on the next day, for he had a matter of great importance to say to him. When Lodovico heard this, both because he did not believe it and because he feared a trap, he sent another in his place, to whom the same Shade appeared and bitterly grieved that his son had not come; for he said that he had been going to tell him much

more, but that now he would only say that after twenty-two years and one month, on a specified day, he would lose the Lordship of the city that he then enjoyed. When the time predicted by the Shade had come, although the greatest precautions were taken on the night indicated by his father's spirit, the Confederate Army of Duke Philip of Milan set up ladders, since the moats were frozen over, and captured the town and its Prince. This is from Marcantonio Cocceius Sabellicus.

Francesco Guiccardini says that there was a popular rumour that the spirit of Ferdinand, King of Naples, appeared on three different nights to Jacopo, the surgeon of his son King Alfonso; and first with mild and gentle words, but afterwards with threats and commands, had ordered him to acquaint Alfonso that he must not buoy himself with a vain hope of withstanding the French power: for it was written in the Book of Destiny that the House of Aragon must be subject to untold misfortunes, and finally be cast out from the Kingdom.

The Ven. Cesare Baronio relates that Michele Mercatis the Elder was bound by a strong friendship to Marsiglio Ficino by reason of their common interest in Platonic philosophy. They happened one day to be discussing, as they frequently did, Plato's theory of the survival of the human soul after death; and not without reverential awe they decided that his opinons could not stand without the support of the Christian faith. (A record is extant of that argument, in a learned letter concerning God and the immortality of the soul written by Marsiglio to Michele Mercatis.) When they had argued this matter for a long time they concluded it in the following manner: they joined hands and agreed that whichever of them died first should, if he were permitted, reassure the other concerning the next life. Having sworn this together, they parted. Not long afterwards it hap-

---

* "Louis XII." This king imprisoned Sforza for the remainder of his life in the Castle of Loches.

pened that, as Michele was engaged in philosophical speculations at high morning, he suddenly heard the sound of a horse galloping and stopping in front of his door, and the voice of Marsiglio crying: "O Michele, Michele, it is true, it is true!" Marvelling at the spirit's voice Michele rose and opened the window, and saw him whom he had heard riding away upon a white horse. He cried after him: "Marsiglio, Marsiglio!" and watched him until he disappeared from view. Wondering at this strange occurrence, and feeling anxious about Marsiglio, he went to seek for him at Florence where he was living when he died, and found that he had died at the same hour that he had heard and seen him.

Not many years ago, when Alessandro Farnese* was conducting his admirable siege of Antwerp, the Hollanders and the English made a fierce onslaught upon him in order to relieve the besieged, who at the same time made a sally; and having captured from the Royal Army their offensive works, they seemed to have won safety. Then a few of the King's soldiers saw standing by the works Pedro de Paz, a Spanish Tribune famous as a soldier and for his piety, who had died a few months before. He was seen fully armed, just as he used to lead his regiment; and beckoning to his former soldiers, he ordered them to follow him. The front rank encouraged the second, and the second the third, and so on; and they all saw the same thing and marvelled and, taking courage, followed their well-known leader. He went in front and led them straight against the enemy. A battle was fought; and the Hollanders were forced to retreat to their ships, leaving the works to the Royal Army. In that moment that impregnable town lost all hope of victory or of defending itself. This is confirmed by the evidence of many soldiers who were eye-witnesses of the event.

In the Diocese, and not far from the city, of Pavia we read that a horrible thing happened in April of the year 1601 at a town called Correto. The funeral rites of a certain notary were being performed in the Church, when suddenly the corpse rose up in its coffin and, turning to one of his relatives who was attending the funeral, said: "Go quickly to my house and take a certain written instrument and restore it to such a place where it justly belongs: for because I suppressed this instrument, when I died I was sentenced by God's judgement to the fires of Hell." Having said this, he laid his head down as before. This was permitted by God that mortals should know what heavy punishment awaits such dishonest lawyers who embezzle the legacies of the pious.

In the year 1590 occurred the following event, which is most worthy to be recorded. It is taken from a collection of Peruvian Letters and the writer is said by some to be Francesco Bencio, and by others Gaspar Spitilli. In a certain lady's house there was a native maid of about sixteen who had been captured in war, and had been baptised in the name of Catharine. As she grew older, she developed a sad freedom and dissoluteness of behaviour, and frequently had to be scolded and punished by her mistress. At last she became so wicked

* "*Alessandro Farnese.*" *This renowned and noble commander was the son of Margaret of Parma. The history of his campaigns in the Low Countries is a tale of heroic genius and victory. He commenced the siege of Antwerp in 1584, and on 17 August, 1585, the city surrendered. Alessandro Farnese was created Duke of Parma in February 1586. He very properly attributed his success to Our Lady, Patroness of Antwerp. The occasion to which Guazzo refers was the great attack, 26 May, 1585, when the Antwerpers endeavoured to make a gap in the Kauwenstein dike. One contingent was headed by Hohenlo and Justinus of Nassau; another containing English auxiliaries under Colonel Morgan, and Scotch under Colonel Balfour, was commanded by Marnix.*

that she associated secretly with certain lost souls: yet she did not neglect confession, although she kept silent as to this sin, lest she should be thought a harlot lost to all shame. On the first of August, 1590, she fell ill and summoned a priest, to whom she opened the sins upon her soul, but not wholly: for though the priest came and went away from her nine times during that same sickness, she laughed contemptuously and said to the other servants that she had committed another thing which she would not confess among her sins; and she added such filthy and obscene words that the others were offended and went and told all this to their mistress. The lady scolded Catharine as she deserved, and then with gentle looks and kind words asked her what were those sins which she would not confess to the Father. She made no difficulty about answering and said that, as often as she summoned the Father in her sickness in order to purge herself with confession, there stood at her left hand one like an Ethiopian who told her not to confess, because they were very little sins of no importance, and if she confessed them the Father would only think her the more dissolute; while on her right hand appeared S. Mary Magdalene urging her to rid herself of whatever sin it was. So the Father was summoned again and the lady told him how matters were; and he tried by every means to induce her to make a full confession, but in vain: for the more he urged her the more obstinate she became, so that she would not even utter the Name of Jesus. Another time when they offered her a Crucifix that she might look upon it and consider in her soul that Christ was crucified for us, she answered with the greatest indignation and perturbation of spirit: "I know that; but what would you have me do?" Her mistress said: "That you should turn to Christ, who will remit you your sins if you acknowledge them in confession." To this Catharine

replied: "I beseech you to cease from troubling me." And when her mistress had gone away, she began to sing about her loves and her shame, and continued to do so for several days, until one night her mistress and some of the maid-servants came to her, and she broke out into these words: "I am in the greatest torture and anguish of spirit because of my violated confession." And from that hour up to midnight her whole body became rigid so that they thought that she was dead and began to think about her burial. But she came to herself, and the priest was called; but she in no way changed her former behaviour with regard to confession. Three hours later, a little before she died, the servants urged her to take in her hand the Cross and a holy candle and to call upon the Name of Jesus; but she said: "Who is this Jesus? I do not know Him." And she sat up on the end of the bed and was heard talking to someone else who was invisible. And another servant who was lying sick in the same room urgently begged her mistress to move her to another room because, she said, she could see certain black demons which terrified her. On the night that Catharine died the house was filled with such a fetid and putrid stench that the corpse had to be placed in the open air: the lady's brother was dragged out of bed by his arm: a serving-maid was struck on the shoulder by a stone, and bore the mark of the blow for several days: a most gentle horse went kicking its heels against the wall and rushing madly about all through the night: and the dogs went running about and barking. After the body was buried one of the maids entered the room where Catharine had lain, and though no one was there, she felt a vessel, which stood on the table, hurled at her. And over the greater part of the town tiles and slates were seen to be hurled about with a great uproar to a distance of two miles (not that there are many tiles or slates in the suburbs of Callao, as the houses of that city are nearly all roofed with palm leaves). Another maid-servant was, in the sight of many people, dragged for a long way by her foot, although no one could be seen dragging her.

On the seventh of October, when a serving-maid went into the wardrobe to fetch a certain garment, she saw Catharine standing stiff upon her feet; and as she ran away the apparition took up a vessel and hurled it against the wall with such violence that it was smashed into a thousand pieces. The next day a Cross was fixed upon the wardrobe door, but it was torn down and rent in three pieces before their eyes. The same day, as the lady was dining in the garden, a brick was hurled and overturned the whole dinner; and at the same time her four-year-old son began to cry out: "Mamma! Mamma! Catharine is suffocating me!" They then hung Holy Relics about his neck, and so delivered him from that pain. These occurrences compelled the lady to change her house, and she went and lodged with a kinswoman, leaving her own house in charge of some servants. On the tenth of the same month one of the servants went into the house-keeper's office and heard herself called three times by Catharine, and was so overcome with fear that the other servants urged her to call upon Our Lord for help and to take a lighted holy candle and go back with two of the boldest of them. This she did safely, and the dead woman then told her to send the others away and throw away her candle, since it hurt her, and to remain alone. Catharine sent out flames from all her joints, with an incredible stench, and was afire from head to foot, and was girt with a blazing girdle eight or ten fingers wide, the ends of which fell to the ground, which seemed to be some punishment for her lust and acknowledged lewdness. Seeing this spectre, the servant began to tremble and grow pale, and the wretched corpse said to her:

"Come here. How many times have I called you?" The servant, nearly dead, replied: "Good Jesus! Who would not be terrified to see you?" When she had said this, there came down to that place a most beautiful youth in white garments who told the servant to lay aside her fear and be of good courage, and to take careful note of what she heard from Catharine and spread it among the others, and to expiate all her sins by confession as soon as she left that place. Then Catharine spoke as follows: "Know that I am sent from Hell, and that I am subjected to the most terrible punishment because, when I went to confess my sins to the priest, I confessed only the least of them, as that I was garrulous and talkative and prone to anger, and such things; but was silent about my lusts and my habitual meetings with young men. Do you then learn to confess well and to keep no sin back: I give you this warning because I am so commanded and am compelled to speak of this matter as an example for others." Then the bell was heard ringing for the Angelus, and the dead woman quickly withdrew into a corner and vanished. And the Angel (for such was that beautiful young man) told the servant to go to her companions, which she did. We have set down this well-attested story, because all the kinds of apparition are found in it: Angels, S. Mary Magdalene, the devil in the form of an Ethiopian, and a damned spirit in an assumed body not, I think, its own, but one formed of air in the likeness of its own body.

At Naples about the year 1370 it happened in a Dominican Friary (as Brother Antonio of Siena says in the *Chronicon Fratrum Praedicatorum*) that, after he had completed his last duty of the day the Friar whose task it was to look after the Refectory entered it, and found it filled with Friars wearing hoods who were sitting down as if it was the hour for supper and they were expecting a meal. He at once ran and told the Prior of it: but the Prior thought he was mad or dreaming; yet, as he insisted, went with him, and saw, and believed. At this he also was perturbed, and at once consulted with the gravest and most prudent Fathers of the House. On their advice he put on sacred vestments and, bearing the Holy Body of Christ, proceeded with all the Brethren to the Refectory and, addressing him who sat in the seat of honour, adjured him to say who they were and for what they had come, and urged him to answer in the Name of that Lord whom he bore in his hands. When the Prior appeared thus before them with the Holy Sacrament, they all rose and bowed their heads, but they kept their faces so hooded that they could not be seen. Then they sat down and, being commanded by the Prior to answer his questions, nodded in agreement. At last the chief among them said: "We formerly belonged to this same religious Order, and were for the most part Masters, Priors, Superiors, Lectors, or holders of other offices." And he went on to say that they had all been judged to damnation because they had been guilty of ambition, pride, envy, and many such mortal crimes; but that by the mercy of God they had been commanded to come there to warn them and all of their Order to be content in their vocation. For because they had thought too little of it, they were all damned and were being burned in eternal flames. And in sign of the truth of this, let them all look upon them. Saying this, they opened their hoods, and each of them was seen to be surrounded by flames of fire. Then their leader struck the table as a signal, and they all vanished: and the whole Convent was mightily disturbed with fear.

In proof of this I will add another no less credible authority. In the year 1599 at Naples, Fra Tiberio, a most holy man who was Superior of the Dominican house, says that the following happened to him. One night when he was going the rounds to see if the Brethren were in bed as usual, he went through the Refectory, and there saw many lights and heard the voice of a man reading from a lectern, and saw men serving. Finally he who sat in the chief place gave a signal upon the table and spoke as follows: "Ambition and gluttony led us to Hell." And even now there is a scar upon the table as if it had been burned.

Blessed Peter of Cluny * tells the following, which he had from a Spanish noble: "When King Alfonso of Aragon† succeeded to the Kingdom of the greater King Alfonso of Spain at his death, it happened that he was gathering an army against certain rebels in Castile, and issued an edict that each house of his Kingdom should send so many horse or foot. Obeying this command, I sent to the army one of my servants, named Sancho. Some days passed, and when all who had been in that expedition were returned to their homes, he also came back; but not long afterwards, as is the way of men, he fell ill and died. Four months after his death, while I was lying in bed near the fire in my winter house near Estella, the same Sancho suddenly appeared to me at midnight, I being still awake, and sat down by the fire and stirred the coals so as to give more light or heat, and so made it far easier for me to recognise him. He was naked except for a slight covering upon his shameful parts. When I saw him, I said: 'Who

---

* "*Blessed Peter of Cluny.*" *Blessed Peter of Montboissier, also known as Peter the Venerable, c. 1092–1156. He was ever honoured as a Saint both by the people and his Order, and thus Pius IX confirmed the cult of this great and glorious monk. His works are in Migne,* "*Patrologia Latina,*" *CLXXXIX.*

† "*Alfonso of Aragon.*" *Alfonso II. Alfonso I, the Fighter ("El Bataleador"), reigned 1104–1134.*

are you?' He humbly answered: 'I am your servant Sancho.' 'What are you doing here?' 'I am going to Castile, and a great army accompanies me on the road, that we may do penance for our sins in the place where we sinned.' 'And why,' I asked, 'have you turned aside here?' 'I have hope,' he said 'of pardon, and if you will have pity on me you can obtain an earlier rest for me.' 'How?' 'When I was lately in the expedition you know of, I was seduced by Satan's wiles to enter a Church with some companions, and despoiled it of its contents and stole away with the priestly vestments; and on this account especially I am punished. And with all my might I pray you, as my master, to help me; for you can give me many spiritual benefits if you will. Further I beg that you will ask my Lady your wife not to delay in paying the eight soldi which she owed me for my service, and to devote that money, which she would have paid me for the needs of the flesh if I were still alive, to the far greater needs of my soul by distributing it amongst the poor.' Taking more courage after this conversation, I said: 'What has happened to our fellow citizen Peter Deioca who lately died? Tell me what you know of him.' He answered: 'Because of his frequent works of mercy, and especially because of his gifts to the poor during the late famine, he has earned the rest of the blessed and is a sharer in eternal life.' When I heard him answer so promptly and easily, I added: 'And do you know anything of our other fellow citizen Bernecio, who died a little while since?' 'He is in Hell: for when he was appointed to determine the boundaries of this town, he gave many unjust decisions owing to having received bribes or favours; and because he did not shrink from taking from a poor widow her only pig, which was the sustenance of her life.' Then, being incited to ask greater things, I said: 'Can you know anything of our King Alfonso

who died a few years ago?' At this, another voice spoke to me from a window near my head: 'Do not ask him this, for he does not know it; for he is but recently come among us and has not yet been permitted to know this thing. But I have been dead for five years and know more than he. What you ask of the King he cannot know.' I was astonished to hear this fresh voice and, wishing to see him, turned to the window and, by the light of the moon which then lit up the whole court very clearly, saw a man sitting on the sill of the window, clothed just as the other was. 'Who are you?' I asked. And he said: 'I am his friend, and am going to Castile with him and many others.' 'And do you know, as you said, anything of King Alfonso?' 'I know where he was, but I do not know where he is. For he was for a time terribly tortured in Purgatory, but was delivered from there by the Monks of Cluny,* and what has happened to him since, I do not know.' Saying this, he addressed his friend who was sitting by the fire: 'Rise, and let us now resume our journey; for the army of our companions fills all the roads to Castile, and we must join them.' At this Sancho arose and tearfully repeated his former request, groaning: "Master, I implore you not to forget me, and that you will persuade my Lady your wife to restore in mercy for my soul what she owed to my body.' When he had said this, they both at once vanished. But I called my wife and aroused her as she lay by me in bed, and before I told her what I had seen and heard, I asked her whether she owed anything to Sancho our servant for his services. She answered what I had never heard

---

* *"Monks of Cluny." The Benedictine Monks of Cluny inaugurated the Solemn Commemoration of All Souls, which was ordered by S. Odilo (died 1048) to be held annually in all the monasteries of his Congregation.*

from any except the dead man, that she owed Sancho eight soldi. I could no longer doubt the truth, since my wife had confirmed the dead man's story. In the morning I took the eight soldi from my wife and, myself adding what I thought suitable, distributed the money among the poor for the soul of him who had appeared to me, and had the priests say Mass for him, and spared no expense to obtain for him pardon of his sins."

In this clear, certain and most edifying vision we are taught that men's deeds follow them in death.

☆

CHAPTER XVIII

Of Apparitions of Demons, or Spectres.

Argument.

IT must be known that there are many kinds of demons differing among themselves by fixed degrees. The first kind is the Fiery, for they dwell in the upper air and will never sink to the lower regions until the Day of Judgement, and these have no dealings on earth with men.

The second is the Aërial, for they dwell in the air about us. These can descend to Hell and, by assuming bodies formed from the denser air, can at times appear to men. More often, with the permission of God, they disturb the air and raise thunders and tempests; and they all conspire together for the ruin of the human race.

The third sort is Terrestrial; and we may not doubt that these were cast from Heaven upon earth for their sins. Some of these devils dwell in woods and forests, and lay snares for hunters; some dwell in the fields and lead nightfarers astray; others dwell in hidden places and caverns; while others delight to live in secret with men.

A fourth sort is of the Water; for they dwell under water in rivers and lakes; and are full of wrath, turbulent, unquiet and fraudulent. They raise up storms at sea, sink ships in the deep, and destroy life in the waters. When such demons appear, they are more often women than men; for they live in humid places and lead a softer manner of life. But those which live in drier and harder places usually appear as men.

The fifth sort is Subterranean, for they live in caves and caverns in the mountains. These demons are of the worst disposition, and chiefly molest those who dig pits or mines and look for treasure in the earth; and they are ever ready to harm the human race. They cause earthquakes and winds and fires, and shake the foundations of houses.

The sixth sort is called Lucifugous, because they chiefly abhor and detest the light, and never appear by day, nor can they assume a bodily form except at night. This kind of demons is altogether inscrutable and of a nature beyond human understanding, being all dark within, and shaken with icy passions; malicious, restless, and perturbed; and when they meet men at night they violently oppress them and, with the permission of God, often kill them by some breath or touch. Of this sort, perhaps, was that Asmodeus* of whom we read in the story of Tobias. This kind of demons has no dealings with witches; neither can they be kept away by incantations, for they shun the light and the voices of men and every sort of noise.

It is further to be noted that the demon manifests himself in many various forms of spectres, such as dogs, cats, goats, oxen, men, women, or a horned owl. But, that his deceptions may be made known to us, Almighty God will not allow him to appear in

---

* "*Asmodeus.*" *Possibly this demon corresponds with the demon called Abaddon, the Destroyer, mentioned in the Apocalypse, IX, ii.*

certain other forms, such as doves, lambs, or sheep; for the true Lamb is Christ, the Good Shepherd, and the Holy Spirit is won to make His appearance in the form of a dove: also, because these animals are without guile and do no harm, God does not permit him to appear in their form. But because the human form is in all respects the most perfect and beautiful, therefore he generally appears in that form to us. For, as Marulli* writes, the human form is adapted to nearly every purpose.

☆

Examples.

A certain wagoner from Nancy was in a fenny copse on the outskirts of the town of Nancy, cutting wood, when a fierce storm suddenly arose. He made haste towards a cottage to find shelter, and on the way rested under a thick wide-spreading tree, and waited for the storm to abate. There he was surprised to see standing near him another woodman; and when he looked at him more closely (as we do when we meet a stranger) he saw that his nose kept shooting out to the length of a stick and then quickly contracting to its former shape and size; that his feet were cloven hooves; and that his whole body was of immoderate size. He was struck nearly dead with sheer terror at this, and then (as is the Christian custom in difficulties) made the sign of the Cross, after which he found himself alone as before. But he remained so stupefied by his experience that, though he was used to say that he could find his way about Nancy blindfold, now he could not do so even with the most diligent attention; but came to that city with his tongue sticking and his eyes staring and so trembling all over that it was easy

---

* "*Marulli.*" *Cesare Marulli, Archbishop of Palermo (1578).*

to believe what he said had happened. This belief was largely borne out by the report of what some other woodmen had seen at a distance; for they said that it had appeared to them that in that place the air had become thick and wrapped in a dense cloud.

In the same chapter Remy tells of a similar occurrence in 1588. One Nicolas Stephen had been commissioned by Master Desiderius, the Mayor's cellarman, to buy some wine vessels for him; and, having done so, he sent his wife Jacobeta (who was a witch) time and again to ask for the purchase money to be paid to him, but in vain. Jacobeta grew tired of asking and angry at so much waste of time and trouble, and turned her whole attention to finding the means and occasion to punish Desiderius for his tricks and subterfuges. Meanwhile it fell aptly enough that Desiderius was forced by an outbreak of the plague in his house to take refuge in the open fields, and lived there away from his household in a hut. As he was there with his only son there appeared to him late at night (through the agency of Jacobeta) a demon with so terrible a shrieking and groaning that it seemed as if the whole heaven had burst from its foundations and was falling upon his hut. And that this was no feigned terror maliciously assumed by Desiderius, as it was emptily rumoured, was afterwards proved by the fact that he and his son became so ill because of it that everybody who saw them despaired of them.

The following happened within our own memory at Colombières, a village six miles from Toul. At the extreme end of the village where the road goes to Salsure, a peasant lived in a humble cottage which was, however, as clean and neat as his means would allow and had never been rumoured to be haunted by spectres. Yet it became occupied by a demon who was at first content with throwing stones at night at the servants without hurting them; but as they grew used to this they ignored it and treated it as a joke. The demon could not tolerate this contempt, so one dark night he set fire to the cottage, which was quickly burned almost to the ground. Some days later I was travelling that way and heard of this from the inhabitants; so I went myself to see the ruins of the cottage so that I could tell the story to others more clearly and with the greater authority.

The Spanish author Antonio de Turrecremata (Torquemada) writes as follows in his native tongue, and this is from his *Jardin de las Flores curiosas.* "At Salamanca there was a matron whose house was popularly said to be haunted by stone-throwing. The Mayor of the city, was incited by this rumour to test for himself whether the persistent report concerning that house was true, or whether it was not rather invented by the servants in order to cover some naughty pranks of theirs; for there were among them two young girls of no mean beauty, and it was suspected that the whole of this story had been fabricated in order to facilitate their meetings with their lovers. So the Mayor went to the house at the time when the stoning was said to be most frequent; and there went with him no less than twenty of the townsmen, some of whom he sent with a light to search the upper part of the house to see who it was who threw stones at the servants. They searched diligently everywhere, and came back and said they had found nothing at all alarming. He then decided to examine the cellars, to which some steps led down from the dining-room, and to spend some time in a further search in that direction. And lo! hardly had they reached the place before there was a great noise and stones began to be hurled at them and swept them off their legs, but without harming them. So they were sent again to see where this shower of stones came from; and although they found no one in the place, the shower of stones kept falling.

This went far to confirm the opinion which many had formed, that the phenomena were all due to devil's work and magic; and this belief they more stoutly maintained as the stones kept falling about their heads. Some of them there rushed from the house in terror; but one of them, feeling bolder at a safe distance, took up and carefully noted the appearance of one particular stone and threw it into the house, saying: 'If this came from you, O demon, throw the same stone back at me.' And when this was at once done, there was no more room for doubt that the house was haunted by demons as the Matron had said."

I remember, when the plague was raging at Toulouse about the year 1563 I was in Auch spending the night gaming and playing in a manner fitting my age and leisure, with my good friend Master Abel, a member of the Cathedral Chapter. And to all of us who were in that house a petulant demon of this sort manifested, as we were playing, no slight disturbance, hurling stones roughly here and there, although they fell to the ground without hurting anyone. The room was locked from the inside and there was no furniture, except the gaming table and the seats, so that there was no place where any mechanical device could have been hidden.

In such ways do good and evil demons approach men, with hatred, terror, hurt and injury. So says Remy as above quoted.

Nider in his *Formicarius* relates that when the Kingdom of Bohemia was shaken with tumults and massacres because of its heresies, near a valley on the boundary of that country there were heard shouts at night, and the clashing together of horsemen, who were often seen to be clothed in various colours. There were two bold standard-bearers in the camp not far from the valley of spectres, who determined to learn the whole truth and what these visions portended; so they went one night to the haunted valley and saw the usual spectres, but before they dared to come near to it one of them grew afraid and said to the other: "It is quite enough that we have seen these things at a distance; I shall not go near to them. For it is an old saying that no one should joke with such matters." The other called him a coward and spurred his horse forward and drew near to the whole ghostly army, whereupon one of them came and cut off his head and returned to his companions. When the one who had loitered behind owing to his apprehensions saw this he took to flight and spread the news of this horror. And the next day they found the headless body and the head in the valley where the armies had been seen, but there was no trace of man or horse; and only the marks of some birds were seen in muddy places.

Nider adds another story worthy of belief, which was told him by the Bishop of Mayence. He said that he knew a soldier from the Rhine, whose son was still living where he heard this story, who was remarkable for his intrepidity in warfare; and because of his boldness and pugnacity others were often involved in quarrels on account of which he used frequently to ride by night to suitable meeting places. One night he was thus riding with his attendants and came into a wood near the Rhine; but before coming out of the wood, since a wide plain lay beyond it, he sent one of his attendants, as is the habit of those who suspect an ambush, to discover if there were any lurking enemies lying in wait for him in the plain at the end of the wood. It was a clear moonlight and star-lit night, and he had no difficulty in seeing: so the attendant spied through the branches of the trees and saw a wonderful army extending right across the plain and advancing on horseback, and came back and told his master, who said: "Let us stand still a little; for it is likely that a rearguard will follow this army, and we will ride up to those and inquire whether the main army are friends or enemies; nor will we be afraid of a few men."

After a short pause the soldier and his attendants came into the plain, and found no one except one man riding a horse and leading another by the bridle. The soldier went up to him and asked: "Are you not my cook?" For so it seemed to him at a distance. That cook had died a little before this, and now answered: "I am he, Master." The soldier then asked: "What are you doing here? And who are those who went before?" The dead man answered: "Master, they who went before are nobles and knights" (and he named many of them by name), "and they and I must this night be at Jerusalem, for that is our punishment." The soldier then asked: "What is the meaning of this horse which you lead without a rider?" "That," he said, "is for your use if you will come with me to the Holy Land. Be assured by the Christian Faith that I shall bring you back alive and safe if you obey my words." Then said the soldier: "In my day I have done marvels, and I will not shrink from adventure too." And though his attendants tried to dissuade him, he dismounted from his own horse and mounted that of the dead man, and they both vanished from their sight. On the next day, as his attendants were waiting by the same place, the soldier and the dead man returned to the place where they had first met, and the dead man said: "Lest you should think that this is nothing but a false phantasm, I give you two rare things which you must keep in memory of me—a small piece of cloth no fire can burn or scorch, and a knife in a sheath. The first, when it is dirty, you must clean in the flames: the second you must handle with care, for whoever is wounded by it, is poisoned."

Cromerus, a diligent author, tells the following. Wratislaw I, King of Poland, was besieging Dramburg, a very strong city of Pomerania. One moonlight night the sentries saw a great host of armed enemies riding over the open fields and attacking the Polish lines: and when this happened many times the Poles became angry because they could never engage these enemies in hand-to-hand fighting. So one night, when this enemy army was announced to be at hand, they charged furiously out of the camp, troop after troop, and pursued the fleeing enemy for a long way in vain. Hearing this uproar in the Polish camp and seeing their charge from the camp, the besieged army made a sudden sortie and set fire to the military works and soldiers' quarters, with burning straw and reeds, and so, since only a few had been left to guard the camp, easily burned all the works and the greater part of the camp. It is said that these were shadows of the night who, with divine permission, disturbed the Poles in this way because, in contempt of the usage and institutions of the Catholic Church, they had dared on a former expedition to desecrate the solemn Forty Days' Fast of all Christians by the ungodly eating of flesh and milk foods. God sometimes permits such apparitions because of sin, either as a trial for the righteous, or to announce plagues, wars, changes in kingdoms, and such things, as the following examples show.

On the night before the sedition of Antioch, a huge woman of formidable appearance was seen, beating a bronze shield so violently that the sound was heard all over the city.

Gennadius, Patriarch of Constantinople, went one night to the altar to pray to God for the public safety, when there appeared to him a horrible spectre which, on being conjured according to the sacred ritual of exorcism, said that as long as Gennadius lived he was not allowed to inflict the injuries which were threatening that Church; but that when he was dead he would rage terribly against it.

Cabades, King of Persia, heard that on the boundary between Persia and India, in a strongly fortified place named, there was a huge treasure of precious stones and gold and silver guarded by demons, who kept all mortals from coming near. He therefore set out with an army and tried to take the place by storm, but the demons fought fiercely and drove him off. He then tried the arts of the Jews and Magicians, but these were equally useless. At last he was persuaded that he could win his desire by the prayer of Christians to God, and asked help from a Christian Bishop living in Persia. This Bishop ordered the Christians to fast, and with prayers performed the Divine mysteries before the congregation, and going to the place conjured the demons living there and drove them out, and with no trouble gave the fortress to Cabades. Of this sort was that demon of Basle which we have already mentioned.

Philinnion,* the daughter of Demostratus and Charito, fell in love with their guest Machates; but since her parents refused to countenance this, she died of grief and was publicly buried. Six months after her death, Machates returned to that house, and Philinnion entered to him and took supper with him and was entwined with him more than once that evening; and Machates gave her an iron ring and a gold cup, while she gave him a gold ring and a girdle. Now as her old nurse came to make sure that the guest lacked nothing, she saw her charge lying in bed with him, and joyfully told it to the girl's parents. They ran up in astonishment, and the next morning found them both, and

---

* "Philinnion." This is from Phlegon of Tralles, "Mirabilia," No. 30. It may be read apud "Fragmenta Historicorum Graecorum." Ed. Carolus Müllerus, Parisiis, Didot, 1849, vol. III, pp. 611–13. See "The Vampire in Europe," by Montague Summers, Chapter I, "The Vampire in Greece and Rome," pp. 34–37.

with cries of joy embraced their daughter as she lay sleeping with their guest. But Philinnion looked at them with stern eyes and said: "O you cruel parents to your daughter! Did you then begrudge me three short days in my father's house with my Machates? Whether it be curiosity or cruelty on your part, it will bring you great misfortune, for you will renew your former grief, and once more bury your daughter." When she had said this, she grew pale and fell down like the dead corpse which she actually was; and her parents were overcome with sorrow. When this matter became known to the people and the Magistrate, they ordered the tomb to be opened, and found it empty of any corpse; for there were in it only an iron ring and a gold cup, the gifts of Machates. But the corpse of Philinnion was found in the bed in his bedroom, and on the advice of a certain seer named Hyllus it was cast out of the city as a prodigy, to be devoured by the birds and beasts. As for Machates, when he saw that he had been mocked by a spectre, he would not bear the ignominy of it, and before long he laid violent hands upon himself.

Such are the many false resurrections of the heathen: and just as it is agreed that the devil has to do with witches in an assumed body, either as Incubus or Succubus, so also in this kind of spectre a nauseating charnel smell is perceived.

Among the writings of the Germans (says Remy, I, 2) there is a popular story of a certain Aulicus, who received news of his wife's death and of the manner of her burial. He at once returned home to see to his domestic concerns; and as he kept thinking of his wife during the night (as is usual when anyone has a deep-seated desire for anything), he saw her undressing herself as usual ready to come to bed with him. He made some effort to prevent her from doing this, since he had been assured that she was dead;

but he was overborne by the sound of her voice and the sight of her body, and allowed her to lie down with him. And so he continued for some days, until the potent words of an Exorcist drove away the demon who had inhabited the corpse in order to delude and, if he could, destroy the husband. And certainly this could not have been done if the body had been informed with its own proper soul. But just as the law has power to eject an usurper, so let no one, who knows the power of adjurations and exorcisms, wonder that the demon can be cast out from his insidious occupation of a dead body.

Philostratus, in the *Life of Apollonius of Tyana*, IV, xxv, records that a similar thing once happened to Menippus, the disciple of Demetrius the Cynic. He was going from Corinth to Cenchreæ, when he met a graceful and apparently rich foreign girl who said that she was seized with love for him, and familiarly invited him to turn aside into her house. Since he in his turn was taken with love for her, he lay with her many times and began to think of marrying her; for she had a house decked like a king's palace. But as soon as Apollonius looked at the house he cried out that she was a Lamia who would soon either entirely devour him, or bring some terrible injury upon him.

Thomas of Brabant,*in his *De bono uniuersali*, II, 57, relates the following history. In Genappe, a sober and noted town of Brabant, a certain young man loved a girl who was a virgin, and spoke to her parents with a view to marrying her; but they refused. In the middle of the night the girl fell into an acute fever and

---

* "*Thomas of Brabant*." A Dominican and suffragan bishop, 1201-70. He is generally referred to as Thomas Cantimpratanus, or Thomas of Cantimpré. His famous work "Bonum uniuersale de Apibus" was immensely popular, but now is of the last rarity. I have used the Douai edition of 1597.

grew so ill that they all thought she was dead; and they mourned and tolled the bell as if for the dead. The young man her lover was going that evening from that town to another, and as he was going by a thicket he heard the sound of a woman weeping. He anxiously ran up and, seeking for the woman he had heard, found the girl whom he thought to be dead, and said to her: "Your parents are mourning you as dead! Whence have you come here?" "See," she cried, "the man going before me, who led me away." The young man was astonished at this, since he saw no one except the girl; and he boldly caught her up and hid her in a house outside the town. Returning to the town, he spoke to his friends, and then went to the girl's father as he sat with his friends at the funeral feast, and asked him if he would give him his daughter whom he was mourning as dead. The father answered in surprise: "Are you God, to raise up and wed the dead?" But the young man said: "Only promise me that I shall have your daughter as my wife if I bring her back alive and safe." To this the father agreed, and confirmed his promise in presence of them all. The young man then raised the shroud which hid the body, and they found an image so wonderful that it could have been the work of no man. For they who have seen such images made by the devil say that they are like rotten wood inside, but are covered outside with a delicate skin. After this the girl was brought back safe and sound to her father, and a few days later married the young man, and lived safely right up to our own times.

An old author tells in the *Life of S. Robert* the Abbot that one night the Holy man saw a foul demon standing at the entrance of the Choir and repeatedly trying to enter, but in vain. He had the form of a peasant in a rough smock with long bare legs, carrying a basket on his back and a piece of wood slung in front of him; and he kept going about the Choir with his neck stretched out, looking attentively at the Brothers to see whether he could find in any of them a quality favourable to himself. The Man of God prayed earnestly and roused the Brothers from their torpor; and when the wicked spy had waited a long time in vain and saw that he was meeting with no success, he mocked the sleepy Brothers with bitter laughter and, leaping about with extraordinary agility, applauded them whenever their thoughts were turning to evil. At last he found among them a young Brother whose thoughts kept wandering upon forbidden things, his body only being present in that place, for he was even meditating a secret flight. Seeing that this man was ripe for his purpose, the devil seized him with his pitch-fork and thrust him into his basket and quickly ran away with him. Perceiving this, the Holy man was in great anxiety for that Brother's safety, and diligently sought for him in the morning. But he had escaped before the dawn and had become an outcast, throwing off the easy yoke of Christ and following the Enemy; for he joined himself with the worst criminals and gave himself up to brigandage, and was not long afterwards captured and miserably punished with death.

Ranulf Higden,† the author of the *Polychronicon*, writes that Count Richard went one night alone into the church to pray, and found there a coffin with a corpse in it. While the Count was praying, the corpse burst from its shroud with a great cry and

* "*S. Robert.*" *Abbot of Molesme; c. 1029–1111.*

† "*Ranulf Higden.*" *Benedictine chronicler; a monk of S. Werburg, Chester; died 1364. The "Polychronicon," a universal history to his own times, was translated into English by John of Trevisa in 1387, and this version was printed by Caxton in 1482, and by Wynkyn de Worde in 1495.*

rushed with arms outstretched as if to embrace him. The Count made the sign of the Cross on his brow, and having adjured it in vain to depart, drew his sword and cut it in two; and he then ordered that the Office for the dead with Requiem Masses should be solemnly sung throughout the whole land.

More wonderful than any is the following, taken from the description of Muscovy by Guagninus.* He writes that certain inhabitants of the Livonian district of Russia die every year on the 27th of November on account of the intense cold, just like swallows and frogs; and on the 24th of April in the next spring they come to life again. He adds that when they feel their annual death approaching, they put their possessions in a certain place; and their neighbours, the Ruthenians and Courlanders, take these away, leaving equivalent goods in their place. When they come to life again, they take their goods if they seem to be just; but if they do not appear just they demand their own back. And therefore much strife and warfare are said to arise between them.

Sigismund, Baron Herbestein,† it is true, relates the same story in his *Rerum Moscouitarum Commentarii,* but he makes it quite clear that he regards it as a mere fable.

☆

CHAPTER XIX

That Cacodemons Exercise their Magic Powers of their Own Will.

Argument.

ON this subject Tostado (on *Job* xl) argues strongly as follows. It must not be maintained that men can constrain or confine a demon to any particular place except by Divine power, that is, by exorcisms and adjurations: but witches do not claim to subject a demon to themselves except by the power of their spells and signs, or by deeds very foreign to the Christian Religion; therefore it is impossible for the lesser power, which is man's, to subject to itself the greater, which is the demon's, since there is no power on earth which can be compared with the power of demons. Therefore there can be no natural or ritual means by which a man can compel the demons to appear or to answer him or to do anything, except, as I have said, by means of the Exorcisms of the Church: for then it may be said that they are put under compulsion either to depart from the bodies of those whom they possess, or to refrain from injuring them; and this was instituted by God to be performed by the Church, and the power of God is in such Exorcisms. But God is not present in the operation of witches by which they claim to master demons, for such are contrary to the honour of God. The demons themselves play

---

* *"Guagninus."* Alessandro Guagnini (or Alexander Gwagnin, as he turned his name) was born at Verona in 1538 and died at Cracow in 1614. His whole life was spent in Poland, and he became a naturalised Pole. For a full study of this curious and most interesting man see Carlo Cipolla's *"Un Italiano nella Polonia e nella Svezia tra il XVI e il XVII secolo,"* Torino, 1887. The work of Guagnini from which Guazzo quotes is the monumental *"Sarmatiae Europeae Descriptio, quae Regnum Poloniae, Lituaniam, Samogitiam, Russiam, Masouiam, Prussiam, Pomeraniam, Liuoniam, et Moschouiae Tartariaeque partem complectitur, Alexandri Gwagnini Ueronensis, Equitis Aurati peditumque praefecti, diligentia conscriptae,"* Cracow, 1578.

† *"Baron Herbestein."* Sigismund, Baron Herbestein was born in 1486. He was promoted and became eminent in the Austrian service, and acted as Ambassador to Russia and to Constantinople. He died in 1566. The De-dication to Ferdinand I, King of the Romans, of his *"Rerum Moscouitarum Commentarii"* (1549) is dated 1 March, 1549, and signed Sigismundus, liber Baro in Herbestein, Neyperg, et Guettenhag.

false and pretend that they are compelled; for in this lies their chief power of persuasion. But demons cannot really be mastered by men through witchcraft; or, if they could, they would not themselves teach men the way to master them, for the demons would be in a sorry case indeed if they could be mastered by men. So they pretend that they are subject when they are not, that they may deceive men: they pretend to be caught, that they may catch you; to be bound, that they may bind you; that they are subject to your commands, that they may make you subject to them; that they are imprisoned, that they may imprison you for ever: they pretend that they are in bondage to your art or image or charm, that they may bring you to Hell bound by the cords of your sins. Therefore, in short, they pretend that they are under compulsion, when they are really serving of their own will and voluntarily until such time as seems good to them.

☆

Examples.

Giovanni Francesco Pico della Mirandola (the younger) in his *De Praenotione* * says that two magicians met in the hall of the Queen of England to give an entertainment, having mutually agreed to obey each other implicitly. The first ordered the second to look out of the window; and when he had done so, stag's horns grew from his head, and he was for a long time exposed to the ridicule and jokes of all. So, since he had been powerless under this outrage and wished to avenge himself with a worse one, he drew a human figure with charcoal on the wall, and ordered the first sorcerer to stand under that figure and walk through the wall. The first

magician saw instant death in this, and was afraid and began to beg to be excused; but when the other reminded him of their agreement he was compelled to obey, and he was seen to walk through the wall. But he was never found afterwards; for the demon with his higher power had killed him and hidden his body in some deserted place or cave.

I will give another example, taken from a certain German jurisconsult.† A conjurer, a man of high estate, for the public amusement and at the request of his fellow guests, cut off the head of his host's servant; but when he wanted to restore his head to him, he found that there was another sorcerer who was preventing this. He asked the man not to do so; but when, after many warnings, he still persisted, the first conjurer caused a lily to grow upon the table and, no sooner had he cut off its head and leaves than that second sorcerer who had been thwarting him fell headless from the table, and the conqueror replaced the head upon the servant with no difficulty. Having done this he immediately fled from the house and city, lest he should be taken by the Magistrate for murder.

This pretended cutting off the head, and its restoration, as well as the production and cutting off of the lily, must all be ascribed to magical illusion. There was a contest between the demons of the two sorcerers, and the weaker of them was strong enough to hinder the success of the glamour, but was compelled by the stronger (though not unwillingly, as I think) to agree to his client's death, which was a matter of fact, and no illusion.

Johan Dubravsky, Bishop of Olmütz, in his *Historia rerum Bohemicarum*, XXIII, tells the following. Wenceslaus, the Emperor and King of the Bohemians, formed an alliance with Prince John of Bavaria by marry-

---

* *"De Praenotione." Libri Nouem. I have used the folio edition, Argentoraci [Strasburg], 1506–7.*

† *"German jurisconsult." John George Gödelmann in his "De lamiis."*

ing his daughter Sophia. And since the Prince knew that his son-in-law took a delight in ludicrous shows and magical illusions, he took a wagon full of buffoons and conjurers to Prague. There the most skilful of the conjurers was giving an exhibition of his power to deceive the eyes, when there came amongst the spectators Zyto, the Magician of Wenceslaus, with his mouth stretched open to the ears. He came nearer and ate up that Bavarian conjurer with all his apparatus, except his shoes, which he spat out because they were muddy. He then retired to rid his belly of its unwonted burden, and voided it into a tub full of water; and thus he restored the dripping conjurer to be laughed at on all sides by the spectators. After this his companions also stopped their tricks.

Now that eating of the conjurer was mere illusion; but the wretched man was really snatched up and thrown into the tub of water by a demon, and was not voided through the other's bowels.

Olaus Magnus (III, 20) writes that a certain magician named Gilbert was quarrelling with his master Catilla as to which of them was superior in their art. The master then threw him a little stick carved with Gothic or Ruthenian characters, which he seized and at once became stiff, and was carried bound to an island in the lake called Wetter in the country of the Ostrogoths, and there imprisoned in an underground cavern.

THE SECOND BOOK, DEALING WITH THE VARIOUS KINDS OF WITCHCRAFT, AND CERTAIN OTHER MATTERS WHICH SHOULD BE KNOWN.

☆

CHAPTER I

Of Soporific Spells.

Argument.

SORCERERS and witches are in the habit of putting others to sleep by means of potions or evil incantations or some secret rite, so that they may then poison them or seize their children, or kill them, or rob them, or pollute them with filth and adultery. And this, as the examples will show, can be effected by natural soporific drugs. For it is a very truth

that there are many natural drugs which, on being applied internally or externally, induce not only sleep, but a torpid insensitiveness to the acutest pain; and this is well known to surgeons, who make use of them when they wish to cut a limb from the human body without any pain. A laughable and at the same time pitiable example of this art is told of a young man of Narbonne who was led into slavery by a Thracian pirate. He was put to sleep by a powerful drug, and his testicles were so neatly cut out that, when he awoke thus deprived of his virility, he mar-

velled at himself as at a new man. Another story is told by Mattioli * of the asses of Etruria which were so put to sleep by eating hemlock that they were carried away for dead; but when they had started to skin them, they at last awoke and stood up on their feet and rushed miserably back to their stalls. Many drugs, then, are known and used by chemists, such as darnel, nightshade, the rush commonly called *Euripice*, mandragora, castor, poppy, etc., but if all these have the property of inducing a compulsory sleep in the daytime simply by reason of the natural powers with which they are imbued, what, I ask, cannot demons effect with their arts and contrivances, since they have perfect knowledge, not only of the secret and hidden powers of nature, but can also, with the permission of God, effect many things without the help or presence of any external thing?

And that witches may the more conveniently pour abroad, spread and disseminate their poisons, they themselves confess, as can be read in Remy (II, 4), that after they have worked with their familiars for some years, they are given by these demons power to penetrate into houses, so they can easily slip through narrow openings by

---

* *"Mattioli." Pietro Andrea Mattioli, the famous Italian physician, born at Siena in 1500; died at Trent 1577. He was especially renowned for his knowledge of herbs and simples. One of the best editions of his "Commentarii" (secundo aucti) is that of Venice, 1538.*

shrinking themselves into mice or cats or locusts or some such small animal as the occasion demands, and once they are inside they can again, if they wish, resume their proper shape and then go deedily about their business. Now they would first anoint all the limbs of their victim whose death they were contriving, so that he should not awake, and next they would pour poison down his throat. And the ointment they use is either given them by the demon or brewed by themselves with devilish art. Wherefore this seems particularly worth noting: that just as Emperors reserve certain rewards for their veteran soldiers only, so the demon grants this power of changing themselves into different shapes, as the witches believe, only to those who have proved their loyalty by many

years of faithful service in witchcraft; and this is as it were a reward for their long service and loyalty. This was amply proved by Henry Carmut in the year 1583 by his own particular confession, coming after that of many others of his sort. Witches used also to make use of strange lights in order to induce sleep, and I think Apuleius * called the smoke of them "a cloud of smoke." Sometimes they set fire to the feet or hands of corpses†

which they have first anointed with an oil given them by the demon: or else they fix candles to each of a corpse's fingers, or light the way before them with enchanted torches made from a horrid fat known to them, or they fix these torches in a certain place in the house; and the sleep lasts as long as those corpse lights burn. Sometimes they hang several parts of the corpse in various places; sometimes they practise other iniquities, all equally abominable, which are efficacious solely because of their pact with the devil. They also use magic characters in order to escape or overcome the tortures to which the Judges sentence them, as will be shown in the examples.

Therefore let those who go to sleep protect themselves by reciting Holy psalm and prayer: such as "*Qui habitat in adiutorio Altissimi*" or "*In te Domine speraui*," or some such orison. Let them make the sign of the Cross, reciting the *Salue Regina Mater misericordiae*, the *Paternoster*, and the *Aue Maria*, etc., if they would be safe from such snares. Let them have by them a waxen Agnus Dei blessed by the Pope, or some Holy Relics. For such devotions are the safest protection and rampart against all the wiles of the Prince of Darkness.

---

* "*Apuleius.*" *The expression used in the* "*Metamorphoseon,*" *II, 30, of the sleep induced by the witches is* "*iniecta somni nebula.*" *Statius,* "*Siluae,*" *IV, viii, 2, has, I remember,* "*Sabaeae nubes*" *for* "*fume of frankincense.*"
† "*Hands of corpses.*" *A Hand of Glory.*

"*Le Petit Albert*" *gives directions how one may* "*se servir de la main de gloire,*" *and other grimoires (such as* "*Le Dragon noir*") *have full receipts for the composition of this horrible charm. It will be readily remembered that in* "*The Ingoldsby Legends*" *there is a striking poem,* "*The Hand of Glory.*"

Examples.

Marguerite Jenin came to hate her son Jaquelin because she had to keep bullying him to go and earn money at the Alsatian markets round about, and by no arguments or demands could she prevail upon him to bestir himself. At last she was taken at dead of night by a demon, together with her associates in crime, to his house in Saxbingen, and suddenly approached him as he slept and roused him from his bed and stood him in front of the fire intending to roast him alive, if it lay in them to do so. But they were by some means prevented from this, and turned to another method of injuring him. They made a cut in his side and inserted a piece of brick which was lying on the ground; and the wound grew together again in a moment. After many months of torture, the piece of brick broke out from under his flesh in the sight of many.

The following history is very similar. At Vorpach in September 1586 Betrande, a barber's wife, confessed that, with the help of her fellow witches, she had fixed a bone on to the neck of a woman named Elisa because she had refused her a pitcher of milk.

Similarly Seneael of Armentières confessed at Douzy on the 30th September, 1586, that he had inserted part of a sheep's hip-bone into the top of the foot of one Philippe, a baker, having first made an incision with a fish's spine; and when the wound hardened, the baker suffered acute and continual pain, as he himself complained.

A man named Benignus was implicated in the murder of a Counsellor of Her Most Serene and Christian Majesty, the Queen of Denmark. He could easily have escaped the death penalty, because he was abroad when the law was set in motion against him: but he preferred to rely upon a magic charm which had been given him by some strolling charlatan, and voluntarily offered himself for trial. And he was in no way deceived in his hope; for he came through all sorts of torture unhurt and without confessing, and was acquitted. But just as he was being released from prison he was unable to bear any longer the burden of so great a crime, and openly acknowledged his guilt, and at length suffered the punishment of death.

In the Diocese of Liège, relates Caesarius of Heisterbach (*Miracul.* III, 40), in a town which some call Hugo and others Dinant, there came one night to an inn two men who pretended that they were tired from their journey; and when they had supped they said that they would not go to bed in another room, but importunately insisted that the inn-keeper should allow them to sleep by the fire in the kitchen. But a maid-servant, who did not like the appearance of the travellers, secretly spied through the key-hole what they would do. In the middle of the night she saw them take from a bag a hand cut from a dead man and anoint the fingers, and light them at the fire; and all of them except one were soon ablaze. The warlocks were surprised at this unusual occurrence, and tried many times to light this finger at the fire, but always in vain. Then one of them said: "What does it matter if there is one person in the house keeping awake?" And setting the hand by the chimney with its four fingers burning with a dim blue flame, they went out of the house and by a whistle signalled to their companions to come and join in the plunder. The maid followed them and, locking the door, shut them out. Then she ran to the room where her master and mistress slept, and found them so fast asleep that she could not awaken them although she dragged them from the bed into the middle of the room. Meanwhile the thieves were trying to get into the house through a window, so she ran and threw down their ladder. But they persisted in their attempts to enter the house. The servant then remembered the light and, suspecting it to be the cause of the deep sleep of those in the house, extinguished all those burning fingers, and after that the sleepers awoke and ran to see what the matter was, and drove from the house the thieves who were thus caught in the act. After some days these villains were captured and confessed their crime. What wonder is it, then, if witches steal by night to the cradles of infants, and to others whom they mean to destroy?

Peter Binsfeld * writes as follows: Anna, the mother of Johann Cuno de Rouer, and two other witches met together one night in order to bewitch a certain zealous witch-hunter. Their Little Master went before them and opened the doors; and Johann Cuno himself was taken as a companion by his mother and the others, that he might hold a lighted candle, made not naturally but by devilish art. They came into the room of him whom they would bewitch, in the town of Trèves; but because he had, after the manner of good Christians, fortified himself with the sign of the Cross and other pious acts before he went to rest, they could do nothing but had to shut the doors again and hurry back without effecting any harm. The good man whom they wished to injure yet lives by the grace of God, and shall live for as long as God pleases. Johann Cuno himself told this; and his mother, when she was questioned concerning information laid against her, confessed to the same matter. Necromancers, who are high in the order of witch-craft, have no need of this candle burning before them; but when they have lit it, they put it in some more remote place, as will be seen in the following example.

What I am about to set down was

* "Binsfeld." "Commentarius in Titulum Codicis Lib. IX. de Maleficis et Mathematicis," Quaestio VIII, ed. 1605, pp. 566–69. Peter Binsfeld, suffragan Bishop of Trèves, was born c. 1540 and died 1603.

taken from grave authors worthy of all belief, and is mentioned also by Martin Delrio (Disqu. Magic. III, 1, q. 3) and should, I think, be especially noted so that we may see the vengeance of God against sorcerers and necromancers. It has seemed to me fitting to conceal the names of the person and place. In a certain town in Spain a very famous man was the intimate friend of a nobleman who had a most beautiful but chaste wife. He began to love her, and not for long keeping this flame hidden, revealed his thought and tried to persuade the woman to sin. She, sure of keeping her chastity, tried her hardest to recall him from his madness to a better state of mind; but it was only throwing oil on the fire. For as flaming naphtha does but burn the more furiously if you throw water upon it, so her admonitions did but the more inflame the man, who continued to press her until she grew weary and determined to be revenged upon the wretch. She told the whole matter to her husband, who was seized with no less a fury than that of the sons of Atreus. At his command the wife made an assignation, and the longed-for night came for the wicked lover. The husband with some of his servants waited well armed in the next room to receive his friend in no friendly manner. And lo, at last arrived the lover girt with sword and dagger: he boldly followed where she led and, when they had sat down, repeated his old refrain: the woman as usual refused and denied him: the adulterer was emboldened by the darkness of night, and resorted to force: she forcefully resisted him until at last she cried out in fear, giving the agreed signal to her husband; but she might as well have called to the deaf, for neither her husband nor anyone else ran to her help. What was she to do? Should she run away? She was held by stronger arms. Should she consent? Rather an honourable death than a shameful sin. So she used her woman's weapons, her nails and teeth, and mutilated his face: but in his madness he hardly felt it. He laid his sword aside; but between her sobs the woman noticed his dagger sticking out behind him, seized it, drew it and stabbed her assailant to death, and his dead body fell to the ground. Having conquered, she regained command of herself and ran to the room where she had hidden her husband, and found him and his servants more like dead men than living. She called them, shook them and dragged them about, and left nothing undone to awaken them; but they remained asleep. Suspecting that this was due to witchcraft (as in fact it was), and seeing that her whole hope rested in herself, she carried the corpse out of the house and threw it into the street with the sword and the bloody dagger. While it lay there some of the night watch came upon it, took it into the guard house and, washing its face, not without difficulty recognised the man. Here the Alcalde exhibited great prudence. He enjoined silence upon all the rest, and next morning went to the man's house and saying that he wished to speak to the master in the presence of the whole household on a matter of the greatest importance ordered them all to assemble together. All the living were assembled, the dead man only being absent. The Alcalde remarked that it seemed to him that someone was missing, and the master of the house noted the fact and said: "All are present except So-and-so, who is probably now getting ready for some business." "Let him also be summoned," said the other. To save time some of them ran to call him, and finding his bedroom locked they beat upon the door; but no one answered. So the Alcalde himself went with the master and forced the door open; but there was no one in the room: and they were all amazed to find nothing but a torch burning with a pale flame by the chimney. Then the Alcalde told the master of the house how and where he had found the corpse: and while they took it from the guard house to bury it in unconsecrated soil, behold there came that nobleman and his wife who related the whole story. On taking note of the times, they found that they had awaked when the torch was extinguished. So the perfidy of that vile hypocrite was exposed to universal detestation, and the chastity and bravery of the lady became renowned and honoured throughout the whole neighbourhood.

Caesarius of Heisterbach (vi, 10) tells that a few years ago there died a simple man named Engilbert, a native of the Province of Tolbiac. Although he was born blind, he was known in many Provinces and esteemed by many noble persons of either sex on account of certain gifts with which the grace of God had illumined his inner life. In a simple hood and a woollen tunic and with bare feet he went both in summer and winter; and following this mode of conduct himself from his earliest years, he often visited distant shrines of the Saints, he never ate flesh, never slept at night on a bed, but only on a little hay or straw, and edified many both by word and example. In the time of his youth he was one night in the house of his aunt, a rich matron, and had gone to bed with her servants, when in the early evening two thieves broke through the wall and entered the house, where they stirred up the fire, lit the lamp, broke open the boxes and talked to each other without any fear. As soon as Engilbert heard them he had no doubt that they were thieves, but being unable to rouse the servants sleeping on each side of him, he cut himself a club from the wooden seat with his knife and, since he was blind, found his way towards the thieves by his ears, and lay about with his club on all sides wherever he could reach, striking like a madman, and so drove them from the house. He followed them to the door where a ladder barred the exit; and when they were outside the house and saw that there was no one awake but him only, they were ashamed at being so driven out. They took counsel and tried to enter again; but when he perceived this from the motion of the rungs, Engilbert so placed the ladder that the thieves would fall into a great corn-bin which was near the hole in the wall; and when they had done so, he pinned them down with the actual steps so that they could move neither forward nor backward. The thieves, fearing that they would be captured in the morning, begged to be pardoned, and after they had sworn a terrible oath never to harm his person or to enter that house, he let them go away. When Engilbert reported this in the morning no one could by any means rouse the sleepers, and so they searched for the magic charm which they were convinced must be the cause of this, and found hanging from the roof above the hole in the wall what appeared to be the backbone of a human corpse; and when this was taken away, they all quickly awoke. Many years later the same thieves, inspired by the fame and virtues of that Engilbert and, as I think, urged to it by his prayers, approached him and confessed their crimes and afterwards embraced the religious life.

Remy writes that at her trial at Gebweiler in January 1589 Marguerite Luondman confessed the following among other crimes. One night she and other wretches entered a house with the intention of pouring poison down the throat of the inmate who was sleeping heavily; and they had nearly accomplished their purpose, since everything seemed to favour them, when they were amazed to see their intended victim waken from his slumber, so that she and her fellow criminals were compelled to make their escape with their purpose un-achieved. The man seized a weapon and pursued them, but not being able to catch them hurled terrible threats at them. To arrive at a more complete knowledge of this matter, the man himself was examined as a witness, and told everything clearly and fully as the witch had told it; namely, that there had been an attempt to poison him, which had been thwarted only by his having awaked (for he had not yet been anointed with their unguent) and his having protected himself by the sign of the Cross and the Lord's Prayer against so great a danger. He said that it was quite true that he had chased them a long way with a halberd without catching them. After this nearly all those who were charged with witchcraft in the German province of Lorraine agreed in confessing that they owed to demons their power of penetrating into houses, as I have said above, and of anointing all the limbs of their victims so that they should not awake, and holding their mouths firmly open so that the poison should not be spilled, and finally pouring the poison down their throats by the light of a lamp burning with a sulphurous flame.

☆

CHAPTER II

Witches use Human Corpses for the Murder of Men.

Argument.

IN our days it is the custom of witches to dig up human corpses to use them for the murderous slaughter of men, especially the bodies of those who have been punished by death or hanged. For not only from such horrid material do they renew their evil spells, but also from the actual appliances used at executions, such as the rope, the chains, the stake, and the iron tools. Indeed it is the popular belief that there is some magic power and virtue inherent in such objects.

Others cook the whole body to dry

ashes, and mix it with certain other matter into a solid lump. Giovanni Battista Porta mentions that this was wont to be done in his day, and Pliny (*Historia Naturalis*, XXVIII, 7) * also

speaks of it. In our own time Remy tells of many who have been tried and executed for such practices in German Lorraine.

☆

Examples.

At Douzy on the 1st October, 1586, Anna Ruffa confessed that she helped a witch named Lolla to dig up in this way a corpse which had recently been buried, and from its burned ashes they compounded a potion that they afterwards used for killing those whom they would.

The evidence of the witch Briceia at Vorpach in August 1587 is clear concerning the digging up of an infant's body which had been buried

the day before by its father, Wolf the Smith. It differs from the case we have just quoted only in the fact that they did not burn the body to ashes, but melted it into a solid lump so that they could more easily make an unguent from it. But they reduced the bones to ashes with which they sprinkled the trees of orchards to prevent them from bearing fruit.

At Guermingen in December 1588 Antony Welch reported what had been told him by the wives of Nichel Gross and Beschess, both of whom were well known to him through his companionship with them in witchcraft. They said that not long before they had dug up from the cemetery of Guermingen two corpses which had lately been consigned to the earth by their relatives Bernard and Antony Lerchen, and that they had burned them in a fire and used them for their own vile spells of witchcraft. But first they cut off the right arm

---

* "*Historia Naturalis,*" XXVIII, 7. "*Quae ex mulierum corporibus traduntur, ad portentorum miracula accedunt, ut sileamus diuisos membratim in scelera abortiuos, mensium piacula, quaeque alia non obstetrices modo uerum etiam ipsae meretrices prodidere ... Cinere eo quidem, si in testa sint cremati, uel cum spuma argenti scabritias oculorum ac prurigines emendari: item uerrucas, et infantium ulcera cum melle.*"

together with the shoulder and the ribs pertaining to it, which they required for the devilish light that we have mentioned above: for if they wished to poison anyone by night they set light to the fingers at the end of the limb, which burned with a blue sulphurous flame until they had completed their work; and when the flame was extinguished the fingers remained whole and unwasted, as if they had never been burned. And this happened in the same manner just as often as they wished.

Johann Müller of Welferdingen had a child but one year old whom he loved very dearly. Agatina of Pittelingen and Maietta of Hoheneck stole this child from its cradle and placed it on a burning pyre which they had prepared for that purpose on a

steep hill called "*La Grise*," and carefully collected its calcined ashes. These they mixed with dew, shaken from the ears of corn and the heads of grasses, into a mass that could be easily crumbled, and with this they dusted the vines and crops and trees, causing their flowers to fade and preventing them from bearing fruit.

leaves and stalks and roots of plants; from animals, fishes, venomous reptiles, stones and metals; sometimes these are reduced to . powder and sometimes to an ointment. It must also be known that witches administer such poisons either by causing them to be swallowed, or by external application. In the first instance they usually mix some poisonous powder with the food or drink: in the second they bewitch their victim, whether man or woman, while he is sleeping by anointing him with their lotions, waters, oils, and unguents which contain many and various poisons. They anoint the thighs, or belly, or head, throat, breast, ribs, or some other part of the body of the person to be bewitched, who being asleep feels nothing; but such is the potency of that unguent that, as it is slowly absorbed by the heat of the sleeper's body, it enters his flesh and penetrates to his vitals, causing him the greatest bodily pain, as Spina has said. They have also a third method of administering poison, namely, by inhalation: and this is the worst of all kinds of poison, for by reason of its tenuity it is readily drawn in through the mouth and so quickly reaches the heart.

☆

CHAPTER III

Of Witches' Poisons.

Argument.

THE poisons used by witches are compounded and mixed from many sorts of poisons, such as the

☆

Examples.

Villamont in his *Voyages*, I, 33, tells of a witch at Venice who was the most villainous of all. He used to buy the souls of those condemned to the galleys, promising them freedom from their earthly punishment of slavery: he used to pay ten pieces of gold for their souls, which they sold with a duly engrossed deed written with blood, making them over to a demon and the witch. Soon after this, lest they should retract, he used to kill them by suddenly touching them with some poison, saying that he had been charged with carrying out the sentence which had been passed upon them. Who ever heard tell of such a thing?

Sprenger relates the history of two midwives who were burned, one in the Diocese of Basle and one in that of Strasburg. One of them had killed forty, and the other a countless number of newly born children, by secretly thrusting great needles into their heads.

According to Xiphilinus and Dio Cassius in the time of Domitian there were arrested many who used to prick whom they would with poisoned needles, so that numbers died without feeling any pain. This was also practised in the time of the Emperor Commodus.

Johann Nider tells that in the territory of Berne certain witches of both sexes killed and ate their own children; and that others did the same in the district of Lausanne.

A certain lawyer of Frankfort, says Gödelmann, de Lamiis, I, 7, narrated a few years ago that a Count of Higher Germany gave to the fire eight witches who had murdered a hundred and forty infants. In the year 1553 there were captured at Berlin two women witches who tried to cause a frost to destroy the fruit: these women secretly kidnapped the child of a women who was their neighbour, and cut it up and cooked it; but by Divine will it happened that the mother, seeking her child, came upon them and saw the pot with the limbs of her child thrust in it. The women were therefore taken and examined under torture, and said that if that cooking had gone forward a great frost would have fol-

lowed, so that all the fruit would have been lost.

About the year of Our Lord 1536 at Saluzzo * some forty men, one of whom was a hangman, and as many women, swore together that, since the plague which had been raging was now abating, they would make an unguent which would cause death when placed on the cornices of the doors. They also made a powder which they secretly sprinkled over persons' clothes. This evil was for some time unsuspected, and many died; but when they had killed the brother and the only son of a certain citizen named Neri, and it was noticed that hardly any but the masters of houses or their sons died; and when at the same time they became aware of an Hermaphrodite which went creeping into the houses, and that they whose house it entered generally died, the plot was at last exposed, and all the conspirators were put to death with the most exquisite torture. They confessed moreover that they had planned to anoint the thresholds during the festival of a Saint much honoured in that district, and so kill all the citizens; and for that purpose they had prepared more than twenty vessels of ointment. Others attempted the same thing at Geneva, and paid the penalty.

☆

CHAPTER IV

Of Tying the Points.

Argument.

I FIND that learned men have given seven immediate causes of this impotence. The first is when one

---

* "At Saluzzo." This is from Girolamo Cardano, 1501–1570, the famous Italian physician, mathematician, and philosopher. "De rerum uarietate libri XVII," lib. XV, c. 80. I have used the Basle edition, "per. H. Petri," 1557.

of a married couple is made hateful to the other, or both hateful to each other, by means of calumny or suspicion, or by the affliction of some disease, as Medea is said to have injected a poison which made all the women of Lemnos smell badly in their breath, and so caused their husbands to neglect them.

The second is some bodily hindrance to their coming together. By this means a husband and wife are either kept apart in different places; or, when they try to approach each other, a phantasm or some such thing is interposed between them, as will be seen in the example.

The third is when the vital spirit is hindered from flowing to the genital organ, and so the emission of semen is prevented. This has been well expounded by John Mayor.*

The fourth is when the fertile semen is dried up and taken away.

The fifth is when the man's penis becomes flabby whenever he wishes to perform the conjugal act.

The sixth is the application of certain natural drugs which in some way deprive a woman of the power to conceive. These are the more common causes mentioned by learned Doctors.

The seventh is rarer, namely, the closing up or narrowing of the female genitals; or the retraction, hiding or actual removal of the male genitals. Sprenger (II, q. 1, cap. 7) and Remy (II, 5) tell various stories of such a calamity to the male. This kind of witchcraft is of two sorts, one temporary and the other permanent. It is called permanent when it lasts up to death and cannot be removed by any natural medicine or other lawful means. It is temporary when it is only to last for a certain time.

☆

Examples.

Vincent of Beauvais† tells the following. At Rome in the time of the Emperor Henry III there was a certain noble and rich young man who had lately married a wife and invited his friends to a sumptuous wedding feast, and they went out after dinner into the fields to play at ball. The bridegroom as leader of the game asked for the ball, and lest his betrothal ring should fall off he put it on the finger of a bronze statue of Venus which was close by, and all

---

* *"John Mayor." Joannes Maior or Haddingtonus Scotus, Scotch philosopher and historian, 1496–1550. For an account of his many literary productions which were all written in Latin see Mackay's "Life of John Mayor" prefixed to Constable's translation of Mayor's "History of Greater Britain," Edinburgh, 1892.*

† *"Vincent of Beauvais." Even the years of the birth and death of this celebrated encyclopaedist are uncertain, but the dates most frequently assigned are 1190 and 1264 respectively. It is thought that he joined the Dominican Order shortly after 1218, and that he passed practically his whole life in his monastery at Beauvais incessantly occupied with his enormous work, of which the general title is "Speculum Maius," containing 80 books divided into 9885 chapters.*

turned to the game. He soon grew tired and stopped playing, and came back to the statue to get his ring; but the statue's finger was bent back to the palm of the hand, and however he tried to recover the ring, he could not bend the finger nor draw off the ring. He went back to his friends, but told them nothing about this. In the dark of night he came back with a servant to the statue, and found the finger stretched out as it had been at first, but without the ring. He kept quiet about his loss and went into the house to his newly married wife; and when he entered the bridal chamber and wished to lie with his wife, he felt himself prevented, and something cloudy and dense rolled between his body and his wife's. He could feel this, but he could not see it. By this obstacle he was prevented from embracing his wife; and he also heard a voice saying: "Live with me, for to-day you have wed me. I am Venus, upon whose finger you placed the ring, which I shall not return." The man (says S. Antoninus, who takes this story from Vincent of Beauvais) was terrified by such a prodigy, and neither did he dare nor was he able to make any answer, but he spent that night without sleep in deep thought. So it continued for a long time, that whenever he wished to have intercourse with his wife he felt and heard the same thing. In other respects he was healthy, ruled his house well, and was diligent in his military service. At last, driven by his wife's complaints, he took the matter to his parents and they, after due consideration, made it known to a certain suburban priest named Palumbus, who was a necromancer and a master of spells. This man, in return for many fair promises, wrote a letter and gave it to the young man, saying: "Go at such an hour of the night to the cross-road where four ways meet, and stand there in silent thought. There will go by you the figures of men and women of all ages and conditions, some on horseback

and some afoot, some rejoicing and some mourning; but whatever you hear, you must not speak. Following that company will come one of greater stature and bulk sitting on a car, and to him you must silently give the letter to read; and he will at once do what you desire." The young man did all this exactly as he had been directed, and he saw there among the rest a woman clothed like a harlot riding upon a mule with her hair flowing loose over her shoulders and bound with a golden fillet in front, carrying in her hand a golden rod with which she drove the mule, and appearing almost naked because of the thinness of her garment, and making lascivious gestures. Last came the Lord of the whole rout, bending terrible eyes upon the young man from a superb chariot made of emeralds and pearls, and asked him why he was there. He answered nothing, but held out the letter to him. The demon recognised the seal and, not daring to despise it, read what was written, and thereupon raised his arms to heaven and said: "Almighty God, how long wilt Thou suffer the iniquities of the priest Palumbus?" He at once sent his servants from his side to wrest the ring from Venus, who after many subterfuges at last yielded it with reluctance. So the young man, having obtained what he sought, at last consummated his long-wished love. But when Palumbus heard of the demon's cry to God about him, he understood that his days were numbered; therefore he himself cut off all his limbs and died in miserable pain, having confessed to unheard of crimes in the presence of the Roman people.

Gotschalcus Hollen,* the Augustinian Eremite, writes as follows (*Prae-*

---

* "*Gotschalcus Hollen the Augustinian.*" I have used two editions of the "*Praeceptorium*" of this Eremite theologian; *Preceptoriū nouum, Cologne, folio, 1481;* and "*Preceptorium gotscalci ordinis heremitarum sancti Augustini,*" *Cologne, folio, 1489.*

ceptorium, fol. 20, litt. A). I know a woman who wished to cause a divorce between a man and a woman who loved each other, and for this she was to receive payment. She wrote upon some cards two strange characters, together with other devout words, and gave them these cards to wear; yet they did not quarrel. Then she wrote the same words on a cheese which she gave them to eat; and afterwards took a black chicken which she cut in half, and offered one half to the devil with certain sacrificial rites, and gave the other half to the man and woman to eat. After this there arose the greatest hatred between them, so that they could not bear to look at each other. And how did this happen, unless it were a sacrificial offering to the devil? So writes Hollen.

Giovanni Battista Codronchi (*De morbis maleficiis*, XIII, 8) relates that there was in the town of Sepino, in the Kingdom of Naples, a man named Jacopo whose wife so detested him that, from the very first day of their marriage, they had been so far from being able to consummate the wedding that they could not even live together; and if ever Jacopo tried to approach his wife, she was filled with such fury and rage that she would rather throw herself from the window than submit to him. This was told to a certain religious man to whom they had given hospitality; and he found it difficult to believe the story, and therefore, in order to prove it, asked that the woman should be approached there and then. The husband accordingly hid himself within the house, lest his wife, knowing him to be present, should refuse to come in. The woman came, and being asked the reason for her hatred of her husband began to bemoan her evil fate and said that she could give no reason at all; but she declared that when her husband was absent she was consumed with such a longing and love for him as she could not express in words; but when she went near him to speak to him and

look at him, there at once appeared in her imagination such deformed, ugly and horrible monsters in the likeness of her husband that she would rather die than endure him; and that her whole soul and all her strength and part of her life seemed to be drawn into her husband as an evil offering to her own ruin: but when he was again absent she again burned with the same love. The good priest wished to prove the truth of the woman's words and told the women who were with her to bind her by her arms and legs with a strong rope to the bed in the form of a cross; and he told the husband to put off all repugnance and quickly have to do with her. For the priest suspected that the woman might be pretending to be affected in that way so that she might conceal some deformity. The wife, in her desire for her husband, let herself be bound and asked that her husband should be admitted to her: but when he came in, never was seen such terrible fury, no wild beast was ever so fierce or so filled with madness and rage as that woman; for she foamed at the mouth and gnashed her teeth and rolled her eyes, whilst her whole body seemed to be shaken and possessed with demons. The women who were present said that when they touched her belly which was twisting under the ropes, it appeared to be crammed full, and all her skin was covered with weals as if she had been beaten. There was no end to this raging until the husband, tired out with struggling and moved with pity for her, went away.

The same author says as follows. In the town S. Gimignano in Etruria a young man so desperately fell in love with a witch that he left his beautiful and faithful wife as well as his children and, forgetting them, lived with his mistress until his wife, persuaded that his conduct was due to witchcraft, secretly searched for the charm which had caused it, and found in a jar under her bed a toad with its eyes stitched up. This she at once took away, opened its eyes, and afterwards burned; and immediately her husband, as if he were awaking from sleep, remembered his family and forthwith came back to his wife and children.

☆

CHAPTER V

Of Incendiary Witchcraft.

Argument.

WITCHES, that brood of hellish vipers, do not only by their devilish work inflame souls, but set fire to bodies, houses, and whole towns; wherefore they are manifestly fuel for the eternal fire.

☆

Examples.

Remy (II, 13) tells that at Montlhéry a certain witch called Black Jeanne Armacuriana quarrelled with one Françoise Huyna and, when she could not get what she wanted, was consumed with a desire for vengeance. She was then given by the demon a piece of linen in which were wrapped some small objects like cut straws, and was told to hide it in Huyna's house and go away quickly; for the house would soon afterwards catch fire suddenly and be burned with all the furniture. She therefore rolled the piece of linen into a ball and offered it for sale as a head ornament to Huyna, who was then busy in the bakehouse. But when she said that she did not need it, as her servants could provide all that she required, Jeanne never-

theless threw it into the bakehouse saying that if she had no use for it she could return it to her; and she had hardly left the house before the bakehouse where that ball was caught on fire, and then the whole house began to blaze so fiercely that it was burned down before any help could be brought. The truth of this matter was established beyond doubt by the separate accounts of the two women and by the event itself.

A less subtle, though equally pernicious work of incendiarism is testified to by Conrad Wolffhart,* who writes as follows in his *Prodigiorum ac Ostentorum Chronicon.* There is a town in Switzerland called Schiltach which, on 13 April, 1533, was suddenly and completely burned; and, according to the report of the townsmen to the Magistrate at Freiburg, the cause of the fire was popularly supposed to be as follows. A demon whistled a signal from a certain part of the house, and the master went up thinking it was a thief, but found no one. But the signal was heard again from the upper dining-room; and the master ran up to find the thief, but again saw no one, yet the whistling was heard from the top

---

* *"Conrad Wolffhart." This famous German scholar was born at Rouffach in Alsace, 1518. He professed Grammar for many years at the University of Basle where he died 1561. In his writings he often adopted a Hellenised name, Lycosthenes, under which he is not infrequently known. I have used the Basle edition, folio, 1557, of the "Prodigiorum Chronicon."*

of the smoke-chamber. Then it came into the master's mind that it was something devilish; and he bade his household keep their wits while two priests were fetched. They began their exorcism, and he answered that he was a demon. Asked what he was doing there, he said that he wished to ruin the town. When they threatened to offer Masses, he said that he cared nothing for their menaces. And soon afterwards he seized a woman with whom he had had intercourse for fourteen years (although she had confessed every year and had received the Eucharist), and bore her up in the air and set her on the top of the smoke-chamber, and gave her a jar which he told her to upset: and when she had done so the whole town was burned down within an hour.

A few years ago some incendiaries were infesting the region of the Rhine. They used to place in other persons' houses a sword or spear or knife, or some other object entirely free from heat or fire; and after a few hours flames would burst from the house and consume it as if it had been made of straw.

☆

CHAPTER VI

The Devil Wishes to Perpetuate the Race of Witches.

Argument.

THE infection of witchcraft is often spread through a sort of contagion to children by their fallen parents, when these study to find favour with their Cacodemons by so doing. For the greed of Satan was ever infinite and insatiable: thus, when once he has gotten a foothold in any family, he is never known to relinquish it except with the greatest difficulty. And it is one among many sure and certain proofs against those who are charged and accused of witchcraft, if it be found that their parents before them were guilty of this crime. There are daily examples of this inherited taint in children, for the devil is always busy to increase the number of his own. And there can be no more fruitful means of attaining this end than by urging and compelling those who are already in his power to corrupt their children.

☆

Examples.

Nicole Morelle confessed at Barr in January 1587 that her father had taken her to the demon's assemblies at night before she had reached puberty. There was another who, although she was not yet of marriageable age, was taken by her mother far into a dense wood, being promised that she would meet a handsome young man, whom she might easily take to husband: and it happened as her mother had said; but as soon as she was embraced by him she felt herself deceived, for she seemed to be embraced by some statue of marble, he lay so stiff and heavy upon her.

At Gebweiler, in July 1568, Henry and Catharine gave their son Hanzel a Succuba for wife. As far as he could see at his first approach, her hair and garments were black, and her feet deformed like horse's hooves; yet he did not on that account repulse her, but immediately lay with her in greedy pleasure, having abjured all holy thoughts: but it was as if he had entered an icy cavern, and he went away ashamed and sorrowful without accomplishing his purpose.

At Girancourt, in October 1586, Domenico Petronius said that before he was twelve years old he had been taken by his mother to those abominable meetings that he might marry a wife. For marriages are often performed at the Sabbat. Colette the Fisher's wife and many others have confessed this. And Bertrande the Barber's wife, and Synchen May reported that they had witnessed a wedding of this sort, when they happened to be present there one night, and that in place of the customary wedding gifts the couple were only required to stoop down and blow upon each other's fundaments.

Near Ribeauville Domenique Falvet was picking rushes with her mother for binding up the vines, and they lay on the ground to rest. After they had talked a little, the mother began to warn her not to be frightened if by any chance she saw something strange, for there would be no danger to her in it. When she had said this, there suddenly appeared something in human form which looked like a shoe-maker, for he was girt round the middle with twine rubbed with pitch. The girl was made to swear an oath to this man, and he marked her on the brow with his nail as a sign of her new allegiance, and then he lay with her in the sight of her mother. The mother in her turn offered herself to be defiled by him in her daughter's presence. Then they joined hands and danced round in a ring for a while; after which he gave them what seemed to be money (but afterwards it crumbled to dust), and disappeared into air and returned to his own place.

At Jouy-aux-Arches, in 1581, Françoise Hacquart, in order to free herself from persecution by a demon, delivered up to the demon her daughter Jeanne, who was not yet seven years old. This was the chief of her many confessions at her trial. Now since there was evidence that the child had consented to this thing, and this was largely substantiated by her own clear statements concerning the witches' Sabbats at which she had been present, it began to be commonly thought that she should be held equally guilty with her mother. But she seemed too young to be tried as a criminal, and no evil act of witchcraft could be proved against her; so a lady of that place took her into her own house to try to wean her from that execrable way of life with every holy means in her power. After her mother had been put to death, therefore, she was kept in the matron's house for some time and urged to lead a good life, and they all thought that she had verily shaken off the demon's yoke and won back her former liberty. But alas! one night as she was sleeping as usual with the serving maids, the demon seized her and lifted her up as if he were about to carry her away with him: and it is believed that he would have done so, if the maids had not prevented him by calling often upon the Name of Jesus. Thus cheated of his prey, he left her hanging between the boards of the roofing and went away. And this was no hysterical vain report of the servant maids, for it was seen by all the neighbours who ran there upon hearing of it. The girl then fell into a sort of stupor, fasting and keeping silent and awake for eight days and nights together; and that this was not assumed by her through fraud or malice was sufficiently indicated by the fact that, according to Pliny, no one can with safety fast for more than seven days, and if anyone should continue to fast up to the eleventh day it must be confessed to be something preternatural.

Remy says that he has read, in the accounts of such trials, of those who have confessed that they had hidden beneath their nails a poison given them by their parents, and that by this means they had often scratched and killed their companions while playing.

In the same place he writes of a child not yet seven years old named Laurent d'Arsonval, who lived at Barr in 1591, and who clearly proved by his own evidence that he had been taken by his parents to the execrable assemblies of demons, where he was set to turn the spit and tend the flesh that was to be eaten; also the presiding Little Master, who had given him the name of Verd Joli, had more than once given him poison with which he afterwards killed the cattle of those

who did him even the very smallest injury. This was proved by the actual event.

☆

CHAPTER VII

Of the Various Ways by which Witches Vent their Spite upon the Human Race.

Argument.

IT is not to be wondered at that witches are everywhere to be feared*: for although they have not an infinite power of doing ill to whomsoever they wish (see the history of Asmodeus and the seven husbands of Sara in Tobit), yet our sins, when God wills, often make us the victims of their malice. For no one is so upright of life and free from sin but that he is pricked and terrified by the conscience of some misdeed; no one is so attentive and diligent in his religious observances but that sometimes the stress of business will cause him to neglect the customary prayers by which he was daily wont to commend himself to the protection and guardianship of God; no one is so secure as to be free from all fear of injury by the wicked. Our daily experience is proof enough that most of us are exposed to no light danger in this direction. For witches do not attack with their poisons only those who are off their guard or asleep at night; but they spread their snares for the vigilant in such a way that they can scarcely be escaped by human counsel or foresight. There are many stories upon this subject in other parts of our book which should abundantly satisfy the reader; but as we are approaching the subject from a fresh angle, and the stories are not altogether without pleasant profit and

---

* *"Witches . . . to be feared." King James in his "Dæmonologie," Book II, v, says that there are three kinds of folk whom God will* permit to be troubled or tempted by witches: *"the wicked for their horrible sinnes, to punish them in the like measure; The godlie that are sleeping in anie great sinnes or infirmities and weakenesse in faith, to waken them up the faster by such an uncouth forme: and even some of the best, that their patience may bee tryed before the world, as Iob was."*

interest, it may not prove wearisome if they are here set out at some length.

☆

Examples.

An old man who was porter at the Château de Bassompierre had married a young wife, but continued to live in adultery with another woman who had been his mistress before his marriage. His wife grieved that a harlot, who could not be compared with her for youth or beauty, should be preferred to her; and, as the custom is, went and told her trouble to a neighbouring woman and asked her advice as to what she should do. Her neighbour, whose name was Laire, told her to be of good heart, for she had ready a remedy for her misfortune; and she picked a herb from her garden and gave it to her, saying that if she made a broth from it and gave it to her husband he would entirely lose his love for the other woman. She gave him the broth the next day at supper; and he then first experienced a heaviness in his head and afterwards sank into a deep sleep. When he awoke from this on the next day he discovered, not without shame, that his virility had been taken from him; yet he told his wife of his misfortune, since he could not hope to conceal it from her for long. His wife, seeing that her imprudence and folly had betrayed her, and that through begrudging another woman a part she had herself lost the whole, told her husband everything that had been done, and asked forgiveness for her fault, saying that it was all due to the great love which she had for him. The husband easily forgave her, recognising that the misfortune had been brought about by his own lasciviousness and lust; and he told the whole matter to his patron, the Lord of the place, François de Bassompierre. This noble man thought it his duty both to attend to the recovery and health of a member of his household, and worthily to punish the witch for so foul a crime; so he summoned the woman and compelled her by his threats to restore to the man that which had to all seeming been lost: and this she did by giving him another herb to eat. She was therefore guilty by her own showing, and was seized and soon afterwards burned to death. It is very clear from this that there is no real actuality in such matters, but that it is all a mockery and a delusion of the eyes. This is taken from Remy, II, 5.

Again, Barbellina Rayel had conceived a vindictive hatred for Jean Louis. As he was crossing a river on his way to a mill house, with the help of a demon she shook a big sack of wheat from his wagon, and then threw over his horses some powder which had been drugged by her Little Master, by which means she killed two of them at once, and the rest were ill for many days. Next, changing herself into a cat, she entered his house by night in that form, and with the same powder killed his two-year-old son. Finally she placed a poisoned pear in his way as he was going to Gerbéviller, as if it had fallen from a traveller's bag; he imprudently took it up and ate it, and at once became so ill that he could hardly crawl home for pain. The demon had foretold all these things just as they happened, and had even himself advised the placing of the pear by the roadside.

Lolla Gelea aroused against herself the hatred and malice of Catharine of Metz, who kept trying to find a means of avenging herself but could not see how to do it without attracting suspicion towards herself, for she knew that the other was on the alert against her wiles. But a demon showed her a safe way, and told her to come the next day and fill a pitcher with burning cinders from the metal furnaces (which at Dieuze are the most famous in all Lorraine), and to go to Lolla and upset the pitcher and breathe in her face: for he said that Lolla would give birth before her time with the greatest pain. And it was as he had said; for no sooner had Catharine overset the pitcher and breathed uncleanly upon her, than Lolla was at once seized with violent parturient pains, and could hardly get into her house in time.

At Conz in July 1582 Jeanne Gransaint went alone to the window late one night thinking how she could be revenged on the comely Barbara, who had insulted her. At once there appeared a demon in the form of a cat, who told her to pound a slug's head to powder and sprinkle it over Barbara's clothes. She followed this advice as closely as she could, and soon found an occasion to make use of it; for she found Barbara sleeping in a mean stable on some straw in the cattles' stall. She therefore blew the powder over her and the cattle that were with her, and they all at once died.

She used the same powder with less harmful effect against the daughter of Antoine Lebossa: for though she thoroughly sprinkled her limbs with it, she only suffered a slight sickness and recovered her health after a few days.

Here it is to be noted that the drugs which they use in this way possess no inherent power either to kill or to heal, neither can the same substance possess such contradictory qualities. But all this is contrived and effected by the power of the demon, who is satisfied if the witch does but lend her hand to the work so that she may be a conscious participator in the crime.

Alexia Belheure used continuously to quarrel with her husband, as is usually the case when there are poverty and want in the home: and her hatred of him grew to such an extent that it was only the difficulty of injuring him, not the will to do so, that restrained her. But a demon agreed to do the work for her, if he should consider her request worthy of execution by him; and when she had extravagantly prayed him to do so, he undertook the business. It chanced that on Christmas Eve the unhappy husband had gone to a neighbouring town to buy household necessities for that Holy Season, and was returning home late at night. The demon violently seized him on his way and beat him and left him half dead in the cave of Donalibaria (as it was called), and flying to his good wife told her what he had done. On hearing this she hastened out to all appearance as if she were anxious about her husband's return, but really that she might see with her own eyes the miserable condition of him against whom she had so long cherished evil thoughts. When she found him lying and bewailing his unhappy lot, she said: "Alas! husband, I was coming to meet you, knowing that you were returning through the country so late at night; but what does this mean? Why do I find you lying thus on the ground and groaning?" When he had told her what she already knew, she raised him up and, supporting him as well as she could with her shoulder, brought him home, where he died on the same night from the intolerable pain of his wounds. The next day she roused the neighbours and showed them the naked body all black and blue with bruises, and said that he had fallen into the hands of brigands the day before and had crawled home in that condition gasping for breath. And they all easily believed her, for she was not young or beautiful enough to be suspected of having entertained adulterers.

Odille Boncœur of Harécourt said that it was the custom of witches, when they feared to be caught in the act, to sprinkle a poison powder in the way by which they thought those persons would go against whom they plotted some calamity. And this agrees with the confession of Rose Gerardine in 1588, that she infected her partner Stephane Obert with a mortal disease by scattering such a powder on his threshold before the dawn.

Jacobus Agathius, again, said that his demon had taught him that this was by far the easiest way to destroy the wife of Hilary à Banno.

Isabella Pardea and Martha Mergelatia affirmed that they had never used this means against anyone without success, especially if they were bidden to do it by their demons.

Francesca Perina took, as she was passing, some pears which had fallen from a tree belonging to a neighbour called Riberianus, and was severely beaten for it. As she was enraged by this and seeking to be revenged by any means, it was not long before a demon showed her a way to obtain her wish, and gave her some herbs which she must scatter on the path by which Riberianus used to go to his work in the morning. This she did; and he, not suspecting anything, walked over the herbs and at once became ill, so that he soon died in great agony.

Barbeline Rayel used similar means against François le Violon, near whom she had lately come to live. She poisoned with a powder the gate through which his cattle used to go to water, and on the next day three of his mares were found in the stable dead on their backs.

In 1586 Claude Morel spread such a powder before the doors of his kinsman by marriage, Wolfgang Hadowille; and when his daughter happened to go that way she at once fell ill and soon afterwards died miserably: for when she passed by that way she broke her leg.

Catharina of Metz was angry because she had been refused by a baker from whom she wished to obtain bread on credit, and asked the help of her demon to pay him out. The demon, as is their nature, came at once ready and eager for any chance of doing ill, and gave her some herbs wrapped in a paper, telling her to scatter them in the place most often used by the baker and his family. She at once took them and spread them in the doorway by which they had to go to the village:

and the baker, and after him his wife and children, walked over them and were all afflicted with the same sickness. And they did not recover until the witch, moved by pity, obtained from the demon another herb to restore them. This she secretly hid in their beds, as she had been told to do, and they were soon all restored from sickness to their former health.

Driget and Odille considered that they were being taxed too heavily by the officials of the village where they lived, and wished to exact some heavy vengeance for that grievance. A demon did not fail to appear and show them how to set to work; for he told them to scatter a poison broadcast in that place where the village cattle most often went to pasture, and that they might readily prepare the poison by pounding a sufficient quantity of grubs and worms. This they did, and within a few days there died of the cattle of that village a hundred and fifty according to Driget, and a hundred and sixty according to Odille. For they were questioned separately but agreed in everything except the number.

Jeanne Foirelle gave a drugged cake to the whole of a neighbour's family to eat, but that one only died whom she had intended to kill.

Huberte of Bussière had been unfairly treated by one of the townsmen, and it seemed to her that she would be amply revenged if she killed by poison the five cows by which he supported himself and his family. But there was a danger of her being caught in the act if she did the business with her own hand by touching each cow with a poisoned wand as was her method in her other poisonings. So her Little Master relieved her of that fear and told her to sprinkle before dawn a poison powder which he gave her about the place where the cattle were usually driven. But she hesitated, fearing lest the poison should affect the whole of the cattle, since she wished to harm none except that of the man against whom she wished to be revenged. The demon then promised that all the harm should be confined to those five cows; and so it proved in the event. For of all the cattle, only those five died or even became sick.

Jeanne Armacuriana had stolen three bundles of faggots from a neighbour's land, and had hidden them in the garden of Alexée Cabuse, which lay most conveniently to conceal her theft; but she did not manage secretly enough to prevent Cabuse, who was at work in a remote part of her garden, from seeing her. After the way of women, she told her neighbours what she had seen; and in consequence, Jeanne was not only ill spoken of, but was even in some danger: for in Lorraine the punishment for the theft of even a cabbage from another's garden is the lash. Her anger and indignation against Cabuse was beyond description, and she kept looking for any means of revenging herself satisfactorily for so great an injury. While she was pondering deeply on this subject, the demon to which she had given herself came to her and twitted her with cowardice in that she had allowed herself to suffer such mental torture for so long when she had so often proved that he was ready to procure her the occasion for vengeance; and he undertook that it would not be long before the other woman should be punished for her evil tongue, if she would allow him to work. Jeanne said that such was her wish, and the demon at once flew to Alexée, who was then tending her cattle in the meadows and was trying to drive back to the herd one which had strayed into a neighbour's corn-field. He caught her up in a whirlwind and dashed her to the ground so violently that her leg was broken, and she was so bewildered by this happening that she had to be carried home half dead.

The following example concerns one Bernard Bloguat. He was driving his cart to Strasburg where he had some business, when he was seen by Jeanne de Bans as she was working in the fields. She then called to mind certain injuries he had done her, which had not been avenged, and by her curses and execrations brought disaster upon him. For she had hardly begun to curse before he fell so violently from the cart in which he was sitting that he was instantly killed. Yet his body was quite uninjured, with no wound or bruise or discoloration or any swelling or dislocation or hurt of any sort, so that it is to be believed that his life and soul were cut off in a moment by a demon. And lest any should think that such a belief was based solely upon that witch's confession, let him know that it was commonly reported that an ostler named Johann, who had lent Bloguat his cart for that journey, was privy to the whole affair. Moreover, the strange and unheard-of manner of his death is itself an argument that it was due to some preternatural power of evil.

At Nancy a certain witch commonly known as Asinaria used to go from door to door begging, and her age and infirmity so aroused the pity of the rich that she received every day enough to live in comfort. One day she was standing as usual begging in front of the Governor's door, when his eldest son, coming out in an unlucky moment, told her to go away and to ask him another time, because it was not convenient just then for his servants to give her money. She became indignant at this treatment and, as witches are always ready to do, cursed him: and immediately afterwards, as if he had pierced his foot with a flint stone, he fell and hurt himself so that he had to be carried back into the house at once. There he told his servants how it had all happened, adding that it was not the result of any imprudent or careless step on his part, but that he had been struck from behind by some higher power and that there was no doubt he would have broken his leg if God had not helped him as he fell; for he said that he had fortified himself with the sign of the Cross at his prayers that morning. Yet after this the witch did not rest: for when her familiar had indignantly upbraided her because he had been foiled in his attempt, she started to beg and beseech him all the more to proceed by any means with the destruction of the young man, a task which would be easy for him if ever the youth came out without the protection of his morning prayers and the sign of the Cross; for the demon himself admitted that these were the causes of his previous failure. Not many days later it happened that the young man put his arm out of the window of an upper room to take some young sparrows from the nest on the wall, when he was lifted up from behind and thrown through the window with such force that he was thought to be dead. But after a few hours he regained consciousness and, looking at his father who was abandoning himself to tears and lamentation, said: "Father, do not think that this evil has happened to me through my own fault, for indeed I am very far from being to blame. Something came behind me and thrust me through the window in spite of my struggles, and I was overpowered by some stronger power and forced out." And indeed they had found near him as he lay prone a piece of wood from a pile which had been stored for household use in the top attic. Constantly maintaining the same story, the youth died after a few days. Not many days later, Asinaria was thrown into prison by reason of the evidence of other witches against her and because of the daily increasing suspicion that she was a witch, and as a result of her careful examination and the evidence taken by Remy, who tells this story. And at last she was induced by persuasion, without any recourse to torture, to make a full confession of all her crimes; and among them was that which had been so often and confidently affirmed by the boy. For she said that as soon as he had accomplished the crime the demon had flown to her in a neighbouring market-place and told her everything that had been done: and she continued to maintain this until she suffered punishment by death in the fire.

There were some peasants, one of whom was lopping off the over luxuriant boughs of a tree, another throwing fruit from a loft down to the yard ready to be pressed, and another loading and arranging straw at the top of a wagon. None of them were acting rashly in any way; but they were taken and hurled to the ground with such force that they had to be carried away half dead. Yet there was no sign of any person or thing to have caused their fall.

There was a pear tree in a remote part of a wood, from which Jean Rotier had long planned to gather the fruit; and he did not think that the tree, being in such a hidden and out-of-the-way place, would be noticed by anyone, and his tit-bit be taken from his mouth. Yet the tree was discovered by Desiré Salet, a man of his own class, who came there first and picked the pears. He was caught in the act, and it was not long before Rotier made him suffer for robbing him of his booty; for this class of men bears such injuries hardly and is easily incited to vengeance. He accordingly cursed Desiré, as he was in the habit of cursing others, and he was suddenly caught in a whirlwind and hurled to the ground, and so hurt in one leg that he could not move until some swineherds ran at his cry and helped him home. And he was not yet healed when Rotier made a full confession of this matter.

The following story of Apra Hoselotte is similar. She had a son in the service of Jean Halecourt, whom his master had cruelly punished for a theft of which he, more than the rest of the servants, was suspected. This grieved the mother and made her wish for revenge, the chance for which she eagerly grasped. When the master was bringing his horses home from pasture and was carelessly riding upon one of them, she and her familiar came invisibly and so bore upon the horse's neck that the rider fell to the ground and broke his leg: and he was still lame and crippled by that fall when he appeared as a witness against that witch.

Claude Fellet of Maizières was always quarrelling with a neighbouring woman, as it so often appears that women of the same class have only to live near each other to find occasion to quarrel and dispute; and she had pondered for a long time how she could privily bring some harm upon her neighbour. For it had to be done very secretly, since all the inhabitants would at once accuse Fellet if any grave accident befell the other woman. She consulted a demon about it, and he told her to go out into the fields and work as usual, while he would play his part in the town; for if she stayed at home she would be suspected. The neighbour's house was shut up and the doors were bolted, when her son, whom the woman had left alone in the house when she went out, was heard crying pitifully. All who heard it ran up and broke open the door to see what had happened to the child to make it cry so; and they found it covered and surrounded with hot coals. They quickly threw these aside and took him from his cradle to save him if possible, but he was already breathing his last and died in their arms. A rumour then began to be spread that Fellet had certainly been at the bottom of this, for it was bruited that she had punished others before in the same way. Accordingly she was brought to trial on account of this and other crimes of which she had long been suspected, and she was at last induced to confess freely that she had wrought this mischief, and to tell everything that the demon had done at her request, particularly the matter of the burning coals which he had taken with a stick from the hearth near by, and had thrown them over the poor child's cradle.

A peasant named Mauletic was going early one morning to a castle by the Moselle to negotiate a profitable deal in milk, since that was his trade, when a violent whirlwind took all his breath away, though everywhere else it was dead calm, so that he lay for a long time between life and death. This misfortune came to him through the contrivance of François Fellet with the help of a demon; for this man had long nursed a rancorous desire for vengeance upon Mauletic for certain injuries, as he himself afterwards acknowledged freely, being induced by penitence to confess his sin.

Colette the Fisher's wife, without coming near her fellow townsman Claude Jaquimine, made him blind in one eye by employing a demon to do that work, as she herself freely confessed when she was tried for witchcraft. And the greater faith was given to her story because the same Jaquimine afterwards said that his eye had been wounded as if pierced by a forcefully driven branch of a tree, although there were no trees for a considerable distance in any direction. Therefore it was suspected that he had received that injury through some black art.

Jacobeta Weher testified as follows: "For many reasons I hated a certain peasant who lodged in the same house as I; but I could not see how to harm him without incurring suspicion, for he kept a keen and careful watch upon me. But at last I found a way; for when he was busy over some work in a thicket, a demon at my request drove a thorn so deep into his knee that he was disabled for a whole three months; and he was not cured until I took pity on his prolonged pain and asked the demon to heal him again. A few days after this, as he was cutting wood in the forest, the demon poured a lotion upon the wound and he was immediately healed."

☆

CHAPTER VIII

Of the Different Diseases Brought by Demons.

Argument.

AVICENNA and Galen and Hippocrates deny that it is possible for any diseases to be brought upon man by demons; and their view is followed by Pietro Pomponazzi * and Levin Lemne,† not because they did not believe that the demons, which they acknowledged to be evil, wished to cause disease, but because they held that every disease is due to natural causes. But that is no good argument: for is it not possible for sicknesses to spring from natural causes, and at the same time possible for demons to be the instigators of such sicknesses? The contrary

opinion is held by Codronchi, Andrea Cesalpino, Jean Fernel,‡ Franciscus Valesius the Spaniard, and other most learned physicians, together with S. Jerome (on Matt. iii), S. Chrysostom (*Homily* 54, on Matt. xvii), S. Thomas (I, 2, 115, art. 5), and other theologians. The jurists also, especially Burchard § (*Decret.* XIX, *de re magica*), argue excellently on the same side. Grilland (2, 6, to number 13) has often been quoted to the same effect: but I prefer the firmer authority of the Holy Scriptures. Did not the devil afflict Job with loathsome sores from the soles of his feet to the crown of his head? Did not the devil put to an alien use the tongue and ears of him whom S. Matthew calls the Lunatic? Did not a devil afflict Saul with a black humour? The account is quite explicit, for it says that an evil spirit afflicted him, which went away when David played the harp.

Let us now see by what method the demon causes sickness. This has been

---

* "*Pietro Pomponazzi.*" *1492–1525. Philosopher and founder of the Aristotelean-Averroistic School. He taught philosophy at Padua, Ferrara, and Bologna. Among his chief works is the "De naturalium effectuum admirandorum causis, siue de incantationibus (1520)" in which he seeks to prove that in Aristotle's philosophy miracles are not possible. The doctrine was condemned and Pomponazzi did not escape in common report the stigma of heresy.*

† "*Levin Lemne.*" *Or Livin Lemmens, 1505–1568. A Dutch philosopher, born at Zirickzee in Zeeland, where also he died. He practised medicine and acquired no small reputation in his day. His "De Miraculis Occultis Naturae Libri IV" was well esteemed, and was translated into French both by du Pinet (Lyons, 1566) and by Jacques Gohory (Paris, 1567).*

‡ "*Jean Fernel.*" *Born in 1497; "le Galien moderne," physician and master astrologer to Henri II and Diane de Poitiers. He published several works on medicine; "La Pathologie"; "Les VII livres de la physiologie"; and after his death a "Uniuersa Medicina" containing his various tractates and monographs appeared at Frankfort in 1592.*

§ "*Burchard.*" *The famous Bishop of Worms; born shortly after the middle of the tenth century; died 20 August, 1025. His celebrated "Collectarium canonum" or "Decretum" is in twenty books, and was long used as a practical guide for the clergy.*

clearly set forth by Franciscus Valesius,* who says that the demon is the
external cause of sickness when he
comes from without to inhabit a body
and bring diseases to it; and if the
sickness has some material source he
sets in motion its inner causes. Thus
he induces the melancholy sickness by
first disturbing the black bile in the
body and so dispersing a black humour
throughout the brain and the inner
cells of the body: and this black bile he
increases by superinducing other irri-
tations and by preventing the purging
of the humour. He brings epilepsy,
paralysis and such maladies by a stop-
page of the heavier physical fluids, ob-
structing and blocking the ventricle of
the brain and the nerve-roots. He
causes blindness or deafness, bringing
a noxious secretion in the eyes or ears.
Often again he suggests ideas to the
imagination which induce love or
hatred or other mental disturbances.
For the purpose of causing bodily infirmities he distils a spirituous substance from the blood itself, purifies it
of all base matter, and uses it as the
aptest, most efficacious and swiftest
weapon against human life: I say that
from the most potent poisons he ex-
tracts a quintessence with which he
infects the very spirit of life, and (as
Cesalpino well observes, *De Daemonum
Inuestigatione, c.* 16) so establishes his
devil-made disease that human skill is
hardly able to find a remedy, since
the devil's poison is too subtle and
tenuous, too swift and sure in killing,
and reaches to the very marrow of the
bones. But those more common maladies which are caused solely by some
external injury or noxious breath, by
means of certain instruments of witchcraft, unguents, signs, buried charms
and such things, have no natural
power for evil in themselves, but are
merely symbols in response to which
the demon fulfils his pact with a witch.
This was pointed out by the same
Andrea Cesalpino in Chapter 17 of the
work above quoted.

☆

Examples.

A certain honest woman who had
been legally married to one of the
household of the Archduke formally
deposed the following in the presence
of a Notary. In the time of her
maidenhood she had been in the service of one of the citizens, whose wife
became afflicted with grievous pains
in the head; and a woman came who
said she could cure her, and so began
certain incantations and rites. And I
carefully watched (said this woman)
what she did, and saw that, against the
nature of water poured into a vase, she
caused water to rise in its vessel, together with other ceremonies which
there is no need to mention. And considering that the pains in my mistress's
head were not assuaged by these
means, I addressed the witch in some
indignation with these words: "I do
not know what you are doing, but
whatever it is, it is witchcraft, and you
are doing it for your own profit."
Then the witch at once replied: "You
will know in three days whether I am
a witch or not." And so it proved; for
on the third day when I sat down and
took up a spindle, I suddenly felt a
terrible pain in my body. First it was
inside me, so that it seemed that there
was no part of my body in which I
did not feel horrible shooting pains;
then it seemed to me just as if burning
coals were being continually heaped
upon my head; thirdly, from the
crown of my head to the soles of my
feet there was no place large enough
for a pinprick that was not covered
with a rash of white pustules; and so I
remained in these pains, crying out
and wishing only for death, until the
fourth day. At last my mistress's husband told me to go to a certain tavern;

---

* *"Franciscus Valesius." A Spanish Doctor of Physic who flourished towards the end of
the sixteenth century. He won a great reputation for his translations of, and commentaries
upon, the older medical writers.*

and with great difficulty I went, whilst he walked before, until we were in front of the tavern. "See!" he said to me; "there is a loaf of white bread over the tavern door." "I see," said I. Then he said: "Take it down, if you possibly can; for it may do you good." And I, holding on to the door with one hand as much as I could, got hold of the loaf with the other. "Open it" (said my master) " and look carefully at what is inside." Then, when I had broken open the loaf, I found many things inside it, especially some white grains very like the pustules on my body; and I saw also some seeds and herbs such as I could not eat or even look at, with the bones of serpents and other animals. In my astonishment I asked my master what was to be done; and he told me to throw it all into the fire. I did so; and behold! suddenly, not in an hour or even a few minutes, but at the moment when that matter was thrown into the fire, I regained all my former health.

The same author tells in the same place the following story. An honest married woman deposed the following on oath. Behind my house (she said) I have a greenhouse, and my neighbour's garden borders on it. One day I noticed that a passage had been made from my neighbour's garden to my greenhouse, not without some damage being caused; and as I was standing in the door of my greenhouse reckoning to myself and bemoaning both the passage and the damage, my neighbour suddenly came up and asked if I suspected her. But I was frightened because of her bad reputation, and only answered, "The footprints on the grass are a proof of the damage." Then she was indignant because I had not, as she hoped, accused her with actionable words, and went away murmuring; and though I could hear her words, I could not understand them. After a few days I became very ill with pains in the stomach, and the sharpest twinges shooting from my left side to my right,

and conversely, as if two swords or knives were thrust through my breast; whence day and night I disturbed all the neighbours with my cries. And when they came from all sides to console me, it happened that a certain clay-worker, who was engaged in an adulterous intrigue with that witch, my neighbour, coming to visit me, took pity on my illness, and after a few words of comfort went away. But the next day he returned in a hurry, and, after consoling me, added: "I am going to test whether your illness is due to witchcraft, and if I find that it is, I shall restore your health." So he took some molten lead and, while I was lying in bed, poured it into a bowl of water which he placed on my body. And when the lead solidified into a certain image and various shapes, he said: " See! your illness has been caused by witchcraft; and one of the instruments of that witchcraft is hidden under the threshold of your house door. Let us go, then, and remove it, and you will feel better." So my husband and he went to remove the charm; and the clay-worker, taking up the threshold, told my husband to put his hand into the hole which then appeared, and take out whatever he found; and he did so. And first he brought out a waxen image about a palm long, perforated all over, and pierced through the sides with two needles, just in the same way that I felt the stabbing pains from side to side; and then little bags containing all sorts of things, such as grains and seeds and bones. And when all these things were burned, I became better, but not entirely well. For although the shootings and twinges stopped, and I quite regained my appetite for food, yet even now I am by no means fully restored to health. And when we asked her why it was that she had not been completely restored, she answered: There are some other instruments of witchcraft hidden away which I cannot find. And when I asked the man how he knew where the first instruments were hidden, he answered: "I knew this through the love which prompts a friend to tell things to a friend."

A tale surpassing all wonder is told in his *De Naturae diuinis character-ismis*, II, 4 by Cornelius Gemma,* who relates that a fifteen-year-old girl of Louvain named Catarina Gualteri was sometime under his charge in the year 1571. She was given by a kinswoman of her own age something to taste, and when she had eaten it she at once showed extraordinary symptoms of sickness; for Gemma himself saw her every day void so many objects of such a size and nature that he would not have believed if it had been told him by anyone else. In the eighth month of her sickness with a great effort she voided from her back passage a live eel, perfectly formed, as thick as a thumb and six feet long, with scales and eyes and tail and everything belonging to an eel. He tells that, three days before it came out, not only the girl herself but also those near her heard the eel utter a sharp thin cry in her belly; and when it was coming out the girl said that she clearly felt that at the first attempt it drew back its head, and then came out with a rush. They killed and disembowelled the eel, and hung it high out of the reach of the animals; but it suddenly vanished. Meanwhile the girl began to vomit an immense quantity of fluid not unlike wine and of an unpleasant taste; and this continued for more than fourteen days, each day's vomiting weighing twenty-four pounds. Besides this she made water copiously two or three times a day. No tumour or external swelling could be seen in her stomach or anywhere in her body, and the girl

---

* "*Cornelius Gemma.*" *Dutch physician and astrologer, born at Louvain in 1535, the son of Régnier Gemma (Frisius or Frizon), Professor at the University of Louvain. The chief work of Cornelius Gemma, "De Naturae diuinis characterismis . . . libri II," was published at Antwerp in 1575.*

ate and drank very sparingly, hardly taking a cup of wine or beer or other liquor; but her excretion of water was such that in two weeks she could easily fill two water-butts. After this flood of water she began to vomit a vast number of hairs of about a finger's length, some longer and some shorter, like those which fall from old dogs; and the quantity of the hairs grew each day so that she could easily have filled many full-sized balls. All this she vomited with much retching and difficulty. After a few days' interval there followed other vomitings of great balls of hair floating in a purulent sanies, and sometimes of the appearance of the dung of pigeons or geese; and in this pus were found bits of wood and tiny pieces of skin, some of the wood being various-sized pieces of living trees, as if they had been broken off from the trunks; these were of the thickness and breadth of a nail, spongy inside and black with old bark outside. Shortly afterwards her vomiting became as black as coal, so that you would have said that it was ink or the excretion of a cuttle fish, with minute pieces of coal in it; and each day she vomited two or three pounds, nearly always accompanied with more hairs than could be put into a walnut, all white and long and stiff. This continued for three days, and then in one single vomit she threw up two pounds of pure blood, as from an opened vein, unmixed with any other matter. After this blood, the black vomiting returned, as if the fluid had been dyed with pounded antimony, and each day there were five or six pounds of the fluid; and this prodigy continued for seven solid hours. The application of human and divine remedies brought some relief, during which the hairs were still ejected, but they were fewer and gradually became blacker and shorter every day, growing from auburn to dark and so to jet black, and it seemed that the vomiting broke them into minute particles, such was her virulent spitting; though at times it was more like mud. About the middle of September she vomited larger pieces of skin which seemed to be torn from her stomach, and they had the appearance of a thick fleshy membrane, tough and difficult to tear, like the choroid envelope of a foetus, and were marked with a network of veins, and were sometimes as much as half a palm in length. Immediately after these followed others much thinner but black right through, but still bearing the marks of veins, and in other respects not unlike the allantoid membrane. Last came membranes of a third kind, devoid of vasa, and thinner than any of the others, like the amnion yet differing from it in appearance and material; for though thin, they were remarkably tough, and in some marvellous manner larger. The fragments differed in size, but two especially were more than two palms wide and were deeply grooved: these split themselves from top to bottom and took the form of cancellated rhombs. I can compare them with nothing better than the slough of a viper, although I had never before seen anything comparable with them. But this was chiefly remarkable in them, that along the length of them there appeared a deeper groove marked sparsely with transverse marks, as appears in hoarseness of the lung. They had a hollow circular cavity within, a little narrower in the fastigium of one membrane, like the mark of a snake's head with a mastoid apophysis or a mamillary processus. In the end of the other there lurked something abdominal and asymmetrical, not unlike a bifurcated vertex. All these joined together clearly attained to the length and thickness of an eel, and I think that it was a papillary tubercle through which the eel breathed and, perhaps, drew into itself the needful solid and liquid nutriment.

After she cast up these membranes, there followed a vast quantity of stones, which she brought up always in the evening and at a fixed hour with much contortion and nausea. These stones were of the shape which is found in the ruins of old houses, and were solid, angular, and of various shapes and sizes, some as big as walnuts; and she vomited them not without danger of suffocation. Sometimes also they were coated with chalk and joined together, so that they could not be distinguished from stones pulled from a house wall.

Once in my presence she brought up an angular stone as big as a double chestnut, with very great difficulty, so that I manifestly saw her vomiting it and heard the sound of it falling into the basin, to the great horror both of my own mind and of those who were standing about. Immediately afterwards she brought up, but with less difficulty, a piece of wood as long and thick as a thumb. This was bound right round with a sort of thread. Meanwhile at intervals she still vomited hairs, but fewer and blacker. Then came that which would surpass all belief, for she brought up a hard triangular bone, hollow and spongy inside, such as was clearly a fragment of ox's leg, and the girl's father said he had seen such a one the day before in his broth. Without delay on the following day she vomited a number of bony objects, some sharp and some round, of various shapes and sizes, still mingled with hairs and stones: and last of all, pieces of glass and bronze. Gemma justly supposes that a demon was, with the permission of God, the originator of these prodigies, but that he nevertheless employed natural causes in their due order as far as he could.

Sprenger (*Malleus Maleficarum*, II, q. 1, c. 13) tells of a woman of Zabern with whom a certain midwife was very angry because she did not engage her to minister to her at childbirth. This midwife came one night with two other witches where she was lying in bed and said that, out of revenge, she was going to put something in her intestines, the pain of which she would feel in six months' time; and she touched her belly. And it seemed to her that she took out her entrails and put in something which she could not see. After six months were gone, in the words of Sprenger, such a terrible pain came into her belly that she could not help disturbing everybody with her cries day and night. And because, as has been said, she was most devout to the Virgin, the Queen of Mercy, she fasted with bread and water every Saturday, so that she believed that she was delivered by Her intercession. For one day, when she wanted to perform an action of nature, all those unclean things fell from her body; and she called her husband and her son, and said: "Are those fancies? Did I not say that after half a year the truth would be known? Or who ever saw me eat thorns, bones, and even bits of wood?" For there were brambles as long as a palm, as well as a quantity of other things.

There is a castle * called St.-Symphorien in the Diocese of Lyons and a few miles from that city, where there lived a man full of faith, a conscientious entertainer of religious men, and of sober and learned conversation and opinions. This man once dragged an Abbot, almost by force, to his dwelling to see his daughter who was troubled with a wretched affliction: for, instigated by her envious mother-in-law, an evil witch-woman had caused her to sink into a hopeless languor, so that she could not endure the presence or sight of her husband. The girl's mother, led by womanly affection to believe that Satan would cast out Satan, sought the help of a famous warlock, who came and examined the girl and pronounced that she was bewitched. He then rubbed

the bark of a tree with a potion of herbs which he gave her to drink, uttering certain enchantments; and with his own teeth bit the poor girl's arm, a marvellous and strange thing unheard of before. She then recovered from her languor; but kept feeling as it were needles coming from her heart, and was in terrible pain while some unseen power drew these needles out through the bite in her arm, upon which no scar had appeared. A cruel remedy, but one worthy of its author. In this way at various times more than thirty needles were expelled, some with and some without an eye for the thread. The Abbot who, as we have said, came to the house where this was happening, is a most eminent and distinguished monk whose good work in this and other marvellous cases is not unknown; but since he is yet living I have thought fit not to divulge his name. The anxious father showed him his unhappy daughter and with tears explained her miserable case, and as he was speaking his words were proved by the fact: for the girl groaned and said that she felt a needle coming. The needle reached the opening, preceded by the usual flow of blood, and had already begun to show part of itself, when one of the lay brothers waiting upon the Abbot drew it out all bloody, to be kept for many years as evidence of the fact. The Abbot touched the wound and promised that by virtue of faith no more iron would come out of it. And so it was; but the material only was changed, for the malady was not yet conquered. Instead of the iron needles there began to come out little bits of wood, like spits of oak or ash, thicker and rather longer than thorns, but not all of the same length or thickness, any more than the needles had been. Within a year and a few months sixteen of these bits of wood came from the woman. At last came the Reverend Bishop Peter who was endowed with grace to perform this miracle. He gave orders in the preceding even-

---

* "There is a castle." This history is given by Laurentius Surius the hagiologist. "De probatis Sanctorum historiis" (Cologne, 1570–77), Tom. III, 8 May, c. xxiii.

ing that the woman should be brought to him as he celebrated Mass; and during the Mass the seventeenth piece of wood came from her body. The Chaplain drew it out in the sight of all, and the Bishop confessed and absolved the woman, and gave her the Eucharist, and bade her henceforth be secure from all extrusion of any matters. In this way she was freed from all spells and sorcery and abode by her husband and gave birth to children, and is said to live to this day testifying to the miracle which she was permitted to experience. Her father's name was Pierre du Fraxinet, a man well known and honoured by his neighbours, as may be verified by any who may find this story too strange to be believed.

Cesalpino writes as follows, in the *De Inuestigatione Daemonum*, cap. 17: This year at Pisa I, with many others, saw the following. A woman possessed by demons used frequently, sometimes while she was being exorcised and sometimes after, to cast from her body objects of a size and nature which precluded the possibility of her having eaten them; such as long iron nails, bones, stones, balls of wool, coals, and many other things. And in her bed, where her breast, and especially her heart, lay, were found many balls cunningly formed from palm leaves in various shapes, but mostly in the form of a rose with many layers of delicate petals, some bound round with thread and others stuck together with glue. Other objects were found on her pillow where her head rested.

☆

CHAPTER IX

Why God Permits the Devil so to Busy Himself with Witchcraft.

Argument.

THERE can be no doubt that there are many reasons for this. First, that glory may be increased even in us, when the glorious qualities of God are manifested in us.

Secondly, it is consonant with the laws of God; for since He created man to be free, He freely permits him to sin.

Thirdly, we may see in this a proof of His benevolent government; for He gave free will even to the devil, and permits him to make use of it at times.

Fourthly, it proves His mercy toward the human race. For if the devil were permitted to do all the harm that he wished and could, no man would escape, but all would be killed. Therefore God often denies him the power to do harm.

Fifthly, it shows God's wisdom. For although He allows the devil to use his natural powers, yet He causes that Father of Pride to be overcome by such foolish little creatures as men.

Sixthly, it shows His power. For although He allows the demon to effect the greater marvels, such as turning water into blood, He does not permit him to accomplish smaller things, such as the generation of gnats.

Seventhly, it shows His justice: for in this way God punishes men's sins even in this life.

☆

Examples.

In 1566, through the mouth of a demoniac woman at Laon, a demon in the hearing of all mocked at the Calvinists, crying out that he had nothing to fear from them since they were his friends and allies. This is too well known throughout Picardy for it to be denied; and it is recorded by Bishop Willem Damasus van Linda * (*De fugiendis nostri seculi idolis*, I, 14).

---

* "Bishop Willem Damasus van Linda" (or van der Lint), 1525–88. Bishop of Ruremonde and of Ghent. He was a staunch defender of the Faith, and the author of many theological and controversial treatises, some of which he wrote in Dutch for the instruction and safeguarding of his people. See Thus in "De Katholiek," CXXV (Leyden and Utrecht, 1904), 435.

It was noted as a fact that when Martin Luther * died at Eisleben, the demons flew to his funeral from those who were possessed, as is recorded by Bredembach, Bk. VII, ch. 37 and 39.

In an ancient Life of S. Zenobius † of Florence, the history is told of a certain heathen woman of that city who was both noble and wealthy. Her husband died, leaving her with two sons whom she reared most carefully; but when they had come to their full growth they fell one day into a rage and terribly beat their own mother with many blows. Unable to endure this outrage she cursed their bodies with horrible imprecations, falling on her knees and beating the ground with her hands, and calling upon Erinnys and the hellish furies to bring madness upon her sons. The demons heard her from the depths of darkness; and they attacked the young men, driving them to a fury so that they immediately became like mad dogs and began biting each other's limbs. The servants ran up, there was a great outcry, and some brought ropes and some chains, and the young men were bound; but even so their madness could not be restrained.

S. Augustine, in *The City of God,* XXII, 8, refers to the following story told by one Paul. While (he said) we were still living at Caesarea in our native country of Cappadocia, our eldest brother began to maltreat our mother in a terrible and insufferable manner, not hesitating to lay his hands on her. The rest of us brothers and sisters bore this patiently without speaking a word for our mother to our brother to ask him why he treated her so: but our mother, goaded by woman-ish anguish, determined to punish her cruel son by cursing him, and went after cock crow to the font of Holy Baptism where she called down the wrath of God upon her son. Then there came to her some demon in the form, as it is said, of our father, and asked her what she wished to do; and she answered: "To curse my son, for his intolerable ill-treatment of me." Then that enemy, since he can easily find a place in the heart of an angry woman, persuaded her to curse all her children; and she, kindled by his viperish counsel, prostrated herself and seized the sacred font, and with her hair all disordered and her breasts bared begged from God the following boon:—that we should be banished from our country and wander about foreign lands as a terrible example to the whole human race. Our mother's prayers soon took effect, and her ven-

---

* *"Martin Luther." Malvenda, "De Antichristo" (Romae, 1604), Liber X, p. 501, writes as quoting Bredembach: "Narrauit mihi uenerabilis Dominus N. aetate, doctrina, et uitae sanctimonia commendatissimus, atque etiamnum superstes, eo ipso die, quo nouus euangelista Martinus Lutherus defunctus est, uniuersos daemoniacos, qui id temporis ad Gheelam Brabentiae spe liberationis, quam apud corpus S. Dymnae diuino beneficio plurimi istic iam inde a multis retro annis consequi solent, aduecti erant, a teterrimis illis et horrendis daemonibus hospitibus suis liberatos. Postridie uero ab iisdem rursus obsessos et discruciatos fuisse: daemones uero, cum interrogarentur ubi pridie delituissent, respondisse, principem ipsorum et archidaemonem precepisse, ut uniuersi spiritus maligni ad sui prophetae et fidelis co-operarii D. Martini Lutheri exequias confluerent, congruere enim, ut qui quam plurimos ad inferos seduxisset, a quam plurimis ad eosdem solemniter deduceretur."*

S. Dympna, Virgin and Martyr, whose Relics are now venerated at Gheel, province of Antwerp, was the daughter of a pagan king in Ireland. In art she is represented with a sword in her hand and a devil chained at her feet. From time immemorial the Saint has been invoked upon behalf of those possessed by demons and lunatics. Miraculous cures and deliverances from demons have without number been wrought at her shrine. The feast of the Saint is 15 May, when many pilgrims visit the sanctuary, as also on the Tuesday after Pentecost.

† "Life of S. Zenobius." Apud Surium; Tom. 3; 25 May. S. Zenobius (died 337) is venerated as one of the Patrons of Florence when his Feast is kept, 25 May, with especial solemnity.

geance at once fell upon our eldest and guiltiest brother; for he was seized with just such a shaking of his limbs as your Holiness saw in me three days ago. Before a year had passed we were all afflicted with the same punishment in the order of our age. But when our mother saw the great effect of her curses, she could no longer endure the conscience of her unnatural behaviour or the general disgust felt against her, but tied a cord round her throat and thus miserably ended her unhappy life. Unable to bear the scandal of these events, we all left our native land and were scattered in all directions, and after long wandering we have won freedom from our afflictions.

In the County of Flanders (hear and tremble!) there is a Monastery (but it is well not to reveal its situation or the name of its Order) where there were three who were monks in name, but in reality beastly gluttons and whore-mongers, who had no shame at all in their crapulence or their lechery. Once when they had sat drinking till late in the night one of them, not quite so hardened in sin, said: "We have given enough to Bacchus and our stomachs. Let us at least thank God." "For my part," said another, who was bolder, "I thank Cacodemon; and I think it is he who should be thanked, since it is he whom we serve." They then left the table with laughter and went to the dormitory, each with his wench. They had hardly lain down when there walked in through the bolted door a demon, in the form of a great fierce black man dressed like a hunter, and with him two little cooks. He looked threateningly at the beds and in a terrible voice exclaimed: "Where is he who gave thanks to me? I am here to repay him!" Then he dragged that man from his bed, quaking and nearly dead with fright, and giving him to the cooks ordered them to spit him and roast him by the blazing fire. They at once obeyed, and the wretched man was roasted and most obviously died. The rest were nearly dead with terror, for the room was filled with the stench of the burned body. At last the hunter turned to the others who were cowering half dead under their blankets, and said: "You also deserve the same punishment, and I would willingly inflict it; but I am prevented by a higher power and leave you against my will. But I warn you to mend your ways, lest an even more terrible fate should overtake you." The demons then vanished; but the men did not recover their courage or even their speech until broad daylight. Then when they arose they found their comrade dead and (to prove that it had been no empty vision) quite blackened and burned. I doubt whether there has been so useful an example as this for hundreds of years.

Geilana, the wife of the Duke of Franconia, ordered SS. Kilian,* Coloman and Totnan to be put to death, and this crime remained hidden until God discovered its author in the following manner. One of those who had struck S. Kilian with his sword was suddenly possessed by a demon and began to cry aloud: "O Kilian, you persecute me cruelly, for I am consumed with fire and cannot hide what I did. I see threatening me a sword red with your blood." He kept shouting like this for a long time, tearing himself with his own teeth, until he passed from present to eternal punishment. Of such it is written, "Destroy them, O Lord, with double destruction" (Jeremiah, xvii, 18). The other associate in the killing fell into a madness and disembowelled himself with his sword, passing from the torments

---

* "S. Kilian." SS. Kilian, Coloman, and Totnan converted the Thuringian Duke Gozbert, who after baptism was bound to put away his brother's widow, Geilana, whom he had wedded, since under the Christian dispensation this pagan marriage was unlawful— Geilana plotted vengeance and in the absence of the Duke caused S. Kilian and his two companions to be murdered, 8 July, 689. S. Kilian is Patron of Würzburg.

of this present time to those of eternity. And what of Geilana when this was known to her? The wretched woman was infuriated to the point of extremest agony; and not long afterwards this ogress was seized with tormenting pains and cried out at the top of her voice: "I am justly tortured, since I set the torturers upon the Holy Men; I am rightly tormented, since I prepared torments for them. O Kilian, you come upon me relentlessly; you light the fire, O Kilian; and you, O Totnan apply the burning coals. Be content with your victory, for you have sufficiently avenged your wrongs. O Kilian, you are named from a cup; but the drink you give me is too bitter." Saying this she was cruelly tortured, so that she could hardly be held by many people; and at last in excruciating pangs passed to the torments prepared for the devil.

Thomas Netter* in his book against the Wycliffites, *De Sacramento Eucharistiae*, cap. 63, vouches that in 1384 he was an eye-witness of the following. He writes in these words: "I tell the story of what I saw myself with the eyes of my flesh in the Cathedral of S. Paul in London. The venerable Archbishop of Canterbury Thomas Arundel of happy memory, whose father and brother were Earls of Arundel, sat there in the Episcopal throne in judgement, with Bishop Alexander of Norwich and others as his assessors, and put some questions concerning the faith in the Eucharist to one William Taylor† from Worcester

who had been charged with heresy. When this man could by no means be turned to the true faith, and persisted in calling and believing the most Sacred Host to be nothing but 'blessed bread,' he was finally ordered to do reverence to the Host. But he blasphemously replied: 'Truly a spider is more worthy to be revered.' Immediately there descended from the top of the roof a huge and hideous spider, and came straight on its thread to the blasphemer's mouth, and persistently tried, while he was yet speaking, to gain an entrance through his polluted lips. Thomas of Woodstock, uncle of the King, was present and witnessed the miracle. The Archbishop immediately arose with the other bishops, and expounded to the whole congregation there gathered what the avenging hand of the Lord had done to the blasphemer. A demon in the form of the spider possessed the blasphemer and so avenged the dishonour done to God."

Sophronius writes as follows of a vengeance taken by the Blessed Virgin Mary. In Heliopolis of Syria (Baalbek) there was an actor named Gaianus who used to blaspheme against the Holy Mother of God publicly in the theatre. The Holy Mother appeared to him and said: "Do not, I beg you, do not such hurt to your soul." He did but the more blaspheme against her, and she came a third time

---

* *"Thomas Netter." Born at Saffron Walden, c. 1375; died at Rouen, 2 November, 1430. Carmelite theologian and controversialist. He took a prominent part in the prosecution of Wycliffites and Lollards, confounding their teachers and refuting their abominable doctrines in many admirable treatises. He died in the odour of sanctity; miracles were wrought at his tomb; and it is hoped that his cult will shortly be confirmed by the Congregation of Rites.*

† *"William Taylor." This horrid heretic graduated M.A. at Oxford and proceeded to*

priest's Orders. Under Archbishop Thomas Arundel he was laid by the heels for his subversive and blasphemous opinions. 12 February, 1420, he recanted and was absolved. 5 May, 1421, he was charged in convocation by the Bishop of Worcester, to which diocese he belonged. Condemned to perpetual imprisonment, he was afterwards pardoned. However, he gave continual trouble by his teaching against prayer, the veneration of the Cross, the worship of the Saints, and other holy doctrines. In the end this pestilent wretch was degraded from his Orders and burned at Smithfield, 1 March, 1423. See Shirley's "Fasciculi Zizaniorum," pp. 412, sqq.; Wilkins, "Concilia," III, 404.

to him repeating the same words. When he would not mend his ways, but even increased his blasphemies, she appeared to him as he was sleeping one mid-day, and without saying anything touched his hands and feet with her finger; and when he awoke he found himself without hands or feet, lying there wretched, maimed and useless. He then confessed to all how and why he had suffered that fate. He was thus mercifully punished for his blasphemy; for so do the Blessed Saints mete out gentle punishment.

Nider says: When I was studying sacred Theology at the University of Cologne, there was a virgin some fifteen or sixteen years old, well enough behaved as manners are now counted, and she was living away from her parents in the house of a kinswoman. She happened to break a common earthenware pot belonging to this kinswoman, who was sore angered when she knew of it, and cried out that it was due to the girl's carelessness. This angered the girl all the more because it was but a very common pot; and in her temper she declared at dinner-time that she would not eat, nor even come to the table. Her kinswoman said to her: "You must eat." But the girl muttered to herself some such words as: "If I must eat, be it so in the name of the devil," and thus came to the table, neglected to asked the customary blessing, and with her first mouthful of bread (as it is thought) felt a fly in her mouth. Being by no means able to eject it, she swallowed this and was immediately possessed; yet she always kept her faculties and reason, although she was often tormented by the demon. She was sorrowfully taken back to her parents' house, and for a long time no one was found who could deliver her. But at last a certain Dominican had pity on the girl and her parents, and undertook to exorcise her on condition that, if she were delivered, no earthly reward should be given to the exorcist, but that the girl should serve God for the rest of her life, if she freely consented to do so, in her present virgin state, and not be given to any in marriage. This good priest then offered the Holy Sacrifice, and the possessed girl made the usual offering and was present throughout the whole Mass without appearing to suffer any torments. But after long exorcism the demon came out of her, leaving every limb of her virgin body bruised; and from that time she began to serve God in virgin chastity.

The same author tells the following. When Peter,[*] the famous Judge of witches, resigned his office, he went back to Berne and lived there. But one day he returned to the Castle of Blankenburg, where a kinsman of his had succeeded him in his office, and there intended to do some business with certain of his acquaintances. Then a witch, together with four men who were her associates in this crime, being busy late one night with the mysteries of their art, searched their brains for a means of grievously harming or killing Peter by witchcraft in some secret manner without being suspected. Accordingly when night came Peter crossed himself and went to his bedroom, but with the intention of keeping awake all night in order to write some necessary letters so that he might be able to leave the place in the morning. As he was thus awake, in the middle of the night it suddenly seemed to him that the day had come, for he was deceived by a fictitious light. Being then angry with himself because he thought he had wasted the night, he put on his clothes without blessing himself as he should, and went downstairs to the place where he kept his writing materials, and found it locked. He then became more angry and began climbing upstairs again to his bedroom, allowing himself, in his irritation, one brief word of cursing, mentioning the name of the devil. At

---

* "Peter." "Formicarius," Lib. V, c. 3, 4, 7.

once he was hurled downstairs in dense darkness so violently that his servant, who was sleeping near at hand by the stairs, was awakened and, coming out to see what was the matter, and lighting a light, saw his master Peter lying senseless on the ground with all his limbs broken and profusely bleeding. Some time later it was discovered through the confession of a prisoner that those four men and that witch had thus hurled Peter down the stairs. Note, reader, what harm came to Peter through neglecting to make the sign of the Cross.

Remy relates the following marvellous story. Jeanne Blaise of Baden had a son-in-law named Rayner with whom she lived in the same house. A fellow countryman of this Rayner, one Claude Gerard, had long ago lent him a pair of breeches, but so far had been unable by any importunity to get him to give them back to him. Weary of so long a delay he at last came to Rayner to ask when he was going to be done with his subterfuges, but found that he was away from home and that only his mother-in-law Blaise was sitting by the fire with their family. He therefore asked her to return him his garment, saying that, as often as her fine son-in-law had made a fool of him, he would find that he was well able to pay him back in his own coin. This enraged the woman; but she decided to refrain from words so that she might be fully avenged in deed upon the man, and asked him to wait a few days more, and he should have what he wanted without any further delay. In the meantime she asked him if he would not sit down with her by the fire for a little in friendly wise and partake of some apples which she had just baked. Gerard declined more than once, saying that he had no leisure to tarry there any longer and that he had no wish for the food which she offered him; but one of the apples stuck to the palm of his hand, and was so hot that he was forced to try to knock it off with the other hand.

Then both his hands were stuck, as if they had grown together, while the apple between them kept waxing hotter until he was driven nearly out of his mind. He therefore cried out on some who were present to have pity on him, and each brought what remedy he could, some bringing water to quench the heat, and others tools for forcing his hands apart; but none of these were of any avail. It then became clear that it was a matter of some evil art, and one of his more understanding neighbours advised that he should be taken to the place where the evil had first come upon him: and when this was done old gammer Blaise began to make fun of what had happened to him; yet she gently rubbed his arm from the shoulder to the hand, and thereupon the apple fell from him and the pain was assuaged, and he was able to use his hands freely as before.

A certain German Jurisconsult (Gödelman, Lib. 1, de Lamiis, cap. de malitia Diaboli) tells the following history. Elizabeth the daughter of John, King of Denmark, Sweden and Norway, was married to Joachim the Elector of Brandenburg; and he left her at his death Queen of the town of Spandau, at the confluence of the rivers Havel and Spree. While she was yet living in this town, a certain soldier came travelling through the Province and was taken ill and had to go to bed; and he gave his hostess a purse of money to keep for him. Some days later, when he had recovered, he asked for his purse. But the avaricious woman was loath to part with so much money and deliberated with her husband whether she must give it back, and they decided that she should deny having received it. Accordingly when the soldier again asked for it she brazenly said that she had never had it and that she wondered at his impudence in daring to ask for something which he had never given her to keep. Moved to indignation, the soldier in his turn accused the hostess of perfidy; and her husband, as if in defence of his wife, thrust the soldier out of the house. Enraged by the hostess's theft, he stood before the door and drew his sword as if to attack the host, and beat upon the door. The host asked for help from his neighbours, complaining that his house was being attacked; and the officers ran up and took the soldier off to prison for causing a public disturbance. After a few days the Mayor of the town sent a report of the case to another place, and asked that a sentence should be passed; upon which it was decided that the house had been publicly attacked and that therefore the soldier must be sentenced to death. When the day of his execution was at hand, the devil came to him in his prison and told him what sentence the Judges would pass upon him, promising that he would free him from that danger on condition that he gave himself to the devil. The soldier firmly answered that he would rather die, although he was innocent. The devil with great eloquence exaggerated his danger; but when he could not influence the soldier's determination he finally promised him his freedom without any condition; saying: "When you come into the Court, say that you are unskilled in pleading and ask for an advocate; and I shall be there wearing a dark hat decorated with feathers. Ask then that I may be permitted to plead for you." Thinking that he might do this without sinning, the soldier said that he would follow this advice. Next day he was led into the Court, where he saw a lawyer wearing a dark hat. The prosecutor demanded that the soldier should be put to death for causing a public disturbance; whereupon the soldier said that he was unfamiliar with legal procedure and asked that his advocate might speak for him. The Judges consented: and then the devil discoursed learnedly on the law, saying that he ought not to be sentenced to death who was neither the origin nor real cause of the quarrel

and disturbance; that the soldier had been turned out and robbed by the host; and he said that they would find the purse if they looked in a certain place. The host violently denied this with terrible cursing. Then the devil added: "Swear then that, if you did rob this man, the devil may seize you and carry you away." And when he had repeatedly sworn this, invoking the devil, that advocate left his learned pleading, suddenly went up to the host and, seizing him, took him away with a great noise through the window and over the market square to the terror of all; and the host's body was never afterwards found.

Three men* were drinking together in a tavern and, being heated with wine, began discussing the immortality of the soul and the pains of hell. One, rasher than the rest, said that it was all nonsense and the invention of priests; and the others laughingly applauded him. Thereupon there came in a man of great stature but slightly built, who sat down and said: "What may you be discussing, and why are you all laughing?" The same bold fellow told him, and added that he would sell his soul cheap to any bidder, so that it were for money. "For how much," said the newcomer, "will you sell it to me?" They soon agreed upon a price, and the man's soul was bought and sold. They drank hard with the purchase money; and at last when it was night the buyer said: "It is time for each man to return to his own place. But do you tell me rightly: if a man buys a horse which is tied up with a halter, has he not the right to take away both horse and halter?" Saying this, he seized the trembling vendor of his own soul before their eyes, and raising him up in the air carried him off to hell to see that which he had refused to believe. For that was a dealer in souls, like the King of

_____

* "Three men." This is from Thomas Cantimpratanus, "Bonum uniuersale," II, 55, Par. 3.

Sodom who said: "Give me the souls, and you may have the rest."

Again, Gödelmann says: A nobleman in Silesia had invited some guests, and the time of the feast had come and everything was ready, when he was disappointed by all his guests excusing themselves. Angry at their failure to appear, he broke out into these words: "Then let all the devils come, if no man can eat with me." So saying, he went out and entered the church, where the priest was addressing his congregation, and listened to him for a while with the intention of calming his anger. But while he was in the church there came into the courtyard of his house some tall black horsemen who told his servant to call his master and tell him that his guests had arrived. The servant went in terror to the church and told this to his master who, not knowing what to do, asked the priest's advice. The priest broke off his sermon and advised that all the household should leave the house. This was done, the servants, men and women, all hurrying out; but it happened that they forgot the baby and left it lying asleep in its cradle. The demons began to eat and shout and look through the windows in the form of bears, wolves, cats and men, holding up cups full of wine, and roast meats and fishes. When the neighbours and the priests and others saw this, the unhappy father cried: "Ah, where is my child?" When he had said this, one of the demons carried the child in his arms to the window as if to show it to its parents. The nobleman was then in the utmost anxiety for the child's safety, and asked a faithful servant of his: "What, I entreat you, am I to do?" The servant said: "Master, I will commend and commit my life to my God, and in the name of the Lord will go in and see whether, with God's mercy and help, I can bring out your child." "Good!" said the nobleman. "God be with you and help you and preserve your soul." After being blessed by the priest and the others,

the servant went in and fell on his knees before the door of the chamber where the demons were assembled, and commended himself to God, and in that mind opened the door. There he saw demons of horrible appearance sitting, standing, walking and creeping about, who all ran together towards him shouting: "Huh, huh! what are you doing here?" Sweating, but still trusting in God, he said to the demon who was carrying the child: "Give me that child." He answered: "By no means, for this child is now mine. Tell your master to come and take it." The servant replied: "I do my duty in that state of life in which God has placed me, and I know that whatever I do in duty is pleasing to God; therefore as in duty bound, and with the help of and in the name and might of Jesus Christ, I take the child from you and restore it to its parents" And he took the child in his arms. The demons made no answer but: "Huh, rascal! Huh, rascal! Leave the child, leave it; or else we will tear you to an hundred pieces." But he took no notice of their devilish threats, and went out unharmed, and gave the child back safe to its noble father. After some days had passed the demons vanished, and the nobleman was able to enter his house again with all his household.*

Again he writes: In Saxony a rich virgin had promised marriage to a handsome but poor young man. The man, fearing what would happen, told the girl that she was very wealthy and, like all her sex, changeable, and would hardly keep her promise, but the girl answered with the most solemn oaths: "If I marry any but you, then may the devil take me in that marriage!" And what happened? After some time she changed her mind and married another man, spurning her former betrothed, although he again and again

---

* "*Household.*" *It will be remembered that in "The Ingoldsby Legends" this history is turned as "The Lay of S. Cuthbert."*

reminded her of her promise and her terrible oath: but she put all that behind her and, leaving him, celebrated her marriage with another. On the day of the wedding, when all her relations and friends and guests were gathered together, her conscience pricked her sorely and made her very sad. Then came two devils to the marriage house in the likeness of horsemen, and were welcomed and led to the table. Afterwards the tables were removed and they fell to dancing, and the bride danced with one of the horsemen to do honour to a stranger. He gave two leaps with her, and then in the sight of her parents and with her friends groaning and lamenting bore her up on high through the door. On the next day her wretched parents and friends looked for the bride to bury her, if they could find where she had fallen; but the same horseman came back with her clothes and jewels, saying: "Not over these things, but over the bride was power given to us by God." So she gave herself body and soul to the devil, because she had broken her promise, and had moreover despised the oath which she had sworn.

Pietro Bizzari* tells the following:

---

* "*Pietro Bizzari.*" A humanist of the sixteenth century who won great repute for his elegant verses as also for his erudite but somewhat diffuse histories and chronicles. He was born at Sassoferrato. Much of his work is conveniently collected in the Antwerp folio of 1589, "Senatus Populique Genuensis Rerum Domi Forisque Gestarum Historiae atque Annales," "cum luculenta uariarum rerum cognitione dignissimarum, quae diuersis temporibus, et potissimum hac nostra tempestate contingerunt, enarratione." I have used this edition. Certain of Bizzari's shorter poems will be found in Gheri's "Delitiae Italorum Poetarum" (1608), I, pp. 436–441; and in the "Carmina Illustrium Poetarum Italorum (Florence, 1719), II, pp. 250–255. Notable among these are the odes to Catherine de' Medici, and to Girolamo Priuli, who was Doge of Venice, 1559–1567. Of particular interest also are the addresses to the Earl of Leicester, Sir Thomas Randolph,

In Suabia, which lies by Bavaria and Franconia, there was a very rich and wealthy nobleman named Richberger, whose yearly returns exceeded thirty thousand gold gulden. Yet, because of his manner of acting, he was not popular with the people; for he was of an unspeakably miserly nature. His one aim was, by fair means or foul, to increase his wealth every day; and he tried to get everything into his own hands. Accordingly, when he foresaw the famine, which followed in the next year, he filled his barns with wheat and fruit and began to sell them at a great profit, so that the poor were compelled by his boundless avarice to buy their food from him; and they must either die of hunger or, if they wished to get food and nourishment, they were reduced to the utmost want and poverty, so dearly did he sell them corn and other necessaries. Among many others there came to him a certain poor man burdened with children, who offered him six thalers, begging him to take the money and let him have a certain measure of wheat, and he would pay him the rest that he owed for it in a short time. But he looked proudly and angrily at him and told him to be gone at once and fetch the rest of the money if he wanted any corn; and so the poor wretch went away, bitterly cursing him. After a few days he sent one of his servants to inspect his granaries as usual, and was told by him that there were three black oxen eating his corn: and the servant who reported this took to his bed the next day and soon after died. The same thing happened to a gentleman whom the master had sent to see whether it was as he had been told: for he saw both oxen and horses. When he was told of this, the master determined to go himself to the place and, coming to the door of the granary, he saw through the chinks the whole

---

and the brief "In mortem Eduardi Curtnaei." Edward Courtenay, Earl of Devon, died in exile at Padua, September 1556.

place full of countless cattle of all sorts, which were eating all the corn. He was so terrified by this sight that he at once became stark mad and rushed away in a frenzy committing many violent acts until he was caught and put in chains. This horrible event aroused great wonder in that province and especially in Aalen, where he had always been known as a most sober and prudent man.

A priest named Epachius* was overtaken by the judgement of God because he presumed to do that which he was not worthy to do. For when he should have been in the church keeping the Vigil of the Nativity of Christ, he kept leaving the church and going into his house where he drank lewdly of foaming cups of wine, so that many said they had seen him drinking that night till after cockcrow. But since he was of noble rank and there was not his superior in secular dignity in that town of Riom, he was asked to celebrate the solemnities of the Mass; and the wretch did not hesitate, although sodden with wine, to undertake that which no man, even after fasting, can approach without fear and searching of his conscience. But when he had pronounced the sacred words and had broken the sacrament of the Lord's Body, and had himself taken It and distributed It to others to eat, he uttered a neigh like a horse and fell to the ground and vomited out the Sacred Mystery, which he had not been able to chew with his teeth, and was carried from the church by his servants. And he never recovered from that epilepsy; but with the waxing and waning of each moon, so his malady increased and abated; for the unhappy man could by no means keep from drinking too much wine.

Not long ago, after the people of Dorpat† had embraced the Lutheran teaching, on the Saturday before Easter Sunday the Lutherans had concluded their meeting and the people were returning from the holy church of the Blessed Virgin Mother, when one of them met another who was his friend and asked him to come home and dine with him, for he had a fine fat Westphalian ham all ready. The other, not at all shocked, answered that he had a plump boiled chicken which he would bring as his contribution to the feast. They sat down to table; and one of them, eating a chicken bone rashly, nearly swallowed it, so that it could neither be extracted nor gulped down, and he was suffocated the same day. The other was seized by an evil spirit on the day after Easter, and soon afterwards, shaken by madness and fury, gasped out both his life and the demon.

Peter of Cluny (*Liber Miraculorum*, II, 1) tells the following as a warning to heretics. A certain Count of Mâcon was sitting in his palace on the town's patronal festival with a large company of soldiers and others around him, when suddenly a stranger on horseback entered the palace gate and, as they all looked on in wonder, rode right up to the Count. When he had come near him he said that he wished to speak to him, and not so much asked as commanded him to arise and follow him. Compelled by some unseen power and unable to resist, the Count arose and went to the palace door where he found a horse ready for him. He was bidden to mount, and did so; whereupon the man seized the reins and in the sight of all began to

---

* "*Epachius.*" This is from S. Gregory of Tours, "*De gloria Martyrum,*" I, 87.

† "*Dorpat.*" This is from Tilmannus Bredenbachius. His work, which was first printed at Douai, has a Dedication, signed at Cologne, *1563,* to Julius Plugh, Bishop of Nuremberg. The "*Historia belli Liuonici quod gestis magnus Muscouitarum Dux,*" "*auctore Tilmanno Bredenbachio,*" occupies pp. *217–239,* of the folio "*Rerum Muscouitarum Auctores Uarii Unum in Corpus nunc primum Congesti,*" Frankfort, *1600.*

carry him swiftly up through the air. The whole town ran up at his loud crying and wretched lamenting to see this strange spectacle, and watched him flying through the air for as long as their eyes could follow him. They heard him for a long time crying out: "Help, citizens, help!" But they could not help him, and he was taken from the sight of men and became, as he deserved, an eternal associate of the demons. So did this man expiate in this life and the next his despoiling of churches and his sacrileges.

In a very old life of S. Calais* we read of a woman named Gunda who was enticed by the subtle Deceiver to mock the Holy Spirit. For she put on man's clothing and tried to enter the monastery of the Saint, to test the truth of his prophecy that no woman would ever be able to enter there. But, by the just judgement of God, before she even came in sight of the closed approach to the cloisters, she was seized by the devil and driven back; and was so shamefully tormented by him that I blush to speak of it. For he thrust her head between her thighs, so that she who had tried to imprint a false kiss upon the holy threshold was forced to kiss the filthy parts of her own body; and she had to exhibit openly to all who wished to see it that sex which she had tried to conceal beneath a man's clothing. The result of this was that no woman thereafter dared to approach the monastery.

---

* "S. Calais" or S. Carileff (c. 540) was a monk of Menat on the Sioule, in Auvergne. For the sake of greater solitariness this holy recluse withdrew and fled away to the desert near Le Mans when he made his hermitage at the place since called Aninsole. His reputation for sanctity became so great that before long a monastery grew up there of which he was forced to assume the government. A life of S. Calais was written by S. Siviard, Abbot of Aninsole, died 687. The feast of S. Calais is observed on 1 July.

☆

CHAPTER X

The Laws Observed by Witches in Causing and in Curing Sickness.

Argument.

EVEN as witches always see their way clearly to any evil, so they find many difficulties and obstacles when they would do good or heal. For what time witches would bring disease or death, everything is ready, everything at hand for them; all kinds of poison, curses, spells, and enchantments. With all these the devil is prompt, and with the witches' consent always undertakes the work of doing harm. This he does to earn their gratitude by gaining them the vengeance they have so ardently desired, and he is able to provide means which, it seems, no human art or skill can combat. At the same time it is in his power to keep the witch clear of all suspicion, when he acts in their absence without their stirring even a finger to help him. But when it is a question of restoring health or saving life, then there are never wanting opposing forces to combat such an intention.

☆

Examples.

Rosa Girardin gave it as the truth that a sickness could not be removed except by the person who had caused it; for no one might thrust his sickle in another's harvest, according to the law which provides that he who binds must also unbind. And therefore we must fear injury and look for help from the same hand.

Dominique Eurea said that no one who had been bewitched could be restored to health unless his sickness were even more grievously transferred to another; and that the sickness always grew in these exchanged. Also the healing power received from the demon always vanished when a priest or a physician laid his hands on the sick to heal him.

Alexée Drigée said that such restorations to health were never absolute and complete, but that there always remained some trace of the sickness.

Catharine Balandre used to say that it was useless to look for any alleviation or cure of a sickness from those who had been brought to trial for witchcraft; for all such power had then passed into the hands of the devil, who is able to perform all such things.

Nicolas Morell agreed with this statement. For when he was asked, in prison, to heal the son of Jean Chemat, whom he admitted that he had bewitched with the sickness from which he was suffering, he answered that he had no more power in such matters since, by confessing his crimes, he had driven the devil away from him, and the sanctity of his place of imprisonment also prevented him from such work. And not even to expiate his crimes could he work those spells which were necessary to heal the boy.

When Cattina Gilotte was asked why it was that she had not healed Canasse Godefreda of the disease which she had brought upon her by witchcraft, although she had more than once given her to eat apples and plums and other such fruit by means of which she was in the habit of curing others, she answered that it was because that Godefreda had not prayed to be healed.

Balial Basol and Colette the fisher's wife mentioned another kind of obstacle. For they said that when they were trying to effect a cure, and some other person, without informing or consulting them, meddled in the matter by making and fulfilling a vow to one of the Saints, then they were prevented by this contempt of their art from doing anything more to heal the sick man. And no doubt they essayed a cure, because such wretches desire above all things the alms and thanks of sick folk, since they are beggars and live entirely on such charity.

When the father of Nicole Morell was charged with witchcraft and was pleading in his own defence, he said that which involved his daughter in suspicion of the same crime; and so the apparitor who was then present persuaded the judge to order her arrest. While Nicole Morell was yet at liberty a demon warned her of this and urged her to be revenged by bringing some harm upon the apparitor, and that he would gladly undertake such work if she bade him. She quickly assented, and he flew to the apparitor's house where he found his wife sitting by the fire giving the breast to her baby. He passed by and blew upon her breasts so poisonous a powder that they at once became dried up and empty of milk. The apparitor soon suspected the cause of this, and went to Nicole Morell, who was now in prison, and offering her a cake to appease her begged her not to begrudge him any help which she could give in the matter; and in his turn he would take care that she had everything to make her life easier while she was in prison. He then left her, wondering what she would do in the matter. The demon at once appeared to her and scolded her for speaking with the apparitor; but at last allowed himself to be persuaded to fill the breasts of the man's wife again with milk, even to superfluity if she wished. And soon after he accomplished this by applying a white powder to her.

Catharine Ocrea had formerly been discharged on her own recognizances, but was again brought to trial by reason of fresh suspicion against her and because of the eloquent mandate of His Most Serene Highness the Prince of Lorraine, who had been advised of the whole matter. Before she was reimprisoned she had smitten with her evil art the arm of one of the witnesses against her so that it became withered: and now she seized this man's arm roughly as if she was angry, and to the astonishment of all who were present it was at once restored to health; so that whereas it had been for many months useless and without strength, it at once became vigorous and fit and able to perform all its former work.

CHAPTER XI

Witches Use something of Religion in Heal-
ing Sickness.

Argument.

MOST cunningly does Satan, that Master of perversity, mask his magic under the appearance of re-ligion: and this he does, both that he may the more easily lead into super-stitious error those who are naturally disposed to that cult; and that, by him-self working miraculous cures, he may avert suspicion from his followers, so that it shall not be thought that he who has removed the sickness was the original cause of it. This we shall later make clear. For witches observe various silences, measurings, vigils, mutterings, figures and fires, as if they were some expiatory religious rite; and worse still, they transfer the sickness to certain pious men, alleging that it is a punishment for having dishonoured their deity. Most intolerable of all, they often mingle with their prayers all sorts of filth and dung and excrement, than which no-thing can be imagined more foreign to the purity which is proper to Divine worship and ceremonies. The follow-ing are examples of this sort.

☆

Examples.

Within the last fifteen years there was at Nancy a woman named The-notte who was a witch. Once when she was asked to heal a sick neighbour (for she was supposed to have such power), she said that the sickness had been caused by S. Fiacre,* who must there-fore be placated with gifts at his shrine; and that, if they bade her, she would gladly undertake the matter. She was induced by payment to attempt this work. First she measured the sick woman cross-wise with a waxed linen cloth, then folded the cloth so many times and placed it in her bosom as though to cherish it. Then for the whole of the following night she lay outside the doors of the house in which the sick woman was, and at dawn went her way in utter silence. When she came to the shrine of S. Fiacre she went in and lit the linen cloth, and with the burning drops of wax traced a cross on the steps of the High Altar; and then went out and walked three times round the chapel, with the cloth still splutter-ing blue flames. When she had done all this she went back to the city.

A peasant of the Vosges named Desiré Finance had cherished a long grudge against a fellow townsman named Valentine Valère and longed to be thoroughly revenged upon him, but had not found any safe or favour-able chance of doing so. But this chance came when Valentine was travelling alone in a solitary place, and a figure like a shadow seized him and hurled him from his horse with such violence that he was lamed in one leg. But some time later he had pity on the man, since he had suffered his mis-fortune for so long, and went to him as if upon some other business. Then he asked him how he came by that acci-dent, and was told at great length the cause, which he himself knew much better; and finally he promised a sure and immediate cure, if he would do as he told him, and that he would take no payment for it. The other anxiously waited to hear what he must do; and Desiré told him to go and beg the horse-dung from nine different stables,

---

* *"S. Fiacre." Abbot in Ireland; died 18 August, 670. He long dwelt in a hermitage on the banks of the Nore of which the memory is preserved in Kilfiachra (Kilfera), Kilkenny. S. Fiacre migrated to France and built an oratory at Brogillum (Breuil), where his shrine is yet a place of pilgrimage. During his life he healed all manners of diseases and numberless* cures *are wrought at his tomb. His shrine was removed in 1568 to the Cathedral at Meaux for safety from the violence and destruction of the Calvinists, and precious Relics have been dis-tributed to other sanctuaries. Feast, 30 August.*

enough to fill a sack, and to limp with it and take it as a gift to S. Benedict, to whom there was a famous shrine in the German town of Berguel; for thus, he said, he would by some secret virtue and power be freed from his affliction and grow strong again. See how it is the custom of witches to cover their cures thus with the cloak of religion; when they have nothing to do with religion, but rather despise and mock at it.

☆

CHAPTER XII

Threatening or Beating Witches is the Best Method of Removing the Spells cast by Them.

Argument.

NEARLY all witches who have been questioned on the matter have confessed that the greater their fear the greater their boldness in doing evil; and that threats and the fear of prison very often cause them to remove their spells. In this connexion there are many points worthy of note.

First, however holy or sacred the reason may be, it does not deprive witches of either the will or the power to do mischief; unless God in His great goodness forbids and turns aside such evil. This is proven by the case of a man who used the aspergillum during the Divine Office to sprinkle and fatally injure a woman whom he could find no other way to harm: and we often find lying about the shrines of the Saints broken fragments of thunderbolts which are believed to have been wielded and hurled by some demon. For in no place are the demons more fain to work their abominations than where they can disguise them under the aspect of some omen of blessing. Aulus Gellius * (IX, 4) and Pliny †

(VII, 2) say that it is no rare thing to find those who, by blessing and extravagantly praising them, have bewitched and destroyed trees, crops and even men.

Secondly, the benefit (if it may rightly be called so) conferred by demons is never lasting, full or complete; but he who has received it must soon suffer a like, or even a heavier injury and incapacity. For hardly ever do they drive a sickness from one man without transferring it to some other man, so that often they give a man health at the expense of another's death. S. Gregory of Tours in his *Historia Francorum* ‡ (VI, 35) writes that this was done by some witches of Paris who, after they had by their black art stricken the prefect Mummol with a mortal sickness, could not restore him to health otherwise than by previously killing, with his consent, the son of King Chilperic, a child scarcely two years old, whom his father was rear-

---

septimo legimus: esse quasdam in terra Africa familias hominum, uoce atque lingua effascinantium: qui si impensius forte laudauerint pulchras arbores, segetes laetiores, infantes amoeniores, egregios equos, pecudes pastu atque cultu opimas; emoriantur repente haec omnia, nulli aliae causae obnoxia.''

† *"Pliny." "Historia Naturalis," VII, 2: "In eadem Africa familias quasdam effascinantium, Isigonus et Nymphodorus: quorum laudatione intereant probata, arescant arbores, emoriantur infantes."*

‡ *"Historia Francorum." The first four books, according to Arndt ("Scriptores Rerum Merouingiuarum"), were written in 575; Books V and VI in 585; and the remaining four books dealing with the years 584 to 591 at intervals which cannot be precisely determined. S. Gregory died in November 593 or 594. On the assassination of Sigebert, King of Austragia in 576, Chilperic, King of Neustria, had seized Tours and held the city until his death in 584. When in 578 a son of King Chilperic died of dysentery Queen Fredegonde instantly accused the general Mummol, whom she hated, of having slain the young prince by evil charms. See "The Geography of Witchcraft," by Montague Summers, pp. 354–55.*

---

* *"Aulus Gellius." "Id etiam in iisdem libris scriptum offendimus, quod postea quoque in libro Plinii Secundi Naturalis Historiae*

ing to succeed to the kingdom. The annals of that time are filled with accounts of such inequitable bargains cunningly driven by men of old time who were infected with the sin of demons. For when a huge chasm appeared through the subsidence of the earth in the middle of the Roman Forum,* it was said that it would never again be filled unless some youth of the greatest promise cast himself into it. In this can easily be seen the great difference between the fatherly kindness of God and the tyrannical cruelty and savagery of the devil: for God calls man through adversity to Heaven, whereas the devil turns and draws man to eternal death through prosperity (if such a man may be said ever to prosper).

Thirdly, with the utmost mockery and derision witches, when they heal, imitate and copy the method used by Elisha and S. Paul and Elijah, and many Holy Fathers, when they brought the dead to life; stretching themselves limb for limb upon the bodies of the dead.

Fourthly, there is no curative virtue in any of the external remedies used by witches for the sicknesses they have caused, such as herbs, unguents, baths and such things; but these are merely a cover for their witchcraft which, through fear of the severity of the law, they dare not show openly.

Fifthly, so tenacious is the demon's hold that he does not easily let go when once he has gripped. Therefore when, at the prayer of his follower, he has sent a sickness, it is on the understand-

ing either that the sickness shall never for any prayers be cured or assuaged, or that it shall be commuted for a graver sickness in another man. Thus the demon provides that in any event he is always the gainer.

☆

Examples.

Claude Morell said that the greatest compulsion he felt to remove the evil spells which he had cast was due to his fear of prison, the lash, or any violence.

On this point Remy (III, 3) writes as follows. I was speaking of this matter with one of the Ministers of His Most Serene Highness the Duke of Lorraine, who told me in good faith that at one time he had been informed that his infant son had suddenly fallen ill, and that it was thought that he had been bewitched by a certain old woman. He first made enquiries from the nurse who had been holding the child when he was taken ill, and then formed an accurate estimate of the nature of the sickness, whether or not it was of the sort which naturally overtakes children of that age. He decided that without doubt it could only be due to magic and witchcraft; and after pondering over this conviction, could not come to any other conclusion save that his son had been bewitched by that old beldame. Accordingly he ordered her to be summoned, and when she was alone with him in the house he at first appealed to her kindly, if she knew of any cure for the sickness, that she would freely use it, and he would not be ungrateful. But when he saw her begin to be very voluble in averting any suspicion of witchcraft from herself, and obstinately refusing to listen to his entreaties that she would find a cure, he took a rope which he had ready for the purpose and so beat her on the shoulders and flanks that she said she was ready to do what he asked: only she

---

* "*Roman Forum.*" *When a chasm appeared in the forum at Rome in 362 B.C. the soothsayers announced that it could only be filled by throwing into it the city's greatest treasure, whereupon a gallant youth, Mettus or Mettius Curtius, in full armour mounted his steed and leaped into the abyss which incontinently closed over him. Varro tells us that the spot was blasted by lightning in 445 B.C. and was enclosed by Curtius, one of the consuls for that year, whence the legend had its origin.*

required a little time to prepare what was necessary for the work. This was granted her and she was given all the opportunity she desired for ministering to the sick child, and soon afterwards she restored him to health by the application of certain matters which were not themselves of any medicinal value, but were used as a cloak for her witchcraft.

Remy in the same place tells the following, which is similar: My friend Antoine Blyestem, the public treasurer of Dammartin and that district, once told me that the same thing had happened to a son of his. For he said that, as children will, the boy had wandered from his mother to play while they were in church, and an old woman came and stroked his head as if to pet him, and after blessing him went out as if she were hastening off somewhere. The boy then hung down his head and, hardly able to stand up, clearly showed by his pitiable crying that he was sick. So he was carried home and, when the sickness grew worse every hour, all who heard what had passed were convinced that it had been caused by that old woman, who was already strongly suspected of being a witch. She was therefore seized by some neighbours and brought to remove the spell; and as soon as she was in the child's presence she began to suffer the same kind of affliction as the little lad was suffering; for her face grew livid and she foamed at the mouth, causing great terror to those who saw her and thought that she had become raging mad. When the night came, she spent it in the same bed as the child, at times lying upon him with arms outstretched, and her mouth upon his mouth as if she were trying to restore his failing life with her warmth and her breath. From the talk of the women who were watching it was learned that a buzzing, such as is made by the gadfly in summer, was heard at times about the boy; and that they ceased to see the fragment of the Gospel which was stitched to his pillow as a godly charm, though they could not tell whether it had been taken away by the witch or her demon. But the truth was that the boy who, the day before, was thought to be sick to death was found at the dawn to be well and strong. Yet this was no advantage to my friend: for it was not long before he had to repay it with interest when he lost through witchcraft the greatest part of his cattle which was stabled there.

At Dammartin, December 1587, Nicole Stephanie of Saint-Pol was induced by a reward to purge the castle from the plague which was afflicting it, since she had a reputation for skill in such matters. She performed this task with great care: but after a sufficient period to prevent any fear of further contagion, and when she had been paid her reward and was allowed to depart, she was angry at being dismissed earlier than she expected and at the thought of losing the good rich living she had been enjoying, and thought that she could provide an excuse for delaying her departure by casting some spell of sickness on the Chatelain's wife, who had been very prompt and eager to dismiss her. So without any hesitation she decided to afflict that lady with a disease, so that she might again be asked for her services in removing it. Accordingly she at once went and stood at her bedroom door and said: " My Lady, the folds of your stomacher are disarranged: let me put them a little in order." And when she was admitted to do this service, she cunningly contrived to shake down the lady's back some grains of a poisoned powder which she had concealed in her hand: and at once the lady was attacked with a trembling in all her limbs, such as is suffered at the height of a sharp fever. Before long she began to feel such pain in her feet that they were horribly curled up so that the toes were twisted round to the heels. All this was seen and noted by the servants; and the woman was seized and kept under observation, and finally put in fear of the lash, and threatened that they would not let her go until she removed the spell from their mistress and restored her to her former health. For their suspicion of witchcraft had been increased by the fact that she had been heard to say that any skill she had in preventing or averting the plague was derived from a certain Matthieu Amant, who not long since had been condemned to death for witchcraft, and that to pay for her initiation she had let him swive her and had been made pregnant by him.

At first she cried aloud that they were wronging her cruelly in repaying her thus vilely for her services to them, and threw out threats of hanging herself. But when they none the less seemed to persist in their opinion, and she saw she could do no good in that way, she changed her tactics and began to ask, if she must needs find some cure for the lady, that they would wait while she tried to call to mind whether she had ever heard tell of a remedy for such a sickness.

Soon afterwards she came back and said that she had found a remedy in which they could put their hope and faith, for she knew a herb which when rubbed into the bath would infallibly cure that sickness: and she begged them not to take it ill if the cure were not instantaneous, since it was not so easy a sickness to cure.

Meanwhile when her son, who was with her, saw his mother thus seized, he feared the same fate for himself since he knew that he was implicated with her. So at dead of night he let himself down by a rope from the battlements. But he was caught the next day and brought back bound, and bidden to confess why he had escaped so secretly: whereupon he explained everything as we have told it; adding that he was entirely responsible for causing his mother to look for an excuse to postpone her departure, and that all those fomentations which she was so meticulously applying to the sick lady had no remedial value, being no more than a pretext to give the impression that the cure was wrought by the appropriate natural remedies. For, he said, she had already begun a secret antidote as soon as they first threatened to beat her; but there could be no shortening of the time which was set at the beginning for the duration of the sickness. Let them, then, wait until the day of the week and the hour had twice recurred; for that was the time set for the spell, and after that their mistress would surely recover her health, being at least freed from all pain although her limbs would still remain weak. In the hope he thus gave he was in no respect found to be wrong: for at the very moment of the day he had foretold the sickness was assuaged.

But on the following night it returned in an acuter form. For, as was discovered afterwards, the witch had repented of undertaking the cure, on the ground that she had been induced to do so in order to provide convincing and indubitable evidence of witchcraft against herself. For, as I have shown above, it is one of their laws that a spell can hardly be removed or assuaged except by that witch who has cast it. This was the reason then why the spell was renewed and re-inflicted by the woman.

The next day when complaint was made to the son of the failure of his prediction he cursed much under his breath and would only say that they should lash his mother as cruelly as possible, for that was the only remedy against her treacheries. So she was again seized, and two lusty peasants went on lashing her with vine birches, kicking her, beating her and shaking her, and finally dragged her to the fire, until she gave her promise to heal their mistress that very day and hour. This she fulfilled, giving her to eat an apple which she had first drugged in the sight of many with a whitish powder. So she was at last allowed to go, as she had been promised, and fell into the hands of the officers of justice waiting at the castle gate. For the Judge, having inquired carefully into her life and manners, had ordered them to seize her and put her in chains; and forthwith she confessed everything as it had happened, and was finally burned together with her son.

Stephane Noach of the district of Châtenois was for three years continually sick and in such pain that he was little short of madness; and despairing of all the usual remedies tried by the physicians, he finally turned to sorcery for his cure. There was at that time at Crainvillers a man pre-eminently famous for witchcraft, and to him he went and told all his story, and was informed that his sickness had been brought upon him by that woman whom on his return home he would find talking with his wife. The warlock made a chain from some pliant twigs, and told him to throw it round her neck as soon as he came to her, and to threaten her fiercely that he would quickly kill her unless she at once restored his failing health. He went home and saw sitting with his wife by the hearth an old woman named Parisette of Neuvillers, and as he had been advised he frightened her as much as he could both by word and deed. She at once fell and embraced his knees and asked forgiveness, and promised that he should be healed of all his sickness if he would do as she told him. First, he must not hesitate to eat a pear which she would give him; for though at first it would appear as hard as a stone, it was not really so, for when he rubbed it it would become as soft as if it had been well cooked. Then, he must at once lie down in bed; for his sickness would then grow worse, even to the point of death. On that account he must summon two chosen women from the neighbourhood to keep watch over him that night. By the presence of these women this vilest of witches cunningly prepared a defence for herself if it should ever be objected that black art had been employed, since such a long and severe illness had been cured so easily and quickly: for she would not expose any of her methods to open view. Noach said he would agree to any condition so long as he was freed from his great pain. But when he took the pear, he at first said that it was impossible to bite it, since it was plainly made of iron: but while he was saying this, and squeezing it a little, he was surprised to feel it become as soft as wool. When he had eaten it (and it was most unpleasant in taste) he at once felt such burning pains in his stomach that live coals could hardly have been hotter. He went to bed at once, and was like a man at the point of death. His trembling wife watched over him that night together with the two other women. She was indeed by her own affection for her husband induced to sit up with them, and her countenance was already full of grief and woe, so that he might see his wife's real tears instead of the forced ones of strangers. They had kept careful watch up to midnight, when the witch secretly sprinkled them with her Lethean powder, like another Mercury, and put them to a deep sleep. She then took the sick man on her shoulders and carried him into the next courtyard, where she placed him upon an immense bear, which carried him backwards and forwards many times, groaning all the time as if the weight were too much for it. But this was the voice of the demon grieving that, against his will, he was compelled to give her help in curing the man. The witch cried out more and more against the demon's tardiness, and kept urging him to proceed with his work, saying: " Come, then, you vile and odious beast, now you are getting your deserts, you who first drove me against my will to afflict this man!" The terrified rider of the beast afterwards testified on oath that he had heard these words. Meanwhile the women who were watching by the bed awoke and, finding it empty, made a hasty search throughout the house for the man in their care: and when at last they found him alone with the witch in the courtyard, they asked him why he had gone from them without their knowledge, thus naked and unattended. The witch made it her business to answer them first, saying: " Do you not see that I brought him here that he might go to stool? " But they did not wait to bandy words with her, turning their whole attention to lifting the man and carrying him as quickly as possible back to bed : but while they all with the greatest effort could scarcely accomplish this, the witch easily did it by herself. In fulfilment of the witch's promise No-a c h, a f t e r what we have just describ-ed, was eased of his sickness, but still there remained no small degree of pain: and the reason for this was that the inoppor-tune arrival of the other women had prevented her from a suc-

cessful conclusion of the work she had begun well. She said, however, that there must then be a delay of eight days, after which he would re-gain his health without any hindrance : and so it happened. Being manifestly guilty of this and other crimes, she was at length put in prison; but she broke her bonds in the very Court of Justice, and escaped.

☆

CHAPTER XIII

*After the Many Blasphemies Committed by Witches, the Demon at last Tries to Induce them to Kill themselves with their Own Hands.**

Argument.

ALL who have given themselves to the devil and have been in bondage to his power confess that he keeps them in such a harsh and unjust slavery that he often puts it into their minds to take their own life, by stabbing, hanging, hurling themselves to the ground, or drowning, so that they may shake off the devil's cruel yoke. And when they make such attempts they are followed by such sudden and instantaneous death that no help, however promptly brought, can be of any avail. It is certain that the devil so insistently urges and goads them to this desperate course, so that, after having spent nearly their whole lives in wickedness and crime, witches may with their own hands cut off what little remains to them, and finally end their abominable lives in an eternal death. Thus the devil contrives that they whose lives were one continual crime shall

---

* "*Induce them to kill themselves.*" See Boguet, "*An Examen of Witches*" (*John Rodker, 1929*), *c. xlv:* "*Satan often Kills Witches when they are in Prison, or else he Inspires them to Kill Themselves. Sometimes he Reveals what will Happen to them at their Deaths*" (*pp. 130–32*).

in death suffer eternal punishment. For death, which men commonly term the end of life and all its misfortunes, is for these poor wretches but a beginning of misery. But the Divine Shepherd in His unspeakable mercy and lovingkindness again and again recalls to the fold His sheep that have been carried away by the wolf, and again He feeds them in the celestial pastures; and so when witches have been cast into prison and have confessed their sins, not grudgingly and under the stress of torture, but willingly and with penitential joy, it may well be said that they obtain the opportunity to avert so great and eternal a calamity from themselves at the small expense of their most wretched lives. For the bow does not always strike where it aims, neither is it always in Satan's power to drive men where he will by his violence. He is permitted to tempt men, but not to coerce them. For this reason it is that he does not himself cast despairing souls against their wills into the waters, or hang them by a rope from a beam, or stab them with knives; but he only lures them to commit such madness. But all his wiles are often thwarted by God, who pities the folly of men and in His wisdom protects them, now in this way and now in that, as will be seen from the examples.

☆

Examples.

Remy says (III, 6) that he saw the body of a malefactor named Sedenarius hanging by the neck from a nail insecurely fixed in the wall, by means of a flimsy and rotten strip of undercloth-ing, with his knees drawn up just clear of the floor. And in this way he had killed himself just as easily as if he had been hanged from a high beam with a short rope, and a skilful executioner had performed the operation. And nearly all such who kill themselves die just as quickly and easily.

I was at Hambach in Lower Germany in the boundaries of Flanders during the reign of the Serene Duke John William, of the Duchies of Cleves and Jülich, being there for the purpose of curing that same Duke, who was bewitched. A ninety-year-old sorcerer priest was summoned, named John, who had a cure of souls at a town named Lauch in the Archdiocese of Cologne; for, according to his own confession, he had by witchcraft made the Duke mad, fearful and panic-stricken. Three days before he was summoned by the Duke there appeared to him in his house at Lauch a demon, who told him that the Duke would shortly send to him, but warned him on no account to go, since he saw danger in it. To him the sorcerer answered: "What is that to you? I shall go where I wish." Hearing this, the demon said no more but, as the witch himself told, pulled down his breeches (for he had taken the form of a nobleman with an attendant servant) and, turning his bum to him, let fly a fart of such an intolerable stink that the sorcerer could not be rid of that stench for three days, although he fumigated the house with incense and other rare perfumes. This ninety-year-old sorcerer came to the Duke and, being questioned, confessed that he had bewitched him, and that at that time he had invoked Lucifer, the Prince of the Devils, to inscribe those characters which comprised the spell. Afterwards, as he was sleeping in a tower in a state of despair because he was to be burned for the crime which he had confessed, a demon appeared to him and tempted him so that on Sunday morning, the 25th September of the year 1605 now passed, he cut his own throat with his knife; and although the wound was not serious enough to cause instant death, yet the demon, in that very act of desperation, seized violently on to his soul and carried it to hell, to the great astonishment of all. I saw the man dead, and still warm, lying on the straw: and as he had led the life of a beast, so he lay upon the provender of beasts. For so did Divine Justice dispose, which rewards every man according to his works; and God willed that he, who had for ninety years lived a follower of Satan, should also end his life at the hands of Satan.

Jeannette Gallee gave a very complete proof of one of my contentions. For she begged and entreated the magistrate who examined her not to delay her well-merited punishment any further, for she was well content to undergo it in order that she might the sooner expiate the terrible crimes which she confessed she had committed against God.

From the moment when she confessed her crimes to the Judge Nicole Morell did not cease to proclaim her happiness in thus being able first to make her peace with God and free herself from all her bondage to the devil. For she said that such had ever been her wish for three years, but she had been unable to accomplish it, or even to attempt it, because that enemy was so tenacious of his prey.

Catharine Latomia of Marques did not deny that for her horrible sins she deserved the extreme penalty and the utmost severity of her Judge; but she asked that, if there was left her any room for mercy, she might be granted one request, namely, that her death should be no longer deferred, so that she might stand as soon as possible before the tribunal of that Judge in Whom all her hope was placed, since her soul was very heavily laden.

Idatia of Miremont implored her Judge to sentence her to death as soon as possible; for she said that even if she were loosed from her bonds she would never be free to mend her ways and bring forth better fruit, because she had pledged her faith to the devil, as to an inexorable creditor, and could not escape her obligations to him as long as she lived.

Apollonie of Freising said that nothing could be more welcome to her than death, by which she could at last put an end to her most wicked life: for as long as she lived she would be unable to abstain from sin and witchcraft, since her demon was so assiduous a persuader, and she could only by death free herself from his domination. On the next day therefore she was the first of all to find a term to her unhappiness, and to open and lay bare her life to her Heavenly Father.

Antonia Mercatrix said that she desired nothing so much as to die placed on the fire as quickly as possible, since she knew that she had long justly deserved such a fate.

Because of his patricide and many foulest mischiefs wrought by witchcraft, the two Supreme Justiciars of Nancy passed a very heavy sentence upon Desiré Finance of the neighbourhood of Châtenois, namely, that he should be punished by being torn with red-hot pincers and then be cast alive on to the fire. Whether he was informed of this by his demon (as it has been and will be shown that it has happened to many), or whether his own consciousness of his horrible guilt foretold it, he determined to die at once by his own hand and so escape that punishment. So he took a knife which his gaoler had carelessly left in the bin with the bread, and thrust it as far as he could into his throat, and so died. In the same year there were in Lorraine more than fifteen who thus killed themselves to escape public execution. But, lest my readers' minds be filled with horror, there is enough of this: let us turn to matters which had a more fortunate outcome.

Jeanne de Ban by her free confession gave evidence that her demon had never persuaded her so importunately to anything as he had that she should throw herself into a well or drown herself in a river, or hang herself with a rope, or destroy herself in some way or other, and that it was impossible to say how insistent he had been when he knew that she was about to be made a prisoner, just as if he saw a morsel being snatched from his jaws: and even after her imprisonment he had not relaxed his efforts, but had rather redoubled them and the more insistently tried to bring his wishes to accomplishment. And when she excused herself by saying that there was no means of killing herself in prison, he showed her in an obscure corner of the prison a neglected chain which she could, if she wished, put round her neck, and so strangle herself. In the end she had consented; but she was prevented from achieving her purpose by the fact that there was nothing from which to hang the chain.

In the same way he tried to persuade Anna Drigée. For he represented to her the horrible torture of the flames in which she was to die, the disgrace of being made a public example, and the infamy she would incur in the eyes of all; and so easily persuaded her to prevent all this by killing herself. But her desire (natural to all of us) to escape present misfortune was combated by the thought that she would certainly lose her soul's safety; and that is a thing feared by even the most abandoned. Therefore her mind was drawn to a contrary decision, and she firmly rejected the demon's advice that she should throw herself out of the prison window, which gave on to a precipice.

When he could by no argument bring Desiré Guerardu to commit this crime, the demon added as a further inducement that, if he killed himself, he would come to be a demon like himself, who would have power to fulfil all his wishes. But not even this promise could make him budge from his determination. For he had so often before been deceived by the wiles of the familiar that he suspected all such advice, holding it certain that the demon would keep no better faith with him in the future. For it belongs to the devil only to persuade, not to compel; as it is said in S. Matthew iv: "If thou art the Son of God, cast thyself down."

☆

CHAPTER XIV

Upon Those who have once Fallen into his Power the Devil keeps a Tenacious Grip, even when They stand Tortured before Their Judges, or in Holy Places, or wherever They may Be.

Argument.

ONCE the devil has acquired power over a man he obstinately guards and retains it, so that he does not lose his hold of, or deny his help to, his bondslave even when such a one stands bound before the Judge; just as a strenuous pugilist does not slacken or relax his efforts so long as his strength endures and he is able to fight. And the demon never leaves those who have once followed him until they are snatched from him as a lamb from a wolf. And when he foresees such an event, he often drives them by base counsel to take their own lives by hanging themselves, or else he actually kills them by twisting their necks, beating them, or (unless God prevents him) persuades them some other way to death, as we have elsewhere shown in our examples. Or if even this is forbidden him he contrives, if he can, to do some horrible thing so that he shall not go away without leaving mischief and misfortune. And although this is so evident as to be apparent to any who have leisure to consider the matter, it will not be tedious to describe certain happenings which may help us to understand better the wiles of our enemy. There is, moreover, no place so sacred or religious but that bold and intrepid old Enemy will try to violate and break into it when he is pursuing his prey. He roams about churches, shrines, the cells of anchorites, and frequently and assiduously haunts them; and this should not seem wonderful to anyone, when it is remembered that formerly he dared to be present when the Sons of God gathered before God, as we learn from Job i. And wherever he may be, he shows himself visible to those whom he wishes, while the rest are able to discern nothing; as will be seen from the examples.

☆

Examples.

As soon as Quirina Xallea was cast in prison a demon came and told her that she would not come out from there except after having endured the most excruciating torture; but if she would only bear in silence a short period of pain, she would certainly be free afterwards; and meanwhile he would not fail her at her need. And, as he had foretold, so it happened before long. For while she was being tortured and was in supreme anguish, he hid himself in her hair-net and did not cease to encourage her and to promise that the torture was just coming to an end. And if it so happened that the examiner signed to them to relax the torture a little, he would foresee this and tell the wretched woman that it was going to happen, just as if he was the cause of it. But when there was no end to her pain and it became more than could be borne by the most hardened, she broke into these words: "Take me away; for that deceiver of mine has given me enough of his words. See, I am ready to confess the truth." And so when she was free from the devil, whom she was bidden to abjure in a solemn declaration, she told the whole in order from that day when she had given herself to the devil.

In the same year and at the same place Anna Xallea told a similar story in nearly the same words. But she said that her devil had hidden himself, not in her hair, but at the back of her throat while she was being tortured, doubtless that he might more easily prevent her from speaking if by chance she felt impelled, through inability to bear the pain, to confess the truth. And in the opinion of those who were

present this was no deception; for they saw her throat swell to a great size until it became level with her chin and so livid and discoloured that they could easily believe there was some large object strangling her.

Among many other women condemned to the fire for witchcraft, whose names I do not now remember, when Claude Simonette and her son were led into prison it was observed that a demon in the form of a fly* buzzed round their temples and repeatedly warned them not to lay their crimes bare by confession even under stress of the direst torture: for if they confessed, it was most certain that they would be condemned to the most terrible death; whereas if they held their tongues they would shortly escape safe and unharmed.

Françoise Fellet said that a demon had impressed upon her a similar need of keeping silent; and moreover that her ears were so deaf to the Judge's words when he first questioned her that she heard no more than if he had not spoken at all: but that when this spell was at length overcome and the truth had been wrung from her by torture, the demon had not ceased from that time to threaten her with death, And for that reason she begged that they would not leave her alone,

---

* "*Form of a fly.*" *Beelzebub was the Lord of Flies, and it was considered that a familiar might often assume the appearance of a fly. In the description given by the Rev. John Gaule ("Select Cases of Conscience Touching Witches," London, 1646) of the methods employed by Matthew Hopkins the watching of witches is particularly described. The suspected witch was placed cross-legged or in some uneasy posture upon a stool or table in the middle of a room. Here she was watched and kept without meat or sleep for twenty-four hours. "A little hole is likewise made in the door for the Impe to come in at; and lest it might come in some less discernible shape, they that watch are taught to be ever and anon sweeping the room, and if they see any spiders or flyes to kill them. And if they cannot kill them then they may be sure they are her Impes."*

especially at night, when she had the greatest fear of being attacked by him.

At the same place, in the year 1587, François Fellet, who had twice escaped a capital sentence by concealing the truth and resisting the torture, was a third time accused, and was convicted and, after a full confession, paid a belated but heavy penalty for his crimes. There have not been lacking others who have endured the stress of their questioning without confessing, and when they were on the point of being discharged have at last discovered the crimes about which they had so long kept silence.

This is exemplified by the case of Marguerite Valtrin, who endured the executioner's fiercest tortures for a whole hour without admitting anything against herself; but when at length she was to be discharged she asked that the Judge should be summoned, and first having asked pardon of him for her obstinacy which was due to the lying promises of the demon, she then unburdened herself by a confession of every sort of wickedness.

Not unworthy of being recorded is what happened in the same year to Alexia Belhore, to the utter amazement of all who were present, when she wished to behave in the same way. For when she had in like fashion prepared herself for a free confession, and had in the manner of Christians prefaced with the Lord's Prayer, she rushed backwards against the wall behind her with such violence that many were of opinion that she should be carried away as a dead woman. But after a little she came to herself and, being asked what had caused her mishap, said: "Do you not see the executioner lying under the bed, who just now seized me by the throat and nearly strangled me? See how he threatens me and does all he can to prevent me from saying a word about him. That is not the first time he has tried to keep me from telling the truth: for while I was being tortured he stood by my left ear as big as a thumb, and

busily warned me to hold my tongue and not allow myself to be overpowered by a short period of not too violent pain.

Remy writes as follows of a case which he witnessed with his own eyes: There was a witch commonly called Asinaria, from her husband the ass-driver, whom I was confounding with the evidence that had been given against her, so that she had no room left for evasion. Accordingly she was preparing herself to make a full confession, when she suddenly changed colour and fixed her eyes in horror upon a corner at the back of the prison, and began to lose all power of speech or thought. I asked her what it was that so suddenly ailed her; and she answered that she saw at the top of that corner her Little Master* threatening her with hands forked and jagged like a crab's claws, and that he seemed about to fly at her. I looked there, and she continued to point her finger in that direction, but I could see nothing. I then told her to be of good courage, and with every confidence spoke a great deal in contempt of that Little Master: and at last she recovered from her fear and was starting to tell her story. But before she had begun she saw him again in a monstrous guise starting out from another corner. He had completely changed his appearance, just as if he had been a play actor on the stage, for huge horns were sprouting from his head, and he seemed on the very point of rushing violently upon her. But

---

* "*Little Master.*" Bodin, "*Démono-manie,*" II, iv, quoting the examination of three witches at the Castello San Paolo, Spoleto, by Grilland, says that the youngest of these made an ample confession concerning her attendance at the Sabbat. "*Et quãd il falloit partir pour y aller, elle oyoit la voix d'vn homme, qu'elles appelloyent leur petit maistre, & quelquesfois maistre Martinet.*" "*Euocaba-tur,*" says Debris (II, xvi), "*uoce quadam, uelut humana ab ipso daemone, quem non uocant daemonem, sed Magisterulum, aliae magistrum Martinettum, siue Martinellum.*"

when he was again reviled and loaded with derision he departed, and was never again seen by her, as she frankly declared when she was on her way to the stake.

Elsewhere there have been told, and will be told, examples of how the demons enter sacred buildings and cloisters.

☆

CHAPTER XV

A Summary in a Few Words of All the Crimes of Witches.

SEBASTIEN MICHAËLIS in his *Pneumalogie** gives an example of a sentence passed at Avignon in 1582, as comprising in a little space the most execrable and abominable of the crimes of Witches and Sorcerers. The extract is as follows:—

We N. N. having considered the charge wherewith you stand charged and accused before us, and having examined both the statements of yourselves and your associates, and your own confessions made to us according to lawful requirements and often repeated upon oath, as well as the depositions and charges of the witnesses and the other legitimate proofs, basing our judgement on that which has been said and done during this process, we are fully and lawfully agreed that you and your associates have denied God the Creator of us all and the Most Holy Trinity our Maker, and that you have worshipped the devil, that ancient and implacable Enemy of the human race. You have vowed yourselves to him for ever, and have renounced your most Holy Baptism and your sponsors therein, together

---

* *"Pneumalogie." "Discours des Esprits en tant qu'il est de besoin pour entendre et résoudre la manière difficile des sorciers. Fait et composé par le R. P. Sebastien Michaëlis, Docteur en théologie de l'ordre des Frères Prescheurs, et Prieur au couvent Royal de S. Maximin en Provence." Paris, 8vo, 1587.*

with your part in Paradise and the eternal heritage which our Lord Jesus Christ bought for you and the whole race of men by His death. All these you did deny before the said cacodemon in the form of a man, and that blatant devil did baptise you anew with water, and you did change the names given to you at the Holy Font, and so took and received another false name in the guise of baptism. And as a pledge of your fealty sworn to the devil you gave to him a fragment and particle of your clothing; and that the Father of Lies should have a care to delete and obliterate you from the book of life you did at his direction and command with your own hands write your names in the black book there prepared, the roll of the wicked condemned to eternal death; and that he might bind you with stouter bonds to so great a perfidy and impiety, he branded each of you with his mark as belonging to him, and you did swear homage and obedience to his behests upon a circle (the symbol of Divinity) traced upon the earth (which is God's footstool); and each of you bound herself to tread under foot the Image of the Lord and the Cross; and in obedience to Satan, with the help of a staff smeared with some abominable unguent given to you by the devil himself and placed between your legs you were enabled to fly through the air at dead of night to the place ordained, at an hour fit for vilest criminals, and on stated days you were so carried and transported by the Tempter himself; and there in the common synagogue of witches, sorcerers, heretics, conjurers and devil-worshippers, you did kindle a foul fire and after many rejoicings, dancings, eating and drinking, and lewd games in honour of your president Beelzebub the Prince of Devils in the shape and appearance of a deformed and hideous black goat, you did worship him in deed and word as very God and did approach him on bended knees as suppliants and offered him lighted candles of pitch;

and (fie, for very shame!) with the greatest reverence you did kiss with sacrilegious mouth his most foul and beastly posterior; and did call upon him under the name of the true God and invoke his help; and did beg him to avenge you upon all who had offended you or denied your requests; and, taught by him, you did wreak your spite in spells and charms against both men and beasts, and did murder many new-born children, and with the help of that old serpent Satan you did afflict mankind with curses, loss of milk, the wasting sickness, and other most grave diseases. And your own children, many of them with your own knowledge and consent, you did with those magic spells suffocate, pierce, and kill, and finally you dug them up secretly by night from the cemetery, where they were buried, and so carried them to the aforesaid synagogue and college of witches: there you did offer them to the Prince of Devils sitting upon his throne, and did draw off their fat to be kept for your use, and cut off their heads, hands, and feet, and did cook and stew their trunks, and sometimes roast them, and at the bidding of your aforesaid evil Father did eat and damnably devour them. Then, adding sin to sin, you the men did copulate with Succubi, and you the women did fornicate with Incubi: moreover, in most bitter and icy connexion and foul coitus with demons you did commit the unspeakable crime of buggery. And, most hateful of all, at the bidding of the aforesaid Serpent thrust from Paradise, you did keep in your mouths the most Holy Sacrament of the Eucharist received by you in the sacred Church of God, and did execrably spit It out upon the ground that you might with the greatest of all contumely, contempt and blasphemy dishonour God, our true and sacred Hope, and promote the glory, honour, triumph and kingdom of the devil himself, and worship, honour and glorify him with all honour, praise, majesty, authority and adoration. All which most grave, abhorred and unspeakable crimes are directly contumacious and contemptuous of Almighty God the Creator of all. Wherefore We, Brother Florus, etc.

☆

CHAPTER XVI.

The Devil Deceives and Seduces by means of False Revelations or Apparitions.

Argument.

TOUCHING revelations or visions and as to the character of the person who sees them, much must be taken into consideration if the true are to be distinguished from the false. In the first place it must be discovered whether such a person is of the true Catholic faith; for no credence can be placed in the visions of devil-worshippers or heretics. In the town of Gretz, in the year 1601, there were a man and his wife who persistently declared that it was through them alone that the Church had endured. Therefore the father baptised their children, with the mother acting as sponsor. They foretold that the world would come to an end in that year; but they were hanged, and by their own death anticipated that of the world.

Secondly, it must be considered fanatic, for no belief may be placed in the revelations or prophecies of such. Firmilian* sent to S. Cyprian many who had been deluded by a woman of this sort (Epistola lxxiv.).

Thirdly, it must be examined whether the person's honesty and virtues point to the sincerity of his faith, or whether his vices and notable imperfections constitute a contrary indication. For we must not believe the proud and ambitious, the impatient, the carnally minded, drunkards, those who cherish anger or stir

---

* *"Firmilian."* Bishop of Caesarea in Cappadocia, died c. 269.

up hatred and spread dissent, or those who defame others; nor hypocrites who display and parade some exceptional proof of devotion and penitence, against the approval of their superiors in the Church.

Fourthly, the state of his body must be considered. For if his health is not robust, if he suffers from a retching of the black bile, if his body is wasted through excessive fasting or want of sleep; if he is injured in the brain, or is excessively timid and subject to a violent clouding of the imagination; none such are to be credited. For it is said that such men, even when they are awake, think they see, hear or taste that which is not there to be seen or heard or tasted; for the devil easily deludes them, since they eagerly accept and believe the images of false appearances.

Fifthly, the consideration of their age and sex must not be neglected. For in their declining years persons are often delirious; and if they are children there is the risk of a light and morbid imagination,since the brains of children are more humid than the normal, and are full of vapours and are influenced by a little thing. Therefore in times past the demons used to love to utter their oracles through children's mouths, as being more adapted to their work. And as for the female sex, it is agreed that this must be regarded with the greater suspicion, as is noted by Johann Nider* in the *Praeceptorum*, I, 11, in the Question *De Diuinatione*.

Sixthly, it should be considered whether the person is an old practitioner of such spiritual exercises, or whether she is only a novice; whether the devil has in other ways attempted, with or without success, to deceive her; and whether her former prophecies were true, and, if not, which of them

were false. If she is a novice there must be suspicion of fraud. For, according to Gerson, the fervour of a novice is soon misled if she has none to control her, especially in the case of the young and of women, whose fervour is too eager, captious and unbridled, and therefore suspect. By this indication Giovanni Francesco Pico della Mirandola (*De rerum praenotione*, IX. 3) discovered the falsity of a certain revelation or vision, after other indications had tended to prove its truth; for the devil, to give his vanities an appearance of verity, had begun to speak in the likeness of our Lord Christ.

I said above that the sex is to be taken into consideration; for, other things being equal, greater faith is to be placed in the revelations of men. The feminine sex is more foolish, and more apt to mistake natural or demoniacal suggestions for ones of Divine origin. Women, too, are of a more humid and viscous nature, more easily influenced to perceive various phantoms, and slower and more loath to resist such impulses. Therefore women are quicker to imagine, but men are less obstinate in holding to their imaginings; and since women have less power of reasoning and less wisdom, it is easier for the devil to delude them with false and deceptive apparitions.

Further, since women are lascivious, luxurious and avaricious in their manner of life (as Apollonius has remarked), it must be noted whether such prophetesses are particularly garrulous, of a roaming disposition, evildoers, greedy of praise, passionate, and whether in their teaching or in their attitude towards the Sacraments of the Church they show themselves in any way opposed to the Apostolic doctrine. For women of this sort not only deceive themselves, but drag even learned men to destruction when these place too much credence in them, as will be shown in the examples.

---

* *"Nider."* I have used the Douai edition, *1612*, of the *"Praeceptorum diuinae legis."* There were seventeen editions of this book before *1500*

☆

Examples.

Father José de Acosta,* in the *De temporibus nouissimis,* Bk. II, ch. ii., relates the following:—

In the Kingdom of Peru there was a man who was at that time held to be of great ability, a learned professor of Theology, a pious Catholic of long standing, and almost esteemed the marvel of his age. This man became familiar with a woman who declared that she had been taught certain mysteries by an Angel and was not infrequently thrown into a trance (or rather she pretended to be rapt) like another Priscilla† or a Maximilla

among the Montanists: and he was so enslaved by her that he often consulted her upon the deepest points of Theology and in all things treated her as an oracle, proclaiming that she was filled with mighty revelations and was very dear to God. Yet in other respects she was mundane enough and had very little intelligence except for constructing lies. But whether she was possessed by the devil (as is the easier to believe) when she went into this sort of ecstasy, or whether she cleverly simulated it (as many prudent men have thought), the result was that the Theologian, hearing from the woman many wonders concerning himself and wishing greatly to enhance his future importance, freely avowed himself a disciple of him whom the woman called her spiritual father. What followed? The man was so far led astray that he tried to perform miracles, and was persuaded that he did perform them, although there was never even the slightest indication of a miracle. For this reason, and because he had taken from that prophetess certain doctrines foreign to the teaching of the Catholic Church, he was, to the amazement of the whole Kingdom, seized by the Judges of the most Holy Inquisition, and was for five years patiently heard and examined, until finally he was clearly proved to be the proudest and maddest of all men. For although he most obstinately maintained that he had been divinely gifted with an Angel from whom he learned all that he wished, and that he was on terms of the most familiar conversation with God Himself, yet he proclaimed the wildest absurdities which no one could believe it possible for any man to give utterance to unless he were quite out of his mind. None the less, as to his intellect, it seemed to all that no one could be saner. He soberly affirmed that he would be King and Pope, when the Apostolic See had been transferred to

---

* "*José de Acosta.*" *1540–1600. It has been said that few members of the Society of Jesus in the sixteenth century have been so uniformly eulogized as Father Acosta. His learning and the philosophic spirit pervading his many works attracted the widest attention. Born at Medina del Campo he became a Jesuit novice at thirteen, and in April 1569 he was sent to Lima, the Jesuits having been established in Peru during the preceding year. In Peru, through which country he travelled extensively, he occupied many important positions. Returning to Europe he filled the chair of theology at the Roman College in 1594, and at the time of his death he was rector of the College of Salamanca. A good biography and a short bibliography of José de Acosta will be found in Enrique Torres Saldanando's "Los antiguos Jesuitas del Perú," Lima, 1882.*

† "*Priscilla.*" *Or Prisca (also called by Epiphanius Quintilla), and Maximilla, two prophetesses, together with the prophet Montanus founded the sect called Montanists, schismatics of the second century. The headquarters of these enthusiasts were in the village of Pepuza, and the ecstatics did not so much speak as messengers of God but vaunted that they were possessed by God and uttered oracles in His Person. It appears that the extravagances of the sect increased after the deaths of the founders (Maximilla must have died about the end of 179, Montanus and Priscilla yet earlier); but Tertullian, the most famous of the Montanists who definitely broke away from the Church in 207, merely emphasised those particulars of the Montanist teaching that appealed to him and almost ignored the remainder which*

---

was presently to degenerate into Gnostic theosophy and other fantastical heresies.

that Kingdom; that he had been endowed with a sanctity above all Angels
and Celestial Choirs and Apostles, and
that God had even offered him a
hypostatic union with Himself, but that
he had declined this : that he had been
sent to be the redeemer of the world
in point of efficacy, whereas Christ (as
he said) had been so only in point of
sufficiency. All the laws of the Church
were to be abrogated, and he would
make new laws which would be easy
and clear : the celibacy of the clergy
should be abolished, and plurality of
wives allowed, and holy confession
should no longer be obligatory. These
and other arguments he maintained so
strongly that all were astonished that a
man with such opinions should not be
mad. Finally after a long exposure of
his frantic behaviour and when he had
been found guilty of more than a
hundred and ten doctrines which were
heretical or foreign to the true teaching of the Church, skilled theologians were bidden, after the manner of
that holy Tribunal, to reason with the
man and try to bring him back to his
senses and his faith. Accordingly the
Judges and the Bishop of Quito* and
three other doctors met together, and
the man was brought into their
presence, where he defended his most
pernicious cause with such fluency and
eloquence that to this very day, says
the writer, I am astounded that the
pride of the human mind could proceed to such lengths. He professed
that he could not prove his doctrine
except by the Holy Scriptures and by
miracles, which were above all human
reasoning; yea, that he had indeed
proved his arguments by the authority
of the Scriptures far more clearly and
effectively than S. Paul proved that
Jesus Christ was the true Messiah :

that he had performed so many and
such mighty miracles that the resurrection of Christ was no greater. For
he said that he had actually died and
risen again, and that he had most
clearly manifested this. He quoted
from memory (for he had no book,
and even his breviary had been taken
from him) so many long passages from
the Prophets, the Apocalypse, the
Psalms, and other Books, that it was
wonderful merely as a feat of memory:
but he so twisted them to his argument, and so allegorised, that it would
have made anyone either laugh or
weep. Finally he said that, if we
wished him to prove his case by
miracles, he was ready to perform
them at once. And then the poor
fellow proceeded to speak in a manner
that suggested either that he thought
we were mad, or that he was mad himself. For he said that it had been revealed to him that the Archduke John
of Austria had been defeated at sea
by the Turks, and that the Kingdom of
Spain had been nearly lost by the in-
vincible Philip, and that a Council had
been held at Rome to consider the
deposition of Pope Gregory† and the
election of another. All that he told
us that we might know just as surely
as if we had received certain news of
them, saying that he could only
through some divine quality have had
knowledge of them. And although all
this was so false that nothing could be
falser, yet he maintained it all as very
truth. Finally when after two days'
reasoning we could do no good, and
he had been taken as the Spanish
law directs, to be shown to the public
with the other criminals, he kept looking up to Heaven waiting for the fire
to descend upon the Inquisitor and
everyone else as the devil had promised him it should. No fire from above
seized upon us, however; but the fire
from below seized upon that King,
that Pope, Redeemer, and Legislator,

---

* "*Quito.*" *The Diocese of Quito was
created by Paul III on 8 January, 1545, at the
request of Charles V, and made suffragan of
Lima. By the Bull "Nos semper Romanis
Pontificibus," 13 January, 1848, Pius IX made
Quito a Metropolitan See.*

† "*Pope Gregory.*" *Gregory XIII, who
reigned 1572–1585.*

and burned him to ashes. So says Father José.

We read in Surius (1 June) that S. Simeon * the Monk of Trèves was sent by divine command to live at the top of Mount Sinai. One night a demon appeared to him in the form of an angel and bade him celebrate Mass. Between sleeping and waking, he objected that no one who was not in Priest's Orders must undertake that office; but the Enemy urged that he was a messenger from God, and that it was Christ's will, for it was not right that the holy place should any longer be without such a celebration. While he yet argued and resisted, the demon, with the help of another demon, dragged him from his bed and set him, now fully awake, before the altar, and put an alb upon him; but there was a dispute about the stole. For the Enemy would have him wear it after the manner of a priest, but Simeon said he should wear it as a deacon. At length the servant of God came to himself by virtue of prayer, and drove off the Enemy by the sign of the Cross, and bemoaned that he had been deceived.

That Deceiving Spirit, seeing amongst the Premonstratensian Canons† certain ignorant triflers whom he had long recognised as his own vessels since they devoted themselves to idleness and pleasure, so filled them with his false illusion of wisdom that they, who had before been scarcely able to read from a book, now quoted grave matters from books and prophesied even greater and more astounding things for the future. One of them maintained that he understood the prophecy of Daniel and, under a lying inspiration, made certain pronounce-ments with regard to the passage where the prophet writes of the four and the seven and the ten horns and the kings and Antichrist; and so he gained the ears of the more simple, and if it had been possible would have led into error even the man of God the Venerable Abbot Simon of S. Nicolas. For his arrogance went so far that, when they were sitting in the presence of the Superior, he dared to preach a sermon upon that Chapter. One who heard and saw it bears witness to the truth of this, and as a proof has given us the beginning of that sermon, as follows :— "Be ye valiant in war, and fight against that old Serpent." These words did that lying spirit utter through this man's mouth; but he was in no way able to proceed to the truth which follows, namely: "And ye shall receive the eternal Kingdom." When the Deceiving Spirit saw that he could not wholly delude his hearers, being wonderfully full of guile he turned with the greater skill to other methods of deceit; so that if he could not openly subvert those who were on their guard, he might at least disturb them in their meditations. Accordingly that same cleric who was his minister in this work was seized with a sudden and very grave sickness; and whereas he had confined his pronouncements to visible matters, he now turned his face to Heaven and did not fear to speak of matters invisible and ineffable. The Brothers, as is the custom, ran up to give him Unction, and to hear his words; for he said much of himself, but more of many of those who stood round him. Of himself he said that on that same evening he would either be with the Angels in Heaven, or he would be standing restored to health with the Brothers in the choir, Of the others, he considered the character of each and said as if prophesying and prognosticating: "This man, when I was lately borne up to Heaven in the church, I saw called to eternity "; and so he foretold various things of the others.

---

* "S. Simeon." In the "Roman Martyrology" under 1 June is inscribed: "At Trèves, of S. Simeon, a monk who was numbered among the Saints by Pope Benedict IX."

† "Premonstratensian Canons." This history is from Surius under 6 June, the Feast of S. Norbert, the Founder of the Order of Prémontré.

Here note, reader, the degree of the devil's pride when he chooses the ignorant and makes them appear learned. Then he causes them to interpret the Scriptures and to preach before their superiors in places where they should be silent.

Ribadeneira * in his *Life of S. Ignatius Loyola* (V, 10) writes that a few years ago in Belgium in one of the cities of Hainault there was a nun who was thought to be possessed, and she was led to the Superior of her Order to be exorcised. But when the ceremony had already been proceeding a long time, she began to speak successively with different voices, in a gentler voice claiming that she was Christ Our Lord God, while her other voice was harsher and more like a demon: and (with this) she openly blurted out many impieties, and much that was apparently devout; and so some who should have known better came to believe that now Jesus and now the devil spoke through her. This matter so full of danger and deception was carried to such an extent that the woman, as if Christ were speaking through her, dared with solemn intention to utter the canonical words and consecrate the Bloodless Sacrifice; and (ah, woe!) certain pious but ignorant or rash persons bowed in adoration before the unleavened bread consecrated (or rather, let it be said, execrated) by this priestess (but not after the order of Melchisedech) and as if it were the live Body of the Lord brought and placed candles upon the altar and venerated it. Yet there were two indications that it was an imposture: first the fact that she was a possessed woman, and secondly that she dared to usurp the priestly office

which belongs to men, not women. But God deliver us from the like!

In two of the above examples we have shown what fruit may come of intercourse with women of fictitious holiness. I will here in a very few words add a third instance, and Tertullian † himself testifies is indeed a signal example. For he, most profound scholar of his time, trusting in the visions of women as concerning the quantity and colour of the soul, forgot all that he had most learnedly and truthfully written against such women and fell into gross and ridiculous errors.

Francesco Benci ‡ adds the following example. During the year 1590, in a certain outlying district near the town of Arona, some thirty women were tormented by the devil. Most of them were girls of the humblest station, and those especially were afflicted who were bound by a vow of virginity; for it was wonderful with what wiles he surrounded them and with what arts he attacked them, assuming various forms to tempt them to sin or to deter them from honesty. Now he would take the appearance and piety of a monk, or even (a thing which the ears shudder to hear) that of Christ Himself upon the Cross persuading them to impious deeds. Now he would appear as a bear or a lion or a serpent about to rush with gaping mouth upon the virgins and devour them in one gulp. At other times he appeared as a soldier with his dishonourable weapon thrust out, threatening them with fire and thunder if he could not achieve his

---

* "*Ribadeneira.*" *Pedro de Ribadeneira, S.J., 1526–1611, wrote his "Life of S. Ignatius" as an eye-witness of many of the events. It appeared for the first time in Latin at Naples, 1572. The first Spanish edition was 1583. The final text may be accounted the edition of 1594. This book was soon translated into almost all European languages.*

† "*Tertullian.*" *Labriolle dates the "De Anima" 208–11, and by 207 Tertullian had definitely broken away from the Church to embrace Montanism, of which sect the prophetesses were Maximilla and Priscilla. Tertullian was indeed in Guazzo's phrase "sui temporis doctissimus" for of him S. Jerome writes: "Quid Tertulliano eruditius, quid acutius? Apologeticus eius et contra Gentiles libri cunctam saeculi continent disciplinam." "Epistola LXX."*

‡ "*Francesco Benci.*" *A Milanese writer of local gazettes and intelligences.*

aim. But their virgin simplicity, with the help of God, overcame all his subtleties. Great indeed was their faith, and with that shield they quenched the fiery darts of the Evil One. Let us relate two of the many stories which are told of these virgins. One of them, who was born of noble parents and had been gently reared, was much disturbed one night by the devil's temptings; and therefore, though it was mid-winter and bitterly cold, she left her bed and slept naked on the bare floor. But when the flame of her desire in no way decreased (for a mighty fire does but burn the more when water is thrown upon it), she stole from her bedroom into the garden and there, in emulation of the great S. Francis who she had heard had done the same, threw her body into a bank of snow; and, although the demon (who was visible to her) raved and gnashed his teeth, she rolled in the snow so long that she wholly quenched her internal fire with the external cold. To another of these virgins the demon likewise appeared at night in the form of S. Ursula bearing the banner of the Cross with a company of many virgins, and spoke to her as follows: "God sees and loves your zeal in keeping your chastity. But because it is somewhat difficult for you in your father's house, with so much bustle of people coming and going, and so many dangers to be encountered, to avoid contaminating your mind in some part, He has sent us to take you to a Convent of Holy Virgins who have put aside all other cares to serve His will with all their strength." The virgin, with the breath of God upon her, feared some ambush of the devil and drew her right hand from her brow to her breast, and then from left to right in the form of the Cross, and protested that she was most unworthy of such a vision and so great an honour. And she added: "Neither have I very great faith in you, for I fear some hidden guile in your specious counsel. But if you are the messengers of God,

then humbly adore these Relics of the Saints." (For she was wearing these about her neck.) Strange to say, the devils knelt in worship before them, and urged her all the more to hasten her departure with them. But she said: "I may not come to any grave decision without the advice of my spiritual father, and it is not seemly for me to go to him at this hour of the night. Do you, therefore, approach him and make known the commands of God; and when it is day I will come and abide by his advice." At this answer the demons threw off all disguise and hid themselves in their own darkness, raging at, and attacking with their tongues only, and pouring insults and vituperations upon the maiden, who mocked at them and humbly gave thanks to God. What greater wisdom could there be than that of this virgin? But indeed true wisdom became hers who bound herself with the girdle of chastity.

I will add an example of a remarkable precaution, by which we are taught that nothing is safer for a man than to mistrust his own judgement, and to preserve his obedience to his superior even in the face of a vision which compels his belief. S. Genebald,* Bishop of Laon, formed a friendship, which arose from the best of motives, with a woman; but such is human frailty that at last he had carnal intercourse with her. Afterwards he came to his senses and confessed to S. Remigius of Reims. He was shut in a narrow cell like a tomb, and there did bitter penance for seven years. In the seventh year at the vigil of the Lord's Supper, while S. Genebald was spending the night in prayer and lamentation, about the middle of the night an Angel of the Lord came to him in a great light in the cell where he lay, and said to him: "Genebald, the

---

* "S. Genebald." As the nephew of S. Remigius, S. Genebald, first Bishop of Laon, who was appointed to that see in 497, is much venerated in the Diocese of Reims.

prayers of your father Remigius for you have been heard, and the Lord has accepted your penitence and your sin is absolved. Arise and go hence, and perform your Episcopal duties and reconcile penitent sinners with the Lord." But S. Genebald was too terrified to answer anything. Then the Angel of the Lord comforted him and told him not to fear, but to rejoice in the mercy of God shown to him. Thus encouraged, he said to the Angel: " I cannot go from here; for my Lord and father Remigius carries with him the key of this door, and he has sealed it with his seal." And the Angel said to him: " Do not doubt: I am sent from the Lord. Even as Heaven is open to you, so also will this door open." And at once the door was opened, the wax of the seal being yet unbroken. Here, then, are the signs of a true vision: for first he was afraid, and then he was comforted; and the unbroken seal and wax was a true and patent miracle.

Ah, how different was that virgin of Ghent in our own times!

This miserable woman spent much time in prayer and frequently assisted at Mass, but either she did not go often enough to a confessor or, if she did, she did not unfeignedly open to him the secrets of her heart, or else she did not follow his good advice. In any case, by degrees and in various visions the devil filled her with spiritual pride, and at last persuaded her that in all other merits she was the equal of the Virgin Mary, but that the one thing lacking to her was fertility joined with spotless virginity; and that, if she persevered, she would achieve that also. Oh madness, worthy of the folly of women! After that she no longer despised confession but used it regularly for some years, at the same time partaking of the Holy Communion. What followed? Once when she was in church awaiting her Communion, and was fervently praying for that one remaining benefit, she heard a voice say: " Be of good heart, beloved; for know that your prayer is heard and you are

permitted to become pregnant with all the prerogatives of chastity. Have faith that you have conceived from heaven." (For she had lain with the demon who was pretending to be an Angel.) She went home, and felt her womb swelling; and after the due period of gestation she went to a pious and discreet citizen who was well known, and told him all, and asked that she might give birth in the interior of his house, begging him to keep it secret. The man did not believe her story about her visions, yet he would not thrust the woman from his house; for the Sectarians were just then gaining ground, and he feared that if this matter were made public it would give rise to blasphemous and injurious utterances by the heretics. Therefore he took her in and, having engaged a trustworthy midwife, awaited her deliverance. The unhappy woman was afflicted with violent pains, and at length, instead of a human child, shed from her womb a great quantity of horrible, ugly and vile worms, so terrible to see that all were appalled, and of so foul a stench that it nearly killed all who were present. So at last the wretched woman understood that she had been deluded, and that she had reaped the merited fruit of her pride from the Prince of Pride. In this way was the woman deceived.

S. Friard* and his companion, the Deacon Secondel, remained perfectly stable in their anchoretic vocation upon an island, each having his own cell at a long distance from the other's. As they were labouring in strenuous prayer, the Tempter appeared at night to the Deacon Secondel in the likeness of the Lord, saying: "I am Christ to whom you continually pray. And now you are a Saint, and I have

---

* "S. Friard." The two holy hermits S. Friard and S. Secondel of Besné (sixth century) are particularly honoured in the diocese of Nantes. Guazzo has his history from S. Gregory of Tours, "De uita Patrum," X, and one may also consult Surius under 1 August.

written your name in the Book of Life with the rest of my Saints. Depart now from this island, and go among the people healing the sick." Deceived by this illusion he departed from the island without telling his companion; and when he placed his hands upon the sick in the name of Christ they were moreover healed. After a long time he returned to the island and came with great glory to his companion, saying: "I went from the island and have done many mighty works among the people." The other was appalled, and asked what he meant; and he told him simply all that he had done. But the old man was amazed, and said with sighs and tears; "Woe to us! How terribly do I hear that you have been deceived by the Tempter! Come now and do penance, lest his wiles prevail over you." Secondel, understanding his error, fell weeping at his feet and begged him to intercede for him with God; and the Saint said to him; "Come, let us both pray the Almighty for the safety of your soul: for He is not a hard God to those who trust in His mercy, as He said by the Prophet.* I desire not the death of a sinner, but rather that he should turn and live." While they were praying the Tempter came again in the same likeness to the Deacon Secondel, saying: "Did I not tell you, because my sheep were sick and without a shepherd, to go out and visit them and heal their sickness?" But he answered: "I know now of a truth that you are a seducer, and I do not believe that you are God, whose image you falsely assume. But if you are Christ, show me your Cross which you have left behind, and I will believe you." And when he could not show it, and the Deacon had made the sign of the Cross upon his face, he vanished in confusion.

Albert Leander† tells us that when Blessed Jordan‡ of Saxony, the Master General of the Order of Preaching Friars, was suffering from an acute fever, there chanced to be with the venerable Father the Superior, or Prior, of a certain friary of the same Order, a discreet man, skilful, provident, learned and of sober behaviour, who brought him some medical assistance. But he could read the mind of Father Jordan and knew that in his very sickness he bore himself very stiffly towards him. Therefore he said: "Father, a sick man must in all things be subject to his physician if he wishes to recover his former health. Wherefore, although you are the chief and head of our religious Order, now that you are sick you must lay aside your headship and subject yourself to me and obey me. And, if you do this, I have no fear but that in a short time you will go away from here cured." The Venerable Father agreed, and at the order of the prudent Prior lay upon a bed of feathers, contrary to the custom of the Order. In the night the devil came in the form of an Angel and said to him, as if in astonishment: "Is this the famous Jordan so renowned among all men? Is this the Master and Father of the esteemed Order of Preachers? I should doubt it if I had not known you before. Oh how vile and imprudent you have become, that you lie upon a bed of feathers and silken stuffs like one of the Lords of the earth. Unhappy man, what an example you give to the Brethren of your Order! Yet God has not forgotten you, for He has sent me to correct you. Rise therefore from your bed and cast yourself in prayer upon the ground." And at once, when the devil had vanished, Jordan threw

---

* "Prophet." Ezechiel, xxxiii, 11.

† "Albert Leander." A Dominican writer and hagiographir of the sixteenth century. The history is from his "Uita B. Iordanis," xxi and xxii.

‡ "Blessed Jordan." The Second Master General of the Dominicans, which Order he ruled from 1222–1237. His cult was confirmed by Leo XII and his feast is kept on 15 February.

himself in terror to the ground, and after the dawn he was found so lying by the Prior and the Brethren. The Prior seized him roughly and compelled him, on his obedience, to lie upon the bed prepared for him. On the following night the devil came again in the same likeness, and chid him more than before for his disobedience, and ordered him to jump down on to the ground. When the Prior again saw him in the morning lying on the ground he was at first angry, saying: "I wonder at your simplicity, not to say ignorance, that you have presumed to act thus in disobedience and to the danger not only of your body but of your soul. For I call God, the Lord of Heaven and Earth, to witness that, for my part, I would not for the whole world sin so gravely against God and the Order." And so saying he burst into a flood of tears. Seeing this, the Venerable Father himself wept and fell at his feet, and told him of his visions, or rather illusions, and how, as he guessed, it had been the devil, transfigured into the form of an Angel of Light. The Prior was then seized with astonishment and became softened to him through pity, and told him to climb into bed: for these happenings had brought him such a weakness of the limbs and such an induration of his humours that he hardly had breath left for sleep. On the third night the devil came as before, but as soon as he saw him the Holy Man said: "O shameless dog! O most wicked foe to the human race! O filthy beast! How have you dared to delude my simplicity under a cloak of zeal for our Order? Had it not been permitted by the dispensation of Almighty God, I should have been more prudent in noting that obedience is far better than the sacrifices of fools." And spitting in his face, he put him to flight. Not long after his death S. Meinolf[*]

the canon of Paderborn and Confessor appeared in a vision to one of his sacristans, urging him quickly to renounce the world and its pomps, and to fight under the banner of the Eternal King. But the man took the vision to be an illusion, and made no attempt to mend his life. The Saint had pity on his infirmity and again warned him as before: but when even so he took no thought for correcting his life, he appeared the third time and said: "You know not, unhappy wretch, you know not how the savage Thief is claiming your soul for himself; for he it is who has persuaded you to disobey the message of God and of me who am sent by Him. When you were plainly going astray in evil living and would not of your own will desist from sinning, a Divine revelation warned you so that you might thus betake yourself to better fruits. But, fool that you are, you allowed yourself to be miserably and perniciously deluded, taking a true revelation to be a fantastic illusion. For none of the faithful can be in doubt that there is no illusion about that revelation which invites a man to Christian piety and religion. But if such a vision were to come to you while you were awake, you ought in no wise to despise it: and since words will not serve to correct you, we must proceed to deeds. Therefore, that I may make it plain that the vision which you affect to misunderstand was a very true one, you shall be left in no doubt at all." When the Saint had said this, the man arose and found that his entire beard had been torn from his chin, and all sleep fled far from his eyes.

Cardinal Jacques de Vitry,[*] in his

---

* "S. Meinolf." S. Meinolf was a canon of the Cathedral chapter of Paderborn in the first half of the ninth century, and the founder

of the Böddeken monastery. His feast is kept on 5 October and his life by Person Gobelinus ("Uita Meinulphi") will be found in the "Acta Sanctorum" of the Bollandists, October, vol. III, 216, sqq.

* "Jacques de Vitry." Historian of the Crusades, cardinal, Bishop of Acre, and later of Tusculum, was born c. 1160 and died at

Book *de Mulieribus Leodiensibus*, I, 9, tells that a friend of Blessed Marie d'Oignies was notably infested by an evil spirit which walked in darkness at noon-tide and was sometimes violently and sometimes cunningly dangerous. For the subtle Enemy transfigured himself into an Angel of light and appeared to him familiarly in dreams under the cloak of piety, sometimes reproving him for certain faults, sometimes fraudulently urging him to good works; so giving him as it were a false seeming antidote that anon he might the more secretly instil his poison, and caressed him with a honeyed tongue that he might afterwards sink his teeth in and bind him securely to his tail. For when the man had put a complete trust in him, then that Betrayer, like a sophist or impostor, so covered his falsehoods with a shadow of truth that at length by his machinations he led that Brother to what would have been a disastrous conclusion of his life, had not the handmaiden of Christ learned through the revelation of the Holy Spirit the deceits of that cunning Enemy. For she told the man that those revelations of his were not from God but were illusions of a wicked demon: but he on the other part objected, guided by his own spirit instead of the Holy Spirit, saying: "That spirit has brought me

so many benefits, and has truthfully foretold so much of the future, that I am sure he does not wish to impose upon me." The woman then had recourse to her customary weapon of prayer (see, what a sure remedy and shield it is!), and watered with her tears the feet of the Crucifix, assailing Heaven with her prayers; nor did she cease until that wicked Impostor with much groaning and shame came to her as she prayed in her cell at night. Seeing him thus clothed in false splendour, she said: "Who are you, and what are you called?" He looking proudly and balefully at her said: "I am he whom you with your cursed prayers have compelled to come to you; and you are trying to take from me my friend by force. I am called Dream; for I appear in visions in the likeness of Lucifer to many, especially to Religious, and they obey me and by my consolations are driven from their senses and consider themselves worthy to converse with Gods and Angels. And I was just about to lead from righteousness that friend of mine who is lost to me through your will." And so it proved in the event. But the adder's eggs were broken, and the evil counsels of the Wicked One were brought to light.

In his *De schismate Anglicano* Nicholas Sander* relates how the heretics formed an unheard of Plot† to rouse a

---

Rome 1240. *After attending the University of Paris he visited Marie d'Oignies, a mystic of the Diocese of Liège, who had won a great reputation for sanctity. Acting upon her advice he became q Canon Regular and from 1210 to 1213 he was one of the most eminent preachers of the crusade against the Albigenses. His "Liber de Mulieribus Leodiensibus" is very famous. The most celebrated of these holy women was Marie d'Oignies, whose visions he relates; see "Acta Sanctorum," June, vol. IV, 636, 666.*

S. Marie d'Oignies was born at Nivelles about 1177 and died at the béguinage of Oignies in 1213. Her feast is kept in the dioceses of Namur and Liège on 23 June. Her holy Relics were enshrined by order of Pope Paul V in 1609.

---

* *"Nicholas Sander." 1530–1581. Educated at Winchester and New College, Oxford, he graduated in 1551. Under Elizabeth he had to fly the country and was ordained at Rome. His writings are very valuable and he did much to help the oppressed Catholics during the Elizabethan persecutions. The most widely known of his books is the "De schismate Anglicano," which was published after his death, first at Cologne in 1585 and in the following year with many additions by Father Parsons at Rome. It has been translated into various languages and frequently reprinted.*

† *"Plot." "De schismate Anglicano." Rome, 1586, "Liber Secundus, Maria" (pp. 342–2), where Sander gives details of this silly and profane plot. Elizabeth Croft or Crofts, an*

turbulent mob to disturb the people of London and urge them to sedition and heresy. They persuaded a girl eighteen years of age, corrupted both by heresy and bribes, to act the following abominable lie. She permitted herself to be shut up for a time between two walls in an obscure corner of a certain house, and through a suitable crack to utter such words as were suggested to her by the plotters. The girl's name was Elizabeth Croft, and the name of the author of the plot was Drake. Accordingly, having been thus instructed and posted in the place convenient for the deception, the girl kept making wonderful utterances from her hiding place, so loudly that all the neighbours could hear her. They ran up from all directions to see what it was, and in their wonder declared that it was not a mortal voice, but the voice of an Angel. That spirit threatened the city and the country with misery, suffering and every misfortune if they permitted the Spanish marriage, or communion with the Pope of Rome. The voice also uttered much in the manner of an oracle against the Holy Sacrifice and the rest of the Catholic Faith. Some of the conspirators took care to mingle with the crowd and interpret the prophetic and darker sayings of this spirit as admonitions for the subversion of religion and the stirring up of sedition. The Lord Mayor, to appease the multitude and to see what the matter was, found some difficulty in exposing the fraud: but at last he decided to pull down the wall and those next to it, whence the voice seemed to come. The wretched girl was then discovered and was questioned as to who had induced and persuaded her to act in that way; and she at once confessed that she had been led to that horrible wickedness by certain seditious sectaries, and especially by the villain who was called Drake.

☆

CHAPTER XVII

Of the Appeal to God.

Argument.

IT is dangerous for men not of proved righteousness to provoke such an appeal. Indeed they commit mortal sin who knowingly and unjustly call others to judgement, for so they cause grievous harm and injustice and the Judges are brought into disrepute as the oppressors of the innocent. But if such action is taken without hatred, desire for vengeance, impatience, anger, despair, vanity or any other vicious motive; or if anyone oppressed by injustice acts in good faith to make his innocence appear, so that his family should not become infamous, or that the world should be rid of such a tyrant, or that he should be turned and through fear become penitent and cease from his oppression and down-treading of the unfortunate; then such a citation is lawful, neither

---

idle wench of eighteen, has found a place in the "Dictionary of National Biography." Early in 1554 she seems to have concealed herself in the thick wall of a house in Aldersgate Street, and through a whistle or trumpet her voice uttering denunciations of the Catholic Faith, King Philip, and the Queen herself sounded so hollow and loud that large crowds collected, amongst which confederates spread the rumour that the locutions were divinely inspired. Before July 1, 1554, the mysterious voice, "the spirit in the wall," was traced, and Elizabeth sent to Newgate. Drake, Sir Antony Knyvett's servant, had supplied the whistle and a rabble of low rascals were numbered among his accomplices. On Sunday, 15 July, Elizabeth Crofts was set on a scaffold by S. Paul's Cross, and there she read her public confession and on her knees asked forgiveness of the Queen. She returned to prison very penitent, but owing to the clemency of Mary was soon released. See Stowe's "Annals," 1554, and the authorities cited in "The Dictionary of National Biography."

did François Feuardent * dare to condemn it, since when the end is good I suppose the means if indifferent are to be commended. There are many examples in Holy Writ. Sarah said: "The Lord judge between me and thee." (*Genesis* xvi, 5). David said to Saul: "The Lord judge between me and thee, and the Lord avenge me of thee." (I. *Samuel* xxiv, 12). So said Zechariah the son of Jehoiada: "The Lord look upon it and require it." (II. *Chronicles* xxiv, 22).

☆

Examples.

Thomas of Brabant in his *De Apibus*, VII, records a most memorable event in the following words: The Monastery of S. James at Liège is well known to all, as is the truth of the following story. A young man who was cousin to the Bishop entered that monastery for the sake of devotion and religion. But when the Bishop heard this he was enraged and collected a strong band of his servants and, forcing his way into the monastery, seized the young man and stripped him of his religious habit and clothed him in secular clothing. The Abbot of the monastery therefore collected the chief men of the city and complained to the Bishop, and appealed to all the clergy concerning this outrage. But the Bishop in his rage

would scarcely listen to him, but rather spoke harshly to the Abbot; whereupon the Abbot knelt down and said with great moderation: "O Bishop, I can have no Judge against you upon earth; and therefore I appeal to God the Supreme Judge against you, that within forty days both of us may appear before him to receive judgement according to our deserts." The Bishop laughed at this, and with his followers mocked at the good man and despised him and drove him away in disgrace. What happened? On the fortieth day about Nones that Abbot died; and as they were solemnly tolling for him the Bishop, sitting in his bath, asked the bystanders what it was. Soon one came in and said that the Abbot of S. James had just died, and that the solemn tolling was for him. The Bishop then remembered that it was the fortieth day since the time he had been summoned by the Abbot, and in terror of soul said to his followers: "Quick! See what I must do. I am dead, and to-day I must appear in the sight of the Supreme Judge." Shortly after these words, as he was hastening out of the bath, he died with a terrible groan in the arms of his attendants, without doubt being compelled to answer for himself there where no causes are cried and the pleadings of advocates are silent, where freedom cannot be won by prayers or by bribery.

Fregoso, I, 6, writes that François I,†

---

* "*François Feuardent,*" *1539–1610. A famous Franciscan theologian who took a prominent part in the religious and political troubles which so disturbed France during his day. He was one of the most zealous preachers in the cause of the Catholic League, and achieved no mean reputation as an eloquent and ardent defender of the Faith. In his old age he retired to the convent of Bayeux which he restored and furnished with a large library. For his own works, both theological and controversial, one may conveniently consult Wadding-Sbaralea, "Scriptores Ordinis Minorum," ed. Nardecchia, I, 80, sqq.; Rome, 1906. The present reference is to his "Entremangeries et guerres ministrales" (Caen, 1601).*

† "*François I.*" *Born at Vannes, 11 May, 1414; the eldest son of John VI of Brittany. When Sir Francis Surienne invaded Brittany on the pretext of redressing the wrongs done by the Duke to his younger brother, Gilles, François appealed for protection to Charles VII of France. The king after remonstrating in vain with the Duke of Somerset on the conduct of Surienne instituted against the English a campaign which led to their expulsion from Lower Normandy. The cruel treatment of his brother by François has left an ineffaceable blot on his memory. But it had terrible results. A month after the death of Gilles in 1450, François, confronted in his sleep by his brother's confessor, was solemnly cited to appear in forty days be-*

Duke of Brittany, with infamous and cruel treachery put to death his brother who was returning from England. But within a year the Duke in his turn perished miserably, for his brother had cited him to the tribunal of God, and thus he most wretchedly lost both his Dukedom and his life.

☆

CHAPTER XVIII

Of the Trial by Single Combat.

Argument.

IN former times, when an accusation was doubtful and could not be proved, no sort of trial was more common than this. For then either the accuser challenged the defendant, or else the defendant offered himself or someone else in his place to fight. It is agreed that this is a most ancient practice, and that it was used in the lands of Palestine; for Alciati * points out in his *De singulari certamine*, II, that David† challenged and overcame Goliath. After the invasion of Italy by the Barbarians it was chiefly practised by the Lombards, the Germans, Franks,

and even Spaniards. But this sort of combat provides no proof; for it is against all law according to the unanimous opinion of the Doctors. Sufius (*De iniustitia duelli*) and Pedro Mexia‡ (*Silva de varia leccion*, *IV*, 9) prove that it is contrary to natural law. All the Doctors agree in proving that it is against the civil law, although that law is not very clear in detail; yet there is no Roman law by which such combats can be justified. That duels are forbidden by the law of God is proved by every argument which forbids us to tempt God, and by the Commandment that we shall do no murder. This is more clearly proved by the Ecclesiastic, or positive Divine Law, as expressed by the Council of Trent as follows: The detestable practice of duelling, introduced by the wiles of the devil that he might win the death of souls together with the bloody death of the body, should be entirely exterminated from the Christian world, etc. (Sess. XXV; De Reform. cap. XIX). And a little later the same holy Council added the following: They who engage in duels, and they who act as seconds thereto, let them be punished with excommunication and the confiscation of all their goods and perpetual disgrace, and may they for ever be deprived of ecclesiastical burial like murderers, etc. There exists that most admirable Bull of Pope Gregory XIII of blessed memory, issued in the year 1582 in the month of December, which begins with these words: *Crescente hominum malitia,*§ *facinorosi non desunt.*

---

fore the tribunal of God, there to answer for his misdeeds. Terror gave full effect to the ghostly citation, which the wretched man perforce obeyed, dying on 19 July, 1450.

* *"Alciati." Andrea Alciati, 1492–1550, the famous Italian jurist.*

† *"David." This Scriptural example was of old quoted by several writers in support of the wager of battle and the duel. But as early as 1240 S. Ramon de Peñafort ("Summa," II, tit. 2) definitely laid down that all who engage in such combats are guilty of mortal sin. Cardinal Henry of Susa is no whit less uncompromising ("Aureae Summae, V, tit. "De Clu. pugnant"). Alexander of Hales ("Summae, III; Q. xlvi, Mem. 3) regarded the precedent of David and Goliath as altogether an exception from which no argument must be deduced. It was to him only permissible to refer to it in an allegorical manner as prefiguring the triumph of Christ over the devil.*

---

‡ *"Pedro Mexia." This famous Spanish author was born c. 1496 and died in 1552. His "Silva de varia leccion," published at Seville in 1543, has been compared to the "Noctes Atticae" of Aulus Gellius. Mexia was a great favourite with Charles V and collected material for a history of that monarch. This, unfortunately, was never written.*

§ *"Crescente hominum malitia." Reference may also be made to the glosses of Pedro Mattei upon the Bull "Mox laudandam" of Gregory XIII. Benedict XIV decreed that duellists, even if they had not perished on the duelling-*

Examples.

In the year 1326, when William III was Count of Hainault, a certain Jew pretended to be baptised in all sincerity into the Holy Christian Faith, and the Count gave him the name of William at the font and appointed him as a servitor in the palace at Mons. Not long afterwards this wicked fellow entered the church at the monastery of Cambrai and in a fit of fury hurled a number of blasphemies against the image of the Mother of God, and (oh, horror!) wounded it with his spear in five several places from which streams of blood at once flowed. This was seen by a carpenter and by a lay Brother named Matthaeus Lobbius. The carpenter was about to cleave the Jew's head with his axe, but he was prevented by the Brother. They reported the matter to the Abbot, John of Mons, and he to the Count. The Jew stubbornly withstood all torture and was therefore released, but four years later an Angel appeared to an old man named Jean Flander D'Esteney who had been bed-ridden with paralysis for seven years, and ordered him to accuse the Jew and challenge him to a duel. After he had been thus warned twice, the old man still, at the bidding of the parish priest, delayed, but the third time the Virgin Herself came and showed him her five bleeding wounds, and commanded him to fight the duel. Full of hope and faith the old man went to Cambrai, and having seen the wounds upon the image obtained an audience of the Count and thereupon accused the Jew of his crime. A day was appointed for the combat; and the weapons, rough clubs* and wooden shields, exist even to this day. The Jew, who although he seemed but a puny fellow was in fact muscular and vigorous, had sewn a number of little tinkling bells to his galligaskins and gambadoes in bitter mockery of the poor old man: but God helped His champion who had undertaken so unequal a fight, for the sick man beat the healthy man, the weak the strong, and the old the young. And as he was convicted terribly blaspheming and impenitent, the Count ordered him to be bound by the hair of his head to a horse's tail and so dragged to the gibbet, and after he had been hanged by the neck with two fierce Molossian hounds rending his flanks, he was cast into the fire. This story is fully told by Robertus Hauport, who wrote a poem in two books on the subject.

Radislaus,† a Prince of Kreis Kaurim (Kolin) and son of Mistibogius, wrongfully invaded Bohemia, so that at last good King Wenceslaus was persuaded to raise an army against him. As they were on the point of joining

---

ground but had lingered and later received absolution, should without exception be denied Christian burial; Pius IX in the "Constitutio Apostolicae Sedis," *12 October, 1869,* excommunicates all who are in any way accessory to a duel, who are present at a duel, or who permit and do not prevent a duel, even though they be kings or emperors; Leo XIII in his letter "Pastoralis officii," *12 September, 1891,* emphasises the fact that the duel is an offence against the Divine Law proclaimed both by the inspired Holy Scriptures and natural reason.

* *"Rough clubs." When champions were employed on both sides, and such would be actually the case here since the old man was fighting in honour of Our Lady, the law of battle restricted the combatants to the club and buckler. See Patetta, "Le Ordalie" (Torino, 1890), for full details. Philip Augustus in 1215 directed that the club should not exceed three feet in length, but in England this baton was often rendered a formidable enough weapon through being furnished with a sharp beak or pick of iron. The wooden shield was generally covered with leather. It may be remarked that the difference of age between the old man and the Jew was altogether exceptional as the punctilio of combat required an equality.*

† *"Radislaus." Guazzo's sources for this history are: Widukind of Corvey, O.S.B., "Res gestae saxonicae siue annalium libri tres," II, which see in the "Scriptores rerum germanicarum," Hanover, 1882; Vincent of Beauvais, "Speculum," xxiv, 70, and Dubravsky, "Historia Bohemorum," v.*

battle, Wenceslaus said: " If the matter cannot be settled except by fighting, why should we two not decide it in single combat without shedding innocent blood?" And without delay he put on a cuirass over his hair shirt and girt himself with a small sword and came out into the battle field. But Radislaus armed himself to the teeth with mighty armour. Wenceslaus made the sign of the Cross on his brow, and suddenly saw Angels who spoke in human voice, saying: " Do not strike." And suddenly Radislaus lay upon the ground and asked pardon for his boldness and yielded himself into the hands of his victor. Wenceslaus raised him up, forgave him and restored him to his dignities, bidding him to turn his contumacy to fitting humility, lest he should thereafter suffer severer punishment from the angry Godhead. Here God declared the justice of the cause by a miracle.

When God does not wish a miracle to take place, it generally happens that the matter remains in doubt, or that he who is in the right submits to the judgement of God. The first was the case in a duel between two noble Spaniards in the time of King Alfonso XI,* the father of King Pedro of Castile. Their names were Ruy Paez de Biedma and Pay Rodriguez de Ambia. The former accused the latter of treason, and the latter retaliated with an accusation of an even more serious crime. They met and fought for three days from sunrise to sunset, and both were sorely wounded; yet the affair remained in doubt and neither could claim the victory. Therefore the King declared them both innocent and equally virtuous, and bade them be friends. This is fully related by Pedro Mexia in his *Silva de varia leccion*, II, x.

---

* "*Alfonso XI.*" *This combat took place in 1342. See the "Crónica de Alfonso el Onceno," cap. CCLXII.*

☆

CHAPTER XIX

Of Vulgar Purgation by Fire.

Argument.

THIS purgation was formerly of three sorts; that by the pyre, that by burning coals, and that by red hot iron: and a man's innocence was proved if he escaped unhurt from the ordeal. The ordeal of red hot iron is still used by the Japanese, as we learn from letters written in the year 1595 by Father Luis Fröes, a Jesuit, which were afterwards printed at Mainz in the year 1598. In France in olden times it was only legal in secular causes, as we learn from the Epistles of Ivo.† I find that this hot iron was called a "judgement," and that this name was applied to all the instruments of these vulgar proofs, as is noted by Pierre Le Loyer in his *De Spectris*, II, 7. It is referred to in various laws of the Northern peoples introduced by the Gauls into Italy after the Barbarian invasions. Radevicus‡ in his *De Friderici Imperatoris Gestis*, I, 26, mentions a military law by which a slave who has not been caught stealing, but is accused of it, was commanded to prove his innocence either by an oath before God or by the ordeal of red hot iron. The laws of the Franks and Lombards provided that a man accused of murder must purge himself by walking over nine red hot ploughshares.

---

† "*Ivo.*" *S. Ivo of Chartres denied the liability of ecclesiastics to the Ordeal, but allowed that it could be properly used on laymen, and even pronounces that there is no appeal from the result. "Iuon. Carnot. Epist." ccxxxii, ccxlix, cclii.*
‡ "*Radevicus.*" *A Canon of Freisingen. His "Libri duo . . . de . . . Friderici Imperatoris gestis" were published, folio, 1515. Another edition is the text given in Tissier's "Bibliotheca Patrum Cisterciensium," vol. VIII, folio, 1660. The work is also included in Wursisten's "Germaniae Historicorum illustrium Collectio," folio, 1670.*

We learn from the Council of Tribur* that in Germany this purgation was not employed for nobles (for whom it was enough that twelve of their peers should swear their innocence), but for the base-born. Yet history proves that even nobles often underwent it, using either red hot blades or red hot gauntlets or some other such thing. In the year 1215 or thereabouts Conrad of Marburg,† the Apostolic Inquisitor, ordered those who had denied a charge of heresy to undergo the ordeal by red hot iron; and if they were burned he at once committed them to the stake. If this is true, he acted against the Canon Law: for Pope Stephen V had already forbidden that practice.

☆

Examples.

A certain Christian‡ was living in the land of Omura with the heathen, and was accused of theft. Now this is a crime most severely punished in Japan, so that if a man be convicted on the very slightest evidence he is condemned to death without hope of pardon. But they could not truly convict this Christian; so the heathen, baffled in all other attempts, insisted upon his being forced to swear an oath after their custom in the following manner: he must write the needful oath upon a paper and, with the paper in his hand, must grip hold of a red hot iron, calling upon his head the vengeance and wrath of Kami if he were guilty; and if his hand were burned they would say that it was a proof that he was guilty, and if his hand and the paper were unharmed it would prove him innocent. Being placed in this dilemma (for either he must take this oath, or else by refusing to do so prove himself guilty and endanger his life), the Christian relied upon his innocence, but said that it was not lawful for him as a Christian to swear by the false Kami, but only by the true God. The heathen agreed that he should swear by his own God. He then made the sign of the Cross on the paper and, being forced to take the red hot iron in his hand, gripped it with the greatest confidence. And by a notable miracle neither his hand nor the paper was burned. He was therefore freed not only from the punishment with which the heathen threatened him, but also from the accusation which they had falsely brought against him.

The Emperor Otto III§ had a wife named Maria, of slippery faith and no conscience. Like another Phaedra this woman tried to entice Amula, Count of Modena, into her embraces, and when she was repulsed conceived a furious hatred against the man whose love she had failed to win; and put her own crime upon him. The Count was aware of her treachery, but was torn between his love for the Emperor and his own honour. His honour gave

---

* "*Tribur.*" *The First Council of Tribur (now Trebur) was held in May 895, and presided over by Archbishop Hatto of Mainz. For the ordinances of this politico-ecclesiastical assembly see Concil. Triburens. ann. 895 apud Harduin, "Concil." VI. i. 446.*

† "*Conrad of Marburg.*" *The confessor of S. Elizabeth of Thuringia, and papal inquisitor. He was assassinated 30 July, 1233. Pope Stephen V reigned 816–17. As recently as 1210 Innocent III prohibited the employment of any ordeal by the ecclesiastical courts ("Regest." xiv, 138). Guazzo has taken this instance from Trithemius ("Chron. Hirsaug." ann. 1215).*

‡ "*A certain Christian.*" *This is from the Japanese letters of Fr. Luis Fröes, S.J., which were collected and printed at Mainz, 1598.*

§ "*Otto III.*" *The date assigned to these incidents is 996. The history is given by several chroniclers: Gotfridi Uiterbiensis Pars xvii, "De Tertio Othone Imperatore"; Siffridi Epit. Lib. I. ann. 998; Ricobaldi Hist. Impp. sub Ottone III. Muratori originally ("Antiquitates italicae medii aeui"; dissert. xxxviii) accepted the old account, but later ("Annali d'Italia"; anno 996) he argues that it is improbable.*

way to his love, for he preferred the honour of Caesar to his own life. But to his wife, a most prudent and (which is rare) brave woman, he told all about the attempt of the Empress, his own answer, her calumnies and his own danger; and said that he had determined to die a thousand bitter deaths rather than bring to light so great a disgrace to the Emperor arising from the incontinence and perfidy of the Empress. And he begged her, if he had deserved her love, to witness that he would undergo the sentence of death which threatened him in all constancy as a faithful husband to her: and when he was dead, he begged her to vindicate the name and honour of her husband and free him from ignominy. Not long afterwards the Count was sentenced to death by a too credulous judge. Afterwards a Court was held at Roncevaux, and on the day set for the hearing of widows' causes, the Count's wife came forward and in legal form before the Court brought a claim of talion against the Emperor, because he had put her husband to death unjustly. Otto in astonishment said: "But how will you prove that your husband was, as you say, innocent?" "By a red hot iron," she answered. At the Emperor's command a well heated iron was brought, and the widow in the sight of all took it and held it in her hand without being hurt at all. This miracle so astounded the Emperor that he avowed that he was worthy to be punished, but he pleaded for delay before he underwent punishment. "I demand a threefold bail from three sureties," she answered, "But I only ask the punishment of the Queen, whose wicked calumnies robbed me of my husband, you of a loyal soldier, and the State of a useful citizen." All thought her demands were just, and the Emperor praised her and offered the security of four sureties in his camp in Etruria. But as for the Empress, who had so evilly burned with the fire of lust, he ordered her to be thrown by the execu-

tioner on to the pyre, there to be consumed in the flames she justly deserved.

In the town of Wittenberg* in Saxony, a man was accused of public incendiarism; but he proved himself on his oath and by ordeal. For he carried a red hot iron for a long way in his hand and put it down on the ground unharmed; but the iron suddenly vanished from sight. Exactly a year later the man who was really guilty of the incendiarism was at work in the town paving the roads with stones, and turned up that iron where it lay hidden, and badly burned his hand. All were astonished, and recognised that iron, and accused the man before the Judge. On being questioned he confessed the truth, and his legs were broken and he was bound to the wheel as guilty. See Kranz, *Historia Uandalorum,* VIII, 30.

Caesarius of Heisterbach (X, 35) describes another equally marvellous instance as follows: Abbot Bernard of Lippe used to say that he knew a fisher in the Diocese of Utrecht who had for a long time fornicated with a woman; and because his sin was too widely known and he was afraid of being accused at a synod which was about to be held, he went straight to a priest and confessed his sin rather, as it appeared later, through fear of punishment than for love of justice; and he received the following advice. "If," said the priest, "you are firmly resolved never to sin again with her, you will be able to carry the red hot iron safely and resist that sin; and I hope that through the virtue of a good confession you will be free." And this was done, to the astonishment of all to whom he had told the matter. He was not hurt by the fire; but when he fell back into a wish to repeat his crime, and boasted that he had no more been burned by the iron than by the water of the river which he was then crossing in a boat, and took up

* *"Wittenberg." This is from the "Chronicon" (Book iv) of Godfrey of Wittenberg.*

some of the water in his hands, the cold water acted as if it were red hot iron and burned all the skin off his hand.

In the same chapter he tells of an abominable hypocrite who hid his crimes under the cloak of a pilgrimage. This man, being bribed by another rascal, burned down the house of his host by whom he had been well entertained: and after he had twice been received into the house, twice showed his gratitude by again setting fire to it. The master in a panic accused many whom he suspected, but they all proved their innocence by safely undergoing the ordeal by red hot iron. The house was built again for the third time, and the iron was put in a corner of it. After some time the false traveller came and was for the third time hospitably received and, seeing the iron, asked what it was for. His host told him, and he replied: "Well, I should put it to some other use, and not let it lie there idle." At the same time he took it in his hand: but it immediately grew hot and badly burned his hand. He dropped it with a yell; and the host in astonishment formed a just suspicion that this man was guilty of having twice burned his house. Therefore he had him seized and taken before the Judge, who ordered him to be tortured on the rack. He then confessed all and was bound to the wheel. So wonderful are the judgements of God.

I will add another instance taken from the abundant store of Caesarius. Rollo the Norman Duke, who was afterwards called Robert, knew that his subjects were given to robbery, theft and rapine. Therefore he made stringent laws against these crimes which he thought would be a sufficient deterrent, and told the peasants that they might confidently leave their agricultural implements in the fields. One of the farmers, on his return home, was immediately asked by his wife why he had not brought his tools with him, and he excused himself on the

ground of the Duke's advice. But she secretly stole the tools from the field and hid them, to teach her husband a lesson in caution. The man went back to the field and, not finding what he had left there, reported it to the magistrate of the place, who in his turn reported it to the Duke. The Duke summoned the peasant to him and gave him the price of what he had lost, and ordered the Prefect to find the thief by means of the ordeal by fire. The first attempt failed to indicate the thief, although all the peasants submitted to the test. Then the Duke turned to the Bishop and said: "If the God of the Christians knows all secrets, why does He not expose the thief?" Since he was not yet well confirmed in the Faith, the Bishop did not reprove him, but said that it was because the fire had not yet touched the thief. So the Prefect was bidden to search more diligently even among the neighbouring villages; but no one was found. The Duke then summoned the peasant and asked him if he had told anyone that he had left the tools in the field; and he answered that he had told no one except his wife. The wife was questioned and confessed the theft. Then the Duke called the peasant and privately asked him: "Did you know that your wife was the thief, or not?" He said: "I knew that she was." Then said the Duke: "Why then did you not either punish her or expose her?" Therefore he ordered them both to be hanged, and by this severity established the law.

There comes to my mind the action of a Spanish Catholic who in the time of Leovigild* challenged an Arian Goth to the ordeal by fire. For when he could make no impression upon him by logic or argument, he said: "I have on my finger a gold ring which I will throw into the fire. Do you take it out

---

* "Leovigild." The Arian King of the Visigoths, 569–86. He was the father of S. Hermengild. This incident is from S. Gregory of Tours, "De Gloria Confessorum," xiv.

red hot." He then threw the ring among the coals and let it become as hot as fire, and turning to the heretic said: "If your contention is true, take it from the fire." But when he refused, he said: "O Almighty Trinity, if I hold any unworthy belief, let it appear; but if my faith is right, let this fierce fire have no strength against me." And he took the ring from the fire and kept it for a long time in his hand, and was not hurt. This was no judicial enquiry, but a cogent argument as to the true and sincere faith.

We read in Polydore Vergil's* *History of England* (Bk. 8) that Robert, Archbishop of Canterbury, persuaded King Edward the Confessor to compel his mother Emma† to undergo the ordeal of walking over red hot ploughshares because she was suspected of having committed fornication with Alwyn, Bishop of Winchester. She was unharmed by the fire, but fled at once from England in terror, and shortly died with a broken heart.

In the Life of S. John‡ the Almsgiver in the month of June, we read that when S. Leontius was sick and felt his death to be at hand, he ordered a thurible full of burning coals to be brought, and in the presence of many took those coals and poured them upon his bosom and said in the hearing of all: "Blessed be God who of old saved the Bush from burning! Let Him be my faithful witness that, even as the burning power of the fire has not touched my garments, so have I never in all my life touched a woman."

In France St. Brice,§ who succeeded S. Martin in the See of Tours, invoked a similar judgement. For the people accused him of fornication with a nun, who used to wash the Bishop's linen, and had given birth to a child by some rascal. S. Brice ordered the child, which was not yet a month old, to be brought among them, and asked it in the presence of the people whether he were its father. The child answered that he was not, but another whom he did not name. This was the work of God, but the people ascribed it to the devil. Then S. Brice filled his biretta with burning coals and wore it all over the city without being hurt; and so he declared himself innocent of the crime of carnal lust, for not even his clothes were touched by the fire.

Peter,‖ a priest of Marseilles, during

---

* *"Polydore Vergil."* Born at Urbino, c. 1470; died there probably in 1555. In 1501 Pope Alexander VI sent him to England as sub-collector of Peter's pence. He settled here, and only returned to his native land owing to the religious changes under Edward VI. The first edition of his "Historia Anglica" was published at Basle in 1533. In the third edition (1535) the work is continued from 1509 to 1538.

† *"Emma."* Giles states (note to William of Malmesbury, anno 1043) that Richard of Devizes is the earliest authority for this story.

‡ *"S. John."* S. Joannes Eleemosynarius, Patriarch of Alexandria (606–16), was born c. 550 at Amathus in Cyprus, where he died in 616. He is said to have devoted the whole revenues of his see to the relief of the poor. He was the original Patron Saint of the Hospitallers, and was commemorated by the Greeks on 12 November. In the "Roman Martyrology" his name is given under 23 January.

§ *"S. Brice."* Bishop of Tours from 397 to 444. Among the principal feasts of his diocese, observed with a vigil, Perpetuus, Bishop of Tours (461–491), sets down: Natalis S. Bricii, 13 November.

‖ *"Peter."* Peter Bartholomew was a follower of Count Raymond of Toulouse. In 1098 during the First Crusade after the capture of Antioch when the Christians were in turn beseiged in that city and sorely pressed by famine, sickness and every need, it was revealed to this humble priest by Our Lord and S. Andrew in a vision that the Lance which pierced the side of Christ upon the Cross lay hidden in the Church of S. Peter. The next day with much toil the Sacred Relic was exhumed, and cheered by this signal manifestation of divine favour the Christians rallied shortly to defeat the Infidels with great slaughter. Yet such was the unhappy rivalry of the leaders of the Crusade that certain of the Frankish princes, jealous of the possession of the treasure by Count Raymond, audaciously presumed to dispute the authenticity of the Relic, blasphemously declaring that the

the First Crusade, at the time of the seige of Antioch (1098), was suspected of heresy. On Good Friday, therefore, he went with the Holy Lance of the

Lord Christ in his hand naked through a pile of burning wood, and escaped unhurt from the fire.

Poppo,* a Danish priest, acted as follows in proof of the Christian faith. He soaked all his clothes in wax and, putting them on, entered a fire in the presence of all the people, and (as he solemnly declared) stood there without feeling any pain while the whole of the clothes upon his body were burned to ashes without the fire having touched his skin. Moved by this miracle, the Danes abolished the ordeal by combat and substituted the ordeal by fire.

From Theodorus† Lector we get the following story. In the time of Marcian‡ two Bishops, one Catholic and the other Arian, began a dispute about the controversies and dogmas of the faith; and at last the Catholic Bishop proposed as a condition of their dispute that they should lay aside all vain arguments and go together into the fire and so prove by the evidence of God which of them had the true faith. The Arian hesitated, but the Catholic went straight into the fire

---

Lance was unworthy of veneration. Peter in order completely to satisfy the doubts expressed as to his veracity offered to vindicate his truth and the identity of the Relic by the fiery ordeal. After a space of three days allowed for fasting and prayer there was built a pile of dry olive-branches, fourteen feet long and four feet high with a central passage one foot wide. In the sight of forty thousand men all hotly impatient for the result, Peter clad only in a tunic and bearing in his hands the Holy Lance boldly passed through the blazing flames. He emerged in perfect safety, but unluckily the frenzied multitude so pressed round him to touch if it were but the hem of his garment that he fell and was trampled in the throng, being injured so severely that he died a few days later maintaining with his last breath the truth of his visions and the authenticity of the Holy Lance. In this account we follow Raimond de Agiles, the chaplain of the Count of Toulouse. He was actually present at the discovery of the Holy Lance and throwing himself into the pit which had been excavated he kissed the point as soon as it was seen in the earth. It was he who officiated at the Ordeal and so delivered the solemn adjuration as Peter entered the pyre. Foulcher de Chartres, chaplain to Baldwin I of Jerusalem, who also has some account of the finding of the Holy Lance, does not write as warmly as he should, and seems a little jealous that the treasure was not granted to his patron. Raoul de Caen who wrote in 1107 and was primed by the party inimical to Count Raymond must not be believed.

The Holy Lance subsequently fell into the hands of the Turks, and there can be no doubt, as all authorities are agreed, that the Sacred Relic discovered by revelation in 1098 was that sent in 1492 by Sultan Bajazet to Innocent VIII to conciliate the Pope's favour towards the Sultan's brother, Djem, who was then a prisoner in the Vatican.

The Holy Lance, preserved at S. Peter's, is one of the Three Great Relics of the Passion which are shown after Matins on Wednesday in Holy Week; several times in the course of Maundy Thursday and Good Friday; and again after Mass on Easter Day. They are exhibited from the balcony over the statue of S. Veronica.

---

* *"Poppo." This is related by Widukind of Corvey, III, 65: Sigebert. Gemblac. Anno 966: Dithmari Chron. II, viii: Saxo Grammaticus Hist. Danic. X. The history is said to be that of Bishop Poppo of Slesvick, the date 962, and the King of the Danes Harold Blaaiand. But the chroniclers of Trèves claim the merit of this conversion for S. Poppo, who was Archbishop of Trèves from 1016 to 1047. "Gest. Treuin. Archiep." xvi (Martène, "Ampliss. Collect." iv. 161). Guazzo has taken as his authority the "Historia Francorum" (iv) of Paulus Emilius.*

† *"Theodorus." A Lector attached to the Church of Santa Sophia in Constantinople during the earlier part of the sixth century. He compiled a "Historia Tripartita," which is mainly an epitome of the historians Socrates, Sozomen, and Theodoret. Fragments of the "Historia" were published by Valesius, who used the book in his editions of the original historians. These fragments may also be found in Migne, "Patres Graeci," LXXXVI.*

‡ *"Marcian." Marcian was Emperor 450–457. Anastasius I was crowned in 491.*

and spoke to many from its very midst, and came out not in the least burned. This is a true story, but some writers say that it happened in the time, not of the Emperor Marcian but of Anastasius I, and indeed they seem to prove their contention from Cedrenus and Nicephorus.

Pietro di Pavia,* Archbishop of Florence, was accused of simony by procuring his dignity with the help of money, and he named a day for his public purgation by fire. In a public place there were built two heaps of wood, ten feet long, five feet wide and four and a half feet high; and between them was a path an arm's length wide strewed with burning coals. When the holy day came, he called upon the help of God to prove his innocence and walked between the masses of flame which rose on high, treading upon the burning coals on the path between the blazing heaps of wood: and when he was about to return by the same way, and there was no sign of burning upon his body or his clothes, he was restrained by the people and went away unharmed. And so the people learned the truth of the matter. See how wonderful is God in his saints.

* "*Pietro di Pavia.*" *This account is slightly confused. Pietro di Pavia, Bishop of Florence, was accused of simony and heresy. Although acquitted by the Council of Rome in 1063, his enemies still continued to denounce him, and when he rejected the ordeal of fire, the monks of Vallombrosa (whose house of San Salvio he had destroyed, butchering many of the religious) determined to decide the question of the bishop's guilt by a public trial, and with the sanction of his abbot S. Giovanni Gualberto, a holy monk Pietro Aldobrandini offered to make the trial. The blazing pyre was lit and before a vast concourse of many thousands he passed slowly through the flames, unscathed, untouched by the fierceness of the fire. It is said that the Bishop now confessed his simony. Pietro Aldobrandini has been canonized, and his feast is kept by the Vallombrosians as S. Peter Igneus, a Double of the Second Class, on 8 February.*

Caesarius† of Heisterbach tells the following:—In the Cathedral City of Cambrai less than five years ago [about 1215] several heretics were taken, all of whom for fear of death denied their perfidy. The Bishop sent a Cleric to examine them with the ordeal of the red hot iron, and if they were burned they were to be sentenced as heretics. They were all examined and all were burned. As they were being led to their punishment, the Cleric kept alive one who was of noble blood in the hope that he might by some means bring him to penitence, and said to him: "You are of noble birth, and I pity you and feel compassion for your soul. I beg and implore you to think better even now of such great perfidy and return from your error to the truth, lest through temporal death you come to death eternal." To this he answered: "I have proved by experience that I was in error. If a belated repentance may avail me at all, I shall not refuse to confess." And he said to him that true penitence was never too late; therefore a priest was called and the man confessed his error with all his heart, promising satisfaction to God if his life were spared. Now as the holy man taught him the power of confession, the man soon began to confess his sins as a penitent; and at the same time the burn upon his hand began gradually and visibly to disappear in proportion as his confession proceeded. When the confession was half made, half the burn was healed; and when he had completed his confession his hand was entirely restored to its former health, all pain and discoloration having vanished. The Judge summoned the man to the fire, but the Cleric asked: "Why do you call this man?" "That he may burn," said the Judge, "since he was burned at the examination." Then the Cleric showed them his hand perfectly whole and freed

† "*Caesarius.*" "*Dialogus Miraculorum,*" *III, xvi and xvii.*

him from punishment; but the rest were consumed in the fire.

Master Conrad Abati tells the following example, which is said to have happened a few years ago at Strasburg. Ten heretics were apprehended in that city, and when they denied the charge they were convicted by the red hot iron and were sentenced to be burned. As they were being taken to the fire on the appointed day one of their escort said to one of them: "Unhappy man, you are damned! But come, and confess your sins now with true penitence, so that after the death of your body, which lasts but a moment, the fire of Gehenna may not eternally burn your soul." He answered him: "I know, indeed, that I have erred; but I fear that God would not accept a repentance conceived under such stress." The other said to him: "Only confess from your heart. God is merciful and will accept your repentance." And lo, a wonder! For as soon as the man had confessed his perfidy his hand was fully healed. He was lingering over his confession, and the Judge summoned him to come to his punishment; but his confessor answered the Judge: "It is not just that an innocent man should be unjustly condemned." And when no trace of a burn was found on his hand, he was discharged. This man had a wife not far from the city, who had heard nothing of what we have just told. When he came to her rejoicing, and saying: "Blessed be God, who has to-day delivered me from the death of my body and my soul!" and told her how it had been, she answered: "What have you done, most unhappy one, what have you done? Have you recanted your true and holy faith because of a moment's pain? It would have been better for you if your body could have been burned a hundred times, than that you should once draw back from the true faith." Alas! who is not seduced by the voice of the serpent? Forgetting the great goodness of God to him, forgetting that

undoubted miracle, he listened to his wife's advice and again embraced his former heresy. But God did not forget to avenge Himself for so great ingratitude, and wounded the hand of each of them. The burn re-appeared upon the heretic's hand, and since his wife was the cause of his returning to his error she was made a partaker in the backslider's pain. The burn was so severe that it penetrated to the bones of their hands: and because they dared not in the town give vent to the cries which the pain wrung from them, they fled to a neighbouring wood where they howled like wolves. What need I say more? They were taken and led back to the city and together cast upon the fire which was not yet quite extinguished, and were burned to ashes. What, I ask, is the truth of the matter? Does the flame follow heresy, even as a shadow follows the body?

In another altogether marvellous happening God manifested the truth, using a demoniac as the executioner of a heretic. Two writers have witnessed to the truth of it: Bernard* of Luxemburg, O.P., in his *Catalogus haereticorum omnium*, under the letter E; and that more ancient authority, Thomas of Brabant, whose words in the *Bonum Uniuersale*, Bk. II, I shall here quote: Near Cambrai there was a very astute heretic who, fearing lest he should be questioned and burned by the Friars Preachers, who at that time were burning many in that city, pretended that he was possessed by a demon; and therefore his friends bound him and took him to Dour to the shrine of S. Aichard who had power to cast out devils, since they thought that his affliction was madness, and not heresy. When a certain cleric, who was possessed by a devil and was bound, heard that Éloi Bou-

---

* *"Bernard."* *Dominican theologian and Inquisitor of the Archdioceses of Cologne, Mainz and Trèves. He died at Cologne, 5 October, 1535.*

gris (for that was the man's name) was in the place, he was by God's will freed from his bonds on the following night, and went and heaped rush mats, straw, and benches from the church upon the bound heretic. Eloi pretended to treat this as a mad joke, until the cleric took a light from a lamp and began to burn the heretic; but upon this he cried out and aroused the gaolers, who ran up and tried to put the fire out. But the cleric seized a sword which he happened to find by the bed, and fiercely drove them all off, and so burned the heretic in the fire. Immediately afterwards, having executed the just judgement of God, the cleric was delivered from his demon and was entirely healed.

S. Gregory of Tours (*De Gloria Martyrum* I, 81) tells how a Catholic deacon disputed with an Arian priest and invited him to prove by his deeds which was the true faith, in the following manner. A fire was lit under a cauldron and each of them was to throw his ring into the boiling water; and he who should take his ring out of the boiling water should be held to have proved his argument. The heretic accepted these conditions; but meanwhile the deacon began to lose confidence, and smeared some unguent upon his hand and arm. The heretic also began to shrink from the danger; but when he saw the Catholic's arm anointed with an unguent, he protested that his adversary was relying upon magic arts and protections, not upon his faith; and a dispute arose. As they were thus quarrelling, there came another deacon from the town of Ravenna named Tacintus, who, when he knew the cause of their quarrel, at once put forth his arm from his robe and plunged it into the boiling cauldron. Now the ring which had been thrown in was very light and small, and was tossed about by the boiling water like a straw in the wind: but he kept searching and groping for it, and within an hour's time found it. Meanwhile the fire under the caul-

dron was burning fiercely and became so hot that it was not easy for his hand to take hold of the ring when he had found it: but at last the deacon drew it out, feeling no pain in his flesh but rather protesting that the cauldron was cold at the bottom and only moderately hot at the top. Seeing this the heretic was quite confounded and rashly thrust his hand into the cauldron saying: "Let this be the proof of my faith." And at once all his flesh was melted and came away from his hand, right down to the joints of his bones. Thus was the dispute ended.

S. Gengulphus* the Martyr tested the violated honour of his adulterous wife in the following manner: He and his wife came to a certain spring, and he addressed her in these words: "O wife, on all sides I hear shameful things of you, unworthy of your birth, but hitherto I am not certain whether they are true or false." She then unblushingly swore that the rumours about her were false, and that she had never defiled herself in another's bed; but S. Gengulphus said: "Divine providence, from which nothing escapes, will clearly show how the matter stands. See, here is a spring, neither very cold nor immoderately hot. Put your hand in, then, and pick up a stone from the bottom; and if you are free from guilt you will suffer no harm, but if you are corrupt God will not allow your crime to be hidden." She ascribed these words of the Saint, as she did all his utterances, to madness, and unhesitatingly plunged her hand into the spring. But as soon as she tried to take hold of the stone, she became stiff in nearly all her limbs, and wherever the water touched her fingers and arm the skin was stripped

---

* "*S. Gengulphus.*" *Originally a warrior and a favourite of King Pepin. He retired from the world and led a life of strictest piety. He is especially venerated in the diocese of Langres. See Pet. Cantor. Uerb. Abbreu. Not. in cap. lxxviii (Migne, "Patres Latini," CCV, p. 471).*

off leaving the bare flesh exposed, and the wretched woman expected nothing but instant death. He put his wife away from him when she was thus convicted of adultery; and not long afterwards, at the instance of his wife, he was murdered by her adulterer.

☆

CHAPTER XX

Of Superstitious Folk.*

Argument.

BE it known to them who lightly use and practise superstitious rites, that the inventor of all superstitious and vain observances is the devil, who at the beginning of the world led nearly the whole human race astray into idolatry. They, therefore, who study and follow superstitious observances show themselves to be disciples not of Christ but of the devil, and they manifest themselves to be lovers of his service and learned in his wiles, and they are alienated from the teaching of the Catholic Church. But it is a marvel that anyone should put faith in such illusions, if he knows of the wretched death of all magicians and conjurers. Zoroaster, the inventor of magic, was at last burned to ashes by the very demon to which he addressed his too importunate supplications, as S. Clement has testified. The fate of Simon Magus is notorious, how he was carried up in the air by demons, and fell and broke his legs, and died in anguish and ignominy. When Heinrich Cornelius Agrippa† was at the point of death he drove from him his dog, a familiar, saying: "Depart, evil beast! You have destroyed me." The citizens knew how Joannes Portantius met his death in prison at Antwerp. William,‡ Archbishop of Tyre, in his *Historia Hierosolymitana* (VIII, 15) tells how two sorcerers tried to bewitch the war machines of the Christians, and were themselves the first to be killed by them.

That conjurer of high estate Zyto lived a consort and companion of devils to the end, when he was taken body and soul from the midst of men. Johann Faust, the famous German sorcerer of our time, was at last dragged from his bed by the cacodemon at night, and was strangled with his face twisted round to his back, and the whole house was shaken and nearly fell, as we are told by Camerarius and others. Francesco Pico tells how he heard from his friends who were actually present that a certain sorcerer had been carried away alive by a demon and was never to be found anywhere again. And Scoto of Parma in our own day had his neck twisted in an ale-house by a demon in Germany, and perished miserably.

☆

Examples.

Johann Pistorius§ the younger in his *Artis cabbalisticae tomus unus* writes

---

* "Of Superstitious Folk." The present Pope, Pius XI, now happily reigning, has recommended (says the "Osservatore Romano," 11 January, 1929) the bishops to condemn superstitions, particularly the prejudice against the number thirteen and the idea that Friday is an unlucky day.

† "Agrippa." But see Weyer, "De Praestigiis Daemonum," II, c. v, 11 and 12. Weyer lived for some years in daily attendance upon Agrippa, and the black dog; "Monsieur," respecting which such strange stories were spread, was a perfectly innocent animal which he had himself often led about on its leash. Agrippa was much attached to his dog, which used to eat off the table with him and of nights lie in his bed.

‡ "William." Born in Palestine of a European family about 1127–30; died in 1190 or a little later. Baldwin IV, who became king of Jerusalem in 1174, appointed William chancellor and then Archbishop of Tyre. His chief work is the "Historia Hierosolymitana" in 23 books.

§ "Johann Pistorius." 1546–1608. The son of a well-known Protestant minister, he was that there was a swineherd who had in his pastoral staff a writing inscribed with the name of S. Blaise; and he thought that the virtue of this staff kept his swine safe from attack by wolves, and placed such confidence in it that he would leave his swine to feed alone in the fields. At last it chanced that, while the swineherd was absent, someone passed that way and saw a demon keeping the herd, and asked what he, the sworn persecutor of human safety, was guarding there. He answered: "I am guarding the swine." The other asked: " At whose bidding?" And the demon said: "Because of the foolish confidence of the swineherd. For he has put in his staff a writing to which he imputes divine virtue because it has upon it the name of S. Blaise; and the fool fast bound in false superstition believes that it supernaturally guards his swine from wolves. And when I had called and called him again, and he did not come, I undertook to keep the swine instead of S. Blaise; for I am always ready to take the place of God and His Saints. And so I most gladly keep his swine for him in the place of S. Blaise, that I may encourage and strengthen the silly man in his vain confidence, and lead him to think more of that writing than of God."

Lucian, in the *Philopseudes*, relates that when a certain Eucrates saw an Egyptian magician named Pancrates do many marvels, he gradually insinuated himself into his friendship until he learned nearly all his secrets. At last the magician persuaded him to leave all his servants in Memphis and accompany him alone, for they would have no lack of servants; and from that time (he said) thus we lived.

"When we came into an Inn, he taking the bolt of the door, or a broom or bar, and clothing it, spoke a charm to it, and to enable it to go, and in all things to resemble a man. The thing going forth, would draw water, provide, and dress our supper, and diligently wait and attend upon us. After his business was done, he pronounced another charm, and turned the broom into a broom again, and the pestle into a pestle. This was an art which, though I laboured much, I could not learn of him. For this was a mystery which he denied me, though in all things else he were open. One day, hiding myself in a dark corner, I overheard his charm, which was but three syllables. He having appointed the bolt its business, went into the market. The next day, he having some other employment in the market, I taking the pestle and apparelling it, in like manner pronounced the syllable, and bid it fetch me some water. When it had brought me a basin full, 'It is enough,' I said, 'fetch no more, but be a pestle again.' But it was so far from obeying me, that it ceased not to fetch water till it had overflown the room. I, much troubled at the accident, and fearing lest if Pancrates should return (as he did) he would be much displeased, took an axe and cut the pestle in two. Then both parts taking several buckets fetched water. And instead of one, I had two servants. In the meantime Pancrates came in, and perceiving what had happened, transformed them into wood again, as they were before I uttered the spell. Shortly after he secretly left me, and vanishing went I know not whither." Here it may be seen how his curiosity was nearly the cause of his being drowned. (*From Sir T. More's translation.*)

Hear another example of how some men were in instant danger of cutting off their own noses. Philippus Camerarius writes as follows: Johann Faust was once with some noted persons who had heard much concerning his magic,

---

converted in 1588. He filled many offices of high responsibility both before and after his ordination in 1591. He wrote several controversial treatises of great value, such as the "Anatomia Lutheri," Cologne, 1595–8. His "Artis cabalisticae tomus unus" was published at Basle in 1587.

and they asked him to show them a specimen of his art. For a long time he refused, but at last yielded to the not too sober company and promised that he would show them whatever they wished. With one accord they desired him to show them a vine laden with ripe grapes: for they thought that, on account of the unseasonable time of year (for it was winter), this would be impossible for him to do. Faust agreed, and said that what they had asked for would presently be seen upon the table: but he made this condition, that they should all keep perfectly still and silent until he told them to pluck the grapes; for if they did otherwise they would be in instant danger of their lives. When they had given this promise, he soon so deceived the eyes of that drunken company and obscured their senses that they thought they saw upon a fair vine as many large and juicy grapes as there were persons present. Greedy for such a novelty, and thirsty after their drinking, they took their knives and awaited his bidding to cut the grapes. At last, after he had kept the fools for some time in suspense in their vain error, the vine and its grapes suddenly vanished in smoke; and each one of them was seen holding, instead of a grape, his own nose with his knife poised over it. So if any of them had forgotten the condition and tried to cut his grapes, he would have sliced off his own nose.

THE THIRD BOOK, TREATING OF THE DIVINE REMEDIES FOR THOSE WHO ARE BEWITCHED; AND OF CERTAIN OTHER MATTERS.

☆

CHAPTER I

Whether it is Lawful to Remove a Spell in Order to Heal One that is Bewitched.

Argument.

WITCHCRAFT is a form of magic whereby with the help of a demon one man does an injury to another. Now the instruments of witchcraft are pots, bands, bars, feathers, little balls, and such things, which the witch uses in order to bewitch a person: and the witch is usually promised that, so long as those bands are knotted in that manner, or so long as a certain matter is buried under the threshold, or certain bolts are barred, for so long will the person affected remain bewitched; or it may cause death to whomsoever is in that place, or enters or leaves it; and so on. Therefore it is asked whether it is lawful, by unbarring the bolt, by burning the ball of hairs, by untying the knotted band, or by digging up the pot and burning or destroying its contents, to break the spell and deliver the person who is bewitched. To answer this question in a few words, I will quote the words of Henry of Ghent.* He says: "It is a Catholic duty to destroy the superstitious work of the devil and thereby to thwart him." (*Quodlibeta*. E.q. 33). And therefore I say that it is clearly lawful to break a spell of witchcraft, just as it is lawful to throw down an idol into the gutter. Duns Scotus* also says (*In 4. Sent. d.* 34): "If the power of the demon be hindered by the prayers of the Saints, it is well: but if God does not hear their prayers, but the charm is discovered and destroyed so that the demon troubles him no more, since by his pact he can only work for as long as the charm endures, then it is not only lawful to remove the spell, but it is even meritorious to destroy the works of the devil. Neither does this savour of infidelity; for he who destroys such evil works does not signify his belief in them, but by destroying them puts an end to the affliction."

☆

Examples.

In the year 1589 a devout young man of Genoa cast wanton eyes upon a woman and conceived such a burning love for her that he forgot his love for God. These two, then, exchanged furtive messages and gifts for the space of three months, after which he was perforce obliged to take to his bed by a grave malady; and it was marvellous what variety of filthy objects he vomited before the eyes of the spectators: women's hairs, sheep's wool, linen, silk, hair-pins, needles, nail-

---

* "*Henry of Ghent.*" Doctor Solemnis; died at Paris or Tournai, 1293. He lived in the golden age of Scholasticism, and as philosopher and theologian ranks only just below his great contemporaries S. Thomas, S. Bonaventura, and the Venerable John Duns Scotus. It has been well said that the writings of Henry of Ghent reflect much deep and searching thought upon the eternal problems of religion and prove that much that has been advanced with great applause by modern inquirers concerning these matters is but a pale reflex of mediaeval knowledge and mediaeval reverent speculation. Of the "*Disputationes Quodlibetales*" or "*Quodlibeta,*" the work to which reference is here made, there are editions Paris, 1518; Venice, 1608 and 1613.

* "*Duns Scotus.*" The reference is to D. 34 of the so-called "*Opus Oxoniense,*" the vast Commentary of Scotus on the "*Sentences*" of Peter Lombard, which was composed at Oxford.

parings, fragments of bone, and no small quantity of iron nails, together with blood. A friend admonished him not to let himself be bound any longer by his pestilent love, and asked whether he had any letters or gifts from the woman. He said that he had received letters, but had torn them up. The other did not believe him and told his servants to search his chest and remove any love tokens that they might find. When the sick man had been made aware of this by some secret voice, he cried out horribly and demanded the key of his chest; and when he had it, at the instigation of the same voice, he threw it into his mouth and would have swallowed it if he had not been prevented. Then he hid it beneath his pillow, and anon lost the sight of his eyes. His mother urged him to restore the key; but when he looked for it he could not find it and thought that it had been stolen. He then cried the louder, yet it could not be found though the whole bed was carefully shaken. At last the chest was forced open and two love letters were found and burned; after which his sight was restored to him and, to his great surprise, the key lay exposed to his eyes. Meanwhile he began to grow better in body and soul, and soon after was entirely healed. Here it was evident to all that the letters were the spell of witchcraft and that the demon had tried to prevent them from being removed; and that when they were taken away and burned the demon had ceased to afflict him.

A certain high-born Count in the ward of Westerich,* in the diocese of Strasburg, married a noble girl of equal birth; but after he had celebrated the wedding, he was for three years unable to know her carnally, on account, as the event proved, of a

certain charm which prevented him. In great anxiety, and not knowing what to do, he called loudly on the Saints of God. It happened that he went to the State of Metz to negotiate some business; and while he was walking about the streets and squares of the city, attended by his servants and domestics, he met a certain woman who had formerly been his mistress. Seeing her, and not at all thinking of the spell that was on him, he spontaneously addressed her kindly for the sake of their old friendship, asking her how she did, and whether she was well. And she, seeing the Count's gentleness, in her turn asked very particularly after his health and affairs; and when he answered that he was well, and that everything prospered with him, she was astonished and was silent for a time. The Count, seeing her thus astonished, again spoke kindly to her, inviting her to converse with him. So she inquired after his wife, and received a similar reply, that she was in all respects well. Then she asked if he had any children; and the Count said he had three sons, one born in each year. At that she was more astonished, and was again silent for a while. And the Count asked her, Why, my dear, do you make such careful inquiries? I am sure that you congratulate me on my happiness. Then she answered, Certainly I congratulate you; but curse that old woman who said she would bewitch your body so that you could not have connexion with your wife! And in proof of this, there is a pot in the well in the middle of your yard containing certain objects evilly bewitched, and this was placed there in order that, as long as its contents were preserved intact, for so long you would be unable to cohabit. But see! it is all in vain, and I am truly glad. On his return home the Count did not delay to have the well drained; and, finding the pot, burned its contents and all, whereupon he immediately recovered the virility which he had lost.

---

* "Westerich." This is from the "Malleus Maleficarum," Part II, Qu. 1, ch. 1. See the "Malleus Maleficarum" translated by Montague Summers (John Rodker, 1928), p. 98.

Martin Delrio* of the Society of Jesus relates the following, taken from the public lectures which have now for many years been delivered at Louvain by Father Robert Bellarmine in refutation of the teaching of Jean Hessels: I remember as a boy seeing at Montepulciano during Lent a certain preacher try to address his congregation: but he was unable to speak, and this happened a second and a third time. Understanding that it was not natural that he should lose his voice only when he tried to preach, he prayed to S. Agnes, the patron Saint of the place, and found in the pulpit certain charms of witchcraft, such as hairs tangled together and the like. These he burned, and recovered his voice, and afterwards was able to preach to the people as before. Now if this had been a sin, God would not have healed the preacher when he called upon Him, nor have revealed the charms to him.

The same author tells of a certain priest who was most evilly bewitched and kept his bed for many months, for none of all the remedies which the physicians gave did him any good. But one month several witches' charms were found in the bed and were burned: after another month, yet more of different sorts were found and likewise burned. After this with the help of God and of the Church's remedies he regained his former health. This happened only a few years ago.

Codronchi (*De morbis uenefic.* I, 8) tells the following of his own daughter: When my daughter Francesca was ten months old and still at nurse, she became very greatly emaciated, and kept heaving great sighs; and she always cried when she was undressed and hated to be undressed, contrary to the nature of children, who however ill they may be or in pain always are soothed when they are rid of their

clothes, and then begin to play. When no preternatural cause of this could be found, her nurse was changed. But she grew worse, and her mother began to suspect that, because she was a very beautiful child, some old witch had been envious and had bewitched her. So she searched the cradle and found not a few witches' charms, such as chickpeas, coriander seeds, bits of coal and dead bone, as well as a certain strange matter which is compounded by evil women from horrid ingredients mingled with menstrual blood. A learned exorcist was called. There were also discovered some feathers such as are usually sewn on to a hat. All these were burned in a blessed fire, and the exorcisms were conducted for three days, other holy remedies being also employed; after which the child began to be better and to take food, so that we thought she was healed. But some days later, since she was very peevish and cried much, the cradle was again searched and other charms were found; and when these were burned she appeared to be restored to health. But at full moon, after she had been awake crying all through the night, she was found in the morning to be the colour of ashes and so altered in appearance from what she had been on the evening before, that it was a matter for tears rather than wonder. The cradle was again searched and there were found two pieces of dry nut and white bone, nine or ten fish-bones formed into a hair comb, and certain little wreaths wonderfully and variously fashioned. All these were burned, we changed our house, and applied, through the learned exorcist, several other more potent remedies; and by the mercy of God the child recovered without any natural remedy.

A certain Nobleman was riding his horse in the outskirts of a city and, passing an ale-house, saw there some of his debtors. He determined to remind them of their debt, and threatened to prosecute them if they did not pay. Some of them found

---

* "*Delrio.*" "*Disquisitiones Magicae,*" *Lib. vi, cap. 2, sec. 1, quaest. 3.*

excuses for their delay; others, who thought he was of a generous disposition, asked to be allowed time to find the money. Among all these there stood out an old woman with a baleful look, who bent her eyes upon the ground as if in admiration of his pawing steed, and asked him whither he was going, at the same time warning him not to trust too much to his horse. He smiled, and said: "What! Do you think I do not know the strength of this brave horse which it seems impossible to tire, seeing that I have been used to ride him for ten miles and more without tiring him?" Yet she answered that she was afraid it would not carry him. The man looked upon this as an old woman's tale, and dug his spurs into his horse; but for the first time in its life it moved very sluggishly, tottering and staggering upon its legs. Wondering at his horse's sudden weakness, he went home leading the horse by hand step by step, and at once summoned a veterinarian who, seeing the horse reeking with sweat, asked whether it had been overworked, or had been suddenly made to gallop after a day's rest, or had drunk too soon after galloping; and made other enquiries about such things as are often the cause of illness in horses. But when he could find no obvious cause of that sort of sickness he asked that the horse be left in his care, and promised that he would not fail in his duty and would leave no stone unturned to discover the reason of the sickness and find a cure for it. The horse was entrusted to the veterinarian, who led him into the stable, where the horse began to suffer acute pain and, after scraping with its hooves, fell flat to the ground panting violently. The veterinarian puzzled his brain to think of the various causes of sickness in horses, and it came into his mind that there was always great danger in such illnesses when there was any inflammation of the bowels or when the animal could not pass water as often as it should. Therefore

he determined to examine whether there were any obstructions in its bowels or bladder, and he thrust his hand into its anus to see whether anything was there to cause such an illness. For when horses are badly constipated it causes them to roll about in agony and to be bathed in sweat. But when he could find no such matter, he began to draw out its genital member with his hand, and found it to be tightly and intricately knotted. First he tried to undo the knots with his finger-nails; but he could not, because the ends of those knots were hidden in the confusion of their coils, and they could only be prised loose with an iron tool. For, as all think, this knot was woven by witchcraft from the roots of hemp, and was thus more formidable than the Gordian knot which was made of reeds which were pliable in every direction, whereas this was made from the root itself and was inflexible. But when the knot was untied, the horse at once jumped up, made water together with a deal of coagulated blood, and did indeed recover; but it was never restored to its full former vigour.

Grilland (*De sortil.* q. 8, num. 16) relates that a lawyer in the diocese of Sabina married a wife but was made impotent by witchcraft, and could not be helped at all by the physician's skill. So he consulted a witch who told him to sleep with his wife that night, but to take a certain potion before he went to bed; only he was to take great care that neither he nor his wife made the sign of the Cross that night, and they were not to be afraid if they heard or saw anything strange. The lawyer obeyed and observed all his instructions to the letter: and about the fifth hour of the night, behold there was a great rain and tempest, with a mighty thunder and lightning, followed by such a quaking of the earth that the house was shaken from top to bottom like a tree which is almost uprooted by the wind. After this there came much shouting and yelling of men;

and when the husband turned his eyes in that direction it seemed to him that he saw in the room more than a thousand combatants struggling and fighting fiercely with their nails and fists and feet, tearing each other's faces and clothes; and among them he saw a woman from a neighbouring town who was said to be a witch: and the husband had formed a strong suspicion that he had been bewitched by this very woman. This woman was howling and shrieking louder than all the rest, tearing her hair and her face with her nails; so that the ensorcelled lawyer said that at first he was afraid that it boded some harm to himself. But then he remembered the sorcerer's warning and took courage again, all the time keeping his wife under the blankets so that she should see nothing. After they had struggled for an hour or more, the sorcerer came into the room at about midnight and at his entrance all those fighting folk, together with the woman, disappeared and vanished at once. But the sorcerer came up to the lawyer and touched his shoulders and rubbed them a little with his hand, telling him to doubt no longer, for he was now cured. After his departure, the husband was healed and able to beget children. In this case the sorcerer compelled the woman who had cast the spell to remove it, by sending demons in the guise of rioters to torment her. But it is not lawful to remove a spell by this means, because of the mortal sin which is committed; and beside the sin, there is great danger when demons are invoked, as will be seen from the following example.

A certain man ordered a witch to summon demons to bring his mistress to him in an underground cavern. A demon came in the likeness of his beautiful mistress and, standing in his sight, strangled the lover by pressing him strongly against the side of the cave, and then threw his body so violently at the witch that he nearly killed him.

CHAPTER II

How to Distinguish Demoniacs,* and Those who are Simply Bewitched.

THE peculiar symptoms of possession by demons through witchcraft are difficult to recognise when the demon which has been sent into a person by witchcraft mingles himself with some unclean substance introduced into the body from another source, or arising from the humours of the sick person himself. For as long as such substance remains hidden in any part of the body, it often happens that there are no signs of its presence beyond some interference with the natural functions of that particular part. Many such persons however, have debased imaginations, especially in their sleep, and so betray the presence of a demon: but this indication by itself is not enough, since it is common also to sufferers from melancholia. But when the evil spirit moves from one place to another in the body, the matter becomes easier to recognise; as follows:

1. If something moves about the body like a live thing, so that the possessed feel as it were ants crawling under their skin.

2. If the part of the body for which the demon is making is stirred by a sort of palpitation.

3. If the patient is tortured with certain prickings.

4. If it is as though wind descended from his head to his feet, and then again went from his feet to his head.

5. If blisters are raised upon the tongue and immediately disappear; or if they are like many little grains, it is a sign that he is inhabited by many demons.

6. If the demon rises as far as the throat and causes it to swell, and brings on a dry cough.

---

* *"Demoniacs." The rubrics of the "De Exorcizandis Obsessis a Daemonio" in the "Rituale Romanum" should be consulted.*

7. If the demon takes hold of his tongue and twists it and makes it swell; or if he causes it to give utterance not to the man's thoughts but to those of the demon; or if the mouth is stretched wide open and the tongue thrust out.

8. If he feels as if cold water were continually being poured down his back.

9. An even more certain sign is when the sick man speaks in foreign tongues unknown to him, or understands others speaking in those tongues; or when, being but ignorant, the patients argue about high and difficult questions; or when they discover hidden and long-forgotten matters, or future events, or the secrets of the inner conscience, such as the sins and imaginings of the bystanders; or if they provoke them to quarrel without cause or become so furious that they cannot be bound or restrained by many strong men.

10. Some say that they hear a voice speaking inside them, but that they know nothing of the meaning of the words.

11. Others, when they are asked what they have done or said, confess that they remember nothing afterwards.

12. Some think that it is an infallible and inseparable sign when those who are possessed are unable to attend Divine worship, so that they can by no means be sprinkled with Holy Water, nor hear nor utter sacred words: but if they are compelled by force to observe the ceremonies of the Church or the Divine Offices, and chiefly if they are forced to be present at the most Holy Sacrifice of the Altar, then they are tormented far more violently. And in support of this opinion is the fact that they themselves testify that they wish to assist and be present at all these Masses and Offices, and to have the help of holy things, but that there is something within them which strongly prevents them.

13. Some demoniacs have terrible eyes; and the demons miserably destroy their limbs and kill their bodies unless help is quickly brought to them.

14. Some pretend to be stupid, and always grow even more so; but they can be detected if they refuse to recite the Psalm *Miserere mei Deus*, or *Qui habitat in adiutorio Altissimi*, or the beginning of the Gospel of S. John, *In principio erat Uerbum*, or similar passages of Scripture.

15. It is a sign of obsession if a man speak in a tongue foreign to his own country, provided that he is not living out of his own country.

16. It is a manifest sign when an ignorant man speaks literary and grammatical Latin, or if without knowledge of the art he sings musically or says something of which he could never have had any knowledge.

17. Abstinence from food and drink for seven or more days is a powerful sign.

18. When some inner power seems to urge the possessed to hurl himself from a precipice, or hang or strangle himself, or the like.

19. Sometimes they become as if they were stupid, blind, lame, deaf, dumb, lunatic, and almost incapable of movement, whereas before they were active, could speak, hear and see, and in other respects acted sensibly.

20. It is also a sign when they are subject to sudden frights, which are as suddenly allayed.

21. A man may very surely be known for a demoniac if he is disturbed when the exorcisms are read.

22. When the priest's hand is placed upon his head, it feels very heavy and ponderous.

23. When the patient feels under the priest's hand something as cold as ice.

24. When a very cold wind descends through his shoulders and reins.

25. When his head swells to an enormous size.

26. When his brain feels as if it were tightly bound, or pierced and stricken as if by a sword.

27. When the head and face, and

sometimes the whole body, swells as if it were filled with hot vapour.

28. Some are afflicted with violent fever and headache, and their whole body is weakened and in pain; but all these symptoms last a very little while, since a conjuration takes away the power of the demon.

29. In some the throat is so constricted that they seem as if they are being strangled.

30. From the abdominal orifice of some there issue certain matters like balls, as if they were worms or ants or frogs.

31. Some have a great vomiting from their stomachs.

32. Many feel acute pain in their guts.

33. The stomach of some becomes forcibly inflated.

34. Some feel a contraction of the heart, as if it had been unmercifully beaten.

35. Sometimes the demon shows himself in some part of the body palpitating like a fish, or like moving ants.

36. Sometimes the bewitched person has a face the colour of cedar wood.

37. Some have very narrow eyes, and appear bound in all their limbs, and their shoulder blades grate dryly.

38. Two very sure signs are the contraction of the heart and of the arms, and when it seems to them that they have a lump upon their stomach.

39. Some have their hearts punctured as if by needles.

40. Some feel as if their heart was being eaten away.

41. Some have great pain in their heart and kidneys, and it seems as if those organs were being torn by dogs.

42. Some feel a lump rising and falling in their throat.

43. In some the genital vein is obstructed.

44. Some are so indisposed in their stomachs that they vomit whatever they eat and drink; but this is a very slight sign unless accompanied by other symptoms.

45. Some have a very cold wind, or one as hot as fire running through their stomach.

46. In some the sign is indigestion of their food; especially when they are given drugs without being relieved.

47. Some have a continuous pulsation about their necks, which seems to inspire them with terror.

☆

The Signs which Show a Man to be Simply Bewitched.

All the above have been far more exactly classified and proved by Codronchi (*De morbis ueneficis*, III, 13) who states that some of those signs are common to all cases of bewitchment, and others peculiar to particular cases. He says that the signs common to all cases are to be found either in the cause of the malady or in its concomitant circumstances. Such signs may be recognised in the cause, when the sickness originates from some inordinate and irrational love or some insensate hatred for another, or from the curses or threats of some witch, or if magic charms are found such as we have often spoken of and are mentioned by Andrea Cesalpini (*De inuestigat. dae-monum.* c. 22). Among the signs which accompany the sickness are paroxysms, and the efficacy or harmfulness of medicines. The commonest signs are the following:

1. In the first place, when the patient's sickness is very difficult to diagnose, so that the physicians hesitate and are in doubt and keep changing their minds, and are afraid to make any definite pronouncement about it.

2. If, although remedies have been applied from the very first, the sickness does not abate but rather increases and grows worse.

3. If it does not, like natural sicknesses, come on by degrees; but the sick man often suffers the severest symptoms and pains from the very beginning, although there is no apparent pathological cause for it.

4. That the sickness is very erratic:

and although it may be periodic, it does not keep its regular periods; and although it may resemble a natural sickness, yet it differs in many respects.

5. Although the sick man is often in the greatest pain, he cannot say in which part he feels the pain.

6. At times the sick give the most mournful sighs without any manifest cause.

7. Some lose their appetite, and some vomit up their food and are so sick in the stomach that often they are doubled up with pain, and a sort of lump may be seen rising and falling from the stomach to the throat; and if they try to eject this when it is risen all their efforts are in vain, although it may very soon shoot out of its own accord.

8. They feel painful pricks in the region of the heart, so that often they say that it is being torn in two.

9. In some the pulse may be seen beating and, as it were, trembling in their necks.

10. Others have excruciating pains in their neck or kidneys or the bottom of their bellies, and often an ice-cold wind goes about their stomach and quickly comes again, or they feel a vapour like a hot flame of fire tormenting them in the same manner.

11. Some become sexually impotent.

12. Some fall into a light sweat especially at night, although the weather and the season are very cold.

13. Others seem to have certain parts of their bodies twisted as it were in a knot.

14. The sicknesses with which those who are bewitched suffer are generally a wasting or emaciation of the whole body and a loss of strength, together with a deep languor, dullness of mind, various melancholy ravings, different kinds of fever, all of which keep the physicians very busy; certain convulsive movements of an epileptic appearance; a sort of rigidity of the limbs giving the appearance of a fit: sometimes the head swells in all directions, or such a weakness pervades the whole body that they can hardly move on any account at all.

15. Sometimes the whole skin, but generally only the face, becomes yellow or ashen coloured.

16. Some have their eyelids so tight shut that they can scarcely open them, and there are certain tests by which such may be recognised.

17. Those who are bewitched can hardly bear to look at the face of a priest, at least not directly; for they keep shifting the whites of the eyes in different ways.

18. When the charms are burned, the sick are wont to change for the worse, or to take some greater or less harm according as their bewitchment was slight or severe; so that not infrequently they are forced to utter terrible cries and roars. But if no change or fresh lesion can be found, there will be great hope that the sick man will with a little attention be presently restored to good health.

19. If by chance the witch should come to see the sick man, the patient is at once affected with great uneasiness and seized with terror and trembling. If it is a child, it cries. The eyes become grey in colour, and other remarkable changes are to be noted in the sick man.

20. Finally when the priest, to heal the sickness, applies certain holy liniments to the eyes, ears, brow, and other parts, if a sweat or some other change is seen in those parts it is a sign that he is bewitched.

The following is the usual practice to determine whether the sick man is possessed by a demon. They secretly apply to the sick man a writing with the sacred words of God, or Relics of the Saints, or a blessed Agnus Dei, or some other holy thing. The priest places his hand and his stole upon the head of the possessed and pronounces sacred words. Thereupon the sick man begins to shake and tremble, and in his pain makes many uncouth movements, and says and does many strange things. If the demon is in his head, he feels the keenest pains in his head, or

else his head and all his face are suf-
fused with a hot red glow like fire. If
he is in his eyes, he twists them about.
If in the back, he bruises his limbs before and behind, and sometimes makes
the whole body so rigid and inflexible
that no exertion of force can bend it.

Sometimes they fall down as if dead,
as though they were suffering from
tertiary epilepsy, and a sort of vapour
rushes up into their heads: but at the
priest's bidding they arise, and the
vapour returns whence it came. If the
demon is in their throats, they are so
throttled as to be nearly strangled. If
he is in the nobler parts of the body,
as about the heart or lungs, he causes
panting, palpitation and syncope. If he
is more towards the stomach, he pro-
vokes hiccoughs and vomiting so that
sometimes they cannot take food, or if
they do they cannot retain it. And he
causes them to void a sort of ball by
the back passage, with roarings and
other harsh cries; and afflicts them
with the wind and pain about the mid-
riff. They are known also sometimes
by certain fumes of sulphur or some
other strong smelling matter.

☆

CHAPTER III

*Recent Examples of the Mercy of God and
the Tyranny of the Devil.*

M ARTIN DELRIO (*Disquisit.
magicarum.* VI. 2, sec. 3) narrates
the following story, and says that it was
both related on paper and told by word
of mouth by the man to whom these
things happened, and that he himself
had that account to his hand as he
wrote. On the 22nd of March in the
year 1600, being the Wednesday in
Holy Week, a young nobleman aged
twenty-two, of the name of Nicolas
Prutenns, entered the College of the
Jesuits, and was seen and heard by one
of the Brothers walking about and
making arrogant gestures in the lower
portico of the College, shaking his
head and rashly uttering desperate
blasphemies against God. He was told
again and again to moderate his behaviour and bridle his tongue, but in
vain; for he became even worse, and
showed every sign of a troubled and
disturbed mind. Therefore one of the
Brethren went up to him and asked
him kindly what was the matter and
what was so troubling him, and why he
kept breaking out into such irreverent
use of the Name of God. He answered:
"Alas, I am lost! I am bound by the
shackles of the devil. And yet he has
not given me the pleasures I desire,
which he promised me." Hearing this
the good Jesuit feared there was something gravely amiss and led him by the
hand into the College, where he gently
asked him not to hesitate to tell him
what was the matter. Then Nicolas
Prutenns with tears and at first wholly
incoherent, but more calmly on the
next day, began to tell him as follows.
That he was of noble birth and had
been brought up richly, elegantly and
delicately; but for certain reasons
(which I need not mention) he had
forfeited his parents' love and had been
driven from his father's house. He had
plenty of money when he set out, but
had spent it and fallen into extreme
want: but at last a demon came to him
with a mighty gust of wind one night
as he was lying under a tree, and
promised him help and assistance for
the ills he had just suffered and those
which he would suffer, and also that
he would restore him to his former
favour with his parents, if only he
would put his signature to certain

small obligations. That time he did not obey the suggestion, which he knew to be full of danger, and the demon departed with the same wind and disturbance as he had come, predicting that he would some day be sorry for not having accepted his conditions. This happened near a village not far from Breslau; therefore he went to that city and lived there for a short space in hardship. One evening he went out reproaching himself for not having put faith in the demon, and weeping because there was no help or hope left to him since he had been offered his chance and had rejected it. It was the dead of night, and a demon of gigantic size appeared to him and reviled him, saying: "Did I not say that the day would come when you would beg for my help? By right I should refuse to help you as being unworthy however much you begged me; but that you may know how I love you from my heart, see, I will help you! You shall have twelve solid years of favour with your parents as before, of pleasures and happiness; but when they are done, I shall have full power over your body and soul. You for your part must freely agree to the stipulations which I exact. First, then, abjure God and His Mother, all the Saints, and the Faith taught you of old. Swear also that you will reveal this pact to no mortal, that you will not read any book of prayers, that you will persecute with implacable hatred all men, especially those who would incite and urge you to piety, and that you will not marry a wife but use concubines hired for money." When the youth had agreed to this vile compact, and it only remained for him to sign the agreement with his own blood, the demon squeezed his left hand as he put it out, with such force that he filled his hand with blood pressed from the ends of three fingers, and gave him a document to sign, I know not of what material, but it was softer than parchment and harder than paper; and the pen wrote as it were

of its own will the terms of the agreement as they affected both parties. After he had signed and delivered the document, he said that he heard a wonderful music of all instruments and was lulled to a deep sleep by the sound; and the next day he at last awoke late in the morning without having been disturbed by the noise of any passers by on the public road. Then he repented of the crime he had committed, and went from Breslau to Olmütz and from there to Vienna. From Vienna he went to Graz where he visited the learned Weninger, and was directed and recommended by him to Master Strassberger. Lastly he came to Marburg to the learned Homelius, and there, weary of his exile, he again lamented that he had not kept his pact with the demon. Again as he lay in bed at night the demon came to him and offered to renew the pact; and he signed a new agreement with the demon in his own blood, and placed it by night in a ruined temple near Marburg. After a few days he again repented of his crime, and in his despair would have killed himself; but someone persuaded him to seek a remedy at Graz. But the day before he left Marburg the demon came to him at night and described to him a certain cottage at Graz near Karlau, telling him to be there on the 30th of March, and then he would fulfil his vow and restore him to his former fortune: but meanwhile he must very particularly beware against approaching any Jesuits, for if he did he would be most severely punished. All this the young man told to our Brother on the day that the demon had appointed to meet him at the cottage; and although our Brother frightened him from going there on that day, yet on the next day (which was Good Friday) after noon, the unhappy man went to the place assigned by the demon, without consulting anyone. The demon appeared and rated him for his want of faith, in that he had disobeyed him by approaching the scoundrelly Jesuits, and asked him to renew his pact for the third time, and to offer his middle finger as a pledge: then he recounted all his sins from the time of his youth, showing him that he must despair of his soul's salvation, and quoted the Scriptures to prove that he ought to live his days in luxury, and at the same time offered him a book containing the names of all the demons, and showing how to summon whichever one he needed. But the young man would have none of it.

On Holy Saturday, when it was known what had happened, they began to take greater care of the young man, never allowing him to be alone, and from that time he was instructed in the Catholic Faith by a Father to whose peculiar care he was entrusted. About the end of April he was ripe for confession, and on the day when he was to make his confession he was bidden to renounce the devil in the presence of some of the Fathers, and righteously to violate his unholy pact. During the recital of the Litanies, at the words *Pater de Coelis Deus*, he fell down nearly dead. We raised the man, trembling in all his limbs; but he would have fallen again at the glorious Name of the Mother of God, if we had not held him up on each side. When he had at last with difficulty made his renunciation and abjuration of the devil, and had been refreshed with food (for all his strength had gone), he was taken in the afternoon to the church to make his confession. But when he had recited the Litanies of the Name of Jesus and of the Angels, and had begun to tell his sins, the demon whispered in his ear: "Do not trust this rogue of a confessor, unless you wish to be foully cheated by him." During the whole of May there was not a day but the Father assigned to him wrestled with him to strengthen him in the faith and that he might by frequent confession purge every corner of his conscience; and there appeared to be some hope of his salvation. Yet he suffered various injuries at the hands of the demon. Three times one night he was thrown from his bed to a distance of three paces, but without receiving any hurt. At other times the demon appeared to him and, pretending great kindness to him, persuaded him to return to Marburg; for why did he afflict himself in that place? "I wonder," he said, "that when you know that you are damned, you take no greater care to make your present life happy, and that you do not return to your former fortunes from which you fell. I am ashamed of you and pity you that, being mine, you lead such a hard life in this place." And as at that very time a most pious and religious man had died in the paupers' house (in which the youth himself was), and certain of the Brethren were praying to God for him all night in the hospital, he added that he neither could nor would remain any longer while those living hell-hounds were barking in the hospital about the dead dog; and therefore he begged him again and again to come even once more to the cottage, where he would hear such new things as had never been heard before.

On Trinity Sunday, the 28th of May, when our Brethren had carefully commended the work to God and had to this end offered to God many other pious exercises and mortifications, he was brought to a public assembly of the Faithful, where first, before many of our good Brethren and the holy congregation in the church of S. Catharine, he abjured the devil in measured words read from a paper, and protested that he repudiated the pact which he had so wickedly made. But he did this with incredible difficulty, for the demon so hindered his faculties that he could not read, and could only repeat the words after another, slowly and with difficulty. Then he made a profession of the Catholic Faith according to the form laid down in the Bull of Pius the Fourth where it is expressed in these words: "The traditions, observations and constitutions of the Church I do most firmly believe and embrace: and that there are seven true and proper Sacraments of the new law: and that in the most Holy Sacrament of the Eucharist there is truly, really and substantially the Body and Blood, etc. And all heresies condemned by the Church, I do also condemn." All his strength had gone from him, and he was deprived of the use of his eyes, ears and tongue; so that, when he regained a little strength, he said that he feared he would die in that place. While he was in that state, and we were vainly urging him to express in words what he believed in his heart, namely that he believed in the presence of Christ in the Eucharist, he agreed to be moved nearer to the Adorable Sacrament. And at Its presence he was so restored that he awoke as it were from a deep slumber and said that he believed and most fully felt the power of Christ's presence. Yet the matter ended otherwise: for when the Eucharist was yet on the Altar, he could both speak and hear; but when the priest approached to offer the Sacrament to the youth, he lost all his senses and his teeth were clenched so tightly that it seemed that no power could unlock them; and when the priest withdrew again with the Eucharist, he could again see and speak and hear. And he said that he knew nothing of all that we had cried in his ears, but had only known that his mouth seemed to be shut as if in a vice. That nothing might be left unattempted, the same priest left the Eucharist upon the Altar and placed his consecrated finger upon the youth's mouth; then when he brought the Host to his lips and offered It to him to eat, the Enemy openly attacked him and began to raise him up in the air, although many struggled against him. When the demon was adjured to leave him in peace and to restore his signed compact, this was seen (but only by the young man) hanging by a great rope from the roof of the church; for no one else saw any such thing. Nothing else was done that day, except that many prayers were offered to God for his safety, and the young man was left with great hope of recovering the pact which he had signed.

On the third of June the young man entered the church, when the Enemy smote him unexpectedly in the face as if with his cloak, and at the same time tore his left hand so grievously that the blood flowed freely; yet there was no one visible who did this. He also felt his neck twisted by some one; but suffered no inconvenience except that for some days the scars remained on his hand, though with less pain than when the hand had been torn. That day our Brethren redoubled their pious efforts that the matter might have a happy end to the greater glory of God. And that night a terrible wind arose without any rain, and the voice of the young man was heard as it were in the wind, woefully lamenting.

On the fourth of June, on the Sunday within the Octave of Corpus Christi, after the offertory and Litanies to each Person of the Most Holy Trinity, he was bidden to read a repudiation of his sins and a profession of faith, and to protest before God, Angels and men that he was a Catholic, and that he would never mistrust the mercy of God towards him. This he did for some time without help from any; and when his sight failed, another read for him and he repeated the words slowly, with difficulty and hesitation, since the demon obstructed his tongue. When he came to the words, "Wherefore, O Blessed Jesu," etc., he could neither read them nor suffer another to suggest them. The demon was adjured by the virtue of God not to hinder the youth in this; and then the young man was violently shaken as if he were possessed, and in a single moment learned the German tongue which, by the help of the demon, he spoke elegantly enough but with his own native idiom. When they saw this all believed yet more firmly in the power of grace, and recited the *Te Deum laudamus*, and bade him proceed. But he could not say "I confess to Almighty God, "etc. and "Lord, I am not worthy," etc. And it was in vain that the priest approached him with the Sacrament, and commanded the demon by the power of God to leave the man alone : for the youth was taken up into the air so violently that ten or twelve men with difficulty held him back.

At the repeated pronouncement of the Name of Jesus and the invocation of the Most Blessed Virgin Mary the demon was broken and departed from him ; and the young man exclaimed in his own tongue : "He has fled from me." Thereupon he at once bent his knees and proceeded in a clear and loud voice to recite : "Wherefore, O good Jesus," etc., and at the end of the prayer added these words : "Praise be to God, I am now another man." And he prepared himself for Communion and confessed, saying the "Confiteor." The demon was adjured not only to leave the young man alone thereafter, but also to restore the written compact; and he confessed again. At length he was so weak that he could not even sit; yet, being now free from the attacks of the demon, he none the less knelt and recited the *Confiteor* and *Domine, non sum dignus*, etc., and protested aloud that he believed with all the strength of his soul that Christ was present in the Eucharist and that he hoped that He would be merciful to him. He took the Eucharist kneeling with the greatest devoutness of spirit, and continued for some time to return thanks and so far recovered his strength that he left the church without appearing to suffer from any weakness. "Now at last," he said, "I do not fear the demon, but scorn him from my heart; but of myself I could never have won this freedom. I am ready now to shed my blood a hundred times for the Catholic Faith." And much

more he said in praise of the charity of our Brethren, who had been so careful for the salvation of a man whom they had never seen before; saying that the like was not to be found among the Lutherans, and much more which modesty forbids me to repeat.

On the 10th of June, the vigil of S. Barnabas the Apostle, our Brethren again armed themselves in the monastery against the Enemy by those methods known to the Society; and the young man wore a hair shirt all day lest he should fail himself, and in the evening scourged himself soundly of his own accord. That evening, and during a great part of the night, a great wind blew upon the college. Before the eleventh hour of the night the Enemy came, together with some man or woman, and walked into the dormitory where the young man was sleeping with three others, and the demon said to the woman with him (who is thought to have been a certain witch) : "Do you see this vile fellow lying here? Oh, if I had managed my business differently it would not have ended like this : they would hardly have driven me off before its fulfilment! Meanwhile I commend the fellow to you. Torment him as much as you can." Then he turned to the young man and said in a terrible voice : "O faithless varlet, O you most light and inconstant wretch who never kept your promise to me, O base and degenerate heart ! Your forefathers would have lost body and soul a hundred times rather than break their word once it had been given. Have, then, what you gave me; but I will keep what is mine." He said this two or three times, and the young man heard him making a sound like the erasure of writing from a paper. Then he said to the woman : "I go to the place appointed for me. Do you meanwhile take care of this fellow." And then again to the young man : "And did you think, you worthless rogue, that you would escape from my hands? I am compelled now to restore to you that which is yours: but meanwhile do you and the vile Jesuits leave me untroubled by the foolish mummery of your ceremonies; for I have nothing of yours. Yet hereafter I shall take much more from you; for the faith which you have embraced is unsound and an invention of these Fathers, whom you revere as holy men, but I drag them to hell as they deserve." Saying this he placed an ice-cold hand upon the young man's neck without at all wounding him, and vanished. To all this the young man made no answer except for telling him at once to depart, for God was upon his side. Then he tried to arouse the others who were sleeping soundly in the dormitory, calling out their names; and one of them, who was sick, heard him and sprang to his feet and, going to the bed of another who was in good health, awakened him. This man struck fire from a flint and kindled tinder; but before he could light a candle it was violently put out by someone. This happened a second and third time, and when at last he had just got the candle alight, both it and the tinder were again extinguished. At last it came into his mind to light a blessed candle; and, when he had done this, it could no longer be put out. On the appearance of a light the Enemy vanished; and although he had again and again said that he was restoring to the young man that which was his, yet the youth had had nothing from him. They then addressed themselves to prayer, and he who had lit the light recited Litanies before an Image of the Blessed Virgin Mary. After about half-an-hour he arose and saw lying upon the floor a bloody paper, which he took up and offered to him whose handwriting it was. He, recognising the writing, began to show great joy, kissing it and pressing it to his bosom; and then they all gave thanks to God, the four of them together reciting the *Te Deum laudamus*, etc. And lest by chance the demon

should recover the paper, they protected it with the sign of the Cross, and sprinkled it with Holy Water, and bound it round with the halo of the Blessed Virgin Mary.

On Sunday morning they called the Father to whose care the young man had been committed, and showed him the recovered paper which he had written at Marburg, with the blood erased which recorded the demon's part of the pact. But lest there should yet remain some evil guile and perhaps there had not been a complete surrender of everything which the young man had written, our Brethren went again as is their custom to the church of S. Catharine and poured out prayers to God, recited Litanies, brought the Sacrament to the young man, and adjured and required the demon, if there was anything further belonging to the young man, by the virtue of Almighty God to restore it. But since the youth said that he was sure that everything had been restored, and he was perfectly at ease in his heart, they decided to proceed no further. Therefore they gave hearty thanks to the Divine goodness for so great a mercy, saying a *Te Deum laudamus*, etc., and we all returned rejoicing. His Most Serene Highness the Archduke Ferdinand, and the Right Reverend Bishop of Seckau determined to make the whole of this matter known to the people. Accordingly this was done at midday on the eighteenth of June, and the very paper written with blood was by the order of the Bishop burned in our church by the parish priest of Graz before a great concourse of men. This is a most true story of what really happened: and you may see from it, reader, the efficacy of each and every of the Catholic ceremonies, of which we could add countless other examples.

☆

CHAPTER IV

Of Divine and Supernatural Remedies.

Argument.

THERE are many remedies of this sort which men ought always to use; for they always help the soul and never harm the body, and often they cure or prevent the sicknesses and other ills of witchcraft. These have been approved by the wiser physicians and catholic-minded men, such as Jean Fernel (*Uniuersa Medicina* II), Cornelio Gemma (*Cosmocrit.*), Baptista Cadronchi (*de Morbis ueneficis*), Andrea Cesalpini (*Disquisit. de nat. daem.*), and others.

The first of these remedies is a true and lively faith, fortified with the love of God and His Son. S. Paul bids us to take this as a shield (*Eph.* vi and I. *Thess.* v). S. Antony the Great also commends this to his disciples, saying: "O my dearly beloved, a sincere life and a pure faith in God are mighty weapons against the devil." Cornelius Chempensis (*De origine et situ Frisiae*, III, 31) affirms the same in the following words: "About the time of the Emperor Lothair there were throughout all Friesland," etc. And the same author proceeds to say how S. Cyprian (*Ad Fortunatum, de exhortat. Martyrii*) and Lactantius (II, 16) and Ambrosius Ansbertus* (*In Apoc.* V, 11) teach that the observance of God's Commandments and innocence of life are the most effective remedies possible. And Nider (*In Epitom. Formic.* cap. 4), quoting a certain Peter, praises the following five most efficacious remedies: To have an entire faith,

and keep the commandments of God; to protect oneself with the sign of the Cross and with prayer; to honour the rites and ceremonies of the Church; to execute public justice truly; to contemplate aloud or in secret Christ's passion.

The second is a lawful use of the Sacraments of the Catholic Church; as, for example, Baptism in the case of those not yet initiated into the Faith. For it is proved by experience that they who are known not to have been baptised are freed from magic spells by means of unconditionally administered baptism: while for such as may with probability be assumed not to have been baptised, the same benefit is obtained from a conditional baptism. When I speak of a probable assumption, I mean that an unsubstantiated conjecture is insufficient to warrant even a conditional baptism.

The third remedy is to have recourse to holy men and to seek help from them who are known to possess the gift of working miracles (a gift which may be found, though rarely, even in those whose life is not upright, so long as they have the true faith; as may be seen from the Gospels (Matth. vii, Mark ix, Luke x)). Although there are hardly any now (at least in Europe) who have this gift, it was formerly much used as a remedy: for all sacred histories are full of examples of men who have profitably had recourse to holy men. And it is agreed that not all they who cast out demons were ordained by the Church into the order of Exorcists. Of old, certainly, holy men put to flight and conquered demons simply by their presence, as we read of S. Macarius of Alexandria in Palladius, chapters 19 and 20; of Aegyptius in Sozomen, Bk. VI, chap. 20; of S. Cuthbert in chapter 15 of his Life written by Bede; of S. Rusticus in John Cassian, Collat. 14, chap. 7; and of many others everywhere in the histories.

The fourth remedy is Ritual Exorcism. Touching this it is to be noted

---

* "*Ambrosius Ansbertus.*" Ambrose Autpert, an early mediaeval writer and Benedictine Abbot; born in France early in the eighth century, and died after ruling little more than a year at his monastery of S. Vincent on the Volturno, near Benevento, 778 or 779. "*Ambrosii Ansberti Galli presbyteri . . . in sancti Ioannis.*" "*Apostoli et Euangelistae Apocalypsim libri decem . . . nunc primum typis excusi*" (*Cura Eucharii Ceruicorni*). *Coloniae, per E. Ceruicornium, folio, 1536.*

that this order of Exorcists has existed in the Church for 1300 years, as is clear from the Epistle of S. Ignatius to Antioch; and the Epistle of Pope Cornelius* to Fabius preserved by Eusebius; (*Hist. Eccl.* VI, xliii.) and from the Letters of Firmilianus to S. Cyprian, and from other Fathers.

The fifth way is to seek a remedy by sufficient works of mercy, by fasting, alms-giving, and prayer. Alms-giving is commended by the authority of the Canon, chapter *si per sortiarias*. With regard to fasting, I find that S. Auxentius† the Abbot prescribed it to a certain countess, as Metaphrastes records in his Life, February 14th. And S. Procopius the Monk very often won the victory against the demon by means of fasting.‡ We have, moreover, Christ to witness in Matth. xvii and Mark xxix. As for prayer, there survives a verse of an anonymous old versifier:

Against the Fiend's might
Prayer is a weapon right.

The sixth is a devout invocation of the Name of the Saviour Jesus Christ, or of the Blessed Virgin Mary, or a prayer for help to the Guardian Angel. All the most ancient ecclesiastical writers assert so firmly and frequently the power of the Name of the Saviour that it would be superfluous to collect their words. There are many examples of the invocation of the Blessed Virgin, especially that famous one of Theophilus § about which, among others, Honorius‖ of Autun treats in the *Seal of Mary*. The help from the Guardian Angel is testified

---

§ *"Theophilus." This history is well known. Theophilus had made so formal compact with Satan that he actually signed away his soul with a written deed. Even in his darkest moments, however, he cherished some love and honour for Our Lady, and at the hour of his doom Mary intervened to save him, since She took the charter from the evil one and signally protected Her servant, who repented and made a good death. This instance of the omnipotent power of the Mother of God and the salutary effects of devotion to Her may be found in one of the earliest collections of Miracles of Our Lady, that which goes under the name of Botho (or Potho), an Abbot of Priefling near Ratisbon in the eleventh century. It is quoted by S. Peter Damian, S. Bernard, S. Bonaventura, S. Antoninus, and many other writers of authority. In "The Glories of Mary" S. Alphonsus Liguori gives it as the "example" in the second section of his commentary on "Ad Te suspiramus." It is also related on the Twenty-fourth Day of "The Love of Mary," a golden treatise by Dom Roberto, a Camaldolese Hermit of Monte Corona. S. Peter Damian cries: "O Mary, Who couldst snatch Theophilus from the very jaws of perdition, what is there that Thou canst not do?"*

‖ *"Honorius." A theologian, philosopher, and encyclopaedist who lived in the first half of the twelfth century. Although many works from his pen have won considerable reputation, of his life practically nothing is known, and it has even been discussed whether "of August" (near Basle) or "of Augsburg" (in Suabia) ought not to be read instead of "of Autun" in Bergundy. The "Sigillum Beatae Mariae" is an exposition upon the "Canticle of Canticles." The works of Honorius will be found in Migne, "Patres Latini," CLXXII.*

---

* *"Pope Cornelius." 251–252. This Pontiff in his letter to Fabius mentions that there were then in the Roman Church forty-two acolytes and fifty-two exorcists, readers and door-keepers, and the formal institution of these orders together with the organisation of their functions was probably the work of Pope Fabian, 236–251. The practice of exorcism, not confined to any one particular order, prevailed in the Church from the very foundation, the power of exorcism being given to the Apostles by Our Lord Himself.*

† *"S. Auxentius." The "Roman Martyrology" under 14 February has: "In Bithynia, of S. Auxentius, Abbot." See the Bollandists for this day.*

‡ *"Fasting." The Homily of S. Basil the Great, "Homilia I de ieiunio," rises to supreme heights of sacred eloquence. Passages are read in the Roman Breviary in the Second Nocturn of Matins on the Fourth Sunday of Lent. "Ieiunium legislatores sapientes facit: animae optima custodia, corporis socius securus, fortibus uiris munimentum et arma, athletis et certantibus exercitatio. Hoc propterea tentationem propulsat, ad pietatem armat, cum sobrietate habitat, temperantiae opifex est."*

by Origen *contra Celsum*, Bk. VI, and S. Golanduch, who is mentioned by his contemporary Evagrius,* Bk. VI. chap. 19.

The seventh is the sign of the Holy Cross,† in commendation of which a whole book could be compiled from the writings of the Holy Fathers and from actual examples. See S. Cyprian, *Serm. de Passione Christi*; Origen upon Job, Bk. III; Lactantius, *De Uera Sapientia* IV, 26; S. Antony as quoted by S. Athanasius; S. Athanasius himself, *De Incarnatione Uerbi* XLVIII; S. Gregory of Naziansus, *Oration*. 1. *in Julianum*, and *ad Nemesium*; S. John Chrysostom, the 8th homily on the *Epistle to the Colossians*, and the 50th homily upon S. Matthew; S. Cyril, *Cathechesis 4*, *de Ascensione*; Diego Niceno the Basilian in the *Life of the Thaumaturges;* S. Jerome in the *Life of S. Hilarion;* S. Augustine, *de Symbol. ad Cathecumen*, Bk. II, and Serm. 81, *de tempore;* Theodoret in the *Life of Macedonius*, and *Hist.* III, 3 and V, 21; S. Gregory, *Dialogues* II, 10, and many others.

The eighth safeguard is the Relics‡ of the Saints, of which we read: "Thy friends, O God, are greatly honoured, and their kingdom is very secure." But care must be taken not to mingle certain superstitious rites with this most sacred worship, as Silvester§

warns us, speaking of the word Relics. For to the Saints superstition is odious, religion is pleasing. This was attested by S. Glyceria the Martyr, from whose personal garments there was distilled a most sweet and healing unguent for all diseases; but one day the Bishop of Heraclea unwittingly tried to collect the unguent in a silver vase which had been used for purposes of sorcery, and the holy ointment at once ceased to be distilled. The Bishop therefore enquired diligently into the matter and found that that vessel had been used for unspeakable purposes; therefore he removed it and put another in its place, whereupon the ointment flowed again as before. This is told by S. Nicephorus,‖ XVIII, 32.

The ninth remedy is of most ancient standing in the Church and is of wonderful efficacy, namely Holy Water blessed by the solemn rite ordained for its benediction. One sort, which is called Baptismal, is consecrated on the Eves of Easter and Pentecost. The other, called Lustral, is consecrated at Prime on every Sunday, and it is avowedly for repelling the attacks of the devil, and for averting other dangers. Its use was known before the time of Pope S. Alexander I,¶ and has always been

---

* *"Evagrius." Scholasticus, born in 536 at Epiphania in Cœle-Syria; died after 594, the exact date being unknown. Of all his works one alone survives, the important "Ecclesiastical History" in six books.*

† *"Holy Cross." O Crux aue spes unica! See also Baltus, "Histoire des Oracles," I, p. 304, etc.*

‡ *"Relics." The virtue of Holy Relics is indeed inestimable. I have myself known and experienced many instances of this. Upon one occasion a Relic of S. Antony of Padua, venerated in the private Oratory of Our Lady of Loreto, healed and restored permanent health to a sick man. Mirabilis Deus in sanctis suis.*

§ *"Silvester." Francis Silvester (Ferrarjensis), Dominican, 1474–1526. It is difficult to see how any superstition could be connected with*

Holy Relics, save indeed these hallowed objects were abused by heretics and witches in their dark rites. Such instances have occurred. No doubt it is to this that Silvester and Guazzo refer.

‖ *"S. Nicephorus." Born about 758; died 2 June, 829; Patriarch of Constantinople 806–815. This holy and orthodox champion of the veneration of Images was sorely persecuted by the abominable iconoclasts, and his dogmatic treatises upon the controversy have the greatest weight. His feast is celebrated both in West and East on 13 March, which day he was interred in the Church of the Holy Apostles at Constantinople.*

¶ *"Pope S. Alexander I." S. Irenaeus tells us that he was the fifth Pope in succession from S. Peter. Duchesne dates his pontificate 106–115; Lightfoot, 109–116. "Constituit aquam sparsionis cum sale benedici in habitaculis hominum."*

retained by all Catholics to their great advantage. It is worshipfully mentioned in the Life of S. Gregory the Great by John the Deacon, a Monk of Monte Cassino, who says that those possessed by devils are delivered when sprinkled with it; and that this miracle is often renewed to-day among the Indians.

Tenthly, there are other things which the Catholic rite is wont to bless for a remedy, as waxen discs which we call *Agnus Deis* because of the print of a lamb on one side. Of their efficacy there is a book by Vincenzo Bonardo,* and Pietro Mattei speaks much of them in 7 *Decretal*.† When the Pope blesses them, he asks God to grant all kinds of favours to those who wear them devoutly. Of the same sort are Blessed Grain, Blessed Candles, Blessed Salt, and Blessed Bread.

Eleventh are pious writings or sacred amulets hung around the neck, such as the Apostles' Creed; the beginning of the Gospel of S. John, "*In Principo erat Uerbum*"; or verses of some Psalm. These were much used of old; and Manuel de Costa‡ writes that in our own time a devil was driven out of a demoniac at Hormuz by this means. But for this remedy to be lawful S. Thomas says that there must be two conditions: first that nothing superstitious is mingled with the sacred words, as that one should put faith in the shape or colour of the letters, or

the manner of writing, or the material of the paper or the ink; and second that the wearer's intention must be righteous, and he must piously observe the sense of the words and put his true hope in God.

Twelfth is the ringing of Bells§ in the Catholic Church (for heretics take more delight in the explosion of grenades). This we know from daily experience to be so hostile and inimical to demons that they are prevented by it from raising up violent storms, and even if they have been already raised it lulls them or turns them aside elsewhere, as has been rightly asserted by the Council of Cologne, chapter 24.

Let us now come to some examples of all these remedies of which we have spoken.

☆

Examples.

1. Of Faith.

Johann Nider in his *Formicarius* (IV) tells the following: A certain witch said: "When a man once asked me to kill an enemy of his, or else to injure him grievously by a stroke of lightning or in some other way, I invoked my Little Master, or demon, who answered that he could do neither: for he said that the man had a pure faith and protected himself diligently with the sign of the Cross; therefore he could not injure him in his body but, if I would, he could destroy an eleventh part of his crops in his field."

The Empress Justina sent against our Father S. Ambrose a witch named Innocentius, who afterwards openly

---

* "*Vincenzo Bonardo.*" *The work here alluded to is this author's famous "Discorso intorno all' origine, antichità e virtu degli Agnus Dei di cera benedetti," Roma, 1586.*

† "*7 Decretal.*" *The collection of Clement V published by John XXII on 25 October, 1317, under the title of "Liber septimus Decretalium," but better known as "Constitutiones Clementis V" or "Clementinae." This is the last official collection of decretals, and the glosses of the canonist Mattei were long highly esteemed.*

‡ "*Manuel de Costa.*" *A famous canonist of Salamanca, who when the University of Coimbra was at the height of its reputation accepted a chair in the faculty of law at the particular invitation of John III (1521–57).*

§ "*Bells.*" *Boguet,"An Examen of Witches" (John Rodker, 1929), tells us: "Satan holds bells in extreme detestation; for by their ringing the people are warned to prepare to observe their duty and pray to God. Also they drive away storms and tempests."*

confessed that he had delegated some demons to kill S. Ambrose, but they had been unable to approach even the door of the house in which the Bishop was; for the house was protected all round by an unquenchable fire which burned there even at a distance; and so their wiles were thwarted, and baffled was the mischief by which he thought to have done injury to the Priest and Bishop of God.

John Cassian relates that two philosophers tried to trouble S. Antony by means of magical illusions and the deceits of demons. But when with all their labour they could effect nothing, and that was all the result of the plots they had sought out with such deep magic, it became very evident to them that there was great virtue in the professions of the Christians; for the same savage Powers of Darkness which could, as they thought, at will obscure the sun and moon, were not only unable to injure S. Antony, but could not even cause him the slightest disturbance in his monastery. Therefore S. Epiphanius denounces the heretical opinion of the Ebionites* that there is no virtue in an invocation which uses the name of Christ and the sign of the Cross.

About the time of the Emperor Lothair Friesland was infested with a great number of Spectres of Hellish Serpent-fiends who lived in an underground cave in a little overhanging brow of a high hill, which they had built by magic without human help. Here lived those whom the ancients called White Nymphs, who used to seize upon night-farers, and such as kept watch over their flocks and herds in the open, and yet more frequently they snared women with the children they had just borne; and the spectres used to take them secretly to their

hidden underground caves, from which there could then be heard the sound of murmuring under the ground, and the wailing of children and the loud weeping and moans of men; and sometimes singing and other uncertain sounds were heard. For this reason a careful watch was set upon pregnant women and little children, lest they should be seized unawares by those hellish Nymphs. But all these devilish illusions vanished and came to nought after they received the true Gospel of God; for erstwhile the Frisians were deluded by the errors of Sabellius and Arius.

2. Of Baptism.

We read in Ecclesiastical History that Tiridates, King of Armenia, afflicted the Christians in the time of Diocletian with various massacres and persecutions, and that he placed S. Gregory† to die of hunger in a deep

---

* "*Ebionites.*" *Early Christian sects infected with Judaistic and (later) with Gnostic errors. In the time of S. Epiphanius only a few obscure communities existed among the scattered hamlets of Syria.*

† "*S. Gregory.*" *Surnamed the Illuminator, the apostle of Armenia. He was born c. 257 and died c. 337. S. Gregory after having been at first persecuted by King Trdat (Tiridates) eventually converted that monarch, and with his aid spread Christianity throughout the country. This happened whilst Diocletian was emperor (284–305). There is a famous life of S. Gregory by Agathangelos which was composed shortly after the year 456 in Armenian, whence it was turned into Greek, used by Symeon Metaphrastes, and translated into Latin early in the tenth century.*

and muddy pit. Moreover, because she would not comply with his desires, he ordered to a most cruel death the virgin Rhipsime, together with many of her pious companions. But he soon felt the vengeance of God. For he was afflicted with madness so that he raged like one possessed, and his body was changed into that of a pig, and in his madness he tore his meat with his teeth. And others who had approved his deeds, the soldiers, magistrates, and officers, were also driven mad and showed the same symptoms; for they too were changed into swine (as Nicephorus will have it), or suffered from a delusion to that effect (as Metaphrastes thinks). But at last they were washed in the font of Baptism and recovered the shape of their bodies and the health of their minds and souls, being baptised and urged to repentance by S. Gregory the Martyr himself;—not the Thaumaturge, as is thought by Nicephorus and some scholiasts, but the other one [S. Gregory the Illuminator], as Metaphrastes teaches. And this evil was not brought upon them by any magic art, as one learned man thinks, but by the vengeance of God working through the evil Angels.

Kazan* the King of the Tartars, otherwise known as the Great Cham, conquered Syria and the surrounding lands with two hundred thousand horsemen; and having thus made himself an object of fear to all, he demanded in marriage the daughter of the King of Armenia, whom he had heard to be very beautiful. The Christian King, fearing the might of this great King, agreed. After some time she bore a son to her husband Kazan, so hideous that the King her husband would by no means acknowledge it as his, since it appeared to be a monster. He summoned his chief men to a council, and on their advice sentenced to death his wife as an

adulteress, and her son as having been conceived in adultery. The innocent woman bewailed her misfortune and took refuge in prayer, and while still unaware of the sentence which had been passed upon her, asked permission to baptise her son. This was granted on condition that there were present some men of known reliability, as well as the King, to see that there was no fraudulent practice. By a miracle, when the boy was baptised he at once became so exceeding comely and beautiful that the King and many others were moved wholly to turn to God, and the Christian cause was very greatly advanced in the land. S. Antoninus tells this story at greater length in his *Historiarum Opus*, tit. 20, c. 8. Let us turn to more recent and equally proved examples. Pedro Cieza de Leon describes a miraculous victory over spectres granted by God by means of this holy sacrament of Baptism. I will quote faithfully from his *Cronica del Peru*.

Near Anzerma, in a place called Pirsa, reigned an Inca who had a youthful brother named Tamaracunga. This young man thirsted eagerly for baptism and therefore tried to seek the company of Christians; but he was frightened by demons which appeared to him in strange forms, for they were visible to him alone, in the shape of huge birds, the condor of the Andes. Seeing the demons thus raging, the young man ordered a poor Christian of the neighbourhood to be summoned; and he came without delay and, hearing the will of the Inca, made the sign of the Cross upon his brow. This did but the more enrage those enemies, whom only the Indian saw threatening him even more furiously; for the Christian saw nothing but falling stones, and heard the whistling of demons. By good fortune there then came to that place a Spaniard named Pacheco who offered to help the other Christian in his difficulty. While these two were striving, Tamaracunga trembled more violently and grew pale with

---

* *"Kazan." This history is from Giovanni Villani, "Croniche," Venice, 1537, Book VIII, chapter 35.*

fear, and was snatched up into the air. This was seen by all, and they heard his prayers and groans, and the howling and whistling of the demons. Once, when the Indian was holding a cup of wine, behold, the cup was lifted up in the air and returned empty of wine, and soon the wine was again poured into it from on high; and the India, full of fear, tried to hide his face with his garment so that he might not see the horrible spectres: yet, without removing the garments with which his face was covered, they took possession of his mouth and nearly throttled him in his throat. At length the Christians, who had meanwhile been praying continually to God, decided to take him to the town of Anzerma and there sprinkle him from the saving font. More than three hundred Indians offered to accompany them, but they were so terrified that they dared not come near the chief who was to be baptised. They came all together to a place where they were hindered by a broken road, and there some human enemies tried to pick up the chieftain and cast him over a precipice: but he cried aloud to the Christians to help him, and while the Indians retreated in terror, they placed him in their midst, binding him with ropes to their girdles, and so guarding him they went on together, bearing three crosses in their hands and not ceasing to pray for the deliverance and salvation of the unhappy man. Not even so did they proceed free from all molestation: for the Enemy often threw him to the ground, and as they ascended a hill on their way they had the greatest difficulty in saving him from some birds that tried to snatch him up and kill him. When they came to Anzerma, the Christians in the town met at the house of Pacheco, where they all saw a violent hail-storm, and heard the demons shouting and whistling, together with that terrible war cry of the Indians— *Hu, Hu, Hu!* The demons threatened him with death unless he abandoned his wish for baptism; they execrated

the God of the Christians who would not permit them to seize the living soul from the Indian's body. With the hail still falling they went to the church where, because it was a thatched building, the Sacrament was not reserved. Some say that before they entered it they heard something walking. When the church was open and the rest had gone in with the Indian, the Indian saw demons of frightful appearance but with their heads bent down towards their feet. When Brother Juan of the Order of the Blessed Virgin Mary of Mercy made ready to baptise him, the demons, unseen by any of the Christians, visibly snatched the Indian into the air and stood him up on high with his head down in the same posture as themselves. The Christians then, relying on their faith, cried aloud: "Jesus Christ, help us!" and dragged back the Indian, and holding him put a sacred stole about his neck and sprinkled him with Holy Water; yet whistlings and groans were still heard in the church. Tamaracunga saw the demons, and received many blows from them; for they brandished darts before his eyes, and spat their fetid saliva in his face. These things happened at night. In the morning a monk put on his sacred vestments to offer the bloodless Sacrifice; and he had hardly begun the Mass when the whistling, groaning, howling and clanking ceased, and the Indian was no more molested. As soon as the Sacrifice was done, Tamaracunga together with his wife and children asked to be baptised: and when he had been baptised he became stronger and bolder in the Faith, and asserted that he was now a Christian and would like to see what the Enemy could do if they would let him brave them alone. But they did not dare to attack him, alone as he was. Unable to contain his joy he marched up and down the church three or four times shouting: "I am a Christian, I am a Christian!" And when he found himself safe and victorious, he went home and was no more molested: so great was the might of Baptism.

At Bungo in the year 1596 there was a heathen woman possessed by a demon, and she was told that she could not be delivered unless she became a Christian. She consented and was already preparing for baptism when, on the following night, the demon dissuaded her from becoming a Christian, saying: "Have you been associated with me in such intimate familiarity for so long, and will you desert me now? You shall not do so with impunity." And as she slept and felt nothing, he cut off her hair leaving but one tress upon her head. When in the morning she saw that her hair had been cut off and woven into the reeds of the opposite bed, she took it as a spur to be baptised the sooner. This she did and, having received that Sacrament, she was immune from all the torments of the demon. This is told by Luis Fröes in his *Japanese Letters* of that year; and he adds the following:

In the island of Chusan there kept appearing to a young heathen, eighteen years of age, a horrible great red dog which spoke with him and led him through the mountains to most remote places, keeping him there for two or three days, and compelling him to lift up his hands and worship him, and to do other unmentionable things. The unhappy youth, seeing that he was so molested by the mortal foe of the human race, at last fled to the church, heard and learned the Christian doctrine, and was bound to Christ by the Sacrament of Baptism; after which he was no more molested by that hell-hound.

At Bungo about the year 1549 a certain man had a serving maid who was familiar with a demon. For the demon used to come to her every night in the likeness of a fox and lead her from the house: but when she embraced the faith through Baptism, she was delivered from this spectre.

In 1583 at Munich in Bavaria a young Jew twenty-three years old was, to the gratification of all, baptised in the College of the Jesuits. A demon laid many wonderful snares for him; and the more the youth sought for Baptism, the more violently did the demon assail him. He threw him nearly naked out of the house; sometimes he nearly throttled him; often he frightened him with visions and spectres so as to drive him out of his mind. The face of the demon was so foully hideous that the youth said that there was no torture to be compared with the sight of him. On the day before he was to be baptised, it was then or never for the demon to gain the victory; and the bitter Enemy so violently took hold upon the youth that he could hardly be held in one place by many men. But when he was made a member of Christ through Baptism, the demon was at once broken and deprived of his strength.

3. Of Confession.

Anno 1591, in a certain Cisalpine Valley in the Diocese of Novara, there was a girl who was quite out of her senses, and seemed to be amazed and stupefied by the spectres and shades which she seemed to see. In the farthest part of this valley of which we speak there was a wise woman, or witch, who claimed to cure with her charms diseases which could not otherwise be cured; and a great many men went to her for help and advice. Although the priests warned them that it was a sin, yet when they had departed, the girl's mother, moved by a mother's care, took the girl to ask the witch's help about the shades. Then the witch said: "Take the girl to the priests and ask help from them." The father and mother took the girl a journey of eight miles, and told the priests what the witch had said: and after they had confessed their sins, they were bidden to fortify themselves with the Holy Body of Christ. And when they had done so the girl became better.

About the year 1591, at Pont-à-Mousson in Lorraine, there was a boy of noble birth but poor fortune who was, at his parents' bidding, taken from school and assigned a position at the Court. But his active spirit rebelled at this and, longing for his former life, he preferred to go and live with the servants in the military camps. As he was on his way, he met a black man in silken garments who asked him why he was sad, and promised to find a remedy. "But," said he, "if I help you, what reward will you give me?" But the boy said: "If you turn me up and shake me, you won't find a farthing." But the other answered: "Only give yourself to me, and no wish of yours shall be in vain." The boy thought he was being asked for as a slave, and demanded time to consider; and the other loaded him with great promises, so that even the boy wondered at such vain words and began to suspect the hidden presence of a cacodemon in the form of the man. He then silently observed the whole of his body, and saw that his left foot was deformed with a cloven hoof; and at once in horror he murmured the name of Jesus and made the sign of the Cross on his brow; and at the same time the terrible spectre vanished. On the third day as he was returning to his own people, the same demon appeared and was again betrayed by his foot, and asked whether

he had made up his mind. The boy answered that he did not require a master; and, on being asked where he was going, named the town. Then the demon threw at his feet a jingling purse containing thirty or forty gulden of bronze (as was later tested by fire). Then he gave him a poisonous powder wrapped in linen, telling him how to afflict whom he would with sudden death, and how to satisfy his base lusts; and warned him to abstain from the use of Holy Water and from adoring the Consecrated Host (which he contemptuously called "The Little Cake"). The boy, shrinking in his pious heart from this blasphemy, and at the same time fearing lest he should have his neck twisted or be strangled by the master, made the saving sign of the Cross upon his breast, and at once fell with a crash to the ground, and could not rise for half an hour. Soon afterwards he came back to his mother and his school; and having obtained forgiveness of his sins by a good confession, rejoiced to find himself freed both from the snare of the hunter and from his fear, through the help of God.

Hear some more ancient examples. "Certane marchandis* wer passand betwix Forth and Flanderis (quhen haistelie came sic ane Thud of wynd) that sail mast and taikillis were blawin in the brym seis, throw quhilk the schip belevit nocht bot sicker derth. The patroun thairof astonist with sa huge and uncouth tempestis againis the season of the yeir because it wes about Sanct Barnabyis day (quhen the seis apperis more calme than rageande) *traistit* the samyn war cumin be illusioun of the devil the ennyme of man, than be violence of weddir. In the mene tyme the voce wes hard of ane woman in the bow of the schip wariand hir self. For the instant hour scho wes conversit with ane devil in

---

* "*Certane marchandis.*" Hector Boece, "*Scotorum Historiae,*" viii. Bellenden's translation (1536).

ymage of ane man. And schew how this devill had usit hir in that maner mony yeris afore. And thairfore besocht the pepill to cast hir in the seis, that be hir deith the remenant pepill in the schip mycht be savit. Than be command of the patroun ane preist went to hir in the hevy cheir. Commandying hir to mak confessioun of hir abhominable lyfe. And to have confidence in God, be quhais mercy all synnis ar purgit, quhen the synnar hes repentance and teris. Quhen this woman wes makand hir confessioun with gret repentance to the preist in sycht of all the pepill ane uglie cloud with ane crak of fyre and reik flew out of the schip and fell down with ane vennomus stink in the seis. Incontinent this tempest ceissit." (*From Bellenden's translation, published* 1536.)

Peter the Venerable, Abbot of Cluny, describing the terrible tormenting of a certain Monk, agonies which could not be relieved either by prayer or by the use of Holy Water, in all sober truth adds the following words: "But lest any should marvel that the demon was not put to flight by Holy Water, let him know that when the plague is seated internally no outward application of salves can avail. And by the plague I mean mortal sin which, as long as it lurks within a man, cannot be removed by partaking of an external sacrament." But the Abbot urged the Monk to make confession of his sins; and after he had confessed he at once ceased to be tormented.

Caesarius tells that at Bonn a priest who had led an abominable life made an end of himself by hanging. When he was dead his concubine entered a Convent, wishing to repent; but by the permission of God she was continually solicited by an Incubus Devil to sin with him. She drove him away with the sign of the Cross and with Holy Water; and when he again returned she devoutly recited the Angelic Salutation, upon which he fled further than a bow-shot: but the importunate fornicator never returned after she had purged herself clean of all the stains of her life by a general confession.

It is recorded that a man at Liège was similarly vexed by a most pestilent Succubus Devil. But let us relate a more recent example. In Austria in the year 1591 a nobleman was enslaved by a great love, near to madness; and no worldly advice or divine admonition could persuade him to cease from it, so entirely was his heart filled with the fire of this poison. But he was cured of his frenzy in the following manner, being stricken with the fear of God. He had contracted a slight fever and was lying in his bed at night, when he saw before him a fiery chariot drawn by a horse blazing with fire, and the charioteer in the form of a hideous monster even more savage than the Evil Spirit himself, than whom there is nothing more fearful to mortals. "Why do you delay," he said, "to mount into a chariot which is worthy of your deserts?" The unhappy man was paralysed with fear, but at last recovered his courage and seized a sword which was by the bed and brandished it, crying aloud the while for his servants to come to his help. The attendants ran up in terror, and the whole household was aroused from sleep; even the neighbours were awakened, some of them asking the reason for the tumult and then covering their ears and eyes with their blankets to hide themselves from the terror. But when the tumult continued and their fear was not appeased, but rather spread to the breasts of others, despite the hour of the night the priests were sent for, being Religious of the Society of Jesus. These came and, by the use of Holy Water, the sign of the Cross, and blessed wax imprinted with the Lamb, calmed the terror a little while the sick man asserted that the demon had departed for the present with a threatening countenance full of savage anger. Then, when he had confessed his sins, he was delivered from his shameful love and from the sad terror in his soul.

At the same time in Bavaria a poor woman was induced, either by the lightness of her nature or by poverty, to give herself to a demon in return for his help; and though she did not at the time perceive his presence, she felt that she was in his power. After she had recovered from her poverty, she paid the penalty for her rash words; for she was not only haunted by sore alarm, but was even beaten with blows and prevented from approaching a church: yet she alone could see the rods that menaced her. She told the matter to a certain matron who led her to a priest, by whom she was purged in confession, and so was delivered from all molestation, having hung about her neck a waxen image of the Celestial Lamb.

The same remedy was used for another who suffered under the same affliction. At the instigation of her kindred a woman broke her vows of chastity and outraged the monastic life by contracting an incestuous marriage. But she was not unpunished; for she had wedded an evil man, and she was in perpetual anguish of conscience, and so lived wretchedly. Weighed down by these cares, and in need of solace, she went one day out of the house and soon, to her utter horror, saw a demon. She drove him away with the sign of the Cross; but immediately she became as one mad, and meditated every abominable crime in her heart. Yet there shone a ray of light in this darkness when she took refuge in prayer; and, like a cloud at the rising of the sun, her fear departed and she suddenly thought of confession and remembered the vow she had broken. But when this hot-bed of vice came to the church, the more she tried to come to the priest the more she was withheld from confession as if by a hand that restrained her: yet at last, with the help and example of others, she conquered both herself and the evil spirit.

4. Of Confirmation.

Thomas of Brabant, *De Bono Uniuersali*, c. lvii, writes as follows: The Venerable Boniface, one time Bishop of Lausanne, related in my hearing a story to the following effect. There was in a certain town a blind man who used to watch the cows of the whole town at pasture, keeping them off the tilled land and leading them to the richest pastures. What was even more wonderful, he could tell the colour and appearance of each separate cow; so that if you asked him for such a cow of such a colour, he would take that cow by the horns and bring it to you without any difficulty. A bishop came to the place and, having heard and proved this marvel of the blind man, asked him if he had received the Sacrament of Confirmation from a bishop; and he said that he had not. The bishop at once confirmed him; and thereupon he lost that power of discrimination between the different cows. For he had done this through the operation and ministry of demons.

5. Of the Eucharist.

Saint Prosper* writes: In our own times a girl of Arab race, who wore

---

* *"Saint Prosper." The dates of his birth and death are uncertain. He is first mentioned in 428 or 429, when he writes to S. Augustine, and he appears to have been living rather later than 455. It does not seem that he was Bishop of Reggio, as was once believed.*

the habit of a handmaiden of God, was once washing herself in a bath when she cast immodest eyes upon a statue of Venus, comparing herself with it, and so offered herself as a dwelling place for the devil. For he who goes about as a roaring lion at once found what he sought and entered into her throat. For nearly seventy days and nights no food or drink passed down her throat, and the devil proved his mastery and possession of her by this fast. The girl's parents, hoping to be able to put an end to this prodigy after so many days, and unable to endure the evil yoke any longer, went with their daughter to a priest and faithfully told him what had happened. The girl only confessed that a bird had appeared to her in the middle of the night and had poured something into her mouth. All were amazed to see the girl showing no signs of her long fast, being neither pale nor wasted nor weakened, but on the contrary organically sound and robust of limb. And when the story seemed incredible, they held a council in a nunnery where were certain Relics of S. Stephen, and the priest and the Prior commended the girl to God. On the first day there she asserted that the bird had appeared to her and rated her because neither hunger nor thirst had driven her to seek that place to which it was not lawful for her to go; and she remained in the convent for two weeks without taking food or drink. But at the dawn of the fifteenth day which was a Sunday, the priest went up with us to offer the customary morning Sacrifice, and the Prior led the girl to the Altar, she adopting the gait and habit of women overcome with shame after feasting and drinking. Then, prostrating herself at the Altar, by the noise of her weeping she moved all those present to groans and tears, with which all the people prayed God to take away so great a misery: for there was an increasing murmuring among the people. After

the Sacrifice had been performed, she, with the other women, received a small particle of the Body of the Lord from the priest; but after chewing It for half an hour she could not swallow It. For he had not yet been put to flight of whom the Apostle says "What concord hath Christ with Belial?" (II. Cor. vi, 15). And again, "Ye cannot drink the cup of the Lord, and the cup of devils" (I. Cor. x, 21). While, therefore, the priest supported her face with his hand so that she should not eject the Holy Element, a certain deacon suggested that the priest should hold the Cup of Salvation to her lips: and no sooner was this done than, at the Saviour's command, the devil left that place which he was possessing, and the girl cried out, praising the Redeemer, that she had swallowed the Sacrament which she had in her mouth. At this there was joy and voices lifted to the glory of God, that after eighty-two days the devil had been cast out and the girl delivered from the power of the Enemy.

In Milan at the church of S. Ambrogio, there was brought to S. Bernard a woman who had been possessed for many years, and was so deformed that she seemed rather a monster than a woman. The Saint turned to the congregation and ordered them to pray fervently to God, then commanding the Clerics to hold the woman near the Altar, he proceeded to offer the Holy Sacrifice of the Mass. Every time he made the sign of the Cross over the Sacred Host, this valiant champion turned also to the woman and fought the Evil Spirit with the same sign of the Cross. At the end of the Lord's Prayer he attacked the Enemy more strongly, placing the Holy Body of the Lord upon the paten and holding It over the woman's head, with these words: "Here is He Who, when about to suffer for our salvation, said: 'Now shall the Prince of this world be cast out.' This is that Body which was formed in the Virgin's womb, and was stretched upon the Cross, and lay in the tomb, and rose from the dead, and ascended into Heaven in the sight of His disciples. By the terrible power of this Majesty I command you, O evil spirit, to depart from the body of this woman, and never to be so hardy as to molest her again!" The demon, being forced to leave her and unable to remain longer, tormented her cruelly, showing the greater fury and rage in that he had but little time to exercise them. The Holy Father returned to the Altar and completed the Breaking of the Host of Salvation and gave the Pax to the deacon that he might communicate it to the people: and at once the woman regained both peace and health. So much says the Abbot William* in his *Life of Blessed Bernard*, Book II, c. 4.

Jehan Molinet† (*Chroniques,*l'an 1491) describes a most pestilent vexation lasting for many years with which God, on account of the sin of one of them who had long fornicated with a demon, permitted Satan to afflict a convent of holy virgins of le Quesnoy. The Dean of Cambrai, a learned and righteous man, came with other Exorcists, and having celebrated the Mass carried the life-giving Host to the possessed community. But the demons could not endure this, and cried out together: "Ah, are you well armed? Have you bread there?" "What are you calling bread?" said the dean. "If this is nothing but bread, remain in possession of this body: but if, as we believe, It is the true Body of our Saviour Jesus Christ, I command you to depart at once from this body and

never more to trouble it." When he had said this (oh, wonderful!) the possessed woman seemed as if she were freed from a great burden, and at once began to breathe freely and to cry aloud on the name of Jesus; and all the others did likewise, being freed when the demons were driven away.

That the like of this happened in our own times at Laon in Belgium is well known to many thousands of Calvinists who witnessed it to their terror and confusion.

S. Auxentius the Abbot had a disciple named Basil who was so terribly afflicted by demons that, with his whole body wounded and broken, he was taken for dead in a cart to S. Auxentius. The holy Abbot ordered him to arise and to take the venerable Body and the life-giving Blood of Our Lord Jesus Christ, and to return at once to his home. Upon this he went away, and the tempter assailed him no more.

A history, surpassing all wonder, is related by Bernard of Luxemburg concerning one Guido de Lachia (*Catalogus haereticorum*, sub littera G). This man obtained such a false reputation for sanctity in the Diocese of Brixen that the people took him to be a second S. John Baptist, and therefore gave him a most honourable burial. After his death the Inquisitors were led by certain sure indications to pronounce that he was a heretic; and therefore, following the advice of the Bishop and other wise men who were his assessors, they passed a sentence that his body should be exhumed and burned. This was done in the presence of the people, and his bones were thrown upon the fire: but behold, certain demons, which were seen by not a few, lifted them from the pyre and held them suspended in the air. This aroused the indignation of the people, who cried out: "Death to the Bishop and these Monks who, out of jealousy, have tried to burn the bones of a Saint! Why do we hold our hands? God is manifesting unto us His sore dis-

---

* "*Abbot William.*" *William of S. Thierry, author of the "Uita Prima" of the Saint.*

† "*Jehan Molinet.*" "*Les Chroniques de Jehan Molinet*" *cover the period from 1474 to 1504. Molinet died in 1507. There were current many MSS. of the "Chroniques" but actually they were not published until they appeared in five volumes, 1828.*

pleasure!" The Bishop was afraid, but the Inquisitors encouraged him to commence Holy Mass, saying that God would perform a miracle rather than permit the cause of the Faith to be imperilled. He then said the Mass of Our Lady; and when it came to the Elevation of the Lord's Body the demons began to shout in the air: "O Guido de Lachia, we have defended you to the best of our power but can do so no longer, for a greater than we is here." At once the bones fell back upon the pyre and were burned to ashes in the flame.

Peter Martyr d'Anghierra, who composed the history of the voyage of Columbus to that Western Land of the Indians, testifies that the following miracle commonly happened: if the Sacrament of the Eucharist was reserved anywhere by the Christians the demons at once were silenced in that place.

Nearly four hundred years ago lived Caesarius of Heisterbach, who in his *Dialogue of Miracles*, IX, 12, wrote as follows: At the time when the heresy of the Albigenses began to manifest itself some malignants, supported by the power of the devil, showed certain signs and portents by which they both strengthened that heresy and subverted the faith of many Catholics: for they used to walk upon the waters without sinking. A certain priest of the Catholic faith and of religious life saw this and, knowing that no true signs could proceed from a false doctrine, carried the Lord's Body in a Pyx to the river where these men were to show the people their powers, and said in the hearing of all: "I adjure thee, thou devil, by Him whom I bear in my hands, that thou work not such phantasies upon this river by means of these men to the subversion of the people." Saying this, and while the men were walking as before upon the waters of the river, the priest in righteous wrath by some inspiration threw the Lord's Body into the river. Marvellous is the might of Christ: for

as soon as the Sacred Host touched the water phantasy gave place to truth, and those false saints sank like lead to the bottom and were drowned. But the Pyx with the Sacrament was immediately borne away by Angels. Seeing all this the priest rejoiced, indeed, in the miracle, but grieved at having thrown away the Sacrament. spending the whole night in tears and groaning. But in the morning, he found the Pyx with the Sacrament upon the Altar.

In the same century, in the year 1231, lived Thomas of Brabant, commonly called Cantimpratanus, who tells the following: At the time that Master Conrad was preaching in Thuringia against the heretics and died a martyr at their hands, a certain heretic, thereto persuaded by demons, invited one of the Preaching Friars to embrace his heresy, and when he saw that he very firmly resisted him, said: "You hold very fast to your faith, and yet you have no proof of it save certain writings. But if you would believe my words, I would show you, as ocular proof, Christ and His Mother and the Saints." The Friar soon suspected some illusion of demons, but wishing to see what it would be, said: "You would verily deserve to be believed, if you fulfilled your promises." The heretic joyfully appointed a day for the Friar; but the Friar secretly brought with him under his hood a Pyx with the Sacrament of the Body of Christ. The heretic led the Friar to a cave in a mountain, as wide as a palace and marvellously lit; and as soon as they reached the inner end of it they saw thrones, seemingly of the purest gold, on which sat a King surrounded with a dazzling brightness, and next to him a most beautiful Queen, serene of countenance; and on each side were seats upon which sat the older Patriarchs and, as it were, Apostles, with a great multitude of Angels standing by; and all shone with a heavenly light: so that they could be thought to be nothing less than demons. As soon as the heretic saw them he fell upon his face and worshipped; but the Friar stood motionless, yet mightily amazed at this spectacle. Soon the heretic turned to him and said: "Why do you not worship when you look upon the Son of God? Fall down and worship him whom you see, and you will learn the secrets of our faith from his lips." Then the Friar came near and drew out the Pyx and, offering It to the Queen sitting upon the throne, said: "If thou art the Queen, the Mother of Christ, behold there thy Son. If thou receive Him, I shall acknowledge thee to be the Mother of God." At these words the whole of that phantasm vanished at once, and the brightness was extinguished, and the darkness was so thick that the Friar and his guide could hardly find their way back out on to the mountain. The heretic was then converted and returned to the Faith, and trembled with terror at the wonderful cunning of the devil.

Here is another story, told by Pico della Mirandola in his *De Strigibus*. Fifteen years since, there dwelt in the Rhaetian Alps a certain good priest, and he had need to take the Eucharist to a man sick unto death, who lived a long distance away. Thinking that if he went on foot he would not reach him as quickly as he ought he mounted his horse, with the most Holy Body of Christ in a Pyx reverently fastened about his neck, and so rode as fast as he could. When he had gone some distance he met a wayfarer who asked him to dismount and go with him to see a most wonderful sight. Rashly, from a desire to see this marvel, the priest obeyed; and hardly had he dismounted from his horse before he felt himself carried through the air with his companion, and in a short time set down upon the top of a very high mountain, where there was a fair plain full of lofty trees and surrounded by forbidding rocks. In the midst was a great company and games of all sorts, and tables loaded with various luxuries of food and drink; and a sound of

sweetest singing was heard; and there came women such as can enslave a man's soul with their beauty and soften his very marrow with the sweetness they exhale. The simple good priest wholly astounded at this unexpected event was speechless for very wonder, not daring to open his mouth; yea, he was quite beyond himself and struck still with astonishment. Then his companion who had led him there asked him if he wished to worship as a suppliant before the Queen who was there present, and to offer her any gift. On a high throne sat a Queen of most beautiful appearance, adorned in royal splendour and marvellous rich jewels: and all who were there went up to her and prostrated themselves to the ground in two or four ranks in the fairest manner, and worshipped her and offered her various gifts. Hearing the word Queen, and seeing her so resplendent and surrounded by so many ministers, the priest thought that she was the Mother of Christ, Queen of Heaven and Earth; for he did not suspect any prestige or devilish glamour, or otherwise he would not have gone near to her. Considering with himself, then, what gift he should offer to her, he thought that none could be more grateful or acceptable than the Body of Her Son; and he went up and, kneeling as a suppliant at her feet, took the Pyx containing the Most August Sacrament from his neck and placed it upon the woman's lap. Everything then at once vanished in a miraculous manner. Astounded at this strange experience the simple man saw that he had been ensnared by an illusion, and tremblingly began to beseech the help of God to bring him safe from such a wandering from the right way. For a long time he strayed through trackless places and vast forests until at last he found a shepherd who put him upon his road and informed him that he was a hundred miles from the place to which he wished to carry the Eucharist. At last he reached home again, and told the whole matter to the

Magistrates. This happened during the reign of Maximilian.

S. Augustine (*City of God*, XXII, 8) tells us that a man named Hesperius, who had formerly been a tribune, possessed a farm called Zubedi in the district of Fussala; and on account of the sickness afflicting his animals and his servants he found that his house was suffering from the visitation of malignant spirits. Therefore, in my absence, he asked our priests to send one of their number; and they granted his request. A priest went, and offered these the Sacrifice of the Body of Christ, and prayed with all his might that that vexation should cease. And God at once had mercy, and it ceased.

S. Augustine says again in the Ninth Book and also in the fifth chapter of his *Collation* that witches confess that they are freed from all vexation by the devil while they are hearing Mass; and therefore they remain as long as they can at about midday in Catholic churches where many Masses are said.

6. It is not Meet to Joke with Demons.

Nider in his *Formicarius* says that he saw a Brother in a monastery at Cologne who was rather ribald of speech, but famous for his power of casting out demons. This man was casting a demon from the body of a possessed person in the precincts of the monastery at Cologne, and the demon asked him to give him a place to go to; whereupon the Brother jokingly said: "Go to my privy." The demon went out; and in the night, when the Brother wished to purge his belly, the demon attacked him so fiercely in the privy that he escaped with difficulty with his life.

Therefore the casting out of demons is a sacred matter, and should be undertaken most reverently.

7. Of Prayer.

In the year 1549 a man confessed to a Jesuit Father that while he was per-

forming in the middle of the night the penance set him by his confessor, he

suddenly saw squadrons of cats, mice, and other beasts, black in colour and of a terrible appearance, so numerous that they seemed to fill the whole bedroom. Terrified by this sight he began to tremble for fear lest he should be seized alive by those beasts; and in his fear he ran to an image of Our Lord crying aloud for His Help. Thereupon all the animals suddenly vanished, with such a commotion and shrieking and outcry that it seemed as if the house would fall down.

At Bungo in Japan there was in the year 1555 a family which had been tormented by demons for a hundred years, so that the evil became as it were hereditary in that family of shepherds. The father had spent all his wealth in placating idols, but the evil rather grew than abated. His son, now thirty years old, was possessed by a demon so that he did not know his father and mother, and took no food for fifteen days. At the end of that time one of the Jesuit Fathers came to him and bade him call upon S. Michael; but when he named the Saint he was struck with a violent trembling and threw his limbs about in such a way as to frighten those who were by. But when the priest invoked God the Father, and the Son, and the Holy Ghost, he was incontinently delivered from the demon. A few days later his sister was beset by the demon's molestations; and in the midst of her agony she cried out in the hearing of the Jesuits that she wished to become a Christian. When she was brought to the sacred font and tried to protect herself with the holy sign of the Cross, she began to shake and tremble violently. The priest poured forth fervid prayers; and she herself strove to utter the Sacred Name of Jesus and that of S. Michael, but the demon only plagued her the more, forcibly sealing her mouth fast. At last, however, she burst out into a kind of refrain and cried: "If we reject the Idols Xacca (Shaka) and Amida, the founders of the Japanese religion, there is no one left who should be worshipped." And much more she said of this sort, which no one could understand. One day, when many Christians were present, the priest celebrated Mass, and the possessed woman also was there. When he had finished he asked her how she was, and she answered: "Very well." But when she was told to pronounce the name of S. Michael, she began to shake and gnash her teeth, and the demon said that he would come out but, because he had for so many years used that family as his lodging, it was against his will to depart. The priest again bade her utter the name of S. Michael, and she answered that it was very troublesome to her, and shed tears and complainingly said: "Whither shall I go?" Then all the Christians joined in prayer; and when they had prayed enough the demon departed from her whom he had till then possessed. The woman at once asked for a drink to be given her; and when she was bidden to invoke the Names of Jesus and Mary, she pronounced them with such sweetness that it seemed like the voice of an Angel.

In the year 1588 there was in a hospital at Brünn in Moravia a woman who was so bitterly plagued by the devil that sometimes she tried to drown herself, and sometimes tried to do away with herself with a knife which she deliberately seized in order to injure herself; but she was prevented by all the others in the hospital. After she had been thus afflicted for three years, she was stricken with apoplexy; and her tongue was tied up so that she could not speak. A request was sent to the priests to ask for the prayers of the people: and God heard their prayers, for first the knot of her tongue was unloosed and then that of her soul, as was proved after she had made a good Confession, and received Sacramental absolution.

In the Letters of Luis Fröes (*anno* 1596) there is the following history:

A certain Nobleman formerly of great honour and authority who lived near Funai had a daughter who was married to a heathen, her mother and all her family being heathens also, and none being a Christian except the said Nobleman, who was a good and religious man. It happened that his daughter fell suddenly ill and in six days was near to death; and it was said that she was possessed by a demon, because her gestures were so frantic and strange that she could hardly be held by two or three men. Her husband and father-in-law implored the Bonzes for help; but they could help her no whit with their vain rites and superstitious trifling. When the woman seemed to be at death's door they told her father, who dwelt eighteen miles away. He hurried to her as quickly as he could and found his daughter alive indeed, but so delirious that she did not recognise her father. He then ordered the Bonzes and the other heathens about the bed to be removed; and taking his Rosary recited the Lord's Prayer three times and was commencing the Angelic Salutation. Meanwhile the woman became no better, but rather was convulsed with more terrible spasms than before, so that now many men could hardly hold her down. Her father again had recourse to the Rosary, and beat her back with it saying: "You seem to me to be some demon. Depart from this body." And the demon answered: "I shall not depart." The father, being a man of eminent virtue, threw the Rosary about her neck, saying: "Whether you will or no, you shall depart." Then the demon said: "Take away the Rosary, for it tears my neck; and then I will depart." The father answered: "I shall not take it away." Then he took some ropes and threatened that he would whip him; and so the demon departed and left the woman free.

8. Of the Guardian Angel.

Ferdinand of Castile,* the Historian of the Order of S. Dominic, relates the following: At Vouzella, a town in the district of Coimbra, was born one Egidius (or Giles) of noble parents. Whilst he was still but a youth, owing to his own natural talents and family influence he obtained no less than three rich benefices and also a Priory. But now he abandoned himself to

---

* "Ferdinand of Castile." "Historia generalis Ordinis Praedicatorum," Pars prima; liber secundus; cap. lxxii. The history of Blessed Gil of Santarem, O.P., who was born c. 1185 and died at Santarem, 14 May, 1265, is related by all Dominican hagiographers and chroniclers. The cult of Blessed Gil was ratified by Benedict XIV on 9 March, 1748. His feast is kept throughout the Order on 14 May as a semi-duplex.

every vice. He was well versed in the humane sciences, and determined to acquire a complete knowledge of Philosophy and Medicine, thinking that this would provide him with greater opportunity to practise his iniquities. Accordingly he set out for Paris with that object in view. On his way he fell in with a demon in human shape; and his evil travelling companion (who knew him well, though Egidius did not know what he was) by degrees began to ask questions; and when he heard the purpose of his journey, he said: "Why do you not rather listen to me? I will give you knowledge which is both easy to acquire and is chiefly of use for obtaining those honours and pleasures which you have in mind, being the very perfection of all medicine. It is Necromancy I mean." With these words he persuaded Egidius, and led him away to a vast cavern near the City of Toledo, where he was joyfully met and received by men and demons in human form; and they entered the cavern. Not only was an oath of secrecy exacted from him, but he was made to swear perpetual allegiance and homage; yet he did this full willingly, confirming his promise with a paper signed with his own blood. For seven years after this he deeply studied the Black Arts and Magic, and then proceeded to Paris where in a short time he made marvellous progress among the followers of Hippocrates and obtained the degree of Doctor. He began to give way to viler and viler enormities and sins, and rushed headlong from crime to crime, so that it was doubtful which waxed the greater, the fame of his learning or the infamy of his wickedness. But oh! the goodness of God! For since He could not lead him by gentleness He would have him by force. Behold there came a horseman brandishing a spear, and, looking at the miserable man with an angry countenance, cried to him threateningly: "Leave this life and these evil ways, and turn again to the practice of good." Egidius was seized with a sudden panic, but as soon as it had passed he was unwilling to change his manner of life and returned to wallow in his filth. Three days later the same horseman appeared looking even more terrible and not only used the same threatening words, telling him to change his manner of life, but pierced his breast with his spear, wounding it slightly. This broke his spirit, and he said: "I yield myself: I shall do what you command, Lord." You would have said that he was Saul fallen prostrate upon the ground. He fully determined to give himself entirely to God and, obeying some inner impulse (which, as I think, was inspired by his Guardian Angel who had appeared to him), resolved to join some Religious Order. In this mind he started back for Paris, and while he was passing through Palencia, where the Dominican Brothers were then building a monastery, he felt a sudden wish to observe the work. He saw men of evident sanctity and learning, some of them aged and enfeebled, who had formerly been delicately nurtured, mixing mortar, cutting wood, shaping stone, and bearing loads upon their shoulders with the greatest cheerfulness and alacrity. He wished to join them, and at once asked to be admitted and was granted his request. He fulfilled his novitiate under the spur of a great hope of future sanctity, and after some years was sent to Santarem in Portugal where he increased in prayer and in his victory over himself. The one regret which tortured him was that that obscene and execrable paper was still in the possession of the demon. Therefore he commended himself the more fervently to the Queen of Heaven, praying not without tears and frequent sighing for some remedy for this evil. What can the Mother of Mercy deny to one who prays in such a manner? One day as he was praying with great fervour in a chapel of the church,

there appeared to him a demon of terrifying aspect howling dismally, who made an outcry against him, petulantly reminding him of the allegiance he had vowed and the benefits he had received. At last, after many idle and impudent threats, he said: "I shall pay you for your monasticism and the violence which compels me to restore to you this paper; for you will never cease to regret it." He then threw the paper down at the feet of Egidius and vanished. Egidius took up the paper and tore it to bits. But the demon's threat was not vain: for he tormented him for more than seven years after in a marvellous manner. Without reckoning his other vexations, he assumed the likeness of a certain friar who dwelt in the same monastery, and so plagued Egidius with every domestic discomfort that can possibly be imagined. After suffering this, Egidius at last, in grief that the evil should lurk hidden and that the Brother (as he thought him) should so continually offend against God, took the matter to the Prior and asked to be sent elsewhere, telling him the reason. Upon this the matter was brought to light; and the calumniator, being exposed and now for the first time overcome not, as before, by Egidius but by them all, ceased to torment his victor. Egidius lived on, and was famous not only for his many virtues, but for various miracles.

In the year 1265 he left this world to be born again in Heaven, and was buried at Santarem where he is worshipped as a Saint. See what a mighty protection against demons there is in the Virgin Mother of God, and what inducement to a good life in a man's Guardian Angel.

John of Salisbury (*Polycraticus*, II, 28) writes as follows: In my boyhood I was sent to learn the Psalms from a priest who unfortunately was given to crystal gazing. One day he made me sit at his feet with one of my companions who was rather older than

I, after having uttered certain spells, in order to use us in those profane mysteries so that we might be able to tell him what he asked. He rubbed our finger nails with some oil or holy ointment, and we gazed at them as also into a highly polished and shining bowl. After the priest had pronounced some strange names which seemed to me merely by reason of the horror I felt at them to be the names of demons, and had muttered some adjurations, which cannot have been in the name of God, my companion told him that he had seen certain ghostly and cloudlike figures; whereas I was so blind to them that I saw nothing but my finger-nails and the bowl and such things as had before been visible to me. From that time I was considered to be of no use for these divinations; and I was forbidden to come near them, as being a hindrance to their sacrilege: and every time they determined to practise these mysteries, I was kept away from them as an impediment. Thus did God (as I think, through my Guardian Angel) show favour to me in my childhood; and from that day the horror which I conceived for this crime increased as I grew older, and was but the more deeply printed upon my soul by the miserable end to which I saw many such Diviners come. For I have never known one who did not die before his time, or through some extraordinary mischance, or by the hands of his enemies; not to speak of others whom I have seen with my own eyes stricken to the ground by the vengeance of Heaven, and destroyed. Yet I must mention two, of whom one was this priest I speak of, and the other a certain deacon, who fled in terror from the horrors of the magic crystal, one to a Chapter of Canons and the other to a cell at Cluny, where they assumed the religious habit. And from that time I have felt great compassion for those two poor men, who have suffered even more than the rest of their companions.

9. The Singular Help of the Blessed Virgin Mary.

Besides other examples which I have already quoted, I will add another most certain story to show the present help of the Virgin Mother of God. Orazio Torsellino,* the writer of the *History of Our Blessed Lady of Loreto*, relates a happening which was as beautiful as it was true:

"Moreover the patronage of the B. Virgin of Loreto saved another young man, whom raging lust drew headlong to utter perdition. For being of desperate affection, desire and audacity, he gave himself wholly to forbidden pleasures; and overcoming many motions with his dishonesty, he burned with the excessive love of a certain woman, whom seeing he could

---

* *"Orazio Torsellino." The historical works of Orazio Torsellino, S.J., are still held in high estimation. Sommervogel's "Bibliothèque des écrivains de la Compagnie de Jésus" (10 vols., Brussels, 1890–1910) may be consulted. For this passage the translation of Thomas Price (1608) has been used. The reference is III, 33.*

gain neither by entreaty nor money, nor force, nor deceit, he determined to experience the most desperate course of all. Making means therefore to the devil by Art magic, he requested to be made partaker of his desire, shewing himself ready to condescend to all, to enjoy that which he so earnestly sought. Whereupon by commandment of the devil, he forsook Christ, and gave and delivered himself wholly to him, and what is more, did also swear unto him by proscript words, and bound himself unto it by hand-writing: so far doth the love of pleasure bind impure minds. But when he had obtained his desire, satiety (as it happeneth) bred loathsomeness, and by the goodness and grace of God he weighed the greatness of his offence with mature consideration. And being truly penitent for his wicked sin, and conceiving some hope of pardon, he began to seek for heavenly help, and to call on Almighty God and His B. Mother, Meantime the B. Virgin of Loreto, and the priests of the sacred House (endowed with most ample faculty to release sins) coming to his mind, without delay made him go to Loreto, Almighty God being the author and guide of his journey; not doubting but there to find remedy against so many evils. His hope deceived him not. For as soon as he came thither, making means to confer with a discreet priest, he declared unto him his mournful state, and asked him, whether he might have any hope to be saved. At first the priest remained somewhat amazed at the grievousness of the offence, but then declaring unto him the greatness thereof; he put him in hope of salvation, if by prayer, fasting, and voluntary punishment of his body, he would wholly give himself to pacify Almighty God. When he refused no punishment at all, the priest promised him, if he did what was commanded, he would willingly hear him, and by the grace of God would also take away so great

an offence. At parting he exhorted him to punish his body, with fasting, with hair-cloth and stripes, for the space of three days, to implore the help of the B. Virgin, and by her to ask humble pardon of Almighty God for his grievous sin; and he also promised to say Mass for his salvation all that time, whereby there was good confidence on either side. The three days being so spent, before he gave him absolution the priest thought good to wrest his hand-writing from the devil, that he might have no right nor interest at all in him. Therefore he exhorted the Penitent to retire himself into the most Majestical Chapel, and earnestly to importune the Mother of God with prayer and tears, until he got his hand-writing out of the devil's hands. He obeyed, very desirous of salvation and security, with undoubted hope to obtain it by the intercession of the B. Virgin Mother of God. Whereupon prostrating his body before the B. Virgin, with flowing tears he earnestly besought her, that she would vouchsafe to get him his wicked hand-writing, and to work his salvation and health. By a great miracle he had his desire. For as he repeated these verses with all devotion:

A Mother show thyself,
He take our plaints by thee,
That being for us born,
Vouchsafed thy Son to be.

he saw the hand-writing fall suddenly into his hands, and scarce crediting himself for the unexpected joy thereof, with new tears he gave manifold thanks to the B. Virgin. Whereupon departing presently out of the sacred Chapel, he went joyfully unto the priest, and showed him his hand-writing gotten again by the benefit of the Mother of God, which was stuffed with so many horrible execrations and curses against Christ, and himself that wrote it, that it may easily appear to be dictated by the everlasting Enemy of mankind. Notwithstanding the power of God, more potent than all diabolical deceit, loosed so great a band, whereby that sinful soul given by vow to hell itself, by favour of the Mother of God was set in the liberty of the children of God, that no wicked nor desperate man should despair of salvation (if he himself will not perish) nor doubt of the clemency of God who hath freely given his B. Mother a Patroness to offenders for their salvation."

10. Of the Sign of the Holy Cross.

Of the many further examples which I could adduce, be content with this one which is both rare and marvellous. A certain priest dwelling at Arona in the year 1591 had made a vow to God that he would enter the Society of Jesus, and made his intention known to one of the Fathers. But the devil took this ill and turned to his wonted weapons; for he so plagued the man with impure thoughts that he prevented him from sleeping. The soldier of Christ arose from his bed and passed sleepless nights reading the lives of the Saints; but the Adversary would not endure even this, for he threw down the lamp which was hanging upon the wall so that the oil

was spilled and dirtied the whole book. Not satisfied with this, he burst into the midst of supper like a foul wind, so that the priest at once went from the table to his cubicle and fell prostrate upon the ground in prayer to God, giving his body stripes instead of food. And when even so he yet felt the fire of blind desire plucking at him, he stood barefoot upon the ground for two or three hours while that importunate heat should be cooled, and then threw himself wearily upon his bed. Lying in the same bed he seemed to see a woman, and to put out his hand and touch her hair; therefore he quickly leaped out in amazement and, turning his eyes to the bed, saw nothing: and this happened two or three times. He feared that he was suffering a delusion of the eyes, and affirmed that the same thing happened on many nights; until at last it reached such a pass that, when the unhappy man went to bed, he used to tie down his arms and hands with bands for fear lest his hands should wander for some vain purpose in his dreams: but it was unavailing, for no sooner had sleep bound up his senses than, in a short time, it unbound his arms. But how wonderful is the mercy of God, who does not allow the devil to tempt us beyond our strength! The priest, obstinately fighting for his chastity, put the devil to flight; but though beaten he returned to the combat with marvellous cunning. One day the priest went out to escape from the heat of the town and was walking by a lake saying the Hours of Our Lady. He had hardly gone two hundred paces when he was overtaken by a man with a long reddish beard, in very costly raiment, and sitting upon a very beautiful black horse like no other in those parts, and accompanied by two foot-servants. Approaching the priest he greeted him with great politeness and asked: "Have you come to the *Jubilate* yet?" Now it happened that the priest was just then reciting that Psalm; but the wonder was that he was doing it so quietly that he could hardly hear himself. Then the horseman and the priest began to converse as follows. First the horseman asked enquiringly: "What is it that is worrying you so deeply?" But the priest tried to put him off, and said: "I am quite well and happy. Your question is wide of the mark." But the other answered: "My friend, it is hard to bandy words with me; for I have long had from God the gift of reading the inmost thoughts of men." The priest stood rooted to the spot with wonder and amazement, staring at the speaker's clothing and his whole person; but at last he took heart and said: "If you have that power, tell me what it is that is troubling me, if you know more about my affairs than I do myself." The other answered him: "It is your vow to the Society of Jesus which is pricking you and will not leave you in peace. But you must order your life in a different manner, for there is no door open to you in that direction." The priest, suspecting that the other had somehow heard that the Jesuits were undecided whether or not to accept his vow, replied: "If the Fathers will not have me, I shall not be disheartened nor torture myself; for there is not only one way of serving God piously and devoutly." "That is right," said the horseman; "put that trouble from your heart. Your mind and body are of such a nature that, even in your present manner of life, you are able to preserve your innocence. But if you will listen to me, you shall see another country where you shall live for God and yourself. Leave Arona and follow me. You shall not have cause to regret it, for you will be excellently placed with me. And here is proof that my promises are not idle." Saying this, he shook a purse full of money in his hand. The priest thanked him, saying: "I do not at present need your generosity, for I must keep faith with the Church at Arona." The horseman at once inter-rupted him, saying: "What obligation have you? It has not been publicly witnessed, or put in writing. Can they claim you in return for fifty-three pounds of bronze? For that is all you receive, and you will never get more." The priest, not without wonder, admitted the truth of this; but was led to suspect that his companion had been told everything by someone in Arona. Then, gaining a little confidence, he asked: "But where are you going? Where do you live?" "In Pallanza," he answered; "and the boat which is approaching us is mine and at the service of my friends." This boat was propelled by an oarsman on each side, and the priest wondered that he had not seen it before. "Now if you accept my condition, you shall have all you desire in Pallanza with me. If you are determined to embrace the religious life, I shall see to it that you are admitted into a famous and most holy House." "I thank your exceeding civility towards a stranger, but I have my reasons for declining." When, after this exchange of conversation, the priest was constrained to wait a little, he said: "Go forward, Master: I shall follow a little behind"; and he did as he said. Then he made the sign of the Cross upon his brow and over his heart, and taking in his hands the rosary with which he had been counting his prayers, followed the other. But at the sign of the Cross, the horseman, the servants, the boat and the rowers all vanished. See how the tortuous wiles of the Serpent were all dissipated like a cloud by one sign of the Cross.

11. Of Holy, or Lustral Water.

At Würzburg in the year 1583 a priest's house not far from the city was haunted either by an evil spirit or by some illusion. The priest himself and his confidential servants used to say that everything in the house was hurled violently to the floor; moreover lighted torches, even when placed in great numbers in a room free from

all draughts, were blown out at one puff; beds were forcibly dragged away from them when they went to lie on them; and many of the servants had such an obstruction in the throat that they were nearly suffocated. Finally many horrible things were seen and heard in the house. The wretched priest, at his wits' end, went to other priests and told them how he was being plagued, and asked the rector to depute some priest to be his protection. One was entrusted with this duty, and towards evening went fasting to the place; but hardly had he crossed the threshold before he himself saw what he had been told of. For in the actual sight both of him and his companion a salver was hurled against the wall with such force and violence that it frightened those present nearly to death. This priest bade them all be of good heart and urged the parish priest to prepare to approach the tribunal of Penance; and then putting on a surplice and stole he went up to the upper part of the house where the demon was chiefly wont to rage. He employed the usual rites of the Church for putting demons to flight; and when there was no answer and no presence was evoked by the priest's voice, he turned to exhorting the servants, especially to throw aside heresy and to expiate their sins by a good con-

fession. Then, having duly purified the place, he returned to his house with a great harvest of souls. For it is agreed that many were reclaimed from heresy to the Church; and that the house was freed from all its former molestation, as the parish priest afterwards testified.

We read in Epiphanus (II) of a certain Josephus who, while he was yet a Jew, restored a sick man to health by making the sign of the Cross upon him in water. Palladius[*] testifies the same of a woman whom through magic glamour seemed to be changed into a mare: for when S. Macarius blessed water and having prayed sprinkled it upon her head, it became clear to all that the woman stood there in her own proper shape.

Theodoret (lib. 5, hist., cap. 21) records that, when Bishop Marcellus was destroying the Temple of Jupiter at Apamea, he saw a black demon restraining the force of the flames so that they should not consume the wooden material. He fortified and blessed water with the sign of the Cross and ordered it to be thrown upon the flames; and the evil spirit could not endure this conduct and fled. But the flames were aroused by the water as if it had been oil, and consumed the Temple in a moment.

S. Theodore the Archimandrite used to drive away all harms with Holy Water, even sickness caused by demons, as he did from that Phentinus near Tantendia who met a demon in the form of a dog which, by merely gaping at him, struck him with a most grievous malady; and as he did from the house of one Theodore, a Tribune, where both men and all the animals were tormented by demons; so that when they would dine, stones were hurled upon the table to the great

---

[*] "*Palladius.*" *Born in Galatia, 368; died probably before 431. Author of the "Historia Lausiaca," an account of the monks of Egypt and Palestine. The first edition was a Latin version by Gentianus Hervetus, Paris, 1555.*

terror of all, and the women's beds were broken, and the house was infested by so many snakes and mice that everybody was afraid to enter it. So the servant of God went in and spent the whole night worshipping and praying to God; and by sprinkling the whole house with Holy Water, delivered it from the unclean spirits. This we learn from Gregory the Priest, whom we have often quoted.

He recalls also the following illustrious miracle: The inhabitants of a village in the district of Como had killed an ox in order to feed upon the roasted flesh, but it so happened that all who ate of it became ill and lay as if they were dead, and whatever meat they had left went black and stinking. Those, therefore, who had not tasted of the meat told what had happened to a holy man; who answered that the misfortune must have come from a company of demons in the cooking pots, and since he could not at that time go with them he blessed water and sent it by one of the Brethren to sprinkle it over those who were in danger and to offer it to them to drink. When this was done they all arose as if from sleep, except one who was dead. For this man's brother, John the Bailiff, would not wait for the blessing of the servant of God but ran for help to a witch; and while he was applying her charm to his brother, he lost his life.

Great armies of devils invaded the dwelling of S. Hubert the Bishop of Liège, a veritable scourge of demons. Seeing this, the man of God said to his page: "Go, and let there be brought here water which a priest has consecrated by mingling salt therewith, and which has been impregnated by the power of prayer for putting to flight the Enemy's malice; and oil (that is, the Chrism) blessed by apostolic authority; for by the aspersion and unction of these the pestilent phantasms of the Enemy will soon be so routed, that he will not dare to renew his machinations." So says the anonymous author, that disciple of S. Hubert who wrote a life of the Saint.

In the year 1583 at Riga one Ruthenus was often admonished to return to the bosom of the Roman Church, but he always refused to listen and went away impenitent. But from that time various spectres were seen by his servants in his house: the tables were removed from them when they sat down, yet there was no one to be seen; the bedroom doors, although secured not only with bolts but with bars across them, were torn right off their hinges; from the top of the house were hurled huge stones covered with pitch, which a Jesuit Father writes that he himself has handled. And a certain Pole, whom that priest asserts that he saw, was so grievously wounded upon the head that he lay half dead for some days. There was also much straw in that house, and this was all cut up into the most minute pieces. In short these and other such terrible manifestations led the man to have no doubt that Satan had taken possession of that house as his by right. The priest whom I have mentioned went into the house with one companion and purified it with Holy Water and incense, and by this exorcism all the disturbance of the demons was allayed, wherefore they returned great thanks in the House of God.

About 1587 the Jesuits established a colony at Patzcuaro in Mexico. Here there was an Indian woman with a child, and every night when she slept it seemed as if the child were snatched from her side and then replaced, but she did not know where he was taken to. Meanwhile the boy himself lost strength every day and was slowly wasting to his death. He was brought into the church and was saved by the application of Holy Water, with prayer.

In 1588, the following year, a peasant woman of Trèves offered a man some eggs. The man's lackey took the eggs in his hat and, after removing them, replaced his hat upon his head; and was at once stricken with such pain that he nearly went mad. Not knowing what he was doing, he rushed into a church and plunged his burning head into the Holy Water stoup which stood there, and was cured. The witch, on being seized and examined, said that the eggs had been so poisoned that they would kill whoever ate them, and would cause those who touched them to swell.

At Pont-à-Mousson in Lorraine in the year 1593 a virgin of advanced age was subject to such fits that she was held to be possessed: another woman was bewitched, and another tormented by an evil spirit. After a priest had recited Litanies, and they had drunk Holy Water, and had hung blessed Agnus Deis about their necks, they came to their senses and, after confessing their sins, soon departed this life while they were intent upon their prayers.

Francisco Lopez Gomara, in his *Historia Mexicana*, testifies that among the Indians there are three chief remedies against the illusions and apparitions of demons. The worshipful Presence of the most potent Sacrament of the Eucharist; the Crucifix, and Holy Water. And he says that the cacodemons themselves have confessed as much to the Indians more than once.

12. Of the Virtue of Salt, Bread, Wax, and the Blessed Agnus Dei

At Trapani in the year 1585 there was a householder in whose house it was reported that certain voices had been heard for some months; and this was a familiar demon who in various ways tried to delude men. He would hurl great stones, but without wounding anyone's head, and would cast down the household vessels from on high without breaking them. And when a boy of the house was wont to sing hymns, the demon trolled out lascivious songs in the hearing of all

to the accompaniment of a harp, and openly boasted that he was a demon. When the master of the house and his wife were starting on their business to a certain town, the demon attached himself to their company; and when the man was drenched with rain and was coming back, the evil spirit went before shouting on his way, and began to warn the servants to build a fire, for the master was at the door soaked through with rain. But so soon as the master of the house understood how he was being deluded, he threatened the demon that he would fetch a priest to drive him from his house: and the demon began to exclaim that he must not do this, and threatened him with his enmity and hatred, saying that he would keep himself hidden for as long as the priest should be in the house. Nevertheless the master went to a priest and told him all that had happened, and even changed his house in order to free himself from that haunting. But the priest, fearing to arouse the curiosity of the ignorant multitude who would flock thither to see what would happen, decided not to go with him; only he advised him and all his household to cleanse their souls by a general confession and strengthen themselves with the Heavenly Bread, and to take care that none of the servants or anyone else should fall into conversation with the Enemy, nor seek to know from him what was hidden, as they had done; but rather they were to laugh at anything he said, and despise it as coming from the Father of Lies. They all promised to do so, and the priest gave them an image of the Celestial Lamb in blessed wax to hang by a thread round the necks of those who were chiefly troubled by the demon. The demon was in terror of that wax and threatened that, if they did not throw it away, he would twist their necks and kill them. But they followed the sage counsel and advice of the priest and gave him no answer, but fortified themselves against the Enemy with the weapons of the Sacraments and were easily saved from his guile and molestation.

The country of Trèves is even now infested with witches, one of whom with her spells and charms enticed a boy, about eight years of age, to that place where, under the cover of darkness and night, they perform their execrable games. The boy was given his part to play; for while the rest joined hands and danced, he beat the measure upon a tabor. Neither was he a looker-on at their dances and games only, but often witnessed the magic with which they do hurt to human bodies and the fruits of the earth. The Archbishop ordered the boy to be kept in custody in his Palace and to be taught the catechism, of which he was quite ignorant. He had an Agnus Dei hung round his neck, and a demon came to him at night and scolded him bitterly for having let himself be deceived so easily, and ordered him to throw away that waxen image if he did not wish to be beaten. The boy, in terror, obeyed; and at once the demon, since the object of his fear had been removed, carried him to the town walls and placed him upon a black goat and took him in a moment to the most obscene spots haunted and infested by witches. After he had remained some time with the witches he was again restored to the Palace, with the cord broken from which the waxen image had hung. At the request of the Archbishop and the whole city, the boy was sent to a house of the Jesuits, and kept till he should learn what was necessary to the Christian discipline, so that he might afterwards return to the Palace piously fortified by the Sacraments and free from the snares of demons. And so, finally, this came to pass; although it is said that after some years he relapsed and paid the penalty of his crime.

In 1586 in the same district there was a young peasant, less than fifteen years old, of very keen intelligence. He had been more than once to the hellish place where men mingled with women, and young with old, with the demon presiding, in feasting at night with all sense of shame forgotten. But he had not yet renounced God and the Mother of God, nor had pronounced after the demon the execrable prayers: only he had eaten the brain of a cat in his food when the moon was waning, and felt that his own brain had become smaller. He entered the city of Trèves which he had never seen before, doubtless being lured to his punishment by the same hand that had led him to the sin of witchcraft; and was taken as possessed into the Prince's Palace to be guarded apart, that the demon might be driven from him. But the demon gave him no rest at night, beating him and tearing the Agnus Dei from his neck. The Archbishop then determined to send him to the College of the Jesuits; but even there the poor boy had no peace until his cubicle was solemnly exorcised. It will be worth while to record some of his statements; for he told the Bishop as follows: "While we were holding our Sabbat there was one of your retainers who boasted that on such and such a night he had poured a poisoned drink into you as you slept, having found the way open to you because you had imprudently left your Agnus Dei on the table when you went to bed; and if the cup had been a little larger, you would not have escaped death." And indeed the Bishop said that he had been so ill after that particular night that he had been forced to keep his bed for some days. When this statement did not convince the great company of nobles who were present, the boy said to the Burgomaster of the city: "And our witches have attacked you twice; but they were repulsed by that little locket which you always wear, containing two images and some consecrated object." (He meant the Agnus Dei.) The Burgomaster admitted that he always wore these holy things.

Another man possessed by a demon appeared more like a snarling, barking dog than a reasoning and speaking man. He was brought from Burgundy to us and with great difficulty forced into the church; and he did not cease to act like a dog until an Agnus Dei was put about his neck. Then at last he grew quiet and behaved like a man again, and purged his soul with the healing grace of confession. The same amulet similarly benefited another who laboured under the same affliction.

In the Province of Innspruck an apt medicine for the gravest maladies is much in use, and the terrors of the devil are counteracted in many places by the use of sacred amulets. Many incidents are told in proof of this. One man asserted that he was destined to hell because of his crimes, and in his convulsions invoked the devil, making it clear by his behaviour to the panic-stricken bystanders that the Fiend had appeared to him. But the man was cured: for a priest soothed him at first with gentle words, and so led him to make his confession, having given him an Agnus Dei to place devoutly in his bosom. Another man had in time past pledged his soul and body to the terrible Snatcher of souls;

and as his time was at hand the unhappy wretch went to a priest and sought his advice with trembling lips and uneasy eyes. In a sudden panic he cried out: "Help! Father, make haste to help a poor wretch with some holy thing." The priest asked what was the matter, and he answered "The Enemy is standing at the door waiting for me to come out, and looking threateningly at me because of my broken vow." This man also was cured by the same remedy. The following story also is not unknown. A certain peasant heard that there were in Innspruck men who had a sure medicine to drive away witchcraft and delusions: so he came to them for the medicine against the devil; for so he called it. When asked what he meant by a medicine, he answered: "I do not know. I only know what I have heard: but whatever it is, it is something that drives the devil away." So he was given a piece of blessed wax, and soon after found great benefit from it: so that now, whenever a Jesuit Father goes through that town, he needs more than seventy pieces of blessed wax to satisfy their clamorous requirements.

About the same time at Avignon a woman was tormented by an evil spirit; and a friend advised her to go to a priest, and meanwhile he gave her parents an Agnus Dei which they sewed in her garment unbeknown to her. She either forgot this advice, or put off going; and she was seized through the window by four seeming cats and carried up on to the roof of the house; then she heard a human voice threatening to hurl her down unless she threw away the waxen image which she had in her clothes. She understood what that must be, and recognised that they were evil counsellors: therefore with great courage she refused to do so, and at once turned to her prayers, and was left perched upon the roof. For there her husband, roused by her cries, found her.

At Trèves in the year 1590 a young man received a great wrong involving much loss at the hands of those from whom he should least have expected it; and he resented this more than was becoming to a Christian. Black with grief and brooding immoderately, as he was walking alone in the twilight he met a demon who, seeing his chance, was not slow to take it. He was in the form of a noble man, very dark, and at first caused the young man some terror; but he greeted him and so removed his fear, and asked him the cause of his sorrow. The young man explained what was the matter; and the demon told him that by himself he had no hope of recovering his money, since it had fallen into the hands of very powerful persons; but if he would follow him, he would very easily recover everything. The young man answered him: "I have been imposed upon by men whom I know, and by my friends: shall I, then, put my trust in a stranger, whom I now see for the first time? Good God——" At these last words the man-monster vanished into the air like lightning. On the next day at the same time, as the young man was pondering the same thoughts, there appeared to him a woman of noble mien who begged him to retire with her for a short time. But the young man refused, and kept resisting her importunate persuasions, until she advised him to draw his sword from the bedside and pierce the wall with it. He refused at first; but at last, not knowing what he did (for he was nearly mad with worry), he obeyed; and as he struck the wall he cried: "God turn it to good!" This again drove off the second demon like lightning. But the demon came a third time (for his moody anxiety was deeply implanted in the man's mind, and the tempter would not leave him alone), and took the form of a woman in the flower of life and of great beauty, who, both by word and gesture, lasciviously invited

him to sin. She did not stop short at words, but forcibly tried to drag him to her. The young man cried aloud for help, and when the servants ran quickly to him that wicked apparition vanished, and the man was found utterly spent and nearly dying. When he was asked the reason of his fear and his screams, he could not even open his mouth, but lay with glazing eyes like a dead man, having lost his voice through fright. He was therefore placed upon a bed and tended, and recovered his courage as soon as he was sprinkled with Holy Water; and the next day he told the whole story, and at the advice of a priest fortified himself with waxen images consecrated by the sacred mysteries, and other weapons feared by the devil, and in this way so frightened his Enemy that he ceased to appear to him. But sometimes it happens, with God's permission, that this remedy is of no avail, especially when God has willed to gain a more glorious victory by some other means, as for example by the bare name of Jesus or of Mary.

This was proved by what happened at Augsburg in the year 1591, where the wearing of consecrated wax stamped with the image of the Lamb was for many a present remedy against the horrid monsters of the devil and his nightly terrors. But to one man the demon appeared openly, as if in contempt, and bribed him with much money to commit a crime, having broken the cord by which the disc hung, and thrown away the Agnus Dei. Yet the man was saved when he called upon the names of Jesus and Mary.

In the year 1589 there was a woman who had written a Deed with her own blood and vowed herself to the devil. After she had repented of this, the demon often showed her the Deed; but she trusted in the protection of the Divine Lamb with whose image she had fortified her breast, and ordered him to return to her her hand-writing. At last she saw it fall at her feet, burned to glowing ashes.

13. Of the Sound of Bells

We have elsewhere given proof of the efficacy of the sound of bells against demons. And this is maintained also by the Council of Cologne, cap. 24; and confirmed by an example quoted by Peter the Venerable, Abbot of Cluny, who writes as follows (*De miraculis*, I, 13): A certain Italian Brother named Giovanni became weary of the severity of the unvarying discipline, and even thought of escaping from the monastery. The devil himself appeared to him in the form of an abbot accompanied by two demons in the guise of monks, while this Brother was sitting alone in a remote part of the monastery in deep thought; and thinking the moment ripe for deceiving him, he appeared to him and said: "Brother, I have lately come here to lodge. But, happening to see you, I recognised that you are in some great trouble and are turning over many thoughts in your mind. Now I have inquired, and in part know the cause of your trouble; but if you would tell it to me openly, perhaps I shall be able to give you some advice. Therefore tell me, as a friend, who you are and why you are so sad and sorry." And when that brother hesitated to open the secrets of his heart to one whom he supposed a stranger, and only answered that he was of Italian nationality; one of the demons in the form of a monk added: "And I am an abbot in that very district, and can be of good help to you in all things: for I know, although you keep silent, that the abbot of this monastery, and the others, treat you badly, not respecting you as you deserve, and moreover putting you to much indignity. Therefore I advise you to consult your own interest and leave this utterly pernicious place and come away with me; for I am ready to take you from these evils to my abbey, which is called Grotta Ferrata where you will receive every honour." To this the Brother answered: "I can by no means leave here; for the gates of the monastery are shut, and I am surrounded with a crowd of monks." Then the devil said: "As long as you remain here, I can give you no help. But find some way to break out of the monastery, and I shall at once be by your side and take you to my place as I said." But merciful God, who does not allow us to be tempted beyond our strength, did not permit the Enemy to proceed any further. But as it is written (*Job* xx, 24), "He shall flee from the iron weapon." For as they were thus disputing, the company of monks were sitting down to supper in the refectory at their accustomed hour, and when they had finished the Prior, as was his custom, struck one blow upon the bell. Hearing this sound, the demon who was pretending to be an abbot, was by the act of God snatched away from the Brother, who was speaking to him, and driven with great speed and violence to the privies which were close by, and in the sight of the said Brother plunged right into them.

It is commonly confessed by witches that if, when they are being carried by a demon to the Sabbat, or back home from it, the sound of bells is heard, the demons carrying them at once set down their foul burdens and escape in terror. This I have already explained in the proper place.

FINIS.

☆

Grant, we beseech Thee, O Lord, That Thy people may escape the contamination of the Devil, and may with a pure mind follow Thee, the only God, Through Jesus Christ, Thy Son, Our Lord, &c.